The Political Economy of Corporation Tax

Excellent technical writing on corporation tax abounds, but it tends to be inaccessible to public lawyers, political theorists and political economists. Although recent years have seen not only an explosion in public law scholarship but also a reawakening of interest in interpretative political theory and political economy, the potential of these perspectives to illuminate the corporation tax debate has remained unexplored. In this important work, John Snape seeks to reconcile these disparate strands of scholarship and to contribute to a new way of understanding and conceptualising the reform of the law relating to corporate taxation. Drawing on important developments in public law scholarship, the study combines elements of political theory and political economy. It advances a new interpretation of corporation tax law as an instrument of rule, through the maximisation of a nation's economic potential. Snape shows how corporate taxation belongs at the centre of any discussion of economic globalisation, not only because of the potential of national tax systems to influence inward investment decisions but also because of the potential of those decisions to shape the public interest that those tax systems might embody. Following public law and politics models, the book looks afresh at the impact of Britain's political institutions, of the processes of its representative government and of the theory that moulds and orders the values that the corporation tax code contains. This is a timely exploration of cutting-edge issues of public policy.

The Political Economy of Corporation Tax

Theory, Values and Law Reform

John Snape

•HART•
PUBLISHING

OXFORD AND PORTLAND, OREGON
2011

Published in the United Kingdom by Hart Publishing Ltd
16C Worcester Place, Oxford, OX1 2JW
Telephone: +44 (0)1865 517530
Fax: +44 (0)1865 510710
Email: mail@hartpub.co.uk
http://www.hartpub.co.uk

Published in North America (US and Canada) by
Hart Publishing
c/o International Specialized Book Services
920 NE 58th Avenue, Suite 300
Portland, OR 97213-3786
USA
Tel: +1 503-287-3093 or toll-free: 1-800-944-6190
Fax: +1 503-280-8832
E-mail: orders@isbs.com
http://www.isbs.com

British Library Cataloguing in Publication Data
Data Available

ISBN: 978-1-84946-028-6

Typeset by Hope Services, Abingdon
Printed and bound in Great Britain by
Lightning Source UK Ltd

MIX
Paper from
responsible sources
FSC® C013056

To Angela

Myrtle grove, or rosy shade, . . .
Yields in sweets, my queen, to thee.

– The poet of Handel's *Solomon*, 1749

Preface

The research for this book unfolded very gradually, around other projects. When embarking on the work, it occurred to me – as a tax lawyer but not an economist – how technical the taxation materials with which I work are. And this not just for general readers, but for specialists in other social science disciplines: other lawyers, political scientists and political economists. That is not to decry the excellence of much of the taxation material, nor its usefulness. I have myself written or co-written a number of technical works for practitioners and students, all well received on their appearance, and I admire and respect the work of many of the leading exponents of a more technical style of tax writing, including Judith Freedman and John Tiley, among others.

However, it did not escape my attention that those who specialise in these other social science disciplines and sub-disciplines have made tremendous strides over the last quarter-century or so in understanding what public law – of which tax law is a branch – is all about. Some of this work, such as that of David Judge, RAW Rhodes, David Marsh and Wayne Parsons, is more associated with public administration or public management, but the nature of public law means it is closely related. Other work on political economy, such as that of Joseph Stiglitz, Amartya Sen and Tim Besley, is aligned to public policy, but again, the boundaries between public policy and public law are becoming ever more porous. Among the most exciting, the most intrepid, of the public law scholars are Martin Loughlin and Adam Tomkins. It was through my critical interaction with their work that I realised that my own intellectual formation, philosophically, historically and culturally, was not merely an adjunct to my study of law but could explain the law and its institutions and workings.

In developing a theory of political jurisprudence, Loughlin shows us that it is possible to make close links between contemporary ways of thinking about public law and those which occupied our forefathers; that, far from being lost in time, they have a relevance and a reality in our modes of working of which we are scarcely aware. Tomkins, appropriately enough the holder of the Glasgow University chair named after John Millar (1735–1801), who was a radical lawyer and the greatest pupil of Adam Smith (1723–90), has similarly sought to use an historical perspective in unearthing the reasons for the dilemmas of contemporary constitutional law. Read with the public policy and public administration material, this new public law scholarship has the potential to illuminate and render universally relevant material hitherto seen, perhaps, as predominantly technical.

I have long been convinced that the key to understanding our present-day public policy dilemmas is to appreciate the sometimes exhilarating, sometimes worrying, ways of thinking of our Enlightenment forefathers. This is not an eccentric whim but the clearly articulated view of a number of contemporary thinkers, pre-eminently the historians and philosophers Tzvetan Todorov and Gertrude Himmelfarb.

More or less in the manner of some vaguely Hegelian ideal, my own legal formation had been first to train as a practising lawyer following my undergraduate legal education. It was only after having become relatively comfortable with black-letter tax law that I began to think more deeply about what it might all amount to. My sixth-form education was greatly devoted to late eighteenth- and nineteenth-century history, much of which reading stayed with me, and on beginning an academic career, I wrote about an eminent member of the Tudor judiciary and drew Adam Smith and his intellectual disciple, Sir Robert Peel, into a student textbook that I wrote on taxation. A copy of the orange-spined Penguin Classics edition – replaced most recently with Oakeshott's 1952 edition – of Hobbes' *Leviathan* was a cherished possession as a younger man, yet it was not until I became immersed in this project that it became clear to me just how many of our contemporary worries about taxation law and policy can be illuminated by familiarising ourselves with the thinking of those who, over the centuries, have shaped the ideas that still dominate, in an attenuated form perhaps, the British state and the economy that it nurtures.

All these insights clarified and made sense to me of another school of public law scholarship that was ground-breaking in its day: the Sheffield school, which, though anxiously searching, lacks the historical insight of the Loughlinian approach. Indeed, it was reading Chris Hilson's book on the regulation of pollution, an avowedly Sheffield school work, that jolted me into realising that something more might be done with the legislative texts on taxation than had hitherto been the case. I indicate in chapter two how aspects of the work of that school withstand Loughlin's and Tomkins' insights. The appearance of Loughlin's second major work in 2003 highlighted ever more sharply the problems with the Sheffield school approach, yet it also highlighted by implication what remains useful in it.

Impressive as much tax law scholarship is, it has not kept pace with these developments, and existing tax reform arguments around institutions, processes – indeed the very nature of tax law itself – leave plenty of room for further theoretical speculation. This situation has become ever more starkly apparent with the publication of Loughlin's magisterial new work in the summer of 2010. I hope that this study will be a useful contribution both to the development of that line of investigation and also to the advancement of public law scholarship more widely. That said, generally speaking, I lay no claim to the originality of the interpretative theory of public law at the core of this book. What I do claim, however, is its application to taxation, specifically to corporate taxation law and policy. Within these areas of specialisation, the interpretative theory in these pages may provide a basis for the further analysis of the monumental Mirrlees review of the British tax system published in 2010 and 2011. I have found it necessary to stress the theory of public law as promoting the public or national interest in relation to particular policies. This again is a reminder of the indebtedness to Adam Smith of a whole branch of legislative endeavour.

The years of New Labour (1997–2007) and subsequently of Labour (2007–2010) put more policy and parliamentary documentation into the public domain, I guess, than any other period of British political history. The new Coalition administration looks set to achieve something similar. In these pages, I do not seek to distinguish between Labour and New Labour. I am not disposed just now to think there was in reality much difference between them – only that latterly the vision and the quality of fiscal decision-making seemed to deteriorate. I hope to return to this material at some point in the future.

I talk about Britain or Great Britain rather than 'the United Kingdom of Great Britain and Northern Ireland'. This seems to have become conventional in critical writing and avoids an air of technicality. I hope readers in the Province will forgive this and make allowances for the stylistic imperative. Another convention to which the reader is asked to acquiesce is my interchangeable use of 'corporate tax' and 'corporation tax'. I do this 'in the interests of euphony', as Anthony Trollope might have said, absent the need to bring out some particular point, in which case I deliberately refer to one or the other. Chris Sanger has pointed out that the government's interchangeable use of the terms in its policy documentation may obscure the need to take account not only of corporation tax but also of the burden on companies of other taxes, such as stamp duty land tax, irrecoverable value added tax, climate change levy and so on. The point is well made, but since I am concerned solely with corporation tax, I think my own generally interchangeable use of 'corporate tax' and 'corporation tax' is nonetheless justifiable.

This study is a substantially edited, updated and revised version of my doctoral thesis, which was examined at the University of Birmingham in 2008. In preparing the work for publication, I have benefited especially from Bill Dodwell's *Business Tax Briefings* for Deloitte, as to factual detail, and from the commentaries in the *Financial Times* newspaper, each of which were particularly useful in making final adjustments to the text in April 2011. For stimulating conversation and fellowship I must thank especially: Julio Faundez, John McEldowney, Dan Priel, Rebecca Probert, Paul Raffield, David Salter and Gary Watt at the University of Warwick; Ann Blair, Jane Frecknall-Hughes (now of the Open University), Oliver Gerstenberg, Roger Halson, Anna Lawson, Amrita Mukherjee and Michael Cardwell at the University of Leeds; and, at Nottingham Trent University, Elspeth Berry, Graham Ferris, Juliette Grant, Peter Kunzlik, Alan Riley (both subsequently at City University, London), Marc Stauch (subsequently at Leibniz Universität Hannover) and James Slater (subsequently at the University of Buckingham). Marc Stauch and Christiane Trüe accompanied my wife Angela and me on a trip on the London Eye, one day of brilliant sunshine in 2005, and this felicitous suggestion on Marc and Christiane's part inspired the pictorial imagery that I hope puts a sunny halo around chapters three to five. I have also benefited from conversations with Dermot Fenlon, who directed me to Ted McAllister's work; Ann Mumford, who encouraged me to reacquaint myself with the work of ERA Seligman; Philip Ridgway, regarding developments in corporate tax law; Michael Sutton, on the history of political ideas generally; and Bill O'Brian and Matthew Clayton, on the so-called 'genetic fallacy'. At a more practical level, I would like to thank Helen Riley and colleagues in the university library at Warwick, especially in document supply and also Jane Bryan, Peter Cook and Gary Watt, who covered my teaching for the period of leave in 2010–11, during which, while taking forward my on-going work on the English philosopher John Locke (1632–1704), I completed the manuscript. It might be that I have other people to thank whom I have not mentioned. If so, I ask their forgiveness for overlooking them.

Richard Hart has been the most patient, helpful and supportive of publishers, suggesting the highly apposite title. On the editorial side, I have benefited from the assistance of Rachel Turner, Mel Hamill, Tom Adams and Lisa Gourd. A special word of thanks, too, is due to David Salter. He has been a conscientious supervisor, a careful observer and a good colleague. Although we do not always agree, our often detailed discussions of corporate tax law and policy, and much else, are a constant source of intellectual stimulation and companionship. And, too, my thanks are due to the examiners of my thesis, Geoffrey Morse and Abimbola Olowofoyeku. Their comments have proved extremely useful. For the same reason, I am grateful to the originally anonymous reviewer, Marc Moore, of University College, London, whose comments on the manuscript were extremely valuable in putting it into its present shape. Neither Marc, nor Geoffrey, nor Abimbola bear any responsibility for its inevitable imperfections and infelicities.

Most of all, I should like to thank my wife, Angela Kershaw, for her love and support over the years that the work has occupied my time. Angela has shown the greatest interest and encouragement at every stage, and I am deeply grateful to her. She is herself a gentle, witty and scholarly companion, and I benefit more from her conversation than I might perhaps realise.

My father, Edward Snape, and my mother, Elizabeth Brigid Snape, died within three weeks of each other, almost to the hour, as the thesis was in its last stages. They were therefore its dedicatees. Nothing if not trenchant, they would certainly have wished that, this difficult time having passed, I should dedicate the book that has come of it to Angela. That is what I do, with a love that I cannot easily put into words. And I do so mindful still of the courage and example that Edward and Elizabeth set when I originally made the thesis dedication. Andrew William Snape and Michael Francis Snape were to me all that brothers could have been over that difficult time, and they continue to be my closest friends.

The text seeks to reflect developments as at 5 April 2011.

John Snape
5 April 2011

Contents

Table of Abbreviations

ACE	allowance for corporate equity
CA 2006	Companies Act 2006
CAA 2001	Capital Allowances Act 2001
CRCA 2005	Commissioners for Revenue and Customs Act 2005
CTA 2009	Corporation Tax Act 2009
CTA 2010	Corporation Tax Act 2010
CTRM	Corporate Tax Road Map[1]
FA	Finance Act
FB	Finance Bill
GAAR	general anti-avoidance rule
GANTIP	general anti-avoidance principle
ICTA 1988	Income and Corporation Taxes Act 1988
ITA 2007	Income Tax Act 2007
ITEPA 2003	Income Tax (Earnings and Pensions) Act 2003
NATP	New Approach to Tax Policy
TAAR	targeted anti-avoidance rule
TCGA 1992	Taxation of Chargeable Gains Act 1992
TFEU	Treaty on the Functioning of the European Union
TIOPA 2010	Taxation (International and Other Provisions) Act 2010

[1] This abbreviation is used in the footnotes for the whole of the document in which the CTRM appears, namely: HM Treasury and HMRC, *Corporate Tax Reform: Delivering a More Competitive System* (London, 2010), available at http://www.hm-treasury.gov.uk/d/corporate_tax_reform_complete_document.pdf (accessed 15 July 2011).

Table of Cases

Table of Legislation

UK STATUTES

EU LEGISLATION

[1] In the text, the directives listed above are referred to compendiously as 'the five Directives' or the 'corporate tax Directives'. They cover mergers, dividends, savings interest, cross-border royalties and interest payments and mutual administrative assistance: they have been variously incorporated in statutory provisions of British law. The Arbitration Convention (Convention 90/463/EEC [1990] OJ L225/10), on transfer pricing, is not discussed separately in the text.

INTERNATIONAL TREATIES AND CONVENTIONS

1

Introduction

THIS IS A book about taxation. More specifically, it is about the controversies that shape Britain's approach to taxing the profits of companies. It aims to analyse these tax policy controversies in such a way as to illustrate their significance, not only for tax lawyers but also for public lawyers more generally, for political scientists and for political economists. Yet it offers nothing as simple as solutions to problems. Instead, it suggests important factors that those who offer such solutions cannot afford to ignore. The ideas at work in its pages, especially perhaps the relationship between government and the British operations of multinational corporations, have an almost universal importance.

But how are we to make sense of this legendarily contentious, arcane and complicated subject matter? I maintain that we have to engage with the historical and contemporary philosophical textures, not only of the corporate tax legislation itself, but also of the processes that bring it into being and of the institutions and other bodies whose processes they are. The effects of the tax planning activities of multinationals are now a major source of public concern, but the issues behind them are to most people highly obscure. So my approach is an interpretative one, firmly rooted not only in our contemporary notions about the design of tax systems, but also in historical ideas of the way that states should be governed. I argue that these insights, second nature as they are to politicians – to those who govern – are very revealing. This is so notwithstanding that the origins of the insights in question are often obscured by ideological dogma and technical detail. That said, the European Enlightenment's most important yet ambiguous philosopher of political economy, Adam Smith, has been invoked by Nigel (now Lord) Lawson, by Gordon Brown and by George Osborne, each to subtly different ends. The last mentioned, in his 2011 Budget speech, even went so far as to restate Smith's 'principles [on the design of taxes] . . . for the modern age'. In doing so, Mr Osborne resolved them, as has become customary, into the values of efficiency and of fairness:

> Our taxes should be efficient and support growth. They should be certain and predictable. They should be simple to understand and easy to comply with, and our tax system should be fair, reward work, support aspiration and ask the most from those who can most afford the most.[1]

[1] Hansard HC vol 525 col 954 (23 March 2011).

Drawing attention to Smith's continuing life on the lips of contemporary politicians is not to mistake rhetoric for reality. He appears, too, in *Tax by Design*, the final statement of the Mirrlees review of 2010 and 2011, set up by the respected economic policy think tank, the Institute for Fiscal Studies (IFS), to evaluate the British tax system. The IFS described Smith's famous maxims of taxation – equality, certainty, convenience and cost-effectiveness[2] – as commanding 'near universal support'.[3] They may not be sufficient in themselves for our globalised economy, but they are nonetheless necessary. Mirrlees' observations come as no surprise, since the tradition to which Smith belongs, and of which the other thinkers in these pages are a part, has been devoted to realising effective public policy amid the shifting values of commercial society. Specific references to the intellectual heritage of tax politics are admittedly rather rare. Most often, public policy discussion of taxation is dominated by fairly unreflective assertion. Much of what follows therefore will be devoted to illuminating the assumptions of tax policy. In this way, I hope, among other things, that the book will contribute to a broadening out of the discussion of the various components of the Mirrlees review.

One of the Mirrlees editors, Tim Besley, has himself paid tribute to Adam Smith's continuing relevance, as well as to that of one of the United States' founding fathers, James Madison (1751–1836). Besley takes the latter as the inspiration for his own political economy, which is directed at designing institutions and processes such that politicians do indeed pursue the 'common good of the society'[4] rather than their own personal advantage.[5] To Smith, too, is owed the particular idea of a theory, as used in this book, as a point of view, as a way of looking at a subject.[6] This might be the viewpoint of a politician intent on achieving a certain end, or it might be that of an impartial critic, trying to make sense of the workings of the reform process. So, when I talk about a theory of corporate taxation, I am referring both to the government's own plan for the transformation of the tax, in line with George Osborne's approach, and to a particular critical standpoint on corporate tax reform. Throughout, I have attempted to take a long-term view of the material, not just by recalling the Enlightenment origins of our contemporary concerns but by using examples from two decades of corporate tax policy, 13 years of which Gordon Brown dominated, first as Labour Chancellor of the Exchequer and subsequently as Prime Minister. The period after 2010 is certainly characterised by the making of inroads on Mr Brown's own personal idea of the appropriate organisation of

[2] A Smith, *The Wealth of Nations Books IV-V* [1776], AS Skinner (ed) (London, Penguin, 1999) 418.

[3] J Mirrlees, S Adam, T Besley et al, *Tax by Design* (Oxford, Oxford University Press, 2011) ch 2 (pre-publication draft chapters available at http://www.ifs.org.uk/mirrleesReview/design (accessed 30 November 2010)) 2.

[4] J Madison, '*The Federalist*, 57' in A Hamilton, J Madison and J Jay, *The Federalist Papers* [1788], L Goldman (ed) (Oxford, Oxford University Press, 2008) 282.

[5] T Besley, *Principled Agents? The Political Economy of Good Government* (Oxford, Oxford University Press, 2006) 1.

[6] A Smith, *The Theory of Moral Sentiments* [1759/1790], RP Hanley (ed) (London, Penguin, 2009) 133; and M Loughlin, *Foundations of Public Law* (Oxford, Oxford University Press, 2010) 93.

Great Britain's national life. Corporations, and the reasons for taxing them, were fundamental elements of this idea.

Some of the assessments of Gordon Brown in these pages may seem generous. Contentious as Labour tax policy certainly was, however, it started by being extremely well informed.[7] Indeed, many of its achievements are likely to be retained, if the political reality of the 2011 Budget[8] – as opposed to its aspirations – was anything to go by. Both Labour and Coalition corporate tax policies have been versions of a vision of the role of taxation in neoliberal ideology, ones that have gained ground since the 1980s and have figured prominently in the foundational text of neoliberalism, the ten principles of the 1980s 'Washington Consensus'.[9] In this discourse, taxes are low and there are few, if any, special treatments for different classes of taxpayer. Its goal is to tax as many things as possible but – and this is the crucial thing – as lightly as possible.[10] Simplicity, stability, 'flatter' tax rates and the exact enforcement of tax liabilities are its watchwords.[11]

Indeed, it was the strand of economic liberalism of which these tax ideals are a part that made the 2010 Coalition between Liberals and Conservatives possible.[12] Its catalyst was a certain reading of Smith promoted by the Austrian philosopher and economist Friedrich von Hayek (1899–1992).[13] There is a story that the Conservative Prime Minister, Margaret (subsequently Baroness) Thatcher, sometime after taking office, slammed a copy of Hayek's *Constitution of Liberty* onto the Cabinet room table, shouting: 'This is what we believe'.[14] And it is undoubtedly the case that, consciously or unconsciously, modern calls for simplicity in taxation owe something to the longevity of the ideals of market liberalism. Certainly, Nigel Lawson took Hayek to be Adam Smith in twentieth-century clothes;[15] Gordon Brown thought it possible to read Smith's teaching, not through Hayek, but alongside the North American liberal political theorists John Rawls (1921–2002) and Michael Sandel.[16] Although the idiosyncrasies of Mr Brown's legacy have continued to be an uncomfortable reality for them,

[7] See below ch 5.

[8] *Budget 2011* (HC 2010–11) 836.

[9] MB Steger and RK Roy, *Neoliberalism: A Very Short Introduction* (Oxford, Oxford University Press, 2010) 19.

[10] Ibid, 24; and R Plant, *The Neo-liberal State* (Oxford, Oxford University Press, 2010) 181–83.

[11] Steger and Roy (above n 9).

[12] D Laws and P Marshall (eds), *The Orange Book: Reclaiming Liberalism* (London, Profile, 2004).

[13] But a contested one: C Petsoulas, *Hayek's Liberalism and its Origins: His Idea of Spontaneous Order and the Scottish Enlightenment* (London, Routledge, 2001); and C Smith, *Adam Smith's Political Philosophy: The Invisible Hand and Spontaneous Order* (London, Routledge, 2006).

[14] S Brittan, 'The Many Faces of Liberalism' *Financial Times*: *Life and Arts* (23–24 January 2010) 13; M Thatcher, *The Path to Power* (London, HarperCollins, 1995) 50–51; and FA Hayek, *The Constitution of Liberty* [1960], 2nd edn (London, Routledge, 2006).

[15] N Lawson, *The View from No. 11: Memoirs of a Tory Radical* (London, Bantam Press, 1992) 13–14; and I McLean, *Adam Smith, Radical and Egalitarian: An Interpretation for the Twenty-First Century* (Edinburgh, Edinburgh University Press) 91.

[16] R Peston, *Brown's Britain* (London, Short Books, 2005) 21; MJ Sandel, *Liberalism and the Limits of Justice*, 2nd edn (Cambridge, Cambridge University Press, 1998); MJ Sandel, *Justice: What's the Right Thing to Do?* (London, Allen Lane, 2009); and *Gordon Brown: Moving Britain Forward: Selected Speeches 1997–2006*, W Stevenson (ed) (London, Bloomsbury, 2006) 145 and 272.

Mr Osborne and the Coalition have aspired to a Lawsonian vision of corporation tax, announcing a prospective decrease in the main tax rate of five percentage points.[17] I do not want to make the expression 'neoliberalism' do too much work, but it is nonetheless a useful compendious term for an ideology in which economics is king and to which even Sandelian communitarianism is only a qualified reaction.[18] The difference between Coalition and Labour has been one of degree, not of fundamental values.

In this introductory chapter, I offer some thoughts on the constituent elements of the book's title. These are intended to give readers an idea of my approach. So, with the taxation of corporate profits as my overall subject matter, I want to talk about the relevance to that phenomenon of three elements: the senses in which the expression 'political economy' is used; what I mean by theory and values in the corporate tax context; and the background to my unfolding discussion of law reform.

I. THE SENSES OF 'POLITICAL ECONOMY'

Uses of the term 'political economy' are perhaps unusually sensitive to the contexts in which they appear. One sense in which the term is used is in reference to the actual craft of governing to promote national prosperity.[19] In this sense it is the expression used by politicians to characterise one of their own practices. This is the sense in which Adam Smith used the term when he said that political economy was that part of the sovereign's task that consisted in providing 'the state or commonwealth with a revenue sufficient for the public services', no less than that of maximising the wealth of the subject.[20] It is as such an oxymoron, as Hannah Arendt pointed out: the political 'stem' (the *polis*) refers to the Greek for the sphere of state and politics, and the economic 'tail' (the *oikia*) to the Greek word for the household and its management.[21] Indeed, economics long consisted of the craft of managing prosperity.[22] After all, Keynesian economics – the contested tradition of John Maynard Keynes (1883–1946) – is specifically directed towards a government's capacity to create the circumstances under which the subjects of a state might be cushioned against inflation and recession.[23]

[17] *Budget 2011* (above n 8) 56; Finance Bill (No 3) 2011, cll 4–5. On Lawson, see P Riddell, 'Commentary' in S Adam, T Besley et al (eds), *Dimensions of Tax Design: The Mirrlees Review* (Oxford, Oxford University Press, 2010) 1284.

[18] Steger and Roy (above n 9) 90; and A Kaletsky, *Capitalism 4.0: The Birth of a New Economy* (London, Bloomsbury, 2010) 40.

[19] Besley (above n 5) 27; S Collini, D Winch and J Burrow, *That Noble Science of Politics: A Study in Nineteenth-Century Intellectual History* (Cambridge, Cambridge University Press, 1983) 68 and 136; and Kaletsky (ibid) 78–79.

[20] Smith, *The Wealth of Nations* (above n 2) 5.

[21] H Arendt, *The Human Condition*, 2nd edn (Chicago, University of Chicago Press, 1998) 30 and 33.

[22] Kaletsky (above n 18) 40.

[23] JM Keynes, *The General Theory of Employment, Interest and Money* [1936] (Basingstoke, Palgrave, 2007).

Since the 1890s, people have tended to talk about 'economics' rather than 'political economy'.[24] However, in 2010, noting its widespread contemporary usage, Nigel Lawson welcomed the return of 'political economy' to the lexicon of politics, characterising it as 'consisting in seeking a rational course of action in a world of endemic uncertainty'.[25] In tax policy terms, political economy has given rise to subtly different principles of taxation, all more or less drawing on Smith's maxims, and all resoluble into the values of efficiency and fairness. However, after what socialist critics regarded as the ideologically suspect example of Philip Snowden (1864–1937),[26] the first Labour Chancellor, the practice of political economy seems to have been identified with Conservative and Liberal politicians rather than with Labour ones.

Reflecting the tension in the very idea of a theory, besides referring to what its practitioners should do, political economy may also describe a way of analysing things.[27] It may refer, in other words, to an academic investigation into tax policy and politics using economic modelling techniques.[28] That is the basis on which Besley's political economy is conceived, and it is the broad sense, too, in which Alt, Preston and Sibieta use the term in their useful and innovative chapter in the Mirrlees review.[29] It is itself part of an honourable tradition, broadly configured around the rival insights of welfare economics and public choice theories, or, as in Besley's case, a sophisticated combination of the two.[30]

Public choice is the explanation of government failures through economic analysis: 'politics without romance',[31] as James Buchanan once described it. Welfare economics, the older discipline to which I return in chapter four, is about remedying market failures through particular policies designed to promote the public interest.[32] What political economy of either stripe produces are useful technical insights into the formulation of tax policy. However, as Alt, Preston and Sibieta readily concede, each approach has its limitations. In particular, public choice is difficult to apply to corporation tax, because the tax 'is not typically electorally salient'.[33] Attitudes to corporate taxes cannot therefore be analysed in terms, for example, of median voter models of behaviour.[34] The political commentator Peter Riddell in his essay on Alt, Preston and Sibieta's contribution therefore asserts that it uses 'too much flimsy political science and

[24] Collini, Winch and Burrow (above n 19) 333; Besley (above n 5) 28.

[25] N Lawson, 'Five Myths and a Menace' *Standpoint* (Jan/Feb 2011) 36, 37.

[26] N Thompson, *Political Economy and the Labour Party: The Economics of Democratic Socialism, 1884–1995* (London, University College London Press, 1996) 79–80.

[27] Besley (above n 5) 29.

[28] CS Maier, *In Search of Stability: Explorations in Historical Political Economy* (Cambridge, Cambridge University Press, 1987) 2–6.

[29] J Alt, I Preston and L Sibieta, 'The Political Economy of Tax Policy' in Adam, Besley et al (eds) (above n 17) 1204, 1208 and 1237.

[30] Besley (above n 5) 43–44.

[31] Quoted in Kaletsky (above n 18) 194.

[32] Besley (above n 5) 24.

[33] Alt, Preston and Sibieta (above n 29) 1245.

[34] Ibid.

not enough well-founded history'. It is just testing 'some tendentious theoretical models', only to find them wanting.[35] This is rather harsh, because economic approaches have become widely applied. Chris Sanger, a former Treasury insider, commenting on the Coalition's approach to corporate tax policy, has suggested another approach, one that might get round the occluded nature of corporate tax policymaking: willingness to pay. How much, in other words, is a corporate group 'willing to pay . . . for the benefits that headquartering in the UK brings'?[36] Even this approach, however, has its limitations, since it is still necessary for politicians to decide what to do with the information thereby retrieved. Interviewed by Evan Davis on the BBC, three former Chancellors – Nigel Lawson, Norman Lamont and Alistair Darling – all expressly disavowed the idea of people responding truthfully when asked about their tax policy preferences.[37]

Another academic approach, a version of which I adopt in this study, seems to me to have the potential to illuminate matters further. It draws on the Smithian idea of political economy as that part of the practice of politics that involves making judgments about the rationale of applying in the real world one or another set of economic conclusions. This is the sense in which Nigel Lawson has warmly endorsed the use of the expression. So I utilise the findings of Besley's political economy, as well as of the Mirrlees review itself, and read them alongside political science and public law material. What factors, in other words, will affect the prospects of Mirrlees' conclusions being applied in the real world? In so doing, I discuss two key contributions: that of Christopher Wales, another former Treasury adviser,[38] and that of the IFS's own committee on the reform of the process by which tax law is made.[39] I want to show how concepts of public law – the law of the state and the subject – founded as they are in politics, assist in the deployment of theoretical economic knowledge. So I refer to Alt, Preston and Sibieta, to be sure, but I give prominence to these other two studies. It is crucially important that the conclusions of Mirrlees are not ignored, even though early signs have not been encouraging.[40] In mapping the relationship between the conclusions of economics and the constraints, and potential, of politics and public law, it may be that an analysis such as the present ensures that Mirrlees continues to be discussed. This may seem like – but is not intended to be – a condescending comment. Mirrlees has certainly had an

[35] Riddell (above n 17) 1280. See also B Manin, *The Principles of Representative Government* (Cambridge, Cambridge University Press, 1997) 224–25; and Loughlin, *Foundations of Public Law* (above n 6) 10.

[36] C Sanger, 'Corporate Tax Road Map' (2011) *British Tax Review* 2, 3.

[37] E Davis, 'The Overall Burden of Tax' *Evan Loves Tax* (BBC Radio 4, 13 September 2010), details available at http://www.bbc.co.uk/news/business-11275040 (accessed 30 March 2011).

[38] C Wales, 'The Implications of the O'Donnell Review for the Making of Tax Policy in the UK' (2004) *British Tax Review* 543.

[39] Tax Law Review Committee, *Making Tax Law: Report of a Working Party on the Institutional Processes for the Parliamentary Scrutiny of Tax Proposals and for the Enactment of Tax Legislation chaired by Sir Alan Budd* (London, Institute for Fiscal Studies, 2003).

[40] Sanger (above n 36) 10.

impact. Indeed, aspects of Alt, Preston and Sibieta's analysis quickly proved influential – their recommendation for an Office for Budget Responsibility was acted on almost immediately when the Coalition took office in May 2010.

So, the political economy of corporation tax, as I portray it, is the analysis of the exercise of political judgment in relation to the application of economic theory to corporate tax policy. It includes those cases where, as some would say, economic theory is all but disregarded in the making of the political judgment. This approach gives a prominent role to politics that not all would accept, but it provides too a context for material that might otherwise seem quite remote from everyday concerns.

II. FIRST THOUGHTS ON THEORY AND VALUES

Corporation tax is, of course, unusual, since it is the only one of the main taxes whose subjects are not – at least, not obviously – creatures of flesh and blood. The taxable person is the limited liability company, or corporation, thought by some to be the most distinctive artefact of the nineteenth-century legal imagination, and now prominent in all developed societies. Indeed, as has often been argued, it would be possible to scratch-build a system that did not include a tax on corporations but relied instead on the income tax liability of the creatures of flesh and blood who have economic interests in companies.[41]

Yet such is not the system we have. This suggests a gap between what we hope for and what actually happens – a gap that this study tries to account for in terms of the realities of politics and the ordering of those realities in public law. The realities have a number of constituent factors: that the public or national interest in corporate taxation is not necessarily the same as what business wants; that the initiation of tax policy by ministers of the Crown tends to be surrounded in secrecy, being in the true sense of the word 'arcane'; and that corporate tax, unlike income tax, has not hitherto been susceptible to the economic analysis of voter preferences.

The gap between what we hope for and what we actually get therefore needs to be conceptualised in some way that anatomises the nature of the engagement between the corporate sector and the government. This, I contend, is the province of theory, in the sense of a particular perspective on corporate taxation. I analyse the choices between corporate tax policies in terms of the insights of politics and history, of how political prudence shapes the divergence in the public sphere between the ideal and the reality. There is no doubt a range of ways of explaining that disparity, and I do not pretend to offer a definitive account. Nevertheless, the reasons for evaluating the purely economic arguments in, for

[41] J Kay and J Sen, 'The Comparative Burden of Business Taxation' (1983) 4(3) *Fiscal Studies* 23; and M Gammie, 'Reforming Corporate Taxation: An Evaluation of the United States Treasury Integration Proposals and other Corporate Tax Systems in an International Context: Part 1' (1992) *British Tax Review* 148, 149. See below ch 2.

instance, Auerbach, Devereux and Simpson's contribution to the Mirrlees review[42] in the light of politics and public law, as unfolded in these pages, seems to me to be compelling. This is why, as Christopher Wales has pointed out, the economics of corporate tax can never be divorced from politics[43] and why Riddell has written that 'tax decisions cannot be taken out of politics'.[44] Indeed, Mr Sanger's comment on the Coalition's commitment to the principle of taxing companies[45] rather than their shareholders direct implies that it is an essentially prudential position: people think 'it is right', he acknowledges, that 'businesses should pay tax'.[46] This type of argument does not diminish the importance of the economic analysis of political decisions on taxation. It merely asserts that such economistic analyses – as for instance Alt, Preston and Sibieta's political economy – are not the only way of critiquing such decisions.

When I use the word 'economistic', I am referring to all discussions of corporate tax in which the non-exclusivity of economic analyses is not given weight, and motivations are instead reduced to essentially economic preferences. Whether, as Charles Taylor has said, such an economism is symptomatic of a generally misplaced faith in scientistic methods,[47] I leave open. But I do not agree with Alt, Preston and Sibieta's premise that the assertion that something is 'political' means it is incapable of systematic non-economistic analysis.[48] I simply argue that, even with corporate taxation, the economistic analysis, though foundational, is not exclusive, and a systematic public law critique can be constructed. Interestingly, the overall tone of the Mirrlees review is much more contextual, if not more political, than its predecessor, the rather technical Meade report of 1978,[49] so the nature of my own work is very much in keeping with the general drift of the contextual study of tax policy over recent decades. The fact that companies rarely operate alone, that most are members of corporate groups and that as multinationals they cross national borders, is another reason for taking a more contextual approach, if only because of unprecedented levels of public concern about multinationals' supposed domination of corporate tax policy.[50]

So-called 'optimal tax theory' is the theory that, taking account of certain 'constraints', it is possible to model the best possible way of achieving tax policy objectives.[51] A creation of welfare economics, it is deployed as the highly

[42] AJ Auerbach, MP Devereux and H Simpson, 'Taxing Corporate Income' in Adam, Besley et al (eds) (above n 17) 837.

[43] C Wales, 'Commentary' in Adam, Besley et al (eds) (above n 17) 1304.

[44] Riddell (above n 17) 1293.

[45] Sanger (above n 36) 6.

[46] Ibid, 5.

[47] Quoted in Loughlin, *Foundations of Public Law* (above n 6) 10.

[48] Alt, Preston and Sibieta (above n 29) 1208.

[49] JE Meade (Chair), *The Structure and Reform of Direct Taxation: Report of a Committee Chaired by Professor JE Meade* (London, George Allen and Unwin, 1978) ch 12.

[50] But (soberingly) see BBC Radio 4, *The Report* (30 December 2010), details available at http://www.bbc.co.uk/Radio4 (accessed 21 Feb 2011).

[51] Mirrlees, Adam and Besley et al (above n 3) 19.

sophisticated basis of the Mirrlees review's recommendations. But it needs to be further contextualised in order to engage public concern. The constraints of which it takes account are 'administrative' and 'political' (eg, the so-called 'revenue constraint', EU membership, etc). Such factors are important, to be sure, but they are not exhaustive, and they do not purport to lead ineluctably to one conclusion or another. Moreover, as we shall see, some such 'constraints' – for instance, EU membership – can actually in the prism of politics be enabling from the government's point of view. In short, therefore, optimal tax theory is not all there is to say about corporate tax policy. It is in danger of dominating discussion, however, because of the generally technical nature of corporate tax discourse. The lack of public understanding of, as well as the lack of wide public involvement in, debates about taxes is a lament of the Mirrlees review itself.[52] A wider, contextual discussion should help to redress the balance. At a profound level, taxation depends upon public consent, if only in its highly stylised parliamentary form. That is why it is never helpful to invoke Colbert's non-consensual doctrine of taxation as the art of extracting the most goose feathers with the least hissing.[53] Taxation has to command consent, which implies a level of public support, which in turn requires a public understanding of the issues.[54]

If the role of theory is to enable the prudential evaluation of different economic possibilities in complex real world-settings, then it remains to say something about values. In this book, values are taken to embody ideological choices about the way we should live, choices settled in large part by the neoliberal ideology already discussed.[55] All positive law of course embodies values in this sense, but critical discussion of them is perhaps most closely associated with public law scholarship.[56] The relevance of values to this study is the result of linking corporate tax policy and tax law to general public law and policy. The role of the theory it propounds is to help both politicians and critics to assess the limitations of otherwise clear conclusions of economics. It also enables each group to sift between the different possibilities that economic models suggest. Theory provides, in other words, an explanation for the choices actually made as between different economic possibilities. Since the possibilities can be analysed in terms of various combinations of efficiency and fairness, some traces of these values are always detectable in the legislative code as it actually exists. Efficiency predicates that corporate taxes do not hamper economic growth, and

[52] Alt, Preston and Sibieta (above n 29) 1206; and Wales, 'Commentary' (above n 43) 1301.

[53] Eg, K Ussher and I Walford, *National Treasure* (London, Demos, 2011) 43. Jean-Baptiste Colbert (1619–83) was the finance minister of the absolutist and fiscally inept regime of Louis XIV.

[54] Wales, 'Commentary' (above n 43).

[55] A Sen, *Development as Freedom*, 2nd edn (Oxford, Oxford University Press, 2001); and N Scott Arnold, *Imposing Values: An Essay on Liberalism and Regulation* (Oxford, Oxford University Press, 2009).

[56] P Cane, 'Theory and Values in Public Law' in P Craig and R Rawlings (eds), *Law and Administration in Europe: Essays in Honour of Carol Harlow* (Oxford, Oxford University Press, 2003) 3; and P Craig, 'Theory and Values in Public Law: A Response' in Craig and Rawlings (eds) (above) 23.

fairness suggests that they reflect a politically appropriate tax burden for the corporate sector to bear.[57]

The content and scope of corporation tax values are shaped in part by the institutions of government and in part by political processes. The corporation tax code itself therefore embodies both the ancient prudence of the institutions themselves and the prudential choices made in the policymaking process. This aura of history indeed was very apparent until the period 2001 to 2010, when except for chargeable gains the fragmented legislation of earlier years was consolidated and rewritten – but not amended – in four Tax Law Rewrite Acts: the Capital Allowances Act 2001; the Corporation Tax Acts 2009 and 2010; and the Taxation (International and Other Provisions) Act 2010.

Political prudence, as a crucial factor in shaping corporate taxation, forms a tangible link between our ideas of government and those of Adam Smith and his friend David Hume (1711–76), as well as three earlier thinkers crucial to their own thought, Niccolò Machiavelli (1469–1527), Thomas Hobbes (1588–1679) and John Locke (1632–1704). All five, in different ways, were searching for a way to ensure an appropriate ordering of the state. Hume and Smith believed that its spontaneous ordering would come from the prudential dismantling of ancient restrictions on commerce; for Machiavelli and for Hobbes, right ordering could be achieved only by the sovereign's prudent wielding of the sword; and for Locke, good order required the prudential limitation of the prerogatives of the Crown. Structuring the discussion in this book around conceptions of prudence at different historical stages gives consistency and robustness to an argument such as Riddell's about the importance of history in understanding the outcomes of tax policy today.

The discussion therefore follows a course marked out by the public lawyer Martin Loughlin. Loughlin, a legal academic with a profound sense of history, steeped in the intellectual tradition I have just described, has been moved to evolve over two decades a broadly Hegelian analysis of public law,[58] incorporating insights from another Hegelian thinker, Michel Foucault (1926–84). In Hegelian thought, political right is 'an elaboration of the working of reason in history'.[59] My own study reflects this Hegelian perspective, but it is Foucauldian only to the extent that Loughlin makes selective use of Foucault's work. It is to Loughlin's thinking that I turn next, in the context of the background to the third component of the book's title: law reform.

III. CORPORATE TAX LAW AND ITS REFORM

Throughout this study, I present corporate taxation as a species of public law. This statement should be understood in both narrow and wide senses, to be

[57] But see Mirrlees, Adam and Besley et al (above n 3) 6.
[58] Loughlin, *Foundations of Public Law* (above n 6) 154.
[59] Ibid, 147.

elaborated in the next chapter. In the narrow and popular sense, it is because corporate tax law 'regulates relations between the individual [including, for these purposes, corporations] and government', rather than 'relations between individuals'.[60] In the wider sense, it is because the substance of corporate tax law, as well as the processes by which it is created, and the institutions involved in enacting it embody something distinctive. What they embody is a particular conception of the contribution of public finance, specifically corporation tax, to the 'right ordering' of the British state.[61] In proposing the wide sense of the term as part of the scope of public law in general, Loughlin has revitalised an ancient conception of public law, an ever-present reality, though one that has often been lost to sight since the eighteenth century.

The inspiration for Loughlin's public law theory, Hegel himself, was aware of Adam Smith's philosophical contribution, naming Smith as an exponent of 'one of the sciences which have arisen out of the conditions of the modern world [ie, political economy]', a science 'of thought working upon the endless mass of details which confront it . . . and extracting therefrom the simple principles of the thing'.[62] Indeed, Hegel might be regarded not so much as an innovator but as a clever manipulator of[63] the Enlightenment spirit in which Smith had written. The essence of Loughlin's thought is that all public law is a striving for the realisation of some collective ideal. Never perfectly realised, the ideal – or value – is yet always detectable in the poor, imperfect artefacts of present legislative endeavours. This, I contend, is the background to all law reform, that of corporate tax no less than any other. The ideal is some way off; the values immanent to what we create.[64] We want something better; we have a plan. Somehow we settle for something second best.

The most distinctive feature, perhaps, of Loughlin's study of public law is its focus, not upon constitutional documents, but on the concept of the state. Public law therefore becomes, as the law of the state and the subject, the embodiment of the principles of political right, of those principles that shape the right ordering of the state. Loughlin takes the defining characteristic of the state to be sovereignty, and the augmentation of sovereignty to be the characteristic function of public law – or, as it has also been called, political jurisprudence. Sovereignty has a legal and a political dimension. Its legal dimension is the relationship between state and subject, whether natural or legal;[65] its political dimension is that between state and people, including corporations and their

[60] Ibid, 2.

[61] Ibid.

[62] GWF Hegel, *Outlines of the Philosophy of Right* [1821], S Houlgate (ed) and TM Knox (trans) (Oxford, Oxford University Press, 2008) 187.

[63] TV McAllister, *Revolt against Modernity: Leo Strauss, Eric Voegelin, and the Search for a Postliberal Order* (Lawrence, University Press of Kansas, 1997) 129–30; and T Todorov, *In Defence of the Enlightenment*, G Walker (trans) (London, Atlantic, 2009) 18.

[64] M Loughlin 'Review Article' (1988) 51 *Modern Law Review* 531, 533.

[65] T Hobbes, *Leviathan* [1651], M Oakeshott (ed) (Oxford, Basil Blackwell, 1955) 112 (pt 2 ch 17).

agents.[66] The legal dimension of sovereignty is the arrangement of the nominal responsibilities of institutions[67] and is referred to as 'competence'.[68] But the establishment of competences relies on a productive or co-operative relationship between the state and the people, on the 'generative conception'[69] that Loughlin designates as 'capacity'.[70] The quality of the relationship between state and corporate sector is crucial to the reform of corporate taxation. In a neoliberal state, it is constituted by those values of efficiency and fairness discussed above.

In the British state, competence is the absolute authority of the Crown-in-Parliament to enact law. The 'sovereignty of Parliament' of AV Dicey (1835–1922) is therefore no more than a half-finished outline.[71] To complete it, says Loughlin, we need to colour the picture with the idea of capacity: 'political sovereignty' or 'constituent power'. Described by an early modern theorist as the ability to shape and order a state,[72] sovereignty is the power that the government holds on trust for the nation, for the purposes of furthering the public or national interest.[73] In this Loughlinian view of public law, the constitution's significance is not as a piece of paper but as 'the complete condition of political unity and order' found in a state.[74] So it is useful to talk about parliamentary sovereignty, just as Dicey intended, but it is even better to think of it in the generative sense of political sovereignty as wielded by the Crown-in-Parliament. The degree of prudence with which the government conducts corporate tax policy is therefore all-important. If a government displays virtuosity in its tax policy dealings with the corporate sector then, given what neoliberalism is all about, the state's sovereignty is maintained. If, instead, the government manages those dealings badly, the state's sovereignty drains away. The possibility of reform, as well as the outline of the imperfect system we already have, is shaped by political prudence.

Sovereignty in this fuller, generative sense – as political sovereignty – expresses the autonomy of the British state, built up through the solidarity of individuals working together in recognised ways of engaging with each other.[75] Such power is enhanced, not dissipated, by the single state's engagement with the EU institutions. Power of this sort is not to be confused with force or with domination,

[66] M Loughlin, *The Idea of Public Law* (Oxford, Oxford University Press, 2003) 67.

[67] Ibid, 160.

[68] Ibid, 84.

[69] Ibid, 160.

[70] Ibid, 85.

[71] Ibid, 84. See AV Dicey, *Introduction to the Study of the Law of the Constitution* [1885], ECS Wade (ed) (London, Macmillan, 1965) 39–40; and generally, J Goldsworthy, *The Sovereignty of Parliament: History and Philosophy* (Oxford, Clarendon Press, 1999).

[72] Loughlin, *The Idea of Public Law* (above n 66) 85, quoting G Lawson, *Politica Sacra et Civilis* [1660], C Condren (ed) (Cambridge, Cambridge University Press, 1992) 47.

[73] Loughlin, *The Idea of Public Law* (above n 66) 85, quoting EJ Sieyès, *What is the Third Estate?* [1789], SE Finer (ed) and M Blondel (trans) (London, Pall Mall Press, 1963) 124–28.

[74] Loughlin, *Foundations of Public Law* (above n 6) 211–12.

[75] A Stewart, *Theories of Power and Domination: The Politics of Empowerment in Late Modernity* (London, Sage, 2001) 6.

since it depends entirely on the quality of the relationship between government and governed.[76] It is 'power to' rather than 'power over', the latter expressing only domination. 'Power to' is 'a phenomenon generated through allegiances amongst and between people', as manifested by the practices of their everyday lives.[77] It is a 'dynamic energy generated through modern political formations'.[78] What political sovereignty means is that the more the government gets right, the more power it is able to wield. The relationship between government and corporate sector is, in Loughlin's word, a 'recursive'[79] one of knowledge and power, in which the government's present and future decisions are being constantly reappraised in the light of decisions already made.

So the state's sovereignty depends on the government managing relations effectively with a range of actors: externally, as regards the European institutions, and internally, as regards the corporate sector and communities of professionals. All of this betokens sovereignty as what Angus Stewart conceives of as the power of concerted action.[80] That idea is foreign to Foucault, as he thinks of power as some or other form of domination. Yet there is still a subsidiary place for Foucault's power-as-domination in Loughlin's theory of public law. This is in the interaction between state capacity and the 'infrastructural power' of systems, the technical and technological domination of human beings.[81] Bear with me if I say that enabling power is constantly interwoven with dominating power. A corporate tax law solicitor or accountant, responding, for example, to a consultation on tax reform, operates within a fairly coercive workplace of billing targets and swipecards, but she is also working in concert, as part of a system that she understands and whose interest she is promoting in helping to shape public policy.[82] Such bonds of practice must indeed be very strong, since '[f]or lawyers and accountants, there are very few rewards to be earned from considering how . . . [things] should be or how to influence change'.[83]

The approach that I have just described highlights the importance of three particular areas of corporate tax reform. First, there is the importance of the role of the institutions of representative government. This is largely a question of competences. Beginning in 2010–11 with the UK Uncut demonstrations,[84] there have been understandable calls for a much wider public debate on corporate taxation law. These calls are echoed even in Mirrlees. However, as Anatole Kaletsky has emphasised, the British system is a representative one, and

[76] Loughlin, *The Idea of Public Law* (above n 66) 112.
[77] Loughlin, *Foundations of Public Law* (above n 6) 220.
[78] Ibid.
[79] Ibid, 416.
[80] Stewart (above n 75) 46. See Loughlin, *The Idea of Public Law* (above n 66) ch 5.
[81] Loughlin, *Foundations of Public Law* (above n 6) 166–70.
[82] M Foucault, *Security, Territory, Population: Lectures at the Collège de France, 1977–78*, M Senellart (ed) and G Burchell (trans) (London, Palgrave, 2007) 66, cited in Loughlin, *Foundations of Public Law* (above n 6) 168.
[83] Wales, 'The Implications of the O'Donnell Review' (above n 38) 559.
[84] M Taylor, P Lewis and A Gabbatt, 'Tax Activists to Target Topshop Boss' *Guardian* (30 November 2010) 17.

the decisions of the government are those of the institutions of representative government.[85] Except in very rare referenda, ours are not the politics of direct democracy, as in the marketplace of ancient Greece.[86] One danger of allowing corporate tax debate to slide into such a marketplace mode is the absence of institutional restraints on the domination of large corporations in particularly sensitive areas of public policy. Another, as shown by the power of the internet to mobilise UK Uncut's street protests, is the contestable nature of claims behind popular protest.[87] As Kaletsky has said, taxation is the price of representation; when governments respond to tax agitation outside the institutions of representative government, they are acting inconsistently with the logic of this principle and not therefore so as to conduce to good order. The 'impersonal fisc', which never dies, was perhaps the first government institution to arrogate an existence distinct from the transient holders of government offices.[88] It is thus that I feel confident in describing corporate taxation as an instrument of rule and in devoting chapter three to the attributes of those involved in reforming it. I explore the study's view of the relationship between rule, in the sense of regulation, and distribution, in chapter two. Of the reforming institutions, the key ones are of course Parliament and the Treasury, but the 'ephorate'[89] of tax specialists and commentators who work with those institutions are important too.

Secondly, it is necessary to pay due attention to the processes of government. This point is closely related to the first but is more a matter of capacity. Reform proposals are sometimes apt to overlook some crucial historical feature of institutions. Much has been made in recent years of the need for pre-legislative scrutiny of tax legislation, and also of the need for greater parliamentary scrutiny of legislative texts. We need to be able to identify the limitations of these arguments. All commentators are agreed that, with British government, enormous competences can be placed in the hands of ministers of the Crown, who have often worked with large Parliamentary majorities.[90] This is why capacity is a more important feature of sovereignty than are competences. If government does take robust corporate tax initiatives, defensible both before and after the event, its capacity will be enhanced. If it does not do so, then its capacity will be weakened. The danger of course is that the corporate sector will capture the exercise of public policy discretion, and instead of being seen to govern in the public interest, the government will be suspected of promoting a sectional one.[91] This is the true significance of accountability, and it is why Loughlin constantly reiterates the point that 'constraints are enabling; apparent limitations on power

[85] Kaletsky (above n 18) 276.
[86] Manin (above n 35) ch 1.
[87] BBC Radio 4 (above n 50).
[88] Loughlin, *Foundations of Public Law* (above n 6) 42n.
[89] Ibid, 454; and Alt, Preston and Sibieta (above n 29) 1269. 'Ephorate' is Loughlin's term, reviving an expression used by Johannes Althusius (1563–1638).
[90] Alt, Preston and Sibieta (above n 29) 1225.
[91] A Smith, *The Wealth of Nations Books I–III* [1776], AS Skinner (ed) (London, Penguin, 1999) 358–59.

generate power'.[92] Developments in corporate tax policymaking, especially since the May 2010 General Election, have augmented concerns that corporate tax policy is skewed towards the interests of multinationals.[93]

Thirdly, given what I have just said about values, we need to be aware that certain aspirations for the corporate tax system are unrealistic. Stability and simplicity are particularly vulnerable aspirations, as the Chancellor's corporate tax measures against oil companies in the 2011 Budget quickly showed.[94] The prudence of the legislator means that legislative texts will inevitably embody sudden and unexpected changes made in response to or in advance of particular events. Similarly, they will tend to become complex, in ensuring that similarly placed taxpayers are treated similarly and that those situated differently are treated differently.

I am therefore concerned with how things function rather than with what they are or what they ought to be. In seeing how things function, I uncover vital clues about their rationale. I would ask the reader to reflect on the book in this spirit. As Hayek's conservative antagonist Michael Oakeshott (1901–90) wrote, this way of writing involves 'seeking to understand a familiar identity in terms different from those in which it is already understood'.[95] The fourth sentence of this chapter is a conscious echo of Samuel Brittan's observation that Oakeshott 'will do nothing so vulgar as to recommend' a particular course of action.[96] So what follows does not seek to present some blueprint for reform or a solution to a perceived problem. Indeed, it questions whether the current condition of corporation tax law can even be viewed as a problem admitting of some solution. It focuses instead on things that it would be folly to overlook. The study seeks to promote a deeper understanding of the issues, especially the relationship between the various disciplines of public law, politics and political economy. It does not, obviously, seek to imitate the economic analysis of private law[97] but is attempting something quite different. I am not implying that this is a definitive view of corporate taxation. Neither am I suggesting that, because things seem to be this way, they can never be any different. The study does not fall victim to the so-called 'genetic fallacy',[98] and its viewpoint is not a deterministic one. Nonetheless, if people want change, they have to know what they are up against. Mirrlees says, wisely: '[T]ax is one area of public policy where the "tyranny of the status quo" is strongest'.[99] As the Coalition discovered soon after taking

[92] Loughlin, *Foundations of Public Law* (above n 6) 231.

[93] Eg: Sanger (above n 36) 7; and Anonymous, 'In the Back: Tax Avoidance: Haven Sent' *Private Eye* (No 1277, 10–23 December 2010) 28.

[94] *Budget 2011* (above n 8) 59.

[95] M Oakeshott, *On Human Conduct* (Oxford, Clarendon Press, 1975) 9. See P Franco, *The Political Philosophy of Michael Oakeshott* (London, Yale University Press, 1990) 5.

[96] S Brittan, 'Why There Are Two Kinds of Conservatism' *Financial Times* (4 March 2011) 13.

[97] Eg, S Shavell, *Foundations of Economic Analysis of Law* (Cambridge, MA, Belknap Press, 2004).

[98] Eg, MR Cohen and E Nagel, *An Introduction to Logic and Scientific Method* (London, Routledge and Kegan Paul, 1963) 388–90.

[99] Mirrlees, Adam and Besley et al (above n 3) 21.

office in 2010, the historical reasons for things being as they are may make a present state of affairs difficult to change.

This book is thus about the basis on which political judgments, based largely on sound economic theory, are enshrined in law. These judgments are prudential ones, and they result in the realisation in the corporation tax code of versions of the values of efficiency and fairness that fall somewhat short of an ideal. While it is true that such prudential judgments cannot be reduced to mathematical formulae, it is also true that they have their own rationale. This rationale is the essence of what the study seeks to lay bare. In chapter two, therefore, I seek to deepen and broaden various aspects of the discussion so far: why corporate tax law has this political quality, and the advantages of viewing it as public law.

In a popular short story, Conan Doyle makes his famous detective, Sherlock Holmes, say: 'It is a capital mistake to theorise before one has data. Insensibly one begins to twist facts to suit theories, instead of theories to suit facts'.[100] If this is plausible for detective stories, it is all the more so for interpretative monographs. So I turn without further ado to some observations about Britain's corporate tax system.

[100] A Conan Doyle, 'A Scandal in Bohemia' in *Sherlock Holmes: The Complete Short Stories* (London, John Murray/Jonathan Cape, 1928) 7.

2

A Theory of Corporate Tax Reform

FOR ALL THE intricacies of corporate tax law, some fundamental points about taxing the profits of companies based in Great Britain can be made fairly briefly and simply. I would like therefore to start with four observations about Britain's corporation tax system, following which I shall sketch out the discussion in the rest of the chapter.

First of all, profits made at home in Britain[1] are generally liable to corporation tax.[2] Every company is treated as a separate taxable entity from its shareholders, and each company within a group of companies is, for most purposes, regarded as being a separate taxable entity from the other company or companies in the group. How widely the profits of companies are defined, which is simply the reverse of asking how generously the exemptions from corporate profits are delineated, has become a significant ideological dividing line among critics of the corporate tax system. If profits are defined widely, such that there are few exemptions, then tax rates – the percentages at which profits are taxed – can be low without loss of public revenue. If, on the other hand, profits are defined relatively narrowly, for instance because there are exemptions designed to incentivise investment in new technologies, then in order to maintain comparably high levels of revenue, corporation tax rates need to be higher. Those on the communitarian Left of politics tend to favour the latter; those on the neoliberal Right tend to favour the former. This, in essence, is what the debate over lower – that is, more 'flat' – corporate taxes is all about. The ideological divide simply means, of course, that rates of corporate tax are something of a red herring. What matters rather more is the definition of the corporate tax base: in other words, of the 'thing . . . which is liable to the tax'.[3]

So far as profits made outside Great Britain are concerned, it used to be the universal rule that these, too, were included in the taxable profits of British-based companies.[4] So if a British company had a branch or subsidiary overseas, the trading profits from the foreign branch, or the dividends paid out by the

[1] In other words, I am referring to the United Kingdom of Great Britain and Northern Ireland. (See the Preface to this book.)

[2] Corporation Tax Act (CTA) 2009 s 5 (formerly Income and Corporation Taxes Act (ICTA) 1988 s 8).

[3] G Morse and D Williams, *Davies: Principles of Tax Law*, 5th edn (London, Sweet and Maxwell, 2004) para 1-09. The corporation tax main rate for financial year 2010 was 28 per cent.

[4] CTA 2009 s 5 (ex-ICTA 1988 s 8(1)).

foreign subsidiary to the British holding company, would be liable to taxation in Britain. This blanket rule has remained the fall-back position, but it has gradually been transformed. Ultimately backed up by stringent controlled foreign company (CFC) rules, the blanket rule was originally a revenue protection measure instituted just before World War I, principally in order to combat the tax avoidance activities of the Vestey brothers.[5] The combined package, however, eventually came to be seen as inconsistent with Britain's commitments as a member state of the European Union.

The Labour Government took a decisive step in the 2009 Finance Act, when dividends from foreign subsidiaries were exempted from corporation tax, subject to detailed conditions.[6] The Coalition Government's Finance Bill 2011 then brought forward matching provisions, designed to enable the exemption by election of profits from foreign branches.[7] Separate legislative initiatives were needed because, whereas an overseas subsidiary is a separate legal and taxable entity from its British holding company, an overseas branch of a British-based company is not. The result is that profits made abroad will now fall within the taxable profits of a British-based company only if it fails to elect to have its overseas branch profits exempted or if for some reason the dividend exemption does not apply.

This evolving limitation on the worldwide sweep of corporation tax is my second observation on the corporation tax system. It is called 'the territoriality principle'[8] and is subject to anti-avoidance provisions designed to tackle abuses of what is certainly a generous approach to corporate taxpayers. Needless to say, the CFC regime, modified in an attempt to comply with EU law, remains in force to deal with British companies deferring corporation tax by leaving profits in offshore subsidiaries rather than paying them out as dividends. Yet the enhancement of territoriality in the British corporate tax system, a move attended by much risk to the government, has accompanied the programmed reduction in the main tax rate as a key component in improving the system's 'competitiveness'. Such a limitation should not of course mean that a company's overseas profits escape tax altogether, since they will continue to be taxed under the tax systems of the foreign jurisdictions where they were made.

[5] S Picciotto, *International Business Taxation* (London, Weidenfeld and Nicolson, 1992) 15; and JF Avery Jones, 'Taxing Foreign Income from Pitt to the Tax Law Rewrite: The Decline of the Remittance Basis' in J Tiley (ed), *Studies in the History of Tax Law* (Oxford, Hart Publishing, 2004) 15, 44.

[6] CTA 2009 pt 9A, incorporated by Finance Act (FA) 2009, s 34 and sch 14.

[7] Finance Bill (No 3) 2011 cl 48 and sch 13, inserting CTA 2009 s 18A.

[8] BJ Arnold and MJ McIntyre, *International Tax Primer*, 2nd edn (The Hague, Kluwer, 2002) 45; HM Treasury and HMRC, *Corporate Tax Reform: Delivering a More Competitive System* (London, 2010) 13 (CTRM), available at http://www.hm-treasury.gov.uk (accessed 30 November 2010). In this book, I generally refer to this document by the abbreviation 'CTRM', which stands for 'Corporate Tax Road Map', because the CTRM is arguably the most important part of the referenced larger document. With the CTRM, the Coalition intended to set out a distinctive approach to corporate tax reform, one that would stand in sharp contrast to that of its Labour predecessor. See C Sanger, 'Corporate Tax Road Map' (2011) *British Tax Review* 2.

My third observation on corporate taxation – not just in Britain, but generally – is that as a matter of economics, it should not be necessary to tax companies at all.[9] Since companies are different legal entities from their shareholders, so the argument goes, a company itself could be exempt from taxation, and the shareholders could be taxed directly. The essence of this rather technical argument is that the tax base of corporation tax – what is and what is not taxed – is the return to the shareholder on her equity in the company.[10] The company itself is just a vehicle for collecting the tax and could in principle be looked straight through, with all attention being focussed instead on the personal tax position of the shareholders. No government has ever dared to go this way, although the first part of the Mirrlees review in 2010 did examine the arguments in its favour.[11] Why no government has gone this way is something that I seek to attribute to history and to political prudence. And, while recognising the economic theory, consistent with the present study's public law approach, I use the expression 'corporation tax base' to refer to the profits actually charged to corporation tax by Corporation Tax Act 2009, section 5. As with many other arguments in the area of corporate taxation, the anomaly pinpoints exactly the relationship between economics, politics and law. This relationship is scoped out of most discussions of the subject, and its dissection is the essence of what I am seeking to achieve in this study.

The fourth and final observation that I would like to make is that within the corporate tax system, the two values introduced above in chapter one – fairness and efficiency – constantly jostle for priority. Efficiency, as we saw, is an outgrowth of the idea expressed by Adam Smith that taxes should not be inordinately expensive to collect. This is one of those principles of taxation that Mirrlees describes as indisputable. Its consequences are, however, striking. In the hands of Gordon Brown, a key influence on this subject until as late as 2010, it meant fine-tuning the corporate tax system so as to eliminate market failures, or inefficiencies, from it.[12] In other, more neoliberal hands, however, it could simply mean stripping back the corporate tax system to a bare minimum, in an attempt to promote economic growth by ensuring that taxation considerations are entirely absent from the commercial ones. Such a view would be championed by followers of another seminal figure already introduced: Friedrich von Hayek. It will be seen from this that efficiency is an economic consideration. Not so – at least not quite – is the rival value of the corporate taxation system: fairness.

The nature and scope of fairness is much more difficult to map. Most arguments about it relate to individuals and the shares of taxation that they bear,

[9] But see J Kay, 'Talk of Raising the Corporate Burden Taxes Logic' *Financial Times* (25 October 2005) 19. See above ch 1 (n 41).

[10] AJ Auerbach, MP Devereux and H Simpson, 'Taxing Corporate Income' in S Adam, T Besley et al (eds), *Dimensions of Tax Design: The Mirrlees Review* (Oxford, Oxford University Press, 2010) 837, 843.

[11] Adam, Besley et al (eds) (ibid).

[12] See below ch 5.

relative to people in the same or a different economic situation. But as already mentioned, this is not possible with companies, since the law has created an artificial layer between a company and its shareholders, and it is very difficult to see how much of the burden of a company's tax bill has been passed on to customers, employees and so on. Questions of fairness therefore tend to centre on rather rough and ready estimates of whether companies are paying a fair share of corporate taxation as a whole and on whether corporate taxation forms an appropriately high share of the overall British tax take. But these are necessarily imprecise arguments and usually disintegrate into extremely abstract and complex anti-avoidance measures. The Labour Administration that left office in May 2010 never succeeded in explaining with sufficient clarity the justification for this aspect of their policy, which became especially prominent in the period 2002 to 2010. Again, this area helps to map with precision where the boundaries between economics, politics and law are to be detected.

Such, then, are four key observations about the taxation of companies based in Great Britain. Foreign companies are not liable to corporation tax unless they generate trading profits through a 'permanent establishment', or branch, in Britain.[13] The profits of such a company are liable to be taxed, if at all, in the country where the company is based. However, if instead of having a British branch, a foreign company has a British subsidiary, then that subsidiary is treated in the same way as any other British company. These supplementary rules, which mirror those I have already discussed, need to be mentioned for completeness, and the rule on branches does of course give rise to issues around whether the home country is subjecting those profits to an adequate level of taxation. This has become a key battleground for nongovernmental organisations (NGOs), such as the Tax Justice Network (TJN) and Christian Aid, campaigning for tax justice[14] and for the co-ordinated efforts of governments worldwide to get certain states to relinquish their tax haven status.[15] One key problem is that of transfer pricing, the price at which goods and services are supplied from one arm of a multinational to another. Very often, possibly in order to take advantage of broken tax systems in the developing world, multinationals will ship goods to Great Britain at manipulated prices.[16] Describing the transfer pricing phenomenon in the context of the shipment of supermarket flowers from Kenya to Britain, the TJN's Richard Murphy had this to say:

> Transfer pricing is completely legal. It simply means that a price is set at which goods are sold, in this case flowers, from one company in Kenya to another company in the UK and they're both owned by the same people. Now, suppose you buy a bunch of flowers in a supermarket for £10. Let's presume that £4 of that will go to the super-

[13] CTA 2009 ss 5 and 19 (ex-ICTA 1988 s 11).

[14] V Houlder, 'Tax Claims Hit at Reputation as well as the Coffers' *Financial Times* (9 November 2010) 16.

[15] N Shaxson, *Treasure Islands: Tax Havens and the Men Who Stole the World* (London, Bodley Head, 2011) ch 10.

[16] Shaxson (ibid) 124–25; and Picciotto (above n 5) ch 8.

> markets, so £6 is left to pay to the supplier of the flowers. Those flowers were grown in Kenya, sold to the supermarket by a British company. Let's suppose that out of that £6, £5 was costs, so they made a profit of £1. Now if that group of companies wanted to pay all its tax in Kenya then the £1 profit would have been added onto the Kenyan costs, and all the profit would have turned up in the Kenyan accounts. And the UK company would have made no profit.[17]

Transfer pricing is indeed a murky business, not necessarily because of any shady dimension to these activities but because the process of establishing transfer prices, and thus of which state should get the tax, is a notoriously difficult one. Besides requiring access to highly specialised product information, it also involves the making of often quite unrealistic commercial assumptions.

In this chapter, I build a theory of corporate tax reform that is rooted in a particular view of the status of corporation tax law as public law. I approach the matter in four stages. First, I demonstrate how and why, given that economic theory is the bedrock of corporation tax, the tax nonetheless has a crucial relationship with politics and law. Secondly, I show what it is that makes corporate taxation a political as opposed to a merely technical subject and, within that framework, what constitutes the reform of the system. Thirdly, I analyse how viewing corporation tax in this way complements its status as public law – as law that deals with the relationship between the corporate sector and the state and, equally importantly, with the ordering of the state itself. This involves expanding on the conception of theory advanced in chapter one, as well as explaining in more detail the public law importance of the rival values of efficiency and fairness. Significantly, however, it also requires me to say something about the critical standpoint adopted in the study, as well as the implications of this for the fairness discussion. I wind up in the final section of the chapter by offering an overview of the rest of the study, in which I explain the significance of and the relationship between its various elements.

I. TENSIONS AND CONVENTIONS IN CORPORATE TAXATION

I mentioned above that at the core of corporate tax reform is the now besieged discipline of economics. This is what provides this intractable policy area with its corpus of technical knowledge that should, one might expect, form the basis of all policy judgments in the area. That these policy judgments must be made as part of the 'practices of politics',[18] of governing, is what justifies my use of the term 'political economy'. This is not, however, an entirely straightforward claim. In this section, therefore, I seek to map out the relationship between the various elements in a little more detail.

[17] BBC Radio 4, 'Companies "Looting" a Continent' BBC File of Four (29 July 2007), available at http://news.bbc.co.uk/1/hiprogrammes/file_on_4/6908997.stm (accessed 9 June 2011). BBC transcript in my possession.

[18] M Loughlin, *The Idea of Public Law* (Oxford, Oxford University Press, 2003) 30–40.

Even before the Mirrlees review, the economics literature on corporation tax was such that, in Jack Mintz's opinion, corporation tax was possibly the subject of more anxious scrutiny than any other tax.[19] 'Countless numbers of professionals', he has said, 'study the impact of corporate tax law on the affairs of the corporation'.[20] In the years between the introduction of corporation tax in 1965[21] and the publication of the first volume of Mirrlees in 2010, there were five major critiques of the tax: the theoretically pleasing though unrealistic discussion of corporation tax in the Meade Committee Report of 1978;[22] the much lauded though inconclusive 1982 Green Paper on corporation tax reform;[23] the discussion of corporation tax in the last edition of John Kay and Mervyn King's widely cited economics textbook;[24] Mintz's own paper on corporation tax,[25] to which I have just referred; and an important, more recent study by Devereux, Griffith and Klemm,[26] which sought to account for the revenue-generating success of the tax while rightly casting doubt on its continuing ability to produce such comparatively high levels of revenue. This particular choice of five examples would not necessarily of course correspond to the choice that another commentator might make. Its importance, however, is that it illustrates the understandable, though necessarily misleading, dominance of economics in the subject area.

The Mirrlees review has continued this trend but has sought to put their economic learning in a somewhat broader context. In their contribution to Mirrlees, Alan Auerbach, Michael Devereux and Helen Simpson provide us with the root of all tensions in the study and practice of corporate tax reform.[27] They do not claim it as an original point, but much of their work has been devoted to examining its implications. Investment capital is a scarce resource, and it is also relatively mobile. It seems likely, therefore, that different countries compete in order to attract it within their borders. Work by one of the trio, Michael Devereux, and others indicates that this is so.[28] Even if the evidence were weaker, it would be a reasonable working hypothesis, and indeed all governmental pronouncements, as well as those of international treaty organisations such as the

[19] J Mintz, 'The Corporation Tax' in MP Devereux (ed), *The Economics of Tax Policy* (Oxford, Oxford University Press, 1996) 137.

[20] Ibid, 137.

[21] FA 1965 ss 46–89. See D Kynaston, *The City of London, Vol IV: A Club No More, 1945–2000* (London, Chatto and Windus, 2001) 300–1, 304, 307 and 311–12.

[22] JE Meade (ed), *The Structure and Reform of Direct Taxation: Report of a Committee Chaired by Professor JE Meade* (London, George Allen and Unwin, 1978).

[23] *Corporation Tax: Presented to Parliament by the Chancellor of the Exchequer by Command of Her Majesty* (Green Paper, Cmnd 8456, 1982).

[24] JA Kay and MA King, *The British Tax System*, 5th edn (Oxford, Oxford University Press, 1990) chs 10 and 11.

[25] Mintz (above n 19).

[26] MP Devereux, R Griffith and A Klemm, 'Why Has the UK Corporation Tax Raised So Much Revenue?' (2004) 25 *Fiscal Studies* 367.

[27] Auerbach, Devereux and Simpson (above n 10).

[28] MP Devereux, B Lockwood and M Redoano, 'Do Countries Compete over Corporate Tax Rates?' (2008) *Journal of Public Economics* 1210.

Organisation for Economic Co-operation and Development (OECD), recognise that it is the case.[29]

This situation invites three main propositions. First of all, being a scarce commodity, investment capital is a source of potential conflict between states, in the same way that the fair distribution of the resources that it creates harbours potential conflict within states.[30] Secondly, the potential conflict exists because the neoliberal value choices implied by open markets for capital and labour are themselves ideological and conflictual as regards the rival claims of communitarianism and, though not now as strong as once they were, social democracy[31] and socialism. And thirdly, the management of the potential conflict by national governments working with international organisations involves political skills that involve isolating the political issues from the merely technical ones.

The first of these propositions has involved a shift of emphasis that the attentive reader will already have appreciated. This is the almost imperceptible transition from the economists' characterisation of the relationship between states as one of tax competition to my characterisation of it as one of potential tax conflict. The shift denotes a very old intellectual divergence. Conflict, so the argument runs, is a zero-sum game, while competition is supposedly a positive-sum game.[32] Martin Wolf and Samuel Brittan have made the point that firms, not countries, compete.[33] The relationship between countries as regards taxation is more a matter of incipient conflict.[34] The weight given to one or other characterisation is what energises debates both about the rates and tax base and about efficiency and fairness. In the 2011 Budget, George Osborne declared that he wanted to make the British system 'the most competitive' in the G20 group of nations.[35] And if the idea of potential conflict seems too emotive, consider, for example, the threat implied by the reported comments of the chief executives of two British multinationals as early as December 2003. According to one, his group's 'investment priorities were in other markets [ie, outside Britain]' because of the additions to his company's 'UK cost base' of '"interventionist" government policies'.[36] To another was attributed the elliptical claim that 'it now "notionally" paid 53 per cent of its profits in taxation', with, again, the threat implied in the comment that he 'would not want to see that going up any

[29] Organisation for Economic Co-operation and Development (OECD), *Harmful Tax Competition: An Emerging Global Issue* (Paris, OECD, 1998); and Shaxson (above n 15).

[30] Editorial, 'Britain's Growing Inequality Problem: The UK has a Problem with its Widening Rich–Poor Gap' *Financial Times* (28 January 2010) 14.

[31] A Giddens, *The Third Way: The Renewal of Social Democracy* (Oxford, Polity Press, 1998) ch 3; and A Giddens, *The Third Way and its Critics* (Cambridge, Polity Press, 2000) ch 3.

[32] J Kay, 'It May Be a Rembrandt to You, But Markets Can Beg to Differ' *Financial Times* (21 July 2010) 11.

[33] See below ch 5.

[34] Shaxson (above n 15) 197–98.

[35] Hansard HC vol 525 col 954 (23 March 2011).

[36] J Boxell and A Jones, 'Domecq Chief Attacks Brown over Tax' *Financial Times* (5 December 2003) 1 (quoting Philip Bowman of Allied Domecq).

further'.[37] Even – or perhaps, especially – in the boom times, examples of such language have abounded, and like the one just quoted, they usually involve the more or less veiled threat of capital flight.[38] 'If you do not play ball with us', these voices suggest, 'we shall take the ball away'. And each example tends to support the claim of the controversial though perceptive German jurist of the 1930s Carl Schmitt (1888–1985), namely that economic factors no less than, say, religious differences, can provide 'energy' to political 'association[s] or dissociation[s] . . . to coalitions and separations'.[39]

However we characterise the nature of the relationship between states – whether as one of competition or of conflict – we need to explain what choices are implied that makes capital such a prized resource. This is the pervasive relevance of my earlier discussion of neoliberalism or, as Steger and Roy emphasise, the various versions thereof.[40] This ideology, traceable ultimately to Smith but given its most powerful expression in modern times by Hayek, is that the political ordering state has a very limited role in the promotion of human prosperity. Instead, a spontaneous order can be created by the operation of the market, an essentially natural phenomenon in which the state's role is limited to the enforcement of contracts and the preservation of property rights.[41] The problem is that in no major developed nation, not even in the United States, has this been adopted in its purest form. Though she regarded it as an ideal, Baroness Thatcher did not in reality even come close to its realisation in the Britain of the 1980s. The slimmed down tax system that it predicates was, however, the ambition of the most intellectually distinguished of her Chancellors, Nigel Lawson, and he did succeed in instantiating some ideas about tax systems that neoliberal ideologies accept. The various ways of taking the fruit of such tax systems – economic growth – without suffering the social consequences have been enshrined in ideas such as the Third Way[42] and the Big Society.[43] The yearning

[37] Ibid (quoting an anonymous executive of Tesco).

[38] A Parker, 'Revenue and Business to Thrash Out Tax Problems' *Financial Times* (24 February 2004) 1 (quoting Jonathan Symonds of AstraZeneca); V Houlder, 'The Tax Avoidance Story as a Morality Tale' *Financial Times* (22 November 2004) 9 (quoting Aidan O'Carroll of Ernst and Young); V Houlder, 'Simpler, Lower, Fairer: Brown's Tax Demand from Business' *Financial Times* (3 October 2005) 17; Editorial, *Financial Times* (9 November 2005) 18; J Eaglesham, 'Employers' Chief Warns over Drive against Tax Dodging' *Financial Times* (6 December 2005) 4 (quoting Sir Digby Jones of CBI); C Adams, 'Energy Industry Angry at Rise in Corporation Tax' *Financial Times* (6 December 2005) 5 (quoting Malcolm Webb of the UK Offshore Operators Association); V Houlder, 'Fright could Turn to Flight as Tax Regime Gets Tighter' *Financial Times* (23 December 2005) 4 (quoting inter alia Chris Spooner of HSBC Holdings); V Houlder, 'Companies Anchored to Tax Regime in Spite of Discontent' *Financial Times* (20 June 2006) 3; and V Houlder, 'Global Corporate Tax Rates Fall' *Financial Times* (23 July 2007) 7.

[39] C Schmitt, *The Concept of the Political* [1927], G Schwab (trans) (Chicago, University of Chicago Press, 1996) 38. See Loughlin, *The Idea of Public Law* (above n 18) 34.

[40] MB Steger and RK Roy, *Neoliberalism: A Very Short Introduction* (Oxford, Oxford University Press, 2010) ch 2.

[41] Ibid, 19–20; and R Plant, *The Neo-liberal State* (Oxford, Oxford University Press, 2010) 168.

[42] Giddens, *The Third Way* (above n 31).

[43] J Norman, *The Big Society: The Anatomy of the New Politics* (Buckingham, University of Buckingham Press, 2010).

for a neoliberal simplicity and the pull of a largely communitarian actuality means, however, that corporate tax law hovers uneasily between two extremes: minimalism and complexity.

Each of the two earlier propositions – about potential conflict as against competition and about the difficulties of prioritising economic values in choices about the way we live – invites some comment about how in practice these antagonisms are to be resolved. This is the topic I want to discuss next; but it necessary to emphasise here that this is the realm of politics, and this requires me to define what I mean by the terms 'political' and 'politics'. The potentially conflictual relationships implied by the first of the propositions discussed above are what I take the essence of the political to be in this context. It is the struggle for the limited resource of investment capital. This agonistic deployment of the political concept has been well explored by Chantal Mouffe,[44] drawing on the perceptive but troubling Schmitt, and it forms what Martin Loughlin calls 'the first order of the political',[45] the potential for conflict in human relations. Likewise, the activity of managing the potential for conflict is what 'the practice of politics' is all about. This is a well-established distinction that Loughlin's theory of public law specifically endorses, designating the management process 'the second order of the political'.[46] Politics, in this context, is therefore precisely coterminous with governing or governance. We are of course using the words interpretatively, meaning that what we say is 'rooted in an appreciation of government and the functions law is expected to perform in respect of those functions'.[47] It is, in other words, about 'making sense' of the factual material,[48] not putting it into some straightjacket. Though not uncontentious, it is suited to interpreting systems of representative government, one of the characteristics of which is that the few govern on behalf of the many.[49]

If economic factors are at the core of corporation tax reform, it is necessary to interrogate further their place relative to politics and public law. This is the task to which I proceed in the next two sections.

II. TECHNIQUE AND PRUDENCE

What distinguishes a political issue in corporate tax reform from a merely technical one is its potential to assume significance in the struggle for investment capital. Only a small number of corporation tax issues, if any, lack this potential. I turn

[44] C Mouffe, *On the Political* (London, Routledge, 2005) 8.

[45] M Loughlin, 'Constitutional Law: The Third Order of the Political' in N Bamforth and P Leyland (eds), *Public Law in a Multi-Layered Constitution* (Oxford, Hart Publishing, 2003) 30.

[46] Mouffe (above n 44); and Loughlin, 'Constitutional Law' (ibid).

[47] M Loughlin, *Public Law and Political Theory* (Oxford, Oxford University Press, 1992) 231.

[48] C Taylor, 'Interpretation and the Sciences of Man' in *Philosophy and the Human Sciences: Philosophical Papers 2* (Cambridge, Cambridge University Press, 1985) 15.

[49] B Manin, *The Principles of Representative Government* (Cambridge, Cambridge University Press, 1997) 41.

next to how such purely technical issues might possibly be isolated. When an issue is not of that technical kind, then the government needs political prudence to manage it. The practice of politics thus invoked draws on two approaches to the subject. The dominant one is that of politics as calculation, but the subject matter often also requires deliberation. Prudence in this area consists in subtle combinations and re-combinations of the two. Distinguishing the technical from the political helps to map out the sphere of economics in relation to the realm of politics and public law.

A. The Technical and the Political

Technical issues can perhaps be characterised as ones where the choice as to a particular course of action are already decided, and the question is how best to implement them. Typically, they require reference to procedural manuals and the careful execution of previously determined solutions.[50] In relation to the government of the state, these elements are the essence of administrative action. Many commentators have argued that forcing economic policy into this technical category and excluding politics from its ambit was a major contributing factor to the 2007–09 financial crisis.[51] Indeed, the political advantage of an entrenched neoliberalism is that political questions tend to be re-characterised technical ones. It produces the illusion of viable, even obvious, solutions to posited problems – a vision of harmony in place of strife.

The salient feature of corporate tax reform as mere technique was the increase in the nature and scope of governmentally promulgated 'educational' material in the 1990s and early 2000s. Some of this was recognisably law in a rather narrow positivistic sense: secondary legislation in the form of statutory instruments, the sheer quantity of these being a striking feature of the regime for the taxation treatment of foreign exchange (FOREX) gains and losses.[52] Other types of technical material, such as statements of practice and extra-statutory concessions, not to mention press notices, have also been features of this phenomenon, abhorrent to the neoliberal imagination but consistent – though lacking legal form – with a communitarian approach emphasising a common political purpose. The corporation tax reform of the 1990s saw a range of other material, too. One of these has been the phenomenon of the explanatory notes that have accompanied new legislation since 1999. That said, explanatory notes, though significant, are not unique, having become commonplace in other areas too. What is unique to the tax context, however, is the publication on the web, subject to certain reservations, of the instruction manuals produced for the staff of the relevant government department, HM Revenue and Customs (HMRC).

[50] M Oakeshott, 'Rationalism in Politics' [1962] in T Fuller (ed), *Rationalism in Politics and Other Essays*, 2nd edn (Indianapolis, Liberty Fund, 1991) 5, 23.

[51] A Kaletsky, 'Goodbye, Homo Economicus' *Prospect* (April 2009) 46.

[52] Now in CTA 2009 pt 5.

The corporate taxation section of the HMRC website includes manuals on taxation treatment of corporate debt, on corporation tax compliance matters, plus the tax treatment of FOREX and financial instruments.[53] All of these different categories of material are technical because they do not challenge but rather facilitate an agreed political end.

Political issues, by contrast, are ones where not only are the means not agreed but the choice of values to prioritise remains highly contentious. This point is closely bound up with my earlier discussion of both the scramble for capital and the division of its fruits as harbouring the potential for conflict. Crucially important to the study is the contention that the significance of corporation tax reform is not encapsulated in the devising of elegant solutions to intricate technical problems. This is, to be sure, one of its most important jobs. At a much deeper level, however, it is also an arena in which, to paraphrase Schmitt, there is an ever-present potential for conflict.[54] Moreover, when government ministers, public servants, lawyers, accountants, corporations and economists engage in the process of consultation and negotiation on corporation tax reform, they are often engaged in the practice of politics.[55]

Readers with a background in political science or public policy will find neither of these statements exceptionable. It is suggested, however, that judging by the economics materials referred to above, for accountants and possibly even for lawyers, these sayings will be controversial. Even outside economic policy theory, the process of corporation tax reform is often presented as a preoccupation of specialist lawyers or accountants, rather than the subject of a wider political discourse. Thus Peters in his study of taxes and politics in OECD countries in the early 1990s[56] devoted only a small part of his analysis to specific issues raised by corporate taxation.[57] The specialist nature of the subject matter means that so far as lawyers and accountants are concerned, the arguments to which it gives rise are such as largely to remove them from the arena of the political. There has been, as we shall see, some discussion of corporate tax politics, notably by Claudio Radaelli in a finely detailed British–Italian comparative study, from the late 1990s;[58] but even this, I would contend, radically underestimated what it is that is political about corporate taxation. In arguing for a political status for corporation tax reform, the present study is not merely saying that it is a practice of 'political economy', since this is of course the case. Rather, its claim is that despite the polished manners and well-tailored suits of its chief protagonists, corporation tax reform is characterised by the need to find 'workable' solutions to profound but skilfully obfuscated antagonisms.[59] The accumulation

[53] Http://www.hmrc.gov.uk/agents/forms-ct.htm#2 (accessed 6 April 2011).

[54] Schmitt (above n 39) 29.

[55] Loughlin, *The Idea of Public Law* (above n 18) 30.

[56] BG Peters, *The Politics of Taxation: A Comparative Perspective* (Oxford, Blackwell, 1991).

[57] Ibid, 31–32.

[58] CM Radaelli, *The Politics of Corporate Taxation in the European Union: Knowledge and International Policy Agendas* (London, Routledge, 1997).

[59] Schmitt (above n 39) 29.

of technical detail may itself give rise to such antagonisms, because of its potential to reduce the return on capital through its attendant costs.

Gradations of neoliberal thought involve the extent to which political judgments are given a place in a sphere of endeavour in which economics and technical solutions seem to rule supreme. The initial contention that corporation tax reform is a political arena, its significance far from exhausted by its technical complexity, relies on the constant potential for conflict, express or implied, suggested by each of the above examples. This potential is not, as we shall see, diminished by the fairly refined and courteous way in which it is handled. And it presents us with the task of providing some interpretation of what has been happening in the reform process, especially over the last decade and a half. For this, we have to turn to politics or, to be more precise, to what politics scholarship has to tell us about the management of the political.[60] One financial journalist has characterised the potential for conflict with a telling example: '[A] quoted company audit committee that puts its tax advice out to tender is likely to be asked by competing firms where, on the spectrum of tax management from "caution" to "extreme aggression", it wishes to be'.[61]

What is striking is that most of the time the policies of the pre-2010 Labour Administration were characterised by a technical kind of neoliberalism. All interventions in the market, as John Kay has explained, had to be justified by reference to market failures.[62] The political had to be recategorised as the merely technical. Since 2010, however, the Coalition's approach has been to re-inject the political into public policy debates, as their bank levy has amply illustrated. In this connection, Chris Sanger has described the Coalition's Corporate Tax Road Map (CTRM) of May 2010 as 'a distinctly political document'.[63] The highest degree of competitiveness, the Coalition's avowed objective for the corporate tax system, is an overtly political conception in a way that promoting the embedded value of efficiency is not.

B. The Role of Political Prudence

If an issue is merely a technical one, the question of how to resolve it is merely a matter of examining the various alternatives and seeing which one is the most efficient. If, however, the issue is political, then its management, within the practice of politics, requires a special skill: political prudence.

[60] Loughlin, 'Constitutional Law' (above n 45) 30.

[61] J Plender, 'Beware the Side-Effects of a Tax Clampdown' *Financial Times* (18 March 2004) 18; and A Parker, 'Tax Probe to Centre on 30 Top Companies' *Financial Times* (4 May 2004) 4. In the latter article, an anonymous 'Whitehall official' is quoted as saying, 'Ernst & Young are probably the most aggressive, creative, abusive provider of schemes and arrangements among the major accountancy firms.'

[62] J Kay, 'The Failure of Market Failure' *Prospect* (August 2007) 36.

[63] Sanger (above n 8) 2.

The idea of prudence in politics, via Loughlin's characterisation of its importance in public law and my argument for the status of corporation tax law as a species of public law, is something that is foundational through the whole of what follows. Many instances will be given, so rather than elaborate in detail on all of its possible implications, I want at this stage to draw attention to some key elements only. Recall that Nigel Lawson defined political economy, as distinct from economics, as 'consisting in seeking a rational course of action in a world of endemic uncertainty'.[64] This is the kernel of prudent politics in the context of economic policy. And note, too, that being politically rational – that is, being able to justify a public policy decision by 'the basic canons of rationality': coherence, consistency and non-self-contradiction[65] – is much more nuanced than the obsession with 'rationalism' that is the mark of mere technique.[66]

Political prudence, as mentioned, is the essential skill of the politician, ruler or legislator. It is, so Loughlin tells us, 'the activity of governing' that has given rise to the practice of politics,[67] and since early modernity every realistic conception of politics has drawn inspiration from Machiavelli.[68] Though rooted in the culture of sixteenth-century Florence, a stream of modern works, of which Jonathan Powell's[69] is only the latest, bear witness not only to Machiavelli's continuing ability to illuminate the practice of politics but also to his continuing usefulness to its practitioners.[70] For Machiavelli, as Fleisher has put it, 'there is no power of [practical] reason superior to *prudenza*'.[71] It is a calculating technique, a process of rapid ratiocination, a weighing of ends and means. Loughlin has quoted Fleisher's summary of Machiavelli's notion of prudence:

> Machiavelli's *prudenza* is rooted in his conception of the human world. Prudence is not to be measured principally by the existing standards of right and wrong but by the requirements of the situation, by necessity, and by the assessment of the best means to achieve one's ends. Prudence is not synonymous with caution, nor is it the dominance of reason over the appetites and passions. It is, instead, the cool calculation of what must be done in a given situation to accomplish one's purposes without judgment of the situation being unduly affected by passions or the contemporary conventions and ideals of right and wrong.[72]

[64] N Lawson, 'Five Myths and a Menace' *Standpoint* (January/February 2011) 36, 37.

[65] Loughlin, *Public Law and Political Theory* (above n 47) 59.

[66] Oakeshott, 'Rationalism in Politics' (above n 50) 8.

[67] Loughlin, *The Idea of Public Law* (above n 18) 32.

[68] N Machiavelli, *The Prince* [1532], P Bondanella (ed and trans) (Oxford, Oxford University Press, 2005) esp chs 25 and 26.

[69] J Powell, *The New Machiavelli: How to Wield Power in the Modern World* (London, Bodley Head, 2010).

[70] L Metcalfe and S Richards, *Improving Public Management*, 2nd edn (London, Sage, 1990) 211. See generally, W Parsons, *Public Policy: An Introduction to the Theory and Practice of Policy Analysis* (Cheltenham, Edward Elgar, 1995) 42–43.

[71] M Fleisher, 'A Passion for Politics: The Vital Core of the World of Machiavelli' in M Fleisher (ed), *Machiavelli and the Nature of Political Thought* (London, Croom Helm, 1973) 139.

[72] Ibid, quoted in Loughlin, *The Idea of Public Law* (above n 18) 39.

It is thus well suited, given its historical origins, to a representative system of government, where competences are concentrated, as in the British system, in the hands of a very small number of government ministers. This is particularly true of the arcane tax policymaking procedure discussed in chapter 3. In a radio interview, Nigel Lawson has described how secretive this process was in the early 1980s:

> First of all, I worked out my Budgets by myself with my small group of ministers and officials. Then, at a fairly late stage, I would discuss with the Prime Minister, with Margaret Thatcher, what I had in mind, after dinner at 11 Downing Street. Then – we'd get agreement, and then the Cabinet would not be told until the morning of Budget day itself what the changes were. And nothing else in Government was done that way, and I'm not sure whether it is still done that way with taxation – I don't know. Perhaps it is. I hope it is because it is a sensible way to do it.[73]

This prudence is quite different from prudence, or practical wisdom, in the Aristotelian sense, as the virtue necessary to take part in a deliberation on the best course of political action, or indeed prudence in its apparently unfashionable accounting sense.[74] Aspects of both are comprised in Adam Smith's approach. This is not quite a middle way, since even his is a rather Machiavellian formulation,[75] but it implies there may be a place in the sovereign's calculations for deliberation and consultation:

> We talk of the prudence of the great general, of the great statesman, of the great legislator. Prudence is, in all these cases, combined with many greater and more splendid virtues, with valour, with extensive and strong benevolence, with a sacred regard to the rules of justice, and all these supported by a proper degree of self-command. This superior prudence, when carried to the highest degree of perfection, necessarily supposes the art, the talent, and the habit or disposition of acting with the most perfect propriety in every possible circumstance and situation . . . It is the best head joined to the best heart. It is the most perfect wisdom combined with the most perfect virtue.[76]

Apart from Radaelli's work,[77] the politics of corporation tax have never received systematic academic consideration in the British context. Though valuable – reference will be made to it later in my own study – it does not attempt to reach into the essence of what is political in British corporation tax reform.

[73] E Davis, 'How Well Do We Make Decisions about Tax in Britain?' *Evan Loves Tax* (BBC Radio 4) (15 September 2010), details available at http://www.bbc.co.uk/news/business-11275040 (accessed 30 March 2011).

[74] Aristotle, *The Nicomachean Ethics*, JAK Thomson, H Tredennick and J Barnes (eds) (London, Penguin, 2004) 187–89 and 215–16. See also J Tiley, *Revenue Law*, 6th edn (Oxford, Hart Publishing, 2008) 408 and 409: '[T]he concept of prudence is no longer in favour . . . [I]t provides that revenue is not anticipate[d] in the profit and loss account, and losses are provided for as soon as they are foreseen – and it is at odds with fair value accounting, which considers income and expenditure in terms of balance sheet movement.'

[75] D Winch, *Adam Smith's Politics: An Essay in Historiographic Revision* (Cambridge, Cambridge University Press, 1978) 159.

[76] A Smith, *The Theory of Moral Sentiments* [1759/1790], RP Hanley (ed) (London, Penguin 2009) 255.

[77] Radaelli, *The Politics of Corporate Taxation in the EU* (above n 58) 125.

Although Radaelli has conceded that '[p]olitics generates conflict',[78] he sees the salvation of the project for harmonised corporate taxation within the European Union as being the slow but steady 'politicisation' of a project originally conceived in purely 'technocratic' terms.[79] In short, like the economics literature, Radaelli understates the political element of political economy in the context of corporation tax reform.

Political prudence, then, is the essential skill in the practice of politics, unless one thinks politics to be chiefly about deliberative decision-making. It is rarely named as such in discussions of public policy, but its presence in or absence from a particular political decision can nonetheless be gauged from the rational coherence of that decision. Smith's formulation of what prudence requires, which has recently been revisited by Amartya Sen,[80] gives prominence to a prudential approach but also accords a place to deliberation: the key is what an 'impartial spectator' would think of the public policy decision in question.[81] It is in this sense, possibly, that an idea of prudence as at once pre-emptive and deliberative has found its way into the language of financial regulation in the wake of the financial crisis. Politicians now refer to prudence only sparingly, and there is a possibility that having – in one sense or another – become so closely identified with Gordon Brown, Conservative and Liberal Democrat politicians will use it even more rarely.

Nonetheless, 'without Prudence', said a sixteenth-century theorist, government is 'not onely weake and feeble, but I may well say none at all', since 'prudential logic . . . binds together the political entity of the state'.[82] It was certainly a lack of prudence that eventually damaged so seriously Labour's credibility in this policy area. David Gauke, appointed Exchequer Secretary to the Treasury in May 2010, has striven not to make the same mistake on behalf of the Coalition. A former City solicitor, he has certainly had a higher profile in corporate tax policy than his Labour predecessors in the office, demonstrating a polished ability to speak to the corporate sector in reassuring language. Nonetheless, he has also shown an acute awareness of the challenge presented by UK Uncut and other groups to the social acceptability of corporate tax avoidance. This can only be viewed as a prudential calculation, given Mr Gauke's minimal state aspirations and Lawsonian views of corporate tax policy.[83]

[78] CM Radaelli, *Technocracy in the European Union* (London, Longman, 1999) 154; and J Snape, 'Corporation Tax Reform: Politics and Public Law' (2007) *British Tax Review* 374, 385 and 391.

[79] Ibid, ch 7. See also CM Radaelli, 'The Political Economy of EU Direct Tax Policy' in A Lymer and D Salter (eds), *Contemporary Issues in Taxation Research* (Aldershot, Ashgate Publishing, 2003) 145.

[80] A Sen, *Development as Freedom*, 2nd edn (Oxford, Oxford University Press, 2001) 262.

[81] A Sen, *The Idea of Justice* (London, Allen Lane, 2009) 44–46.

[82] Quoted in M Loughlin, *Foundations of Public Law* (Oxford, Oxford University Press, 2010) 412n.

[83] D Gauke, 'Check against Delivery' *The Philip Hardman Memorial Lecture* (16 November 2010), available at http://www.hm-treasury.gov.uk/speech_xst_161110.htm (accessed 18 April 2011). See also V Houlder, 'Large Companies Pay Lower Rate of Corporation Tax' *Financial Times* (2 March 2011) 3.

C. The Idea of Reform

The distinction between the technical and the political coalesces in the idea of reform. The term implies both technical and political change and therefore requires different degrees of prudence to manage it. The reason for this is that reform is sometimes seen as the bottom-up reconstruction of a system, sometimes as the restoration of a system to its 'true nature', as highlighted in chapter one.

The references to 'corporation tax reform' should not be taken to imply a tightly unified reform process. Although attempts at greater efficiency and greater fairness in the system imply, as we shall see, the realisation of a 'vision' for the tax, they have been 'incremental' and often reactive in nature. Good illustrations of this point are the effect on corporation tax legislation of the compulsory adoption of international accounting standards (IASs) for quoted companies after 31 December 2004, and the problematic abolition, without consultation, of advance corporation tax (ACT) brought about by Labour's landslide General Election victory in May 1997.[84] The now shelved Tax Law Rewrite project, which resulted in much of the code being consolidated in the four mammoth statutes referred to in chapter one (among them, the Corporation Tax Acts 2009 and 2010), was not presented as a case of reform, even though it had efficiency implications.

III. CORPORATION TAX LAW AS PUBLIC LAW

What distinguishes political from merely technical issues, therefore, is their potential to generate conflict. Potential conflict in the sphere of corporate tax policy is revealed in threats from multinationals to invest – or reinvest – outside Great Britain. What is unusual about corporate tax in comparison with other strands of public policy, however, is that a simple accumulation of technical detail is itself capable of assuming a political significance. Indeed, the essence of corporate tax politics has become the skill with which successive administrations manage this antagonism. The question is thus how the management of the incipient threat reflects institutions and processes and produces a code of corporation tax with certain characteristics. This is the province of public law in general and, at successive levels of specificity, tax law and corporate tax law in particular. It is why Loughlin has characterised constitutional law as 'the third order of the political', after the practice of politics as the second and the conflictual political core as the first.[85]

So I next need to examine three different but related areas: the particular view of public law that this approach embodies; the justification for taking tax law as

[84] See below ch 4.

[85] M Loughlin, 'Constitutional Law' (above n 45) 30; and Loughlin, *The Idea of Public Law* (above n 18) 40–42.

part of the broader category of public law; and why corporate taxation, from the particular public law perspective, can be seen primarily as an instrument of rule or of regulation, rather than as one of distributive justice.

A. Public Law as the Law of the State

Public law has long been an arena of vigorous theoretical dispute. However, in the space of around 30 years, two propositions have gradually gained acceptance. These too have been highly contested, but the arguments have tended to be about their wider significance rather than the essential content of the propositions themselves.

First, although conventional wisdom had it that the laws of Great Britain admitted of no distinction between the legal rules applicable to private citizens and those applicable to government,[86] it is generally agreed that this is no longer true. Private and public law are now generally held to function as separate categories of law.[87] Secondly, given the reality of the public law and private law divide, public law itself has two components: the law of the constitution and the law relating to the exercise of executive discretion.[88] What divides public law scholarship is the cumulative significance of these propositions.

The former idea that private and public law are separate categories of mostly positive law is a specific part of the Loughlinian theory outlined above in chapter one. It will be recalled that the focus of the theory is the state[89] and that it emphasises the role of public law in building up the state's capacity. So conceived, public law's significance is that positive law rules, marking out the relationship of state and subject and constituting the institutions of government,[90] are distinctive precisely because they embody the same theoretical assumptions as the principles of political right by which the state – or public sphere – is ordered.[91] The intricate patchwork of rights and duties thereby created, as placed on state and subject alike, tends to be created as much by longstanding political practice as by positive law. The theoretical assumptions of these rights and duties are those of 'reason of state',[92] a reasoning shaped simply by the

[86] RC van Caenegem, *An Historical Introduction to Western Constitutional Law* (Cambridge, Cambridge University Press, 1995) 3. See also HP Glenn, *Legal Traditions of the World*, 2nd edn (Oxford, Oxford University Press, 2004) 234n.

[87] Loughlin, *Foundations of Public Law* (above n 82) 438.

[88] E Barendt, 'Constitutional Fundamentals' in D Feldman (ed), *English Public Law* (Oxford, Oxford University Press, 2004) para 1.08. See also *Davy v Spelthorne Borough Council* [1984] AC 262, 276 (Lord Wilberforce); and *O'Reilly and Others v Mackman and Others* [1983] AC 237, 273–85 (Lord Diplock).

[89] Loughlin, *Foundations of Public Law* (above n 82) 208.

[90] JF McEldowney, *Public Law*, 3rd edn (London, Sweet and Maxwell, 2002) para 1-003.

[91] Loughlin, *Foundations of Public Law* (above n 82) 159, 228 and 231–32.

[92] Loughlin, *The Idea of Public Law* (above n 18) 148. See generally, N Malcolm, *Reason of State, Propaganda, and the Thirty Years' War: An Unknown Translation by Thomas Hobbes* (Oxford, Clarendon Press, 2007) ch 6.

Ciceronian maxim that the state exists for the protection of its people: *salus populi suprema lex esto* ('Let the welfare of the people be the first of laws').[93] So Loughlin's crucial insight is that the informing spirit of public law is that of political prudence,[94] since public law is no more and no less than 'political jurisprudence'. It is a distinctive practice of politics, the third order of the political, existing to consolidate the second, namely the practice of government. Public law cannot be, in other words, independent of or above politics.[95] In the words of the Justinian code, *publicum ius est quod ad statum rei Romanae spectat*: 'public law is that which relates to the Roman state'.[96] And if public law is primarily about prudence, it might not primarily be about justice. Loughlin's public law theory is therefore different from John Rawls' and Jürgen Habermas' systems, and indeed different from the tradition of Immanuel Kant (1724–1804),[97] since it seeks only to interpret the reality, not to suggest ways of building new legal orders. It is a functionalist and interpretative theory of public law as it works in the world.[98] This is a way of thinking to which most lawyers have strong reactions. Their instinct, of course, is to think normatively, to make statements about what 'ought' to be the case. As such, Loughlin's theory provides a functionalist and interpretative standpoint. It is fundamentally different, therefore, from the normative systems of liberal constitutional theorists such as Dicey, Hayek and Robert Nozick (1939–2002), systems 'rooted in a belief in the ideal of the separation of powers and in the need to subordinate government to law'.[99] Again, unlike the perspectives of TRS Allan, Jeffrey Jowell and John Laws, all three of whom are public law followers of Ronald Dworkin and Michael Sandel, Loughlin's functionalist theory predicates no higher or normative idea of law against which to measure the reality. Most importantly, Loughlin's theory is different from Dicey's constitutional law, since, unlike his Scottish predecessors Adam Smith and John Millar,[100] Dicey deliberately restricted his inquiry to positive law[101] and, having done so, naturally enough – given his own ideological position – found no public law/private law distinction.[102] Loughlin's Hegelian theory can therefore certainly be regarded as a

[93] MT Cicero, *de Re Publica; de Legibus* [54–51 bc], CW Keyes (ed and trans) (London, William Heinemann, 1928) 466.

[94] Loughlin, *The Idea of Public Law* (above n 18) 38.

[95] Loughlin, *Public Law and Political Theory* (above n 47) 60.

[96] *The Digest of Justinian* [528–34 ad], T Mommsen, P Krueger and A Watson (eds and trans) (Philadelphia, University of Pennsylvania Press, 1985) 1 (bk 1, I.1.2)).

[97] Loughlin, *Foundations of Public Law* (above n 82) 87 and 129.

[98] M Loughlin, 'Theory and Values in Public Law: An Interpretation' (2005) *Public Law* 48, 60.

[99] Loughlin, *Public Law and Political Theory* (above n 47) 60 and 144; and R Barker, *Political Ideas in Modern Britain* (London, Methuen, 1978) 193.

[100] J Millar, *An Historical View of the English Government* [1812], MS Phillips and DR Smith (eds) (Indianapolis, Liberty Fund, 2006) 796. See Loughlin, *Foundations of Public Law* (above n 82) 5n.

[101] AV Dicey, *Introduction to the Study of the Law of the Constitution* [1885], ECS Wade (ed) (London, Macmillan, 1965).

[102] Loughlin, *Foundations of Public Law* (above n 82) 442.

development of the Scottish Enlightenment tradition,[103] mentioned at the beginning of this chapter.

The notion that private and public law are separate categories of positive law is in turn intimately related to the distinction between constitutional law and administrative law. In Loughlin's theory, the significance of the constitution is that it is not restricted to a 'slim constitutive document',[104] something of course that Great Britain has historically lacked.[105] Instead, as mentioned in chapter one, the constitution comprises 'the complete condition of political unity and order' found in a state.[106] That unity is explicable in part by the political facts as they obtain at any time, but it also relies on the restless yearning for ideals that is formed by a political consensus. This is the immanent dimension to the neoliberal values discussed in chapter one, with the 'well-being of state and its population' as 'the ultimate value'.[107]

It is thus that Loughlin advocates a critical investigation into 'empirical understandings of the functions of government and law'[108] and, in doing so, again reveals a point of connection with the line of investigation started in eighteenth-century Scotland. '[T]he only infallible criterion of the excellence of any constitution', wrote one of Adam Smith's younger contemporaries, 'is to be found in the detail of its municipal code' and in 'those legislative improvements which the general interests of the community recommend'.[109] Or to put it another way, the actual legal ordering of the state embodies politically determined beliefs and values.[110] The duties and the rights of both government and subject in any area of politics, including public law, are 'constitutional' to the extent that out of such material is wrought the order of the state. Identifying the contribution to order and unity of the corporation tax code entails testing the relationships between the values immanent to it against the rational canons of coherence, consistency and non-self-contradiction.[111] It is this relational quality of order and unity in the state that augments the state's sovereignty. The rights and duties of governors and governed alike are shaped by the rationale of prudence.

With Loughlin, moreover, the significance of administration, the exercise of the prerogative or executive power, is not its restraint by judges so much as its

[103] Loughlin, *Public Law and Political Theory* (above n 47) 5.

[104] Ibid, 241.

[105] But not England: SR Gardiner, *Constitutional Documents of the Puritan Revolution 1625–1660*, 3rd edn (Oxford, Clarendon Press, 1906) 405.

[106] Loughlin, *Foundations of Public Law* (above n 82) 211–12.

[107] Ibid, 87.

[108] Loughlin, *Public Law and Political Theory* (above n 47) 36.

[109] D Stewart, 'Account of the Life and Writings of Adam Smith, LL.D' [1793] in IS Ross, DD Raphael and AS Skinner (eds), *Essays on Philosophical Subjects* (Liberty Fund, Indianapolis, 1982) 263, 310–11, quoted in S Collini, D Winch and J Burrow, *That Noble Science of Politics: A Study in Nineteenth-Century Intellectual History* (Cambridge, Cambridge University Press, 1983) 36.

[110] Loughlin, *Foundations of Public Law* (above n 82) 196.

[111] Loughlin, *Public Law and Political Theory* (above n 47).

potential to implement big legislative programmes of social amelioration.[112] This is also distinctive to Loughlin among contemporary theorists. It means that the focus of his discussion moves away from the separation of powers and the rule of law – keystones of Hayekian and Diceyan analysis – and towards the socially beneficial exercise of executive power.[113] The executive is, in Loughlin's view, the most important of the state's competences, not just because of its potential to allocate resources – part of the eighteenth-century science of police[114] – but because of its potential to further the democratic will. Loughlin's approach brings out one of the richly interpretative foundations of Habermas's normative theory: the notion that, while constitutions are idealistic, lofty and forward-looking, administration is materialistic, practical, largely technical and earthbound.[115] Thus, although not an entirely satisfactory distinction, it is certainly true that administrative law can largely be identified with the technical and constitutional law with the political.

In Loughlin's theory, therefore, public law 'operates in accordance with its own conceptual logic'; as such, it should remain 'free from gross manipulation by power-wielders',[116] its 'even-handedness' helping to 'create intimacy, shape identity, generate trust and strengthen allegiance'[117] to the British state.

B. Taxation Law as Public Law

The reader will probably already have conjectured the relevance of each of the preceding public law points to the specific category of tax law. That said, it is useful to spell them out in full and to take the opportunity to elaborate somewhat on the role of tax law in the state.

Tax law is radically different from the archetypal private law subjects of contract law and tort.[118] Its purpose of 'defining the reciprocal duties of State and individuals',[119] as regards the former's prerogative of taxation, marks it out as a branch of public law.[120] Traditionally, this was because, in DEC Yale's words, the latter term referred to 'the sum of the king's powers both prerogative and statutory', and these included the power of taxation as one of a range of powers unique to the sovereign.[121] An important feature of public law, in Smith's theory

[112] Loughlin, *Foundations of Public Law* (above n 82) 391–93 and 397–98.
[113] Ibid, ch 14, esp 416.
[114] Ibid, 409 and 420–23.
[115] Ibid, 12, 164 (referring to J Habermas, *Between Facts and Norms*, W Rehg (trans) (Cambridge, Polity Press, 1997) 38–41) and 451.
[116] Loughlin, *Foundations of Public Law* (above n 82) 41.
[117] Ibid, 40–41.
[118] Eg, EJ Weinrib, *The Idea of Private Law* (Cambridge, MA, Harvard University Press, 1995).
[119] CK Allen, *Law in the Making*, 7th edn (Oxford, Clarendon Press, 1964) 300. See Loughlin, *Foundations of Public Law* (above n 82) 446n, quoting the 6th edn.
[120] Loughlin, *Foundations of Public Law* (above n 82) 254; V Thuronyi, *Comparative Tax Law* (The Hague, Kluwer Law, 2003) 60; and *Ferrazzini v Italy* [2001] STC 1314, 1319c and 1320g–j.
[121] Quoted in Loughlin, *Foundations of Public Law* (above n 82) 377.

of the subject, is that, while it is relatively easy to delineate the subject's duties as regards the sovereign, the duties of the sovereign as regards the subject are much more problematic. They have to remain open-ended because of the sovereign's policymaking prerogative.[122] So although the subject has certain basic rights in relation to taxation, these cannot be spelt out in detail and must be qualified to varying degrees.

The interpretative focus of Loughlin's theory is uniquely valuable in relation to tax law, and its use in the present study marks out the differences between the approach in this book and other legal discussions of corporate tax law and policy. Most often, such discussions of corporate taxation are not theorised, consisting instead of finely detailed analyses of legislative texts. The absence of theory is unsurprising, since the readership of this material is the practising tax profession.[123] I refer to this type of work, at its most distinguished, as 'analytical jurisprudence'.[124] It is invidious perhaps to select examples, but appropriate ones would be two loose-leaf publications: Bramwell et al on the taxation of companies and corporate reconstructions;[125] and Johnson, Ghosh and Miller on the taxation treatment of corporate debt and financial instruments.[126] More theorised is a second category of work, directed at students, the often tacit assumptions of which are largely of a normative kind. John Tiley's work, notably the successive editions of his leading tax textbook, provides an outstanding example,[127] but another would be Davies's elegant and brief introduction to the subject.[128] Each of these, to varying degrees, seem to fit a broadly Diceyan and Hayekian framework, since they do not explicitly recognise a public and private law dichotomy, and they evidently regard simplicity and lighter taxation as desirable ends in themselves. A third category, more theorised still, is also of a normative kind, but more in the North American jurisprudential tradition. Despite perhaps her involvement with the Mirrlees Review, Judith Freedman does not place a comparable premium on simplicity,[129] but her advocacy of a

[122] A Smith, *Lectures on Jurisprudence* [1762–63/1766], RL Meek, DD Raphael and PG Stein (eds) (Indianapolis, Liberty Fund, 1982) 102–49 and 91–99; and K Haakonssen, *The Science of a Legislator: The Natural Jurisprudence of David Hume and Adam Smith* (Cambridge, Cambridge University Press, 1981) 127–33.

[123] J Freedman, 'Taxation Research as Legal Research' in M Lamb, A Lymer, J Freedman et al (eds), *Taxation: An Interdisciplinary Approach to Research* (Oxford, Oxford University Press, 2005) 13, 19–20; and BI Moran, 'Taxation' in P Cane and M Tushnet (eds), *The Oxford Handbook of Legal Studies* (Oxford, Oxford University Press, 2003) 377. See also DM Schneider, 'Interpreting the Interpreters: Assessing Forty-Five Years of Tax Literature' (1999) 4 *Florida Tax Review* 483.

[124] Haakonssen (above n 122) ch 5.

[125] R Bramwell, A James et al (eds), *Taxation of Companies and Company Reconstructions*, 8th edn (London, Sweet and Maxwell, 2002).

[126] J Ghosh, I Johnson and P Miller, *Ghosh, Johnson and Miller on the Taxation of Corporate Debt and Derivatives* (London, LexisNexis, 2010).

[127] Tiley (above n 74).

[128] See Morse and Williams (above n 3).

[129] J Mirrlees, S Adam, T Besley et al, *Tax by Design* (Oxford, Oxford University Press, 2011) 1, pre-publication draft chapters available at http://www.ifs.org.uk/mirrleesReview/design (accessed 30 November 2010) ch 1, 21.

general anti-avoidance principle (GANTIP) relies somewhat upon a Dworkinian theoretical model.[130] By contrast with all three of these styles, my own approach in this study is avowedly functionalist:

> [It] views [tax] law as part of the apparatus of government. Its focus is upon [tax] law's regulatory and facilitative functions and therefore is oriented to aims and objectives and [it] adopts an instrumentalist social policy approach.[131]

Functionalism thus 'reflects an ideal of progressive evolutionary change'. It is difficult to find precise parallels in other tax literature, but the approach taken by Ann Mumford in her work,[132] as well as by one of her own inspirations, the early twentieth-century theorist ERA Seligman,[133] might be regarded as broadly consonant with the present study. Sol Picciotto's work on international taxation is also coming at the material in a similar direction.[134] I would still claim some distinctiveness for my Loughlinian standpoint, however, relying as it does on the Loughlinian theory of public law and, in turn, upon the thinkers of the Enlightenment.

In my study, therefore, taxation law is in part an instance of constitutional law, not in the sense of the law relating to a brief written list of constitutional fundamentals, but as emblematic of the overall situation of order and unity obtaining in the state. It is also in part an instance of administrative law, a proposition to which European jurists would certainly assent. A robust example of a constitutional fundamental involving tax would be the wide scope given to the concept of a tax in British law[135] and the attendant necessity for the government to exercise extreme caution in obtaining Parliamentary consent to anything that could be interpreted as tax legislation.[136] Whether the reference to 'local taxes to fund local authority expenditure' in the Scottish devolution scheme[137] or those

[130] Eg, J Freedman, 'Defining Taxpayer Responsibility: In Support of a General Anti-Avoidance Principle' (2004) *British Tax Review* 332.

[131] See Loughlin, *Public Law and Political Theory* (above n 47) 60.

[132] Eg, A Mumford, *Taxing Culture: Towards a Theory of Tax Collection Law* (Aldershot, Ashgate, 2002).

[133] Eg, ERA Seligman, *Essays in Taxation*, 9th edn (London, Macmillan, 1923); and ERA Seligman, *Progressive Taxation in Theory and Practice*, 2nd edn (Princeton, American Economic Association, 1908).

[134] Picciotto (above n 5).

[135] Eg, *Brewster v Kidgill* (1697) 88 ER 1239; *Baker v Greenhill* (1842) 114 ER 463, 470; *Coltness Iron Company v Black (Surveyor of Taxes)* (1881) 1 TC 287, 316–17; *Bowles v Bank of England* [1913] 1 Ch 57; *Attorney-General v Wilts United Dairies Ltd* (1921) 124 LT 319, 322–23 (overruled by CA and HL at [1922] WN 217, 218); *Ormond Investment Company v Betts (HMIT)* (1928) 13 TC 400, 422 and 434; *Scott v Russell (HMIT)* (1948) 30 TC 394, 419; *Congreve v Home Office* [1976] QB 629 (EWCA); *Daymond v South West Water Authority* [1976] AC 609; *IRC v Océ van der Grinten* [2000] STC 951; and *Aston Cantlow and Wilmcote with Billesley Parochial Church Council v Wallbank and Another* [2001] EWCA Civ 713; [2002] Ch 51, para 40, overruled by HL at [2003] UKHL 37; [2004] 1 AC 546. And see Tiley (above n 74) 29n.

[136] P Jackson and P Leopold, *O Hood Phillips & Jackson: Constitutional and Administrative Law*, 8th edn (London, Sweet and Maxwell, 2001) para 2-001.

[137] Scotland Act 1998 Sch 5, pt II, head A1.

to 'taxation' in the European Treaties[138] will eventually require the courts to pin the idea of taxation down more precisely, as the federal constitutions of a number of Commonwealth countries have done,[139] remains to be seen. For the present, the significance of a tax in British law centres on the prohibition in the 1689 Bill of Rights on 'the levying of money for or to the use of the Crown by pretence of prerogative without grant of Parliament'.[140] The Bill of Rights prohibition simply refers to the 'levying of money', without distinguishing between taxes and other kinds of levy (such as fees). This wording has not invited the making of fine distinctions between taxes and other types of levy but has instead directed attention to whether Parliamentary consent has been duly given to the levy in question.[141] The presence or absence of consent is of course an expression of the idea of public law as political right: levies as the price of representation. Another example of tax as political right would be the historic ban on the House of Lords intervening in legislation involving taxation, whether 'money Bills' strictly so called or not.[142] This latter example has gained a particular topicality, and I return to it in chapter four.

Other, less obvious examples would be the issues discussed in detail in chapter five: the relative weight, depending on the current ideological consensus, to be accorded to the political values[143] of fairness and efficiency in tax legislation. The present study therefore envisages the British constitution as what might be described as a purposively shaped and ordered configuration of values, imperfectly realised but ever striving to get closer to the ideal.[144] Except that their conception of immanence was evidently confused,[145] the distillation of values from public law is an insight still largely owed to the Sheffield school,[146] and it emphasises that these values are what WB Gallie characterised as 'essentially contested concepts'.[147] In other words, the content of these values, as well as

[138] Treaty on the Functioning of the European Union (TFEU) Art 110 (ex-Art 90 EC); and, eg, Case C-10/65 *Deutschmann v Germany* [1968] CMLR 259; and Case C-74/76 *Iannelli and Volpi v Meroni* [1977] 2 CMLR 688.

[139] *Re Eurig Estate* (1999) 165 DLR (4th) 1. See also Tiley (above n 74) 3; and Thuronyi (above n 120) 45.

[140] Bill of Rights 1689, fourth indent, reprinted in G Wilson, *Cases and Materials on Constitutional and Administrative Law*, 2nd edn (Cambridge, Cambridge University Press, 1976) 2. But see *Bates's* case (1606) 2 St Tr 371; *R v Hampden* (1637) 3 St Tr 825; and A Tomkins, *Our Republican Constitution* (Oxford, Hart Publishing, 2005) 74 and 83. See also T Barnard, *The English Republic 1649–1660* (Harlow, Longman, 1982) 38 and 46.

[141] Eg, see the cases listed above at n 135.

[142] Parliament Act 1911 (as amended by Parliament Act 1949) s 1(2). See also Jackson and Leopold (above n 136) para 8-034).

[143] Loughlin, *Foundations of Public Law* (above n 82) 456.

[144] T Daintith and A Page, *The Executive in the Constitution: Structure, Autonomy and Internal Control* (Oxford, Oxford University Press, 1999) 18.

[145] M Loughlin, 'Review Article' (1988) 51 *Modern Law Review* 531, 533.

[146] I Harden and N Lewis, *The Noble Lie: The British Constitution and the Rule of Law* (London, Hutchinson, 1986).

[147] WB Gallie, 'Essentially Contested Concepts' (1955–56) 56 *Aristotelian Society (Proceedings)* 167. See also WE Connolly, *The Terms of Political Discourse*, 3rd edn (Oxford, Blackwell, 1993) 10–12 and 225–31.

their relationship with each other, is conditioned by the ideologies, opinions and beliefs that shape people's practices and way of life. I can illustrate this with two examples from the broadly neoliberal debate about tax policy. Those of a Hayekian disposition will tend to favour efficiency and simplicity, with the idea of tax as fostering the spontaneous order of the market. Sandelian communitarians or social democrats, by contrast, will favour fairness and possibly the attendant complexity, mistrustful of the vagaries of the market. Indeed, as Loughlin points out, fairness in 'the distribution of goods between social classes' has come to be the language of public policy debate,[148] even though it evidently does not translate into support for strongly redistributive tax policies.[149] Indeed, this may be a manifestation of the idea that the 'underlying motivating principle of the modern state' is a very thin version of fairness, namely egalitarianism.[150]

Whether fairness or efficiency gains pre-eminence in the corporation tax code at any particular time depends in part on the prevailing political consensus and, in part, on the prudential decisions of representative government. The 2010 Coalition Agreement provides a precise example in relation to taxation, since it specifically refers to values in the context of taxation and explicitly aims to prioritise and shape the content of those values,[151] an objective that was subsequently pursued in the Corporate Tax Road Map.[152] But context is everything in assessing 'the complete condition of political unity and order' found in a state, and political statements and policy documents must be parsed to discover the true shape and prioritisation of the immanent values in question. As Loughlin points out:

> In the interpretative mode, theory is to values what grammar is to vocabulary. The meaning of words such as . . . [efficiency, fairness and] accountability can be determined only by observing their grammar, the way in which they are set to work within a defined field.[153]

The strength of this use of Loughlin's public law theory in relation to corporation tax is that it enables the transcendent and idealistic, constitutional law aspects of the code, as well as the gritty, administrative law ones to assume their proper spheres. It also draws attention to the institutional and procedural value of accountability, doubtless the key legitimising factor in practice. The constitutive is generally concerned with the political; the administrative in large part with the technical. I return to these arguments in chapter five.

[148] Loughlin, *Foundations of Public Law* (above n 82) 396 and 450.
[149] J Alt, I Preston and L Sibieta, 'The Political Economy of Tax Policy' in Adam, Besley et al (eds) (above n 10) 1204 and 1226–45.
[150] Loughlin, *Foundations of Public Law* (above n 82) 198.
[151] HM Government, *The Coalition: Our Programme for Government* (London, Cabinet Office, 2010) 7, available at http://www.cabinetoffice.gov.uk/news/coalition-documents (accessed 5 March 2011) para 29.
[152] CTRM (above n 8).
[153] Loughlin, 'Theory and Values' (above n 98) 65.

It will be apparent from all of this that normative and functionalist ways of working are intimately related to views on the role of taxation in the state. Like Loughlin, I accept the strongly based Foucauldian idea of the state as having three constituent elements: the 'apparatus of rule'; the territory; and the people.[154] Debates on tax policy tend to concentrate on the levels of public revenue necessary to maintain and secure the second and third of these. They tend, too, to embody what Michael Oakeshott referred to as the 'unresolved tension' between the 'irreconcilable' conceptions of a European state' as a 'civil association' or as an 'enterprise association'.[155] A state conceived merely as a civil association would require comparatively little public revenue; a state conceived as an enterprise association might require a great deal. This is because the latter – but not the former – implies that the state exists to pursue some shared goal, some permanent good.[156] In this prism, the use of tax policy to fulfil certain objectives, especially that of greater fairness in society and greater efficiency in its economic policy, shines especially bright. By contrast, what characterises the state as a civil association is not the pursuit of a common objective but the cementing of loyalties as between its members.[157] This, of course, is much more consistent with a neoliberal idea of the state. That said, I do not think it quite corresponds to the Hayekian model, since a plan not to plan anything is still a plan[158] and since a purely civil association would tend to reject even this. The contemporary pull in all European states, even markedly neoliberal ones, towards the enterprise association, means that a government's power of initiating tax legislation and its use in shaping social outcomes assume considerable importance.[159] It has the consequence that, whereas in the state as civil association, tax legislation will be restricted to statutory form, in an enterprise association, the very notion of the category of tax legislation will be much wider. The pronounced tendency of both the Treasury and HMRC under the Labour Government to produce detailed non-statutory technical material, together with the dislike of this in some places, highlights the ideological divergence. So, too, do divergent attitudes to tax avoidance and the kinds of measures necessary to combat it. Whether the state as civil association or the state as enterprise association is uppermost at any one time depends on the values commanding widest acceptance at that time and how those values are deployed and embodied in particular decisions of government. In neoliberalism, the pull of the civil association is strong, but the enterprise association is still there. Some would

[154] Loughlin, *Foundations of Public Law* (above n 82) 189 and 205.

[155] M Oakeshott, *On Human Conduct* (Oxford, Clarendon Press, 1975) 200. See Loughlin, The Idea of Public Law (above n 18) 17–19. See also P Franco, *The Political Philosophy of Michael Oakeshott* (London, Yale University Press, 1990) 179; and S Brittan, 'Why There are Two Kinds of Conservatism' *Financial Times* (4 March 2011) 13.

[156] Oakeshott, *On Human Conduct* (ibid) 203. See also Loughlin, *The Idea of Public Law* (above n 18) 17–19.

[157] Oakeshott, *On Human Conduct* (above n 155) 201 and 203.

[158] Oakeshott, 'Rationalism in Politics' (above n 50) 26.

[159] Loughlin, *Foundations of Public Law* (above n 82) 407.

say, nearly a half a century on from Oakeshott's heyday, that the enterprise association was no more eradicable than its antagonist, the civil association.

C. Corporation Tax as Economic Regulation

Even though I identify fairness issues in this book, it is not an investigation into what a just or fair corporate tax policy would be. This will be disappointing to high-minded readers. Instead, I am trying to interpret how and why matters stand as they do in the area of corporate tax law. This does not preclude a discussion about what would be just or fair. But that is not this discussion. The most important consequences of the present line of inquiry are threefold. First, the corporate tax discussion in this book is realistic and interpretative, rather than normative and idealistic, though the pull towards the ideal is expressly acknowledged. Secondly, the discussion is chiefly about regulation and prerogative rather than about distribution. Thirdly and most importantly, it is about understanding current political practices rather than about the possibilities for just outcomes. None of these points means that these other conversations, especially about what a just outcome might be, cannot be had. They just mean that I am concerned with one rather than the others.

Regulation has been analysed both from a law and economics perspective[160] and from a public law perspective, where the emphasis has been on regulatory legitimacy.[161] Most scholars, notably Picciotto, have long thought that the taxation of corporations, especially multinationals, can be regarded as a self-evidently 'regulatory system'.[162] What might at first sound like a dissentient voice is that of Giandomenico Majone,[163] who, taking tax policy to be in essence 'redistributive', might be understood to view regulation as involving somewhat distinct considerations. However, on close reading, it is clear that this comment is not made from the standpoint taken here and is made solely with regard to an observation about the majoritarian nature of the EU procedures by which regulatory policy, as opposed to tax policy, decisions should be reached.[164] Even this point does not, however, relieve us of the obligation of deciding on what are taken to be the defining characteristics of regulation.

Consistent with the idea that politics is concerned with the art of government or of governance, the contention in the study will be that 'regulation' is a large enough term to cover all ways of bringing about a particular policy objective. Cast in wide terms though it is, Parker and Braithwaite's definition of regula-

[160] A Ogus, *Regulation: Legal Form and Economic Theory* (Oxford, Oxford University Press, 1994). See also JM Black, 'An Economic Analysis of Regulation: One View of the Cathedral' (1996) 16 *Oxford Journal of Legal Studies* 699.

[161] Eg, C Hilson, *Regulating Pollution: A UK and EC Perspective* (Oxford, Hart Publishing, 2000).

[162] Picciotto (above n 5) 83.

[163] G Majone, *Regulating Europe* (London, Routledge, 1996) 294.

[164] Ibid, 285.

tion as 'influencing the flow of events',[165] as well as Baldwin, Scott and Hood's definition of regulation as 'an authoritative set of rules, accompanied by some mechanism, typically a public agency, for monitoring and promoting compliance with these rules',[166] seems no less apposite to the case of taxation than to any other policy arena. Mirrlees regards it as axiomatic that 'most taxes influence people's behaviour'.[167] As a form of regulation, corporation tax counts as economic rather than social regulation.[168] It is designed to maximise the economic potential of the nation and, at the same time, to collect a reasonable – that is, politically feasible – amount of tax (about eight per cent of total tax receipts in 2010 to 2011, or £42.1 billion).[169] Of this, found the Oxford University Centre for Business Taxation in the spring of 2011, almost 90 per cent has come from multinationals.[170] Its immediate policy objective might at a fairly superficial level be stated as the fair and efficient raising of revenue. Taxation is one form – perhaps one of the earliest forms[171] – of economic regulation,[172] and English law has made no general distinction between regulatory and other taxes since the seventeenth century.[173]

If what has just been said is well-founded, the next question is what additional elements taxation might have, above and beyond other forms of economic regulation. The pre-eminent contribution to this debate has been from Liam Murphy and Thomas Nagel's provocatively entitled interrogation of two pervasive ideas: those of 'pre-tax ownership' and of tax justice.[174] Although the two are closely intertwined in Murphy and Nagel's account, we need here to place the accent on the former, since it offers a theory of the nature of taxation itself. The taxation of corporations is scoped out of Murphy and Nagel's inquiry,[175] but both main elements of their theory have interpretative resonances even in this area. Most importantly, they ask us to accept the 'conventionality of property', as contrasted with a concept of it being in some sense 'morally fundamental'.[176] 'We have to think of property', claim Murphy and Nagel, 'as

[165] C Parker and J Braithwaite, 'Regulation' in P Cane and M Tushnet (eds), *The Oxford Handbook of Legal Studies* (Oxford, Oxford University Press, 2003) 119.

[166] R Baldwin, C Scott and C Hood (eds), *A Reader on Regulation* (Oxford, Oxford University Press, 1998) 3.

[167] Mirrlees, Adam and Besley et al (above n 129) ch 2.

[168] T Prosser, *Law and the Regulators* (Oxford, Clarendon Press, 1997) 4–6. See also Picciotto (above n 5) 83.

[169] Mirrlees, Adam and Besley et al (above n 129) chs 1 and 8. The overall tax burden in Britain, as a percentage of GDP, is in the high 30s: ibid, 5.

[170] Houlder, 'Large Companies Pay Lower Rate' (above n 83), discussing MP Devereux and S Loretz, *Corporation Tax in the United Kingdom* (Oxford, Oxford University Centre for Business Taxation, 2011), available at http://www.sbs.ox.ac.uk/centres/tax (accessed 19 April 2011).

[171] Parker and Braithwaite (above n 165) 120.

[172] Baldwin, Scott and Hood (eds) (above n 166).

[173] *Bates's* case (above n 140) 389, noted in Loughlin, *Foundations of Public Law* (above n 82) 379n.

[174] L Murphy and T Nagel, *The Myth of Ownership* (Oxford, Oxford University Press, 2000).

[175] Ibid, 10.

[176] Ibid, 175.

what is created by the tax system, rather than what is disturbed or encroached on by the tax system. Property rights are the rights people have in the resources they are entitled to control after taxes, not before.'[177] Their argument, heavily consequentialist as it is, can easily be assimilated into the present functionalist perspective on tax law as public law, despite having much in common with what we are content to accept is the 'liberal normativist' tradition of Rawls and Dworkin. Contentious as it is,[178] this conventional rather than natural view of property rights is therefore accepted in this study.[179] It is a key contention that it is not even possible to begin to articulate a convincing interpretation of, say, tax avoidance measures without rejecting the notion that taxes involve the 'exactions'[180] of property, which can be said to be the absolute moral entitlement of its holder. Instead, I accept that there is a closely interwoven relationship between property rights and taxation.

The reality of this point is borne out by the exception for taxation in the right to property enshrined in the European Convention on Human Rights (ECHR), always qualified as it is by public interest considerations.[181] What is plainly inadequate is the kind of Hayekian attitude to tax avoidance embodied in older judicial decisions, which reflects an absolutist, or natural, idea of property rights.[182] As Andrew Simester and Winnie Chan have forcefully pointed out, few, if any, lawyers really believe this type of statement any more.[183]

IV. THE OUTLINES OF THE INTERPRETATION

Most coherent statements about what corporate taxation policy should be, whether by politicians or by professional critics, make implicit reference not only to the intended policy or legislative outcome but to the role of institutions and processes in bringing it about. George Osborne's declaration in Budget 2011 of his ambition to make Britain's corporation tax the most competitive among G20 nations is a statement of this kind.[184] It implies assumptions about what it is in the power of the ruling party to accomplish, how it may be achieved and what the outcome might be. Equally referential to institutions and processes are the common statements to the effect that better scrutiny of corporation tax by Parliament would produce a simpler, more stable corporation tax code. At the most basic level, the rest of the study, which makes a threefold division between the role of institutions, the nature of processes and the sig-

[177] Ibid.

[178] But see, eg, R Nozick, *Anarchy, State, and Utopia* (Oxford, Blackwell, 1980) 169.

[179] See AP Simester and W Chan, 'Review Article' (2003) 23 *Oxford Journal of Legal Studies* 711.

[180] *CIR v Newman* 159 F 2d 848, 851 (1947) (Learned Hand J).

[181] ECHR First Protocol, Art 1.

[182] *Ayrshire Pullman Motor Services and DM Richie v IRC* (1929) 14 TC 754, 763. Cf Shaxson (above n 15) 203.

[183] Simester and Chan (above n 179) 711.

[184] See above n 35.

nificance of the outcomes, is a deconstruction of the components of these statements. The division into institutions, processes and policy solutions – but certainly not the mode of its execution – is a tangible link to Sheffield school writers such as Chris Hilson and Norman Lewis, whose characteristic mode of operation this has been.[185] Where the study differs from that body of work, however, is in its rejection on historical and interpretative grounds of a Sheffield school methodology. This allows me to say rather more about the relative importance of the values at work in corporation tax reform, as well as their content, than might otherwise have been the case.

With these points in mind, chapter three offers an analysis of the significance of the institutional ordering of corporation tax reform. It is centred on the idea of Crown and Parliament being locked in a perpetual tension, one against the other, while Government vies to manage, and possibly even to exploit, the economic power of the corporate sector. As long ago as 1973, the Royal Commission on the Constitution[186] highlighted the importance of the relationship between the state and the corporation in promoting national prosperity and managing the economy.[187] The coinage, so to speak, of this tension is the mobile investment capital that I earlier identified as the source of the political dimensions of this area of public policy. Everyone knows that, prudently managed, corporate tax reform encourages capital to come or to stay; imprudently managed, it flies away or does not come to Britain in the first place. Right ordering, as I mentioned when discussing the significance of public law to corporation tax law, is about both the ways in which the institutions of government are set up – how government is constituted, in other words – and how its institutions go about their business in a particular policy area.

Loughlin accepts that since the eighteenth century, Britain has been a 'constitutional bureaucratic state'[188] (what David Judge calls the 'Parliamentary state'), with Parliament as the symbol of the 'political nation'.[189] Parliament occupies a central place in this scheme. The competences of the various government institutions are a matter of public law in the sense not so much of positive law but of political right,[190] with one of Parliament's main functions being to construct an account of the Crown's taxing activities.[191] Parliament is traditionally therefore a mediator between the state, in the sense of the people, and the state as government apparatus.[192] The broadening of the tax base, in the sense of the bases of

[185] Eg, C Hilson (above n 161); ND Lewis, *Law and Governance: The Old Meets the New* (London, Cavendish Publishing, 2001); and N Lewis, *Choice and the Legal Order: Rising above Politics* (London, Butterworths, 1996).

[186] *Royal Commission on the Constitution 1969–1973, vol I, Report: Presented to Parliament by Command of Her Majesty October 1973* (Cmnd 5460) (London, HMSO, 1973) 76.

[187] Loughlin, *The Idea of Public Law* (above n 18) 12.

[188] Loughlin, *Foundations of Public Law* (above n 82) 242.

[189] D Judge, *The Parliamentary State* (London, Sage, 1993).

[190] Loughlin, *Foundations of Public Law* (above n 82) 272.

[191] Ibid, 247.

[192] Ibid, 250.

all taxes, was only possible after 1688 because Parliament was competent to scrutinise the Crown's taxation activities,[193] which is why, as Tim Besley has affirmed, good government requires individuals of 'character and wisdom',[194] or as we might say, prudence.

The subject matter of chapter three is intimately related to that of chapter four. Here Parliament's role is to give consent to decisions made under the prerogative,[195] since it was not specifically designed as a democratic institution. The system potentially concentrates power in a very few hands, and this is reflected in my analysis of how corporate tax reform proposals become law. These institutional forms generate power, if used prudently.[196] But they do so in a way that is often hidden. Consultation and debate are essentially inroads into a process that is essentially secret. Although there is less secrecy than once there was, it is not known exactly what corporate tax measures will be in the annual Budget until the Chancellor stands up to deliver his Budget speech. The Coalition was committed, on its election in May 2010, to instil the value of stability into corporate taxation. Yet this did not prevent Mr Osborne in spring 2011 from making a surprise attack on the profits of North Sea oil and gas companies.[197]

Given what I have said about values and the shape that they take in the corporation tax code, it follows that 'posited law . . . can never fully comprehend' what Loughlin calls the 'living law', which is a 'representation of . . . [the political] values of the majority'.[198] I therefore demonstrate how the corporation tax code, which realises a certain scheme of economic values, can be viewed as a map of what is politically possible, whatever the merits of the economic arguments at any particular time. The code is nonetheless obeyed because of its legitimation in its 'ethical justification'.[199] Commentators complain about its complexity, its instability, but they obey it 'not only because it is their own work, but because it may be changed if it is harmful'.[200] There is therefore a perpetual tension in this way of looking at matters between the corporation tax code as it exists and as it might yet be.

[193] Ibid, 261–62.
[194] T Besley, *Principled Agents? The Political Economy of Good Government* (Oxford, Oxford University Press, 2006) 2.
[195] See, eg, *Vestey (No 2) v IRC* [1979] 2 All ER 225, 233 (Walton J); but also *R v IRC, ex parte Fulford-Dobson* [1987] STC 344, 351 (McNeill J). But see E Simpson, 'Making Sense of the *Ramsay* Principle: a Novel Role for Public Law?' in M Freedland and J-B Auby (eds), *The Public Law/Private Law Divide: Une entente assez cordiale?* (Oxford, Hart Publishing, 2006) 165, 178.
[196] Loughlin, *Foundations of Public Law* (above n 82) 231–32.
[197] Channel 4 (Siobhan Kennedy), 'Oil Company Speaks Out on "Easy Hit" Tax' (4 April 2011).
[198] Loughlin, *Foundations of Public Law* (above n 82) 230.
[199] Ibid, 234.
[200] Ibid, 231.

3

The Reformers

A VISITOR TO London in 2011 might still take a ride on the London Eye, one of the capital's remaining millennium attractions. From the gondolas of this gigantic fairground wheel, mounted above the brown-green waters of the River Thames, can be seen, does one choose to remark them, the tangible manifestations of the political institutions associated with corporation tax reform, and thus with the project of attracting investment to Great Britain.

The view to the south of the Eye is dominated by the Victorian Gothic splendour of the Palace of Westminster and the Houses of Parliament. There, in committee rooms and in Westminster Hall, individual Finance Act provisions have been debated by at least some of the elected representatives of the people. There too the Law Lords used to hand down judgments in the most important corporation tax appeals. The fact that since October 2009 their former jurisdiction has been transferred to the justices of the Supreme Court of the United Kingdom has not deprived the judiciary of its central place in the vista though. The Supreme Court judges are still close by, at the former Middlesex Guildhall in Parliament Square.[1] Just to the right of the Houses of Parliament, clearly discernible to the northwest of Westminster, are the modernised New Government Offices on Horse Guards Road, the western part of which houses the Treasury.[2] The Treasury building in Whitehall is nearer to the Houses of Parliament than any of the other Departmental buildings; it is also, with the exception of the Foreign Office, the most imposing of them. The Treasury is where the incremental project of corporation tax reform has been co-ordinated, and also the place from which the economic policies that shape that project have been developed.

Further to the northeast, by Waterloo Bridge, no more than a mile away, can be discerned the classical lines of Somerset House in the Strand, the western part of which, in Lancaster Place, has been the seat of the Inland Revenue and its successor, HM Revenue and Customs (HMRC).[3] Just visible behind it are the Royal Courts of Justice, the principal seat both of the Court of Appeal and of the High Court. The Government buildings are not, however, all that a curious

[1] To date, just two Supreme Court decisions have involved corporation tax: *Holland v HMRC* [2010] UKSC 51; and *HMRC v DCC Holdings (UK) Ltd* [2010] UKSC 58.

[2] S Bradley and N Pevsner, *The Buildings of England – London 6: Westminster* (New Haven and London, Yale University Press, 2003) 270.

[3] Ibid, 324. But the Business Tax Unit is based in Kingsway.

visitor might see. Signs of the presence of influential non-governmental bodies are visible too. Located somewhere between the Treasury and Somerset House, above Charing Cross railway station and looking out over the Golden Jubilee Bridges, is the headquarters, in Embankment Place, of one of the 'Big Four' accountancy firms, PricewaterhouseCoopers.[4] Ernst and Young, another Big Four firm, has its headquarters on the other side of the river in Lambeth Palace Road, near Tower Bridge. If the location of the Treasury building is symbolic of the 'centrality' of tax policy to the British state,[5] then the presence of the imposing premises of two Big Four accountancy practices so close to the nerve centre of the government is surely emblematic of the importance of accountants in the formulation of tax policy.

The presence of other professionals, though less visible from the Eye, is no less striking. From the Treasury in Whitehall to St Paul's, in the heart of the City, is a little over a mile and a half – a cab-ride away for busy civil servants, accountants or solicitors with the inevitable 'pilot case' of A4 policy documents and multi-volume taxation statutes. Within the City's 'square mile' are the offices of no less than 40 major international and European and domestic banks, including Goldman Sachs, Merrill Lynch,[6] Nomura and Deutsche Bank; no less than two dozen fund managers, including Fidelity Investments, Henderson Global Investors and Schroders; at least a dozen international law firms, including Allen and Overy, Freshfields, and Slaughter and May; and the other two Big Four accountancy practices, Deloitte and KPMG. Even Canary Wharf, the City's Docklands extension, with its 50-storey, 800-foot tower and its two slightly smaller 42-storey companions, each dominating the eastern horizon seen from the Eye, is only two miles or so from St Paul's, and not much more than two and a half miles as the crow flies from Whitehall and the Houses of Parliament. Canary Wharf, once 'unfashionable', is now home to at least ten other major banks, including Credit Suisse and Morgan Stanley,[7] as well as the law firm Clifford Chance.[8]

Faced with this rather obvious commercial might, which has been battered, though unbent, by events since 2007, it might appear counterintuitive to begin by highlighting certain analytical problems in interpreting the significance of institutions to the reform of corporation tax. We certainly have to be able to understand their make-up, functions and values, but we need too to be able to interpret the significance of the relationships between government institutions

[4] Ibid, 300.

[5] E Fisher, 'Book Review' (2001) 13 *Journal of Environmental Law* 115, reflecting on the status of the US Environmental Protection Agency.

[6] Merrill Lynch, Goldman Sachs and Morgan Stanley (all investment banks) were known as 'the super bulge' even before the 2007–09 banking crisis focussed public attention on bankers' salaries. See P Augar, *The Greed Merchants: How the Investment Banks Played the Free Market Game* (London, Allen Lane, 2005) 37–39.

[7] J Pickard, 'Notably Global Set of Owners' *Financial Times* (3 April 2007) 19.

[8] A Sampson, *Who Runs This Place? The Anatomy of Britain in the 21st Century* (London, John Murray, 2004) 181.

and those of the corporate sector.[9] Describing the duties and powers of political institutions is something that comes rather easily to devotees of public law – briefly turning up a standard constitutional law or tax text will illustrate the truth of this point. Since, however, I want to offer an interpretation of these phenomena, and since Martin Loughlin's references to political institutions occur in the context of discussions of concepts such as representation, sovereignty and constituent power,[10] I need to look beyond the public law texts themselves, to find ways of understanding the wider significance of institutions and the ways in which they interact, in the reform of corporation tax.

My task is complicated by the fact that the discourse on institutions, the so-called the 'new institutionalism', in the field of politics has as many as six distinct strands.[11] These range from the 'normative institutionalism' of March and Olsen,[12] which emphasises 'the "logic of appropriateness" as a means of shaping the behaviour of the members of institutions',[13] via the 'rational choice institutionalism' of, for instance, Tsebelis and Money,[14] to the 'empirical institutionalism' of Weaver and Rockman.[15] All have insights to offer, and all are in the interpretative tradition of political thought. A further complication arises, though, from the fact that there is little published material that applies new institutionalism to the particular phenomena visible from the London Eye. Fortunately, David Judge makes a valuable attempt to interpret these institutions in terms that combine various elements of new institutionalism.[16] Using what he calls an 'organising perspective'[17] rather than a theory as such, Judge takes new institutionalism to imagine political institutions in terms of formal structures and organisations, 'mediated' by all sorts of wider contingencies, including 'social, economic and political conditions and forces'. In relation to corporate tax reform, these contingencies imply that the considerations of conflict and of prudence outlined above in chapter two will call forth particular qualities from the individuals concerned, to discharge the relevant legislative competences effectively. The activities of particular structures and organisations are delimited and defined by their 'interactions' with other institutions, and insofar as they correspond to 'normatively appropriate behaviour', they

[9] CJ Fox and HT Miller, *Postmodern Public Administration: Toward Discourse* (Thousand Oaks, Sage, 1995) 91–92.

[10] M Loughlin, *The Idea of Public Law* (Oxford, Oxford University Press, 2003) chs 5 and 6. But see M Loughlin, *Foundations of Public Law* (Oxford, Oxford University Press, 2010) ch 9.

[11] BG Peters, *Institutional Theory in Political Science: The 'New Institutionalism'*, 2nd edn (London, Continuum, 2005) 19.

[12] Especially JG March and JP Olsen, *Rediscovering Institutions: The Organizational Basis of Politics* (New York, Free Press, 1989) esp ch 9.

[13] Peters, *Institutional Theory in Political Science* (above n 11) 19.

[14] See generally, G Tsebelis and J Money, *Bicameralism* (Cambridge, Cambridge University Press, 1997).

[15] RK Weaver and BA Rockman, *Do Institutions Matter? Government Capabilities in the United States and Abroad* (Washington, DC, Brookings Institution, 1993).

[16] D Judge, *Political Institutions in the United Kingdom* (Oxford, Oxford University Press, 2005) 21–22.

[17] A Gamble, 'Theories of British Politics' (1990) 38 *Political Studies* 404.

reflect 'internal organisational norms and values', shaped by 'wider societal understandings and expectations'.[18] It is these expectations and understandings that both set bounds to the competences of the institutions involved in corporation tax reform and shape the roles of those who engage with them in the reform process.

The insights that Judge offers, as well as the approaches that he synthesises, though useful in interpreting how institutions function, do not, however, set out to identify the true 'source of authority' when it comes to public policy decisions.[19] The need to pinpoint this brings us back to texts that are foundational to public law as a political practice. In Thomas Hobbes's analysis of 'the seat of power',[20] as Loughlin reminds us,[21] authority originates from the 'commonwealth',[22] the entity that Hobbes himself refers to as 'the state'.[23] Although the state is a 'fictitious person', it is not like other persons, since both it and its representative, the Crown-in-Parliament,[24] 'are instituted precisely for the purpose of creating law'.[25] This is a particularly important point, since much of the material in the politics field, especially as it relates to governance, tends to underestimate the pre-eminent place of the state in the policymaking process.[26] Whatever the objectives and values of the non-state actors in corporation tax reform might be – whether as accountants, bankers, lawyers or 'policy networks' that draw in each of these groups – it is important to recognise that they may or may not be the same as the functions of the state. Divergences and similarities in the purposes and functions of institutions, as well as in the values that they promulgate, form the first important strand in the following discussion.

When the visitor to London catches sight of the Palace of Westminster, the New Government Offices, Somerset House or the Royal Courts of Justice, what he or she is seeing is the physical location of the institutions that represent the Leviathan[27] – that is, the state – in this particular area of policymaking.[28] Only the state, the 'United Kingdom of Great Britain and Northern Ireland', the 'fictitious' personality[29] represented by the Crown-in-Parliament and created by the 'authorization . . . [of the] multitude',[30] may be sovereign. The power to impose

[18] Judge (above n 16) 21.
[19] Loughlin, *The Idea of Public Law* (above n 10) 54.
[20] T Hobbes, *Leviathan* [1651], M Oakeshott (ed) (Oxford, Basil Blackwell, 1955) 2 (Dedication).
[21] Loughlin, *The Idea of Public Law* (above n 10) 55.
[22] Hobbes (above n 20) 109 (pt 2 ch 17).
[23] Ibid, 81.
[24] Loughlin, *The Idea of Public Law* (above n 10) 84.
[25] Ibid, 60.
[26] J Pierre and BG Peters, *Governance, Politics and the State* (Basingstoke, Macmillan, 2000) 82. See also M Loughlin, 'The State, the Crown and the Law' in M Sunkin and S Payne (eds), *The Nature of the Crown: A Legal and Political Analysis* (Oxford, Oxford University Press, 1999) 34.
[27] Hobbes (above n 20) 5 ('The Introduction') and 112 (pt 2 ch 17).
[28] Loughlin, *The Idea of Public Law* (above n 10) 56.
[29] Ibid, 59.
[30] Ibid, 58; and Hobbes (above n 20) 112 (pt 2 ch 17).

or repeal taxes is one of its most fundamental attributes.[31] A second important strand in the discussion is thus the sovereign status of the Crown-in-Parliament and the point – all too easily elided – that the 'transfer of jurisdiction and competence' in matters other than taxation[32] to the institutions of the European Union has not necessarily affected the sovereign status of Great Britain in corporation tax matters.[33] These are not problems of sovereignty but rather ones of jurisdiction and of competence.

Crucial to Loughlin's conception of public law is the idea that, over the years, lawyers have drained the idea of sovereignty of its true significance. Sovereignty must, he says, be thought of separately from the person of the sovereign. As I explained in chapter one, Loughlin has argued that sovereignty has both a political dimension, namely 'capacity', and a legal dimension, 'competence'. A third significant element of the discussion is therefore how the state's sovereignty in corporation tax matters is not merely a matter of competence. Whatever competence the government may have in corporate tax policy is in turn founded on capacity and thus upon the quality of the relationship between state and non-state participants. The challenge to public lawyers is to be alive to the precise significance of each of these ideas.

Developing a productive relationship between state and non-state institutions therefore depends on constantly augmenting the ties between the government and the governed.[34] Such a process goes to the heart of promoting the public interest, of governing. The nature of corporation tax reform, as involving considerable tensions, means that augmenting these ties is no easy task. Nonetheless, as Loughlin has stated, the 'vital function of the established framework of constituted authority is that of being able to generate trust between governors and governed'.[35] Generating trust depends on a range of factors, including effective action, the cultivation of certain neoliberal values,[36] the creation of suitable systems of accountability and even, in appropriate situations, the transference of jurisdiction or competence to the European Union. A fourth – indeed the most important – strand in the discussion is therefore the extent to which the structures, functions and values of the institutions help to build up trust in and strengthen allegiance to the state in the corporate tax arena. Such a task is, of course, an exercise in constitutionalism,[37] an aspect of state-building, albeit in

[31] J Bodin, *On Sovereignty: Four Chapters from The Six Books of the Commonwealth* [1576], JH Franklin (ed and trans) (Cambridge, Cambridge University Press, 1992) 81. See also Hobbes (above n 20) 117 (pt 2 ch 18) and 119 (pt 2 ch 18). See generally, D Bräutigam, 'Building Leviathan: Revenue, State Capacity and Governance' (2002) 33(3) *IDS Bulletin* 10.

[32] Treaty on the Functioning of the European Union (TFEU) Art 114(2) (ex-Art 95(2) EC).

[33] Loughlin, *The Idea of Public Law* (above n 10) 94.

[34] Ibid, 85.

[35] Ibid, 104, reflecting the traditional Lockean position. See generally, J Dunn, *Locke* (Oxford, Oxford University Press, 1984) ch 2; and J Dunn, 'Trust and Political Agency' in J Dunn, *Interpreting Political Responsibility: Essays 1981–1989* (Cambridge, Polity Press, 1990) 26.

[36] Loughlin, *The Idea of Public Law* (above n 10) 85.

[37] Ibid, 69, referring to S Holmes, *Passions and Constraint: On the Theory of Liberal Democracy* (Chicago, University of Chicago Press, 1995) xi.

an unusually arcane area of public policy. It complements the discussion below in chapter four, where the emphasis passes to the processes by which corporation tax policy goals are determined. Generating trust and confidence in the institutions in an area with so great a corporate sector involvement is difficult, precisely because of the accountability questions to which it gives rise.

I. INSTITUTIONS, OBJECTIVES, FUNCTIONS

Within the framework just constructed, I now seek to analyse the institutional dimension of corporation tax reform. Fundamental to a government's power to initiate successful processes for realising policy objectives (the subject matter of chapter four) is the effectiveness of the institutions thereby engaged. An introduction to the 'governance perspective',[38] which I take throughout the study, forms the first part of my discussion. This is an attempt to understand the divergences and alignments between the functions and values of the state, on the one hand, and the objectives of the corporate sector, on the other. Surprisingly perhaps, for a discussion that began with a mental image of central London, this first part requires us to modify a strict 'Westminster model' of the institutions of the government in favour of one that is 'fragmented' and predicates 'a maze of institutions and organizations'.[39] Isolating how institutional structures, purposes and values may strengthen or weaken sovereignty from the processes by which policy goals are set is no easy task. Yet each is no less important than the other in enhancing trust and confidence in corporation tax policies. Chris Hilson, in his discussion of a different policy area, one of 'social regulation',[40] isolates these factors with considerable success, but his analysis, which emphasises institutional accountability without convincingly explaining its relationship to institutional effectiveness, is squarely based on the Sheffield school approach, which I rejected in chapter two.

This brings me to an attempt to encapsulate in section III the objectives and values of the corporate sector, especially those of multinational corporations and the City of London. This is in a sense about how far government may be dominated by economic power, but it is also about whether, prudently managed, the corporate sector may serve the public interest. What we find, I suggest, is rather surprising. Although contemporary political debate is dominated by the tensions between the nation state and the multinational corporation, we discover that, given the political choices discussed in chapter four, there is a fundamental unity of interest in this particular area between public and private sector institutions. There are tensions, to be sure, but there are also commonalities. To try to pinpoint what these may be, it is necessary to distinguish between

[38] G Stoker, 'Governance as Theory: Five Propositions' (1998) 50 *International Social Science Journal* 17.

[39] Ibid, 19.

[40] C Hilson, *Regulating Pollution: A UK and EC Perspective* (Oxford, Hart Publishing, 2000) ch 4.

different constituencies of economic power, between inward investment by multinationals and the allocation of funds by international fund managers. Although the differences between these two constituencies could be over-stated, what cannot be denied is the fundamental importance of identities of interest to current political choices.

The difficulties, given that governments seek to build up trust and confidence in their corporation tax policies, are highlighted in sections IV and V of the chapter, where I examine the constitutional opposition between the structure, functions and values of Parliament, on the one hand, and, on the other, the Treasury and HMRC. The study takes as axiomatic the view of Great Britain's constitutional arrangements that has been so elegantly articulated by Adam Tomkins.[41] This is that Parliament holds power that has over centuries been 'forced' from the Crown,[42] and '[t]o the extent that there is a separation of powers in English political jurisprudence it is a separation between the Crown on the one hand, and Parliament on the other'.[43] What need to be identified in sections IV and V, therefore, are the characteristics of Parliament and of the government that may contribute to or detract from generating trust and confidence in corporation tax reform. So far as Parliament is concerned, my main preoccupation is the effectiveness with which it holds the government to account. With the Treasury and HMRC, however, the concern is rather with the qualities that may contribute to their effectiveness in the art and science of governing. My discussion of the Treasury begins, therefore, with power and how it is wielded effectively; my discussion of Parliament starts with how the government is made to account for the wielding. The discussion of Parliament is therefore mainly about Parliamentary Select Committees, while that of the Treasury and HMRC is about prerogative power and how it is constrained.

What I am envisaging, then, is an institutional framework in which there is a pervasive tension between Parliament and Crown. The Crown perceives that it needs to involve the corporate sector, given the similarities in their respective interests. Parliament, however, fears the lack of accountability that this may bring. Accordingly, in section VI, I look a little more closely at the objectives and values of those who are often seen merely as 'technicians' in the reform process, as well as at their relationships with the government. These are specialist lawyers, accountants, etc, whose presence near the seat of power is so striking to the visitor looking across London from the Eye. The technical expertise of these specialists, as well as of 'policy networks more generally', means that they have a crucial role in bringing to prominence certain policy issues and coordinating representations thereon. Their contributions will be referred to again in the discussion of policymaking in chapter four. For present purposes, however, it is policy networks as institutions that claim our attention. This is because, besides private sector bodies, some such networks incorporate public

[41] A Tomkins, *Public Law* (Oxford, Oxford University Press, 2003).
[42] Ibid, 42.
[43] Ibid, 44.

servants. Others, however, do not; recent years have seen the emergence of extremely well-informed 'issue networks', anxious to highlight what they perceive to be injustices caused by the manipulability of the corporation tax system.

By the end of the chapter, the main actors and the dynamics between them will have been established. The foregoing has posited the fundamental Crown–Parliament opposition: the opportunity of the former to involve the corporate sector in tax policy; and the concerns of the latter at the accountability problems that this may cause. One other important institution needs to be reflected, however: the judiciary. In section VII, I look at the role of the judges in corporation tax reform. Following Tomkins and Loughlin, I place them closer to the Crown than to Parliament. Judiciary and Crown are linked simply by mutual trust,[44] and I consider how the judiciary's presence may affect the range of reform alternatives. Judicial review of legislation is important here, but even more so, I contend, is the judicial approach to interpreting tax legislation.

Corporation tax law as a political practice, as the area of political jurisprudence tasked with enhancing the state's capacity to ensure that the corporate sector assumes a 'fair share' of the overall tax burden, thus operates in a complex institutional setting. I begin, therefore, by explaining one way of interpreting the interaction between state and corporate sector: the 'organising perspective' of governance. According to Andrew Gamble, such an organising perspective provides 'a framework for analysis, a map of how things relate'.[45] In the words of Judge and others, it provides 'a language and frame of reference through which reality can be examined and [which] lead[s] [us] to ask questions that might not otherwise occur'.[46]

Readers will readily appreciate that this governance perspective both complements and illuminates the interpretative inquiry in which I am engaged. What I would like to do in this chapter is to render explicit certain dominant ideas that subconsciously influence the ways we think about governance,[47] ideas that we would otherwise uncritically accept. For this, it is necessary to turn to politics and, in particular, to new institutionalism, to test governance values for coherence, consistency and non-contradiction, while appreciating the role that political jurisprudence plays in shaping and prioritising these values. Britain may well retain its sovereignty in tax matters, but this depends on the government's capacity to shape corporation tax policy; and this in turn is a question of how institutional structures, purposes and values help to build up trust and to strengthen allegiance to the British state.

[44] *In re M* [1994] 1 AC 377, 425D (Lord Woolf). See Tomkins, *Public Law* (above n 41) 85; and Loughlin, *The Idea of Public Law* (above n 10) 152.

[45] Gamble (above n 17) 405.

[46] D Judge, G Stoker and H Wolman, 'Urban Politics and Theory: An Introduction' in D Judge, G Stoker and H Wolman (eds), *Theories of Urban Politics* (London, Sage, 1995) 3.

[47] I Berlin, 'Does Political Theory Still Exist?' in H Hardy and R Hausheer (eds), *The Proper Study of Mankind: An Anthology of Essays* (London, Pimlico, 1998) 76.

II. GOVERNANCE AND CORPORATION TAX REFORM

John Tiley, when discussing the 'constitutionality' of extra-statutory concessions, has described the running of the British system of taxation with characteristic pungency. The system is, he says, 'a club', one whose membership consists of 'the professions and the department',[48] namely accountants and lawyers, on the one hand, and the 'Commissioners for Her Majesty's Revenue and Customs',[49] on the other. Professor Tiley's subtle imagery implies a keen understanding of what a governance perspective entails. He has an obvious alertness to the implications of involving both state and non-state actors in corporation tax reform. Gone, I reiterate, is the 'Westminster model', with its ideals of public administration,[50] and in its place is something of a 'differentiated polity',[51] organised in terms of the neoliberal New Public Management as discussed in chapter four. These contrasts get at the heart of the state's role in governance theory, and they are just two of the main strands in an extensive, searching, but not always consistent governance literature.[52] What a governance perspective does, claims Gerry Stoker in the first of five 'propositions' that are designed 'to present a number of aspects of governance for consideration',[53] is to sensitise observers to the implications of involving a range of institutions in – in this case – the process of reforming corporate taxation. Though Stoker's approach was applied to a particular analytical context, it is recommended by a number of students of institutions.

Governance, Stoker first points out, 'refers to a complex set of institutions and actors that are drawn from but also beyond government'.[54] The term therefore highlights the 'complexity' created by an institutional framework that includes not only the Treasury and HMRC but also regulatory bodies such as the International Accounting Standards Board (IASB), the Accounting Standards Board (ASB) and even supranational and international institutions, such as those of the European Union (especially the European Commission

[48] J Tiley, *Revenue* Law, 5th edn (Oxford, Hart Publishing, 2005) 64 (removed from the 6th edn, 68).

[49] Commissioners for Revenue and Customs Act 2005 s 1(1).

[50] See generally, R Thomas, *The British Philosophy of Administration: A Comparison of British and American Ideas 1900–1939* (Cambridge, Centre for Business and Public Sector Ethics, 1989); H Finer, *The Theory and Practice of Modern Government*, 4th edn (London, Methuen, 1961); and RAW Rhodes, *Understanding Governance: Policy Networks, Governance, Reflexivity and Accountability* (Maidenhead, Open University Press, 1997) 166.

[51] Rhodes (ibid) 7–22.

[52] Ibid; J Pierre, 'Introduction: Understanding Governance' in J Pierre (ed), *Debating Governance* (Oxford, Oxford University Press, 2000) 1–10; Pierre and Peters (above n 26); A Gamble, *Politics and Fate* (London, Polity, 2000); and A Gamble, 'Economic Governance' in J Pierre (ed), *Debating Governance* (above) 110; J Kooiman, 'Societal Governance: Levels, Modes, and Orders of Social-Political Interaction' in J Pierre (ed), *Debating Governance* (above) 138; and D Richards and MJ Smith, *Governance and Public Policy in the UK* (Oxford, Oxford University Press, 2002) ch 2.

[53] Stoker (above n 38) 18.

[54] Ibid, 19.

and the European Court), the Organisation for Economic Co-operation and Development (OECD), the International Monetary Fund (IMF) and the World Trade Organization (WTO). Complexity is not, however, to the range of these institutions. On another level, the governance perspective highlights the different *loci* of 'strategic decision-making'.[55] When he proposes a significance for the 'complex set of institutions and actors' involved, Stoker does not particularly have corporate taxation in mind. Had he done so, he might have drawn attention to the fact that the IASB, the body responsible for formulating 'international GAAP (Generally Accepted Accounting Practice)', is not an agency of the government, and its funding comes from a range of central banks, but also corporate sector sources.[56] Nonetheless, the various documents that it produces play a significant, though not decisive, part in shaping the corporation tax base. None of this is to detract, of course, from the point that sole competence in corporation tax matters remains with the government.

Thus sensitised, both to the complexity of the institutional framework and to the fact that strategic decisions are taken outside the institutions of the government, we are presented with what Stoker has designated 'the first dilemma of governance'[57] – namely, that whatever efficiency gains may result from a reliance on expertise, a division of responsibility that requires strategic decisions to be made by people other than government ministers, may not be recognised as legitimate. An ambiguous attitude to public deliberation in non-governmental institutions has a long history in British political discourse. Mistrust of it prompted Parliament's 1642 demand that King Charles I concur that 'the great affairs of the kingdom may not be concluded or transacted by the advice of private men, or by any unknown or unsworn councillors'.[58] However, although the principle that the Crown should thus be fully subject to Parliament's control was briefly enshrined in section 4 of the 1701 Act of Settlement, the section was, as Loughlin has related, deleted in 1706 as inexpedient and unnecessary, ministers of the Crown being removable anyway on a no confidence vote.[59] Nonetheless, the possibility of unelected, unaccountable people helping to shape the public interest has left lingering worries in the minds of successive generations. What is unusual about corporation tax reform is that the nature and scope of the involvement of a body such as the IASB is largely hidden from

[55] Ibid, 18.

[56] International Accounting Standards Committee Foundation, *Annual Report 2009* (London, IASCF 2010) 51; and N Shaxson, *Treasure Islands: Tax Havens and the Men Who Stole the World* (London, Bodley Head, 2011) 251–52.

[57] Stoker (above n 38) 19.

[58] Proposition 2 of 'The Nineteen Propositions Sent by the Two Houses of Parliament to the King at York', reprinted in SR Gardiner, *Constitutional Documents of the Puritan Revolution 1625–1660*, 3rd edn (Oxford, Clarendon Press, 1906) 249 and 250. The text of Proposition 2 is quoted in Tomkins, *Public Law* (above n 41) 130). See generally, GE Aylmer, *Rebellion or Revolution? England 1640–1660* (Oxford, Oxford University Press, 1986) 35.

[59] Loughlin, *Foundations of Public Law* (above n 10) 264; and Tomkins, *Public Law* (above n 41) 45.

sight. Its role is not, in contemporary parlance, transparent. It may therefore be that, valuable as IASB assistance is, the shadowy nature of its influence, in Peters' words, compounds the widespread difficulties 'of citizens . . . understanding and influencing the actions of their governments'.[60] As corporation tax policy comes increasingly to be recognised to involve political rather than merely technical issues, the IASB's involvement will increasingly be scrutinised.[61]

Given this context of complexity, of fragmented responsibility for 'strategic decision-making', the tasks of Parliament and the government are particularly sensitive. Stoker has characterised the problem in terms of the absence, as regards both the media and society, of 'a legitimation framework in which to place the emerging system of governance'.[62] At a general level, 'tensions' have emerged over the last decade and more about the implications of Public Management for 'separating policy and operational matters', about 'unaccountable quangos' and about 'the nature of ministerial accountability'.[63] These general concerns are particularised in corporation tax reform in terms of concerns about the demarcation lines between politics and administration, which are blurred when government is seen in terms of management; of concerns about the nature and influence of the IASB;[64] and of the worries about the relative unaccountability of the Chancellor of the Exchequer for the conduct of fiscal policy.[65] If the influence of the IASB has tended to be discussed in financial reporting circles rather than in tax circles, it may be because its expertise was until recently a source of greater trust and confidence in tax circles than in other policy areas. However, one 'only has to mention the name "Enron" '[66] or to refer

[60] BG Peters, 'Managing the Hollow State' in KA Eliassen and J Kooiman (eds), *Managing Public Organizations: Lessons from Contemporary European Experience*, 2nd edn (London, Sage, 1993) 46 and 55.

[61] Eg, the arguments over IAS 39 and the subsequent adjustments to the special corporation tax code on derivatives. See B Jopson, 'Banks and IASB in Stalemate on Derivatives' *Financial Times* (17 September 2005) 30.

[62] Stoker (above n 38) 20.

[63] Ibid.

[64] Editorial, *Financial Times* (31 March 2004) 17; J Pierce and R Knight, 'Letter' *Financial Times* (7 April 2004) 16; D Hargreaves and H Tricks, 'New Accounting Rules Raise Questions of Accountability' *Financial Times* (9 December 2004) 20; T Buck, G Parker and C Mai, 'EU Internal Market Chief Fuels Debate over Accounts Rules' *Financial Times* (17 January 2005) 6; B Jopson, 'McCreevy Turns on the IASB' *Financial Times* (27 January 2005) 26; T Buck and B Jopson, 'Brussels Seeks Greater Role in IASB Decisions' *Financial Times* (3 February 2005) 27; B Jopson, 'IASB Committee Expands Europe Representation' *Financial Times* (22 February 2005) 30; Editorial, *Financial Times* (10 March 2005) 18; DE Tyrrall, 'Letter' *Financial Times* (17 March 2005) 42; P Thal Larsen, 'Accounting Bodies under Fire' *Financial Times* (13 June 2005) 21; B Jopson, 'EU Calls for Caution over IFRS Move' *Financial Times* (21 October 2005) 30; B Jopson, 'New IASB Trustee Calms Nerves' *Financial Times* (30 January 2006) 26; S Fearnley and T Hines, 'Accountability at the Heart of a Complex Debate' *Financial Times* (25 May 2006) 12.

[65] V Cable, 'Britain's Fiscal Policy Network Needs to be Less Opaque' *Financial Times* (6 December 2006) 19. See also C Wales, 'Commentary' in S Adam, T Besley et al (eds), *Dimensions of Tax Design: The Mirrlees Review* (Oxford, Oxford University Press, 2010) 1300, 1313.

[66] Tiley, *Revenue* Law (above n 48) 392 (deleted from 6th edn).

to the megaphonic effects of marking-to-market assets and liabilities of banks[67] to illustrate the assertion that that time may now be past.

Whilst Stoker frames the problem in terms of how to ensure the 'legitimacy' of institutions involved in governance,[68] this is only a version of the point made at the end of section I above:

> [T]o be effective in the long run, power-holders must be seen to be legitimate. A legitimation deficit undermines public support and commitment to programmes of change [,] and ultimately undermines the ability of power-holders to mobilise resources and promote co-operation and partnership'.[69]

In other words, as we shall see, ensuring that institutions are effective, whether because of their skill in governing or their ability to hold other institutions to account, is a *prudential* approach, which helps to augment trust and confidence, and thus to enhance the government's sovereignty in tax matters. Effectiveness and capacity are closely related concepts. In essence, therefore, the governance approach alerts us, first, to the challenge that institutional complexity presents to analysing corporation tax reform and, secondly, to how, within that context, responsibilities become 'blurred' as between state and non-state participants.

What Stoker asserts in his second proposition is that '[g]overnance recognises the blurring of boundaries and responsibilities for tackling . . . economic issues'.[70] Corporation tax reform of course raises crucial economic issues, it being, in common with other areas of tax reform, an aspect of 'microeconomic' – that is, 'supply-side' – economic policy.[71] Whilst the importance of this second proposition to illuminating the values and priorities of the actors in corporation tax policy may seem obscure, it does highlight an important dimension to the respective roles of the state and the corporate sector: the views of the Treasury and HMRC of their responsibilities to the corporate sector, as well as the corporate sector's views of its responsibilities to the state.

Stoker sees this second proposition in terms of the respective responsibilities of state and private sector in the specific context of public service provision. The 'unbundling' of public utilities offers an obvious and periodically contentious example. But the 'blurring' of responsibilities is important, too, in relation to the present area of inquiry, even though this involves the Crown provision of goods and services only in some rather general sense. This is because there is an increasing acceptance among writers on corporation tax reform of the need for greater mutual respect between the Treasury and HMRC, on the one hand, and the corporate sector, on the other. This is manifested by demands for the former

[67] A Kaletsky, *Capitalism 4.0: The Birth of a New Economy* (London, Bloomsbury, 2010) 139.
[68] D Beetham, *The Legitimation of Power* (Basingstoke, Palgrave, 1991) 19.
[69] Stoker (above n 38) 20.
[70] Ibid, 21.
[71] HM Treasury, *Microeconomic Reform in Britain: Delivering Opportunities for All*, E Balls, J Grice and G O'Donnell (eds) (Basingstoke, Palgrave Macmillan, 2004) esp ch 1. See also N Lawson, 'Changing the Consensus' in H Davies (ed), *The Chancellors' Tales: Managing the British Economy* (Cambridge, Polity, 2006) viii, 113 and 115.

to ensure that market-sensitive information on big taxpayers does not become a matter of public knowledge, for instance through 'leaks' to the press, etc;[72] by calls for the Treasury to justify much more carefully the introduction of any statutory measure that has an obvious anti-avoidance dimension; and by suggestions for a 'much lighter touch' in compliance and enforcement matters.[73] The emphasis on responsibilities is no less forceful, however, in the mouths of the officials of HMRC. Companies should look to their social responsibilities, they say; companies should not go around looking to purchase tax avoidance 'products';[74] and they should be much more willing to disclose fully to HMRC the details of their taxation activities.[75] Since there is a responsibility on the government to raise a 'fair share' of tax from the corporate sector, there is also a responsibility on the corporate sector not to seek to cast off that burden.

However, as Stoker says:

> [T]he dilemma suggested by the blurring of responsibilities is that it creates an ambiguity and uncertainty in the minds of policy-makers and public about who is responsible and can lead to government actors passing off responsibility to [the corporate sector] when things go wrong.[76]

Therefore, initiatives of the Labour administration such as HMRC's Large Corporates Forum, the assessment of high risk and low risk taxpayers, as well as the secondment of HMRC officials to individual companies, have all had the capacity to build up trust and confidence between the 'Revenue Departments' and the corporate sector. Equally, however, they have also had the potential to create precisely the opposite effect. Labour became extremely critical of the corporate sector's use of tax avoidance techniques when corporation tax receipts suddenly dropped, while the corporate sector increasingly blamed the Labour administration for the adverse effects of tax policy on Britain's 'competitiveness'. Again, this is a matter of building up the foundational, political aspect of sovereignty. It is of course too early to see how the Conservative–Liberal

[72] A Parker and R Budden, 'Business Warning over Tax Crackdown Tactic' *Financial Times* (2 April 2004) 2. See also C Wales, 'Building or Bombing Bridges?' *Tax Journal* (20 November 2006) 9.

[73] J Eaglesham, 'Employers' Chief Warns over Drive against Tax Dodging' *Financial Times* (6 December 2005) 4; V Houlder, 'Gold Star Tax Award Proposed' *Financial Times* (31 March 2006) 5; V Houlder, 'Inquiries into "Closed" Returns Prompt Alarm' *Financial Times* (21 August 2006) 3; V Houlder, 'A Charm Offensive from the Taxman' *Financial Times* (17 November 2006) 3; and V Houlder, 'Watchdog Criticises Excessive Business Tax Probes' *Financial Times* (25 July 2007) 4.

[74] A Parker, 'Tax Probe to Centre on 30 Top Companies' *Financial Times* (4 May 2004) 1; A Parker, 'Tax Collectors Clash with "Aggressive Avoidance Promoter"' *Financial Times* (4 May 2004) 4 (FA 2002, sch 26, para 22A); J Croft, A Jolliffe and PJ Davies, 'Action on Loopholes will Target Financial Products' *Financial Times* (17 March 2005) 9; J Plender, 'Double Non-taxation is a Global Issue' *Financial Times* (17 March 2005) 19 (F(No 2)A 2005 ss 24–31); V Houlder, 'Crackdown in Structured Finance Arena' *Financial Times* (15 March 2006) 21; and P Thal Larsen, 'Sprinter's Dash for Tax Advantages has Admirers Watching in the Stands' *Financial Times* (15 March 2006) 21 (FA 2006 s 76 and sch 6).

[75] Eg, the 2006 'interventions' initiative. See A Hubbard, 'Interpreting Interventions' *Taxation* (2 November 2006) 111.

[76] Stoker (above n 38) 21.

Coalition will fare in this regard, but there are few early signs of a more tolerant attitude to tax avoidance.

It is the debate on the types of issue just referred to that highlights another consequence of 'blurred' responsibilities. This is that the blurring enhances the scope for '[t]hose in a position to interpret and lead public debate . . . [to], often with considerable effectiveness, blame others for failures and difficulties'.[77] Corporation tax policy provides a rather interesting context for this type of problem. It is an area of public policy where those best placed to 'interpret and lead public debate' are multinationals, especially, as we shall see in a moment, through their spokespersons in parts of the press and in the legal and accountancy professions. In this connection, the role of the *Financial Times* newspaper cannot be underestimated. Although its subtle and studiously detached coverage, which often makes use of interviews with leading tax professionals, strives to avoid any element of the partisan, it is extremely effective at shaping issues for debate. For instance, its policy suggestions[78] after the European Court's decision in *Cadbury Schweppes*[79] in September 2006 were largely adopted in the Pre-Budget Report of December that year.[80] Only occasionally, by contrast, does corporation tax policy achieve comparable coverage in more widely consumed media.[81] In this connection, too, PricewaterhouseCoopers and the Hundred Group of Finance Directors have been publishing a glossy, if strangely-premised annual survey of 'the tax contributions made by Britain's largest businesses to government revenues'.[82]

The approach that I have so far taken should have dispersed any lingering impression of transparency or linearity, whether as regards the range and the roles of institutions involved in corporation tax reform or as to responsibility for the results. Each of these points raises problems of sovereignty, partly because of 'gaps' in the legitimation of power and partly because of the tendency of each of government and corporate sector to blame the other, in the event that corporation tax reforms have unintended and undesirable consequences.

Problems of sovereignty also arise, however, through the power relations between institutions of government and those of the corporate sector. This brings us to the third of Stoker's interpretative propositions: '[g]overnance iden-

[77] Ibid, 22.

[78] Editorial, *Financial Times* (14 September 2006) 16.

[79] Case C-196/04 *Cadbury Schweppes plc and Another v CIR* [2007] 1 CMLR 2.

[80] HM Treasury, *Investing in Britain's Potential: Building Our Long-Term Future (Pre-Budget Report, December 2006)* (Cm 6984, 2006) para 5.102.

[81] BBC 2, 'No Tax Please, We're Rich!' *The Money Programme* (2 March 2006), discussing, inter alia, the personal tax affairs of John Caudwell, the founder of Dextra Accessories/Phones 4U. See *Macdonald (HMIT) v Dextra Accessories Ltd* [2005] UKHL 47; [2005] STC 1111, para 8 (Lord Hoffmann).

[82] P Broadley and R Collier-Keywood, 'The Hundred Group and its Total Tax Contribution' *Tax Journal* (12 February 2007) 7, referring to the survey's website at http://www.pwc.com/uk/ttc (accessed 21 August 2010); and V Houlder, 'Large Companies Pay Lower Rate of Corporation Tax' *Financial Times* (2 March 2011) 3.

tifies the power dependence involved in the relationships between institutions involved in collective action'.[83] '[G]overning is an interactive process [he contends] because no single actor, public or private, has the knowledge and resource capacity to tackle problems unilaterally'.[84] I have already noted one example of this phenomenon in the apparent willingness of the Treasury to entrust part of the responsibility for shaping the corporation tax base to the IASB. This is a form of 'principal-agent' relationship,[85] and as we shall see, it raises accountability issues of a classical kind. I shall, however, be noting a subtly different type of power dependency, which involves a 'partnership' between the government and the corporate sector, and each negotiates 'joint projects in which by blending their capacities they are better able to meet their own . . . objectives'.[86] This is the spirit of the various forms of enhanced co-operation suggested both by the Varney Review of November 2006[87] and by the emerging concept of 'tax governance', which is gradually being fashioned at the hands of tax professionals.[88] Some of the issues of power and its legitimation to which they give rise are considered in section III. Again, our concern is with the 'generative' aspect of sovereignty, with capacity.

The fourth of Stoker's interpretative 'propositions' is closely linked to the power relationships to be examined later in the chapter. It is that partnership relationships such as those referred to above tend to lead to the development of 'autonomous self-governing networks of actors'.[89] The idea that public policy is influenced by 'policy communities', or policy networks, has been explored most rigorously by Marsh and Rhodes.[90] Two main possibilities are postulated: first, the existence of groups whose purpose is to influence policy; and secondly, what are referred to as 'governance networks', the purpose of which is 'not just influencing government policy but taking over the business of government'.[91]

In the specific context of corporation tax reform, governance networks clearly exist – comprising representatives of bodies such as the Institute of Chartered Accountants in England and Wales (ICAEW), the Law Society and the Chartered

[83] Stoker (above n 38) 22; and C Thain and R Christie, 'Treasury Power: Past, Present and Future', JUC PAC Conference (Belfast, 3–5 September 2007) 13, available at http://colinthain.com/images/pub_uploads/pacpaper.pdf (accessed 5 July 2011).

[84] Thain and Christie (ibid), who refer to J Kooiman, 'Social-Political Governance: Introduction' in J Kooiman (ed), *Modern Governance: New Government-Society Interactions* (London, Sage, 1993) 4.

[85] Stoker (above n 38) 22.

[86] Ibid.

[87] HM Revenue and Customs, *2006 Review of Links with Large Business*, Sir David Varney (Chair) (November 2006).

[88] DF Williams, 'Developing the Concept of Tax Governance', Discussion Paper of KPMG's Tax Business School (London, KPMG, 2007); and V Houlder, 'Tax Claims Hit at Reputation as well as the Coffers' *Financial Times* (9 November 2010) 16.

[89] Stoker (above n 38) 23. See also Thain and Christie, 'Treasury Power' (above n 83) 13.

[90] D Marsh and RAW Rhodes, 'Policy Communities and Issue Networks: Beyond Typology' in D Marsh and RAW Rhodes (eds), *Policy Networks in British Government* (Oxford, Clarendon Press, 1992) 249. See also Rhodes, *Understanding Governance* (above n 50) 43.

[91] Stoker (above n 38) 23.

Institute of Taxation (CIOT) – all of which have both the resources and the expertise to take an active part in this particular area of public policymaking. The nature of tax policy is such that, whilst reliant on such bodies for their expertise, the government retains a more pre-eminent position than it does in the other areas of policymaking discussed in the literature. Indeed, corporation tax reform has become an area in which the type of partnership just identified is a key feature of the institutional framework. This point will be underlined in chapter four when I detail somewhat further the involvement of policy communities' membership in the policymaking process. Two illustrations will suffice at this stage. First, there are the discussions under the 'Chatham House rule', conducted at the Centre for Tax Law at Cambridge University, involving members of the Treasury and HMRC, academics and members of the practising professions, as well as the conferences with a similar constituency organised at the Oxford University Centre for Business Taxation. Indeed, it was in a speech at the latter institution in July 2010 that the incoming Exchequer Secretary to the Treasury, David Gauke, announced the establishment of a Tax Professionals Forum and a tax forum for multinationals, the Business Forum on Tax and Competitiveness, the latter reviving an idea of the previous Labour administration.[92] Secondly, there is the regular transfer of distinguished individuals between the Revenue Departments and the corporate sector. So, for example, Chris Sanger, currently in charge of tax policy at Ernst and Young, was previously an adviser to the Treasury[93] and is now a member of the government's Tax Professionals Forum; Edward Troup, who was in charge of tax policy at Simmons and Simmons, a City law firm, moved to the Treasury in 2005 and is now the Treasury's Budget, Tax and Welfare Directorate Managing Director; Sir David Varney, Chairman of HMRC from September 2004 until September 2006, was formerly the chairman of a mobile phone company;[94] and Mike Clasper, CBE, now Chairman of the Board of HMRC, was previously the Operational Managing Director of the private equity company Terra Firma Capital Partners.

It does not therefore seem too much to argue that corporation tax policy is a strong example of an 'autonomous self-governing network of actors'. But as Stoker has pointed out, '[t]he dilemma created by such self-governing networks is that of accountability'.[95] This 'accountability deficit' is problematic both for

[92] Available at http://www.hm-treasury.gov.uk/speech_xst_020710.htm (accessed 20 August 2010). See also http://www.hm-treasury.gov.uk/tax_forums_business_tax_competitiveness.htm (accessed 25 February 2011). For the Labour antecedent, see HM Treasury, *Multinational Business–Government Tax Forum*, available at http://www.hm-treasury.gov.uk/tax_governmenttaxforum_index.htm (accessed 23 February 2010). January 2011 saw the constitution of a study group 'to explore the case for a GAAR in the UK': HM Treasury, 'Details of Avoidance Study Group Set Out' Press Release 04/11 (14 January 2011), available at http://www.hm-treasury.gov.uk (accessed 21 January 2011).

[93] V Houlder, 'Brown Urged to Consider Foreign Dividend Tax Reform' *Financial Times* (4 December 2006) 3.

[94] C Adams, 'MM02 Chief to Head Merged Revenue' *Financial Times* (14 May 2004) 3.

[95] Stoker (above n 38) 23.

'the individual constituent elements of the network and . . . [for] those excluded from any particular network'.[96] Thus, not only may dissatisfied individual members of the network find it difficult to act, for instance in relation to the now halted Tax Law Rewrite,[97] but there may be wider disquiet over the fact that 'all networks are to a degree exclusive. They are driven by the self-interest of their members rather than a wider concern with the public interest or more particularly those excluded from the network'.[98] The controversy just before the banking crisis broke in 2007 over corporation tax relief for interest payments in 'private equity' acquisitions offers a good example, given the nature and extent of trade union intervention in the debate.[99] The perceived self-interest of the network members, whatever the reality may be, is a major challenge to the capacity of the government in this particular policy area.

Complex and opaque interactions, fuzzy responsibilities, a dependence on outside experts, unwelcome perceptions. What, then, is the result? The fifth and final of Stoker's propositions assists in going some way to answering that question:

> Governance recognizes . . . [a] capacity to get things done which does not rest on the power of government to command or use its authority. It sees government as able to use new techniques and tools to steer and guide.[100]

Government as 'steering'[101] is a key aspect of governing by 'governance'.[102] Stoker refers to the work of Kooiman and van Vliet[103] as elaborating on the institutional aspect of Public Management. Besides 'identifying key stakeholders', 'steering' involves 'influencing and steering relationships in order to achieve desired outcomes'. Most importantly, perhaps, governance is 'about what others call "system management". It involves thinking and acting beyond the individual sub-systems, avoiding unwanted side-effects and establishing mechanisms for effective co-ordination'.[104] It is in this context possibly that the biggest perceived failure of corporation tax, arising perhaps out of the Labour administration's desire to bring about particular political results, has occurred: the systemic complexity to be discussed later.[105] This in turn can perhaps be attributed to

[96] Ibid.

[97] But see T Bowler, 'Tax Policymaking in the UK' Tax Law Review Committee (TLRC) Discussion Paper No 8 (Institute for Fiscal Studies, 2010) 11.

[98] Stoker (above n 38) 24.

[99] B Barber (TUC General-Secretary), 'Europe Must Rein in the Power of Private Equity' *Financial Times* (16 March 2007) 15; and J Dromey (Unite Deputy General-Secretary), 'Protect Workers from the Private Equiteers' *Financial Times* (3 July 2007) 13.

[100] Stoker (above n 38) 24.

[101] CD Foster and FJ Plowden, *The State Under Stress* (Buckingham, Open University Press, 1996) 46.

[102] BG Peters, 'Politics is about Governing' in A Leftwich (ed), *What is Politics?* (Cambridge, Polity, 2004) 24.

[103] Stoker (above n 38) 24. See also J Kooiman and M van Vliet, 'Governance and Public Management' in Eliassen and Kooiman (eds) (above n 60) 58.

[104] Stoker (above n 38) 24.

[105] See below ch 5. See also V Houlder, 'Rules Getting "More and More Complicated"' *Financial*

mutual suspicion between the Revenue Departments and the corporate sector, as well as to the inability of the two to achieve a close working relationship. That they must do so in order for the system to work is dictated by the need to build up the state's capacity in the area.

The purpose of this part of the discussion has been to highlight the institutional trends that have the greatest implications for sovereignty, for the ability of the government to shape corporation tax reform and, in doing so, to augment the state. As Stoker says, however, the map constituted by his five propositions, the governance perspective, 'applies a simplifying lens to a complex reality', identifying several 'key' features of that reality and posing 'significant questions about that reality'.[106] The key element that now requires further elaboration is the exact nature of the challenge to sovereignty presented by the objectives and values of the corporate sector institutions visible from the London Eye.

III. THE CORPORATE SECTOR AND THE GOVERNMENT

If, as is likely, some of the civil servants, accountants and lawyers whose workplaces we imagined at the beginning of the chapter were listening to the *Today* programme[107] at around 6.35 on the morning of 8 March 2007, they would have heard a familiar pre-Budget exchange between Sir Digby Jones,[108] then famous as a former Director-General of the Confederation of British Industry (CBI), and Stuart Wheeler, a City financier and major Conservative party donor. The discussion dealt with the broad outlines of some central issues of the study: the nature of the power of the corporate sector and the extent to which it facilitates or hinders the government in achieving its policy objectives. Although the respective contributions, inevitably perhaps, were directed at the contrasting personalities of the then Chancellor of the Exchequer, Gordon Brown, and David Cameron, then the leader of the Opposition, they were about the extent to which Mr Brown, as Prime Minister, would be able to rely on the constructive engagement of different corporate sector constituencies.

Times (21 October 2004) 3; C Giles, 'Brown Yet to Grasp Thorny Problem of Corporation Tax' *Financial Times* (21 October 2004) 3; Lord Howe, 'Bipartisan Support is Needed to Clear the Tax Jungle' *Financial Times* (22 March 2006) 17; J Eaglesham and V Houlder, 'Four in Ten Companies Make Errors in Corporation Tax Returns' *Financial Times* (31 January 2006) 4; V Houlder, '"Confusion Layered on Complexity" with Growth of Legislation' *Financial Times* (24 March 2006) 2; V Houlder, 'Tax System Complexities Threaten to Dull Competitive Edge, Say Directors' *Financial Times* (21 April 2006) 3; V Houlder, 'Britain Remains Competitive on Tax Even as Law Book Expands' *Financial Times* (8 November 2006) 4; V Houlder, 'Fewer Tax Laws as Treasury Reacts to Criticism' *Financial Times* (15 August 2007) 3; and C Giles, 'Chancellor Pledges to Simplify Tax System' *Financial Times* (26 July 2007) 2.

[106] Stoker (above n 38) 26.

[107] See the BBC Radio archives at http://www.bbc.co.uk/radio4/today/listenagain/listenagain_20070308.shtml (accessed 12 July 2011).

[108] H Williams, *Britain's Power Elites: The Rebirth of a Ruling Class* (London, Constable, 2006) 185; and G Monbiot, 'They Still Rage about the Class War, but Keep Funding Their Class Enemies' *Guardian* (10 July 2007) 29.

While conceding that the Chancellor had demonstrated 'economic competence', the former CBI Director-General stressed Mr Brown's status as what he described as 'one of the great taxing Chancellors' and hinted at the long-stop possibility of businesses dissatisfied with Britain's taxation climate relocating to other, more 'business friendly' jurisdictions. Properly interpreted, this contribution could perhaps be seen as no more than a voicing of the predictable concerns of a corporate sector operating within the governance context discussed above. Mr Wheeler's approach was, however, rather different. Mr Brown may well have been a 'taxing Chancellor', he opined, but what was much more significant was that he was 'not at all trusted in the City', and Mr Cameron would, in this respect, be a breath of fresh air. Moreover, the Chancellor faced the real risk that the headquarters operations of multinationals, though probably not fairly small businesses operating solely in Great Britain, would look to relocate in other countries in order to avoid corporation tax.

Setting aside the inevitable media preoccupation with personalities and bearing in mind the partisan nature of the radio discussion, it nonetheless distilled some important realities about the relative power of corporate sector and governmental institutions. The 2007–09 banking crisis has reconfigured, though not effaced, these realities. They arise in the context of debates about the continuing significance of the nation state, under conditions created by that nebulous[109] but much discussed idea of economic globalisation.[110] From Saskia Sassen, who maintains that 'the major dynamics at work in the global economy carry the capacity to undo the particular form of the intersection of sovereignty and territory embedded in the modern state',[111] to Hardt and Negri, who proclaim the end of the 'centuries-long dialectic' between capital and the state,[112] a succession of commentators[113] has asserted that the sovereignty of particular states has been eviscerated, or at least transformed, by global economic power. Moreover, as Anatole Kaletsky has recently argued, one effect of the banking crisis may have been to reconfigure and redefine the values already embodied in the global economic phenomenon.[114]

The view taken in this study is that, in the context of corporate tax policy, the state does indeed retain its importance, but in this fragile global economy, new

[109] JA Scholte, *Globalization: A Critical Introduction*, 2nd edn (Basingstoke, Palgrave Macmillan, 2005) 15.

[110] See generally, JE Stiglitz, *Globalization and its Discontents* (London, Penguin, 2002); M Wolf, *Why Globalization Works* (London, Yale, 2005); and JE Stiglitz, *Making Globalization Work* (London, Penguin, 2007).

[111] S Sassen, *Losing Control? Sovereignty in an Age of Globalization* (New York, Columbia University Press, 1996) 5.

[112] M Hardt and A Negri, *Empire* (London, Harvard University Press, 2000) 306.

[113] See generally, K Ohmae, *The End of the Nation State: The Rise of Regional Economies* (London, HarperCollins, 1995); S Strange, *The Retreat of the State: The Diffusion of Power in the World Economy* (Cambridge, Cambridge University Press, 1996); Sassen (above n 111); J Gray, *False Dawn: The Delusions of Global Capitalism*, 2nd edn (London, Granta, 2002); and Hardt and Negri (ibid) 306.

[114] Kaletsky (above n 67) 21.

demands are made upon its sovereignty in that particular policy area. Difficult issues arise, nevertheless. If, as was suggested earlier, the first dilemma of corporation tax reform governance is that we or, more accurately, Parliament cannot effectively interrogate certain key areas of policy, then the possibility that global economic power may be working against the public interest must give cause for concern. In order for the government to maintain the trust and confidence of the governed, therefore, a prudent management of the corporate sector's economic power is called for, as well as the effective scrutiny of that management by Parliament. The decisive intervention of the government to support the banking sector in 2008 is a clear indication of the importance of the former point,[115] and as I shall demonstrate, there are signs that parliamentary scrutiny will be tightened in response to the regulatory failures that necessitated that intervention.

Secondly, in speaking of economic power, it is crucial to make a careful distinction. Hobbes, as already discussed, differentiated between power as capacity, which is enabling, and power as domination, which is not.[116] How the relationship between state and corporate sector is interpreted depends essentially on whether the corporate sector's influence is seen in terms of capacity or domination. Those who take one viewpoint will hardly be persuaded of the truth of the other. Power is a fundamentally agonistic concept. Either viewpoint is perfectly plausible. The idea that the corporate sector dominates government has a long pedigree.[117] Indeed, even in the seventeenth century, Hobbes deplored 'the great number of Corporations; which are as it were many lesser Commonwealths in the bowels of the greater, like wormes in the entrayles of a naturall man'.[118] Thanks largely, however, to the influence of David Hume and Adam Smith, this idea was a minority one by the end of the eighteenth century. It will be recalled from chapter one that in stabilising political society, commerce did for Hume and Smith what for Hobbes only the sword could achieve.[119] This was unsurprising, since by the nineteenth century, the joint-stock company had become, in Peter Drucker's words, 'the first new autonomous institution in hundreds of years, the first to create a power center that was within society yet independent of the central government of the national state'.[120] What had intervened was the development of the political values that I discussed in chapter two. To someone who subscribes to these values, economic power will seem enabling; to others, it will appear constricting. The idea that it is enabling has, however, been the pith of the neoliberal economic consensus for upwards of

[115] Ibid, 101.

[116] See above ch 1. Capacity is 'power to'; domination, 'power over'.

[117] J Micklethwait and A Wooldridge, *The Company: A Short History of a Revolutionary Idea* (London, Phoenix, 2005) 2.

[118] Hobbes (above n 20) 218 (pt 2 ch 29).

[119] See above ch 2.

[120] PF Drucker, *The Frontiers of Management* (London, Heinemann, 1987) 170. But see AA Berle and GC Means, *The Modern Corporation and Private Property*, rev edn (New York, Harcourt, Brace and World, 1967) 313.

40 years.[121] Though thinkers on the Left deplore it, that consensus is even today surprisingly durable.[122]

Keeping the confidence and trust of the governed, in corporate tax, as in any policy area, is essential to a government's capacity,[123] and it involves managing the concerns of the corporate sector. To the profound disapproval of many,[124] the government's commitment to private sector economic growth[125] is at least consistent with the corporate sector's interests. The potential for conflict is real enough; but it is capable of being managed. If taxation policies provoke conflict, it is the flight of capital that will damage economic growth;[126] given the neoliberal consensus, an important aspect of the government's task is to see that that does not happen. Attracting overseas investment, as discussed in chapter two, is the mainstay of economic policy. What is most likely to emerge from the financial crisis is, as Kaletsky has said, a reinvented capitalism,[127] not a different economic system.

Thirdly, some important distinctions need to be drawn between various constituencies of economic power. The key distinctions here are the ones implied by the radio discussion referred to earlier, between the power of multinationals and that of the City, and between multinationals and the power of firms operating exclusively in Britain. So far as multinationals are concerned, one important relationship might be that between the government and 'foreign-owned subsidiaries', but given certain historical factors, the relationship between the government and the parent firms of corporate groups[128] might possibly be even more important.[129] The nature and extent of the economic power of multinationals has spawned an extensive literature,[130] ever since the rapid expansion into Europe of US firms in the decades after the Second World War.[131] Only relatively

[121] See generally, MB Steger and RK Roy, *Neoliberalism: A Very Short Introduction* (Oxford, Oxford University Press, 2010) ch 6. See also A Turner, *Just Capital: The Liberal Economy*, rev edn (London, Pan Books, 2002).

[122] See generally, C Leys, *Market-Driven Politics: Neoliberal Democracy and the Public Interest* (London, Verso, 2001) ch 3.

[123] Loughlin, *The Idea of Public Law* (above n 10) 76.

[124] Leys (above n 122) 44.

[125] W Grant, *Economic Policy in Britain* (Basingstoke, Palgrave, 2002) 34.

[126] A Smith, *The Wealth of Nations, Books I–III* [1776], AS Skinner (ed) (London, Penguin, 1999) 463–64; and A Smith, *The Wealth of Nations, Books IV–V* [1776], AS Skinner (ed) (London, Penguin, 1999) 442, 505 and 529.

[127] Kaletsky (above n 67) 312.

[128] R Vernon, *In the Hurricane's Eye: The Troubled Prospects of Multinational Enterprises* (London, Harvard University Press, 1998) 2.

[129] Ipsos MORI, 'UK Corporate Taxation and International Competitiveness', Research Study (Confederation of British Industry (CBI), 2006) app s 2. See also B Dodwell, 'The UK: New Holding Company for the World?' *Tax Journal* (2 July 2007) 15.

[130] Eg, C Tugendhat, *The Multinationals* (Harmondsworth, Penguin, 1973); D Julius, *Global Companies and Public Policy: The Growing Challenge of Foreign Direct Investment* (London, Pinter, 1990) esp ch 3; Vernon (above n 128) esp chs 4 and 6; and PJ Buckley and M Casson, *The Future of the Multinational Enterprise*, 3rd edn (Basingstoke, Palgrave Macmillan, 2002) esp ch 5.

[131] See generally, J-J Servan-Schreiber, *The American Challenge,* R Steel (trans) (London, Hamish Hamilton, 1968) esp 3 and 199. See also R Vernon, *Sovereignty at Bay: The Multinational Spread of US Enterprises* (London, Longman, 1971) esp ch 8; and Micklethwait and Wooldridge (above n 117) 163.

recently, however, in the work of Nathan Jensen, has its political significance been identified with some precision.[132] What Jensen has proposed is a certain identity, rather than an opposition, of interests, between multinationals and civil society. This is not to deny that multinationals have 'policy preferences', nor that their prime objective is profit-maximisation, but it does assert that 'the consolidation and maintenance of democratic institutions' are crucial factors in the willingness of multinationals to invest in particular states, in Britain no less than any other.[133] In other words, there is little more unappealing for foreign direct investment (FDI) than wide 'executive discretion'.[134] What Jensen does assert, against the arguments of Rosanne Altshuler and others,[135] is that 'there is very little empirical support for claims that taxes or other forms of government fiscal policy seriously affect FDI inflows'.[136] Such matters are far less important, from multinationals' viewpoint, than institutions structured in such a way as to minimise 'political risk': 'Institutions affect policies, and policies affect multinational operations'.[137] I have already explained the significance of this issue in relation to international tax competition,[138] and I shall touch on it again in chapter five.

If the power of multinationals has given rise to extensive debate, so too has the power of the City of London[139] and the issues raised by the possibility of capital flight. In this connection, Layna Mosley's work[140] provides useful complementary insights to those offered by Jensen. Mosley's analysis is not specifically concerned with the relationship between the government and the City.[141] Nonetheless, it does seek to throw light on the weight given to matters such as 'the structure of a nation's tax system' '[w]hen a bond trader at Goldman Sachs, or a fund manager at Fidelity, sits at his desk, contemplating where to allocate investment'.[142] Just as the territory of Jensen's analysis is FDI, Mosley is con-

[132] NM Jensen, *Nation-States and the Multinational Corporation: A Political Economy of Foreign Direct Investment* (Woodstock, Princeton University Press, 2006).

[133] Ibid, 153.

[134] Ibid, 152.

[135] R Altshuler, H Grubert and TS Newlon, 'Has US Investment Abroad Become More Sensitive to Tax Rates?' in JR Hines Jr (ed), *International Taxation and Multinational Activity* (London, University of Chicago Press, 2001) 9–32 and 28.

[136] Jensen (above n 132) xii. See also V Houlder, 'Global Corporate Tax Rates Fall' *Financial Times* (23 July 2007) 7.

[137] Jensen (above n 132) 2.

[138] See above ch 2.

[139] See generally, D Kynaston, *The City of London, Vol IV: A Club No More, 1945–2000* (London, Chatto and Windus, 2001). See also M Buckle and J Thompson, *The UK Financial System: Theory and Practice*, 4th edn (Manchester, Manchester University Press 2004) chs 7–13.

[140] L Mosley, *Global Capital and National Governments* (Cambridge, Cambridge University Press, 2003).

[141] See generally, Augar (above n 6) 183; and P Diamond, 'The Political Power of Economic Ideas: Understanding Relations between "New" Labour and the City in the Post-War Era' in S Barber (ed), *The City in Europe and the World* (London, European Research Forum, 2005) 65. See also Shaxson (above n 56) 257 (drawing attention – uniquely, in my experience – to the office of the City Remembrancer, dating from 1571).

[142] Mosley (above n 140) 25.

cerned with 'portfolio investment',[143] in particular with 'the Government bond market [and] the causal pathways associated with it'.[144] Her conclusion is perhaps surprising:

> In the advanced capitalist democracies, market participants consider key macroeconomic indicators, but not supply-side or microlevel policies. . . So, whereas many governments have converged cross-nationally in the pursuit of lower inflation and lower government budget deficits, they have not converged in a variety of other areas, including overall government consumption, the structure of tax systems, and the role of labour market institutions within the economy.[145]

Fourthly, it is clear that the corporate sector cannot legitimise itself by making decisions based on rather narrow 'economistic' calculations. This is particularly true of banks in the wake of the 2007–09 financial crisis. Increasingly, as the 'governance' phenomena referred to earlier, as the PricewaterhouseCoopers/Hundred Group 'total tax contribution' database and as the evolving notion of 'tax governance' illustrate, the corporate sector must seek more subtle and broader-based ways of legitimating its activities. These are usually gathered together under the umbrella term of 'corporate social responsibility',[146] an expression that is coming to include the payment of 'appropriate' levels of taxation.[147] For example, although said to be attributable to unusually large deductible pension contributions, reports such as that in 2007 of the retailer J Sainsbury, having 'paid no corporation tax in 2005–06',[148] cannot be said to have enhanced the firm's reputation for corporate social responsibility. Short-term considerations over maximising shareholder value have wider implications, themselves of an economic nature. Even banks, says Kaletsky, 'must accept a fiduciary duty of care to the Government and the public'.[149]

Finally, assessing the potential impact of corporate taxation on levels of inward investment and on capital flight is to some extent a matter of reflecting on experience. Such experience suggests that, with about a dozen major exceptions since mid-2008, including Henderson, Ineos and Shire, companies still do not leave this jurisdiction simply because of corporation tax policy.[150] The

[143] Jensen (above n 132) 23.

[144] Ibid, 17.

[145] Mosley (above n 140) 305.

[146] Micklethwait and Wooldridge (above n 117) 79, 153 and 174. See also Berle and Means (above n 120); PF Drucker, *The Concept of the Corporation* (New York, Mentor, 1964) ch 3; PA French, *Collective and Corporate Responsibility* (New York, Columbia University Press, 1984) ch 3; S Wheeler, *Corporations and the Third Way* (Oxford, Hart Publishing, 2002) 72; Henderson Global Investors, *Responsible Tax* (London, Henderson, 2005); Financial Times, 'Responsible Business: Special Report' *Financial Times* (3 July 2007); and Houlder, 'Tax Claims Hit at Reputation' (above n 88).

[147] V Houlder, 'The Tax Avoidance Story as a Morality Tale' *Financial Times* (22 November 2004) 9.

[148] V Houlder, 'One-Third of Biggest Businesses Pays No Tax' *Financial Times* (28 August 2007) 3.

[149] Kaletsky (above n 67) 299. See also above ch 2.

[150] P Stafford, 'Swiss Tax Rules Lure McDonald's from UK' *Financial Times* (13 July 2009) 15. See also A Sakoui, 'Ineos Looks to Cut Tax Bill with Swiss Relocation' *Financial Times* (4 March 2010) 1.

problem for the government is how to retain the trust and confidence of society as a whole, in circumstances such that the influence of the corporate sector appears to be so great. If there is a solution, it would appear to lie in the extent to which the objectives, structure and values of Britain's political institutions are such as to enable them to uncover the true extent to which that influence is exercised.

IV. PARLIAMENT

For some commentators such as David Marquand[151] and Will Hutton,[152] the turrets and pinnacles of the Palace of Westminster epitomise a state whose political institutions are ill equipped, either to work with the corporate sector or to define and safeguard the public interest against the encroaching influence of corporations.[153] Much impatience on the former count, though noticeably less on the latter, has long been detectable in commentaries on corporation tax reform.[154] I now turn to assessing how well placed Parliament is, as the key institution of Britain's representative government, to scrutinise the various aspects of corporation tax reform. For some time, indeed, it looked as if this rather specialist issue would itself be undercut by the fundamental and more general controversy over MPs' improper expenses claims.[155] Though still simmering away, that issue has cooled somewhat, following attempts to improve accountability and the departure of a large number of sitting MPs in the May 2010 General Election.[156]

What constitutes a representative as opposed to a direct democracy, Bernard Manin has written, 'is not the fact that a few govern in the place of the people, but that they are selected by election'.[157] However low our opinion of representative government, we need to remember that the strength of representative institutions is that they 'subject those who govern to the verdict of those who

[151] D Marquand, *The Unprincipled Society: New Demands and Old Politics* (London, Fontana, 1988) ch 7.

[152] W Hutton, *The State We're In*, rev edn (London, Vintage, 1996) ch 11; and W Hutton, *Them and Us: Changing Britain – Why We Need a Fair Society* (London, Little, Brown, 2010) 333–37.

[153] Eg, Monbiot, 'They Still Rage about the Class War' (above n 108); S Muggeridge, 'Letter' *Financial Times* (31 July 2007) 10 (regarding efforts to 'bridge the gap'). But note Shaxson (above n 56).

[154] See further, M Gammie, 'Has Nigel Lawson Really Reformed Business Taxation?' (1984) *Fiscal Studies* 82–93; and D Hole, 'Finance Act Notes: Corporate and Government Debt, Sections 80–105 and Schedules 7–15' (1996) *British Tax Review* 347, 358.

[155] See generally, Daily Telegraph, *The Complete Expenses Files* (London, Daily Telegraph, 2009).

[156] J Pickard and A Barker, 'Legg Orders 390 MPs to Repay £1.1m' *Financial Times* (5 February 2010) 2; G Parker and J Eaglesham, '"Committee of Chairmen" Set for Select Role' *Financial Times* (11 June 2010) 2; and J Pickard, 'Query on £14m Stirs Spectre of Expenses Scandal' *Financial Times* (16 December 2010) 2.

[157] But see B Manin, *The Principles of Representative Government* (Cambridge, Cambridge University Press, 1997) 41.

are governed'.[158] It is the latter, ultimately, who will pass judgment, if not on corporation tax reform in particular, then on the government's management of the British economy in general, the stability and growth of which corporation tax reform is intended to support.[159] Britain's constitutional arrangements mean that the relationship between the government and Parliament is peculiarly close, the Crown-in-Parliament being 'the sole representative of the person of the state'.[160] It is the fact that members of the executive both sit and vote in the legislature that, as Walter Bagehot pointed out long ago, is the key to the efficiency of these arrangements.[161]

The objection to the governance trends that I discussed earlier is in part precisely that the non-state actors involved are not ministers and therefore do not have a seat in one or other of the Houses of Parliament. Although Parliament tends to be thought of mainly as a legislature, its real strength, as Tomkins has argued, is as a scrutinising body.[162] This scrutinising role includes, of course, the ex ante scrutiny of legislation, but it also comprises its ex post scrutiny of governmental policy through select committees.[163] Parliament is the body that, in Bagehot's words, 'has . . . an informing function . . . to inform the Sovereign what . . . [is] wrong [and] to lay . . . grievances . . . before the nation'.[164] It is in this sense that Parliament holds the government to account, and not exactly, as John Stuart Mill claimed, by 'watching' and 'controlling' it.[165] Select committees, in advising the government of failures in policy and thereby guiding it along the most prudent path, are thus a source of capacity, of political power. The ability to rely on Parliament's collective wisdom was what made the Tudor monarch Henry VIII opine that he was never more powerful than when he had Parliament to advise him.[166] Tomkins' proposal for interpreting the role of Parliament in this way relies on the ancient idea that more people are available to advise the Crown when Parliament is sitting than at any other time.[167] In no policy area is this more important than taxation. England's 'ancient constitution' envisaged that taxation, the archetype of a measure that touches and concerns everyone and which therefore needs political power in order to be effective,

[158] Ibid, 234; and Sampson, *Who Runs This Place?* (above n 8) 14.

[159] Eg, HM Treasury and HMRC, *Business Tax Reform: Capital Allowances Changes* (July 2007) 3.

[160] Loughlin, *The Idea of Public Law* (above n 10) 84. See also AF Pollard, *The Evolution of Parliament*, 2nd edn (London, Longmans, 1926) 229–34.

[161] Tomkins, *Public Law* (above n 41) 38.

[162] A Tomkins, 'What is Parliament for?' in N Bamforth and P Leyland (eds), *Public Law in a Multi-Layered Constitution* (Oxford, Hart Publishing, 2003) 53.

[163] Hilson (above n 40) 52.

[164] W Bagehot, *The English Constitution* [1867] (London, Kegan Paul, 1919) 133.

[165] JS Mill, 'Considerations on Representative Government' in J Gray (ed), *On Liberty and Other Essays* (Oxford, Oxford University Press, 1991) 282.

[166] MAR Graves, *The Tudor Parliaments: Crown, Lords and Commons, 1485–1603* (London, Longman, 1985) 80; and Loughlin, *Foundations of Public Law* (above n 10) 252.

[167] Tomkins, 'What is Parliament for?' (above n 162) 56.

should be considered by the Crown-in-Parliament.[168] This was why Charles I's attempt to impose taxation in reliance on the royal prerogative, with the allegiance of the judges but without Parliament, provides the classic illustration of the consequences of ignoring this principle.[169] Thus, the 1689 Bill of Rights,[170] which invokes the principles of the ancient constitution, bans the raising of taxation 'by pretence of prerogative'[171] and insists that Parliament grant taxation and 'supply' to the Crown.

In case all of this sounds romanticised, it is useful to reflect on the kind of representative institution that the House of Commons has become. Manin finds the principle that '[t]hose who govern are appointed by election at regular intervals' as one of the key 'constants' of representative government.[172] David Judge has related Manin's insights to the contemporary House of Commons[173] to show us why, even in times of exceptional political disillusionment, the Commons might nonetheless be a source of trust and confidence. The situation today, Manin tells us, is not one of 'parliamentarianism', nor yet one of 'party democracy'. Instead, what we experience today is ' "audience" democracy',[174] which nonetheless retains a key legitimating feature of those earlier models. The electorate chooses the currently 650 MPs because people think that those individuals are 'special', and it also decides the basis on which that status is to be awarded.[175] This has, as we shall see, resonances for corporation tax reform when it comes to the qualities of the ministers of the Crown – the Treasury ministers – who sit on the government front bench and deal with corporation tax matters. But it applies, too, to the individual MPs who carry out the Commons' scrutinising function in relation to this particular area of public policy: the House of Commons Treasury Select Committee.[176] This representativeness is currently lacking, to be sure, in the House of Lords Select Committee on Economic Affairs; it is very doubtful whether the Committee's undoubted technical expertise is adequate compensation.[177]

[168] Manin (above n 157) 86; and Tomkins, *Public Law* (above n 41) 41. See also Loughlin, *Foundations of Public Law* (above n 10) 36 and 44; JH Baker, *An Introduction to English Legal History*, 4th edn (London, Butterworths, 2002) 205; Magna Carta 1215, cl 12 (JC Holt, *Magna Carta*, 2nd edn (Cambridge, Cambridge University Press, 1992) 455); and Loughlin, *Foundations of Public Law* (above n 10) 246.

[169] J Adamson, *The Noble Revolt: The Overthrow of Charles I* (London, Weidenfeld & Nicolson, 2007) 7–12, 35n. See also Tomkins, 'What is Parliament for?' (above n 162) 58.

[170] GM Young, 'The Liberal Mind in Victorian England' in *Last Essays* (London, Rupert Hart-Davis, 1950) 211.

[171] Bill of Rights 1689, 4th indent (full text reproduced in G Wilson, *Cases and Materials on Constitutional and Administrative Law*, 2nd edn (Cambridge, Cambridge University Press, 1976) 2).

[172] Manin (above n 157) 6.

[173] Judge (above n 15) 34.

[174] Manin (above n 157) 218.

[175] Ibid, 236. The Parliamentary Voting System and Constituencies Bill 2010–11 will reduce the number of MPs to 600.

[176] Eg, of the Committee's 14 members, as of 1 July 2007, at least 10 were graduates (eight of these from Oxbridge), and one was a Scottish aristocrat.

[177] Judge (above n 16) 76. But see Coalition proposals for the election of a senate in place of the Lords: J Chapman, 'House of Lords to be Abolished and Replaced by Elected Senate' *Daily Mail* (4 December 2010) 20.

Select committees, these days Parliament's main scrutiny mechanism,[178] have increased in importance as ministerial responsibility has declined. Summarising their strengths and weaknesses as accountability mechanisms, Tomkins has had some useful comments. Reflecting on reports of governments, via their whips, historically seeking to control committee membership, he has revealed a paradox. Whilst Government whips went to great lengths, the fact that membership was so controlled, at least historically, simply meant that the committees were not the formidable bodies they might otherwise have been.[179] That this situation may change, however, is suggested by the recent wresting of the committees from the whips' control. One effect of the disillusionment produced by the 2009 expenses scandal has been the 2010 amendment of the House of Commons Standing Orders to provide for the election of select committee chairs.[180]

Accountability, '[t]he rendering of accounts', is, in Manin's view, nothing less than 'the democratic component of representation'.[181] Departmental select committees,[182] which date only from 1979, take their cue from the Public Accounts Committee, instituted by Gladstone in 1861.[183] In common with other select committees, the Treasury Committee deliberates in private;[184] but it hears evidence in public,[185] and these proceedings are widely reported.[186] It has summarised its 'first and most important objective' as being 'to examine and comment upon the economic policy of the Government'.[187] Treasury ministers do well to weigh the Committee's findings carefully, since if one thing at least is certain, it is that representative government 'still entails that supreme moment when the electorate passes judgment on the past actions of those in government'.[188] Such was Labour's fate in May 2010. Indeed, the effectiveness of the Committee can be illustrated by considering how well equipped it is to illuminate the problems raised by the governance trends in corporation tax reform discussed earlier.

One group of issues, it will be recalled, arises from the Chancellor's accountability for the conduct of fiscal policy, in a climate in which Public Management ideas have tended to blur questions of policy and administration. During the

[178] See generally, Standing Orders of the House of Commons (SOs), Nos 121–52C; W McKay et al (eds), *Erskine May's Treatise on The Law, Privileges, Proceedings and Usage of Parliament*, 23rd edn (London, LexisNexis UK, 2004) ch 26; Judge (above n 16) 55; Tomkins, *Public Law* (above n 41) 162 and 166; M Rush, *Parliament Today* (Manchester, Manchester University Press, 2005) 225; and C Turpin, 'Ministerial Responsibility' in J Jowell and D Oliver (eds), *The Changing Constitution*, 3rd edn (Oxford, Clarendon Press, 1994) 109.

[179] Tomkins, *Public Law* (above n 41) 164.

[180] SO Nos 122A–C; R Kelly, 'Standard Note SN/PC/3719 Nominations to Select Committees', House of Commons Library (2010).

[181] Manin (above n 157) 234.

[182] SO No 152; and McKay et al (eds) (above n 178) 779.

[183] HCG Matthew, *Gladstone: 1809–1874* (Oxford, Clarendon Press, 1986) 117; and HCG Matthew, *Gladstone: 1875–1898* (Oxford, Clarendon Press, 1995) 166.

[184] McKay et al (eds) (above n 178) 738 and 755.

[185] SO No 125(1); and ibid, 755.

[186] Both in the 'print media' and on a dedicated BBC TV channel (http://news.bbc.co.uk/tv).

[187] Treasury Committee, *2nd Report: The 2005 Pre-Budget Report* (HC 2005–06, 739) 5.

[188] Manin (above n 157) 234.

previous Parliament, Gordon Brown, when still Chancellor of the Exchequer, appeared before the Committee on at least four separate occasions, corporation tax featuring to a greater or lesser extent each time. The strengths and weaknesses of the Committee in addressing the issues on each occasion mirror those analysed in an extensive literature on select committees in general.[189] What was striking, first, was the limited scope of the inquiry into corporation tax. The focus tended to be on tax rates rather than on more detailed aspects of the corporation tax base,[190] although as in Angela Eagle's 2007 questioning of Mr Brown, this could raise interesting questions about the possibly detrimental effects on the public finances of continuing to drive corporation tax rates down.[191] Secondly, it was noteworthy how, despite claims to the contrary, the discussion could take on a party political character. This was particularly noticeable in the attempts by a Conservative Member in 2006 to get the Chancellor to admit that he was manipulating tax rates for political advantage,[192] something the latter was never going to do and which would have required the clearest of evidence to substantiate. Such partisanship was not peculiar to Conservative Members, however. In the same debate, Sally Keeble gave the Chancellor the opportunity to say why his approach to corporate taxation was better than Germany's,[193] while John McFall's questions in 2007 seemed designed to enable the Chancellor to emphasise still further the importance of economic growth.[194] Such examples highlighted the inadequacy, at least during the last Parliament, of the approach to the Chancellor of backbench MPs, of whom they were then clearly in awe. If Ms Keeble was intent on doing more than enabling the Chancellor to justify his policies still further, it was not apparent from her failure to follow up on Mr Brown's replies.

The failure to interrogate the Chancellor's answers was a third striking feature of the Committee's discussions. It was true, too, of the very limited follow-up to the Chancellor's answers to Peter Viggers' questions in 2006[195] and also of a failure by the same honourable Member to quiz a passing reference by Mr Brown in 2007 to a large number of companies not paying tax.[196] Again, this may be set to change, again possibly as a result of Parliament's need to regain integrity in the wake of the events of 2009. Early signs from reports of the Treasury Committee, constituted in the summer of 2010 under the chairmanship of the Conservative MP Andrew Tyrie, reveal a rather different reality. Mr Tyrie, the first chair of the Treasury Committee to have been elected by MPs

[189] Tomkins, 'What is Parliament for?' (above n 162) 61.

[190] Treasury Committee, *4th Report: The 2006 Budget* (HC 2005–06, 994-II) Ev 44 (Q330) (Sally Keeble) and Ev 55 (Q394-Q395) (David Gauke).

[191] Treasury Committee, *5th Report: The 2007 Budget* (HC 2006–07, 389-II) Ev 44 (Q299).

[192] Treasury Committee, *4th Report*, 2006 (above n 190) Ev 55 (Q394–95) (David Gauke).

[193] Ibid, Ev 44 (Q 330).

[194] Treasury Committee, *2nd Report: The 2006 Pre-Budget Report* (HC 2006–07, 115) Ev 58 (Q473–75). See generally, 'Gavel Basher' *Private Eye* (28 September–11 October 2007) 6.

[195] Treasury Committee, *2nd Report*, 2005 (above n 187) Ev 63 (Q416).

[196] Treasury Committee, *5th Report*, 2007 (above n 191) Ev 36 (reply to Q248).

under the new rules, has consistently subjected the new Chancellor, George Osborne, to extremely close questioning, not as yet on corporation tax matters, admittedly, but on the fairness or otherwise of proposed cuts in public spending.[197] However, corporation tax policy is due to come under the spotlight, as an open letter of Mr Tyrie's to the Exchequer Secretary, David Gauke, has indicated.[198] Historically unsatisfactory, the scrutiny of tax policy provided by the Treasury committee may be about to intensify.

The second and third features mentioned above, namely, the taking of evidence in public and the publishing of reports, illustrate two further criticisms: the discussion is skewed by the absence of legal representation for committee members, unlike in the US;[199] and although the committee chair has a role in shaping the discussion, questions from individual Members are largely uncoordinated.[200] The result, it might be inferred, is that Committee hearings have been little more than opportunities for the Chancellor to pursue familiar topics: the need to combat tax avoidance;[201] the overwhelming importance of promoting economic growth,[202] and (at least for Gordon Brown and Alistair Darling) the categorical assertion of Britain's relative competitiveness. Such criticism would carry considerable weight if the Committee's role were simply the Millian one of 'controlling' and 'watching' the government. However, if the Committee's role is seen instead, as Bagehot says, as that of letting the sovereign know of the problems with its governing and of alerting the public to particular areas of concern, then the Committee's reports, no less than the transcripts of its hearings, assume a considerable significance. What the relatively light treatment of Mr Brown at the hands of a Labour-dominated select committee indicated is what Tomkins called a 'fault line' in the constitution, blurring the distinction between Crown and Parliament.[203] Whether the election of Mr Tyrie as Treasury Committee chair and Mr Osborne's greater willingness to answer the committee's questions inaugurate a period of more effective scrutiny remains to be seen.

Finally, consider the problems presented by the second of Stoker's governance propositions: the 'blurring' of the respective responsibilities of state and corporate sector. These illustrate the tendency of one side to seize the initiative, in order to blame the other for policy failures. Here, I would contend that the 'informing function' of the Committee is significant, since it enables a dispassionate account of the strengths and weaknesses of the arguments on either side. The broad

[197] Treasury Committee, *1st Report: June 2010 Budget* (HC 2010–11, 350) 44.

[198] Treasury Committee, *Letter from the Chairman to the Exchequer Secretary regarding Tax Policy* (4 November 2010), available at http://www.parliament.uk (accessed 20 December 2010).

[199] See generally, K Bradshaw and D Pring, *Parliament and Congress* (London, Constable, 1972) ch 5.

[200] Sampson, *Who Runs This Place?* (above n 8) 19.

[201] Treasury Committee, *2nd Report,* 2005 (above n 187) Ev 64 (reply to Q418); and Treasury Committee, *5th Report,* 2007 (above n 191) Ev 36 (reply to Q248).

[202] Treasury Committee, *2nd Report*, 2006 (above n 194) Ev 58 (Q473–75).

[203] Tomkins, *Public Law* (above n 41) 164.

question of tax fairness provides an illuminating example of this idea in practice. When, in its report on the 2005 Pre-Budget Report, the Committee asked the government to say 'whether it now [had] any intention to introduce a general anti-avoidance rule [GAAR]',[204] the latter was careful not to accede to the invitation. Instead, it said simply that the 'current approach [namely, to anti-avoidance] . . . [was] sensible, proportionate and fair'.[205] Conversely, the House of Lords Select Committee on Economic Affairs was able, with reservations, to commend a 'modest step' in the 2007 Finance Bill towards the simplification of corporation tax. Whether each of these contrasting responses, in its own particular sphere, proves to be the right one, only time will tell. The important point for present purposes is that the problem was highlighted by the relevant Committee, and those Committees' accounts of the problem, as well as the Chancellor's response to them, were matters on the effectiveness of which the electorate ultimately passed judgment. This is the paradoxical nature of parliamentary scrutiny, reflecting as it does the tensions of 'Crown versus Parliament'. It is the combination of Parliament's support for the Crown, by voting supply, and its opposition to it through representation.[206] It helps to explain the strength of the two acting together, as the Crown-in-Parliament, to be discussed in chapter four.

This discussion has necessarily been somewhat selective. It has, however, underlined the point that the Treasury Committee's role should properly be seen as an advisory one rather than as a 'policing' one,[207] as helping to construct the story for which the government of the day will be held to account. This is what the British constitution is all about: safeguarding liberty by facilitating 'constitutional accountability', the accountability of the government to Parliament.[208] To be sure, the Public Accounts Committee has a similar role but within a somewhat different remit; the Treasury Committee is the body tasked with advising the government on the strengths and weaknesses of its corporation tax reforms. The capacity of the government is enhanced by Parliament's ability to cast light on the potential for domination discussed in section III above. Clearly, there are problems, but overall, the functions, structure and values of Parliament go some way to enhancing trust and confidence in corporation tax policy, not least perhaps because the discussion is that of the people's representatives rather than that of 'experts'.

V. THE TREASURY AND HM REVENUE AND CUSTOMS

Effectiveness – that is, the capacity of a representative institution to advance its political objectives – means different things for different institutions. If

[204] Treasury Committee, *2nd Report*, 2005 (above n 187) 46.

[205] Treasury Committee, *3rd Special Report: The 2005 Pre-Budget Report: Government Response to the Committee's Second Report of Session 2005–06* (HC 2005–06, 1013) 19.

[206] Tomkins, *Public Law* (above n 41) 90.

[207] MD McCubbins and T Schwartz, 'Congressional Oversight Overlooked: Police Patrols versus Fire Alarms' (1984) 28 *American Journal of Political Science* 165.

[208] Tomkins, *Public Law* (above n 41) 47.

Parliament's scrutinising role evolved from the bloodshed of the seventeenth century, the function of the relevant Department of the government – what Colin Thain categorises as 'the constitutional Treasury' – is of even more ancient lineage.[209] For Parliament, effectiveness means the ability to construct a narrative of the Treasury's conduct of corporation tax policy, to which the latter can react and on the basis of which, come a General Election, the electorate can make its judgment, most likely in the prism of the policy's impact on Britain's economic performance.[210] For the Treasury,[211] effectiveness means the capacity to create in voters' minds the impression that the former's actions or inactions matter and that they produce optimal results in terms of the attainment of political objectives.

In the corporation tax sphere, while Parliament's task is to identify the problems with corporation tax policy, the Treasury must address the ones it considers important, discount unimportant ones and anticipate yet others. Under Britain's constitutional arrangements and, as a Department whose powers originate in the royal prerogative,[212] the Treasury has considerable freedom of action in the initiation of policy.[213] The prerogative is, as Tomkins says,[214] the basis of executive power; it is noteworthy for its resilience to supervision by the courts.[215] Taxation policy is significant because it is an aspect of the Treasury's powers that is amenable to law, not least because of the constitutional struggles referred to above. Policy initiation, however, lies largely beyond the scope of law. As Joseph Jacob has said, the prerogative's boundaries 'are defined by law and certainly . . . its scope is diminishing; but [at the centre of government], the rule of law does not operate'.[216]

The reasons for this freedom of action may owe less to any lust for power and more to some uncomfortable realities. But there is one overarching, ineluctable

[209] C Thain, 'Letter' *Financial Times* (18 February 2008) 10; and Thain and Christie, 'Treasury Power' (above n 83) 3. See generally, M Loughlin, 'Constituent Power Subverted: From English Constitutional Argument to British Constitutional Practice' in M Loughlin and N Walker (eds), *The Paradox of Constitutionalism: Constituent Power and Constitutional Form* (Oxford, Oxford University Press, 2007) 29.

[210] See generally, A Sentance, 'UK Macroeconomic Policy and Economic Performance' in T Buxton, P Chapman and P Temple (eds), *Britain's Economic Performance*, 2nd edn (London, Routledge, 1998) 35; and Grant (above n 125) ch 10.

[211] A Tomkins, 'The Struggle to Delimit Executive Power in Britain' in P Craig and A Tomkins (eds), *The Executive and Public Law: Power and Accountability in Comparative Perspective* (Oxford, Oxford University Press, 2006) 16.

[212] Ibid, 25; P Jackson and P Leopold (eds), *O Hood Phillips & Jackson: Constitutional and Administrative Law*, 8th edn (London, Sweet & Maxwell, 2001) paras 18-007–18-008; RA Chapman, *The Treasury in Public Policy-Making* (London, Routledge, 1997) ch 2; and T Daintith and A Page, *The Executive in the Constitution: Structure, Autonomy and Internal Control* (Oxford, Oxford University Press, 1999) 32 and 113.

[213] T Daintith, 'Public Law and Economic Policy' (1974) *Journal of Business Law* 9, 13; and Ussher and Walford (above n 162) 21–23.

[214] Tomkins, *Public Law* (above n 41) 78.

[215] Ibid, 81–83.

[216] JM Jacob, *The Republican Crown: Lawyers and the Making of the State in Twentieth-Century Britain* (Aldershot, Dartmouth, 1996) 1.

difficulty. No one knows, in this changing world, what will happen tomorrow. Or the day after. Or the day after that. Yet a government must somehow move through these radical uncertainties to realise its political objectives. This is the fundamental difference, in the corporation tax sphere as much as any other, between Parliament and the Crown – between, in the present context, the Treasury Committee and the Treasury; between Westminster and Whitehall.[217] In its scrutinising role, Parliament looks over its shoulder; the government stares into an inscrutable future. The latter does so, moreover, in the knowledge that however it responds to or anticipates events, it must retain the trust and confidence of the governed.

I maintain that what Machiavelli said about the qualities that a sovereign requires in the face of these uncertainties is as relevant now as ever it was. Machiavelli thought of such unknowns in terms of *fortuna*,[218] of the unpredictable woman[219] – what Bernard Crick has synthesised as that 'sudden, aweful [*sic*] and challenging piling up of . . . [economic] factors and contingent political events in an unexpected way'.[220] Is it to be supposed, for instance, that so soon after his appointment as Chancellor, Alistair Darling could have known the extent of the complex of issues that would be thrown up in what became known as the 'Northern Rock crisis'?[221] In the face of such calamities, what the ruler must show, said Machiavelli, is *virtù*. It is not, as Crick again reminds us, goodness as such that is called for but rather something nearer perhaps to 'virtuosity'.[222] *Virtù* has many facets, the most notable, as already observed, being the facility of *prudenza*,[223] of 'prudence'. It is not the same as having no policy; it is reactive, to be sure, but it is proactive, too, should circumstances demand. It is a crucial element in the generation of capacity, of sovereignty.

If, in this interpretation, prudence is the key to understanding the type of policy decisions to be discussed in chapter four, it becomes important to consider the extent to which this seems to be a characteristic of the key decision-makers in the Treasury and HMRC. Given the competences residing in individuals, the strength of their personalities – their political style – matters no less than their policies.[224] Ministers, Philip Norton has said, fall discernibly into one of a number of different 'styles': 'commanders', 'ideologues', 'managers',

[217] The 'segmented' nature of policymaking means that it is appropriate to concentrate on HM Treasury: JJ Richardson and AG Jordan, *Governing under Pressure: The Policy Process in a Post-Parliamentary Democracy* (Oxford, Basil Blackwell, 1985) 73.

[218] N Machiavelli, *The Prince* [1532], P Bondanella (ed and trans) (Oxford, Oxford University Press, 2005) esp ch 25. See also B Crick's introduction to N Machiavelli, *The Discourses* [1517], B Crick, LJ Walker and B Richardson (eds and trans) (London, Penguin, 2003) 57–59.

[219] Machiavelli, *Discourses* (ibid) 86–87. If this is right, then James Naughtie and others are precisely *wrong* to suggest that *prudence* is female. Eg, J Naughtie, *The Rivals: The Intimate Story of a Political Marriage* (London, Fourth Estate, 2001) 203.

[220] Crick (above n 218) 58.

[221] A Porter and D Reece, 'Chancellor who Wants a Return to Prudence' *Daily Telegraph* (13 September 2007) 14.

[222] Crick (above n 218) 60.

[223] See above ch 1.

[224] Manin (above n 157) 219.

'agents' or 'team players'.[225] The fact that they are all, at least at the Treasury, elected Members of the lower House means that their constituents have identified in what Thain calls 'the political Treasury' some special quality,[226] which sets them apart from other people. This is one reason why it is important to maintain the difference between ministers and civil servants, between those who are elected – literally, the 'elite'[227] – and those who are not. The elected are, as has long been recognised, an 'aristocracy'.[228] Labour's Treasury ministers amply reflected this aristocratic conception, this 'principle of distinction', to which reference has already been made. For example, Kitty Ussher, briefly the Economic Secretary to the Treasury in 2009, was the very model of a Labour metropolitan intellectual.[229] Despite this, she represented the historically economically deprived and culturally and socially diverse constituency of Burnley and Pendle. Alistair Darling, MP for Edinburgh South West, was both socially and professionally distinguished,[230] though the representative of a much more affluent constituency. His political skills were extraordinarily tested throughout his time in office,[231] but most would concede that on Norton's classification, he was the nearest to a 'manager', albeit a beleaguered one.[232] Most importantly, there was the MP for Kirkaldy and Cowdenbeath, one Gordon Brown, who as Chancellor of the Exchequer from 1997 to 2007, dominated the period covered by this study. Mr Brown, working with the former *Financial Times* leader writer and special adviser Ed Balls,[233] transformed a department that, although already in WH Greenleaf's famous words, 'the Department of Departments' and 'basically a ministry of finance',[234] became something more akin to a continental

[225] P Norton, 'Barons in a Shrinking Kingdom: Senior Ministers in British Government' in RAW Rhodes (ed), *Transforming British Government Volume 2: Changing Roles and Relationships* (Basingstoke, Macmillan, 2000) 101, 109. See also P Dorey, *Policy Making in Britain: An Introduction* (London, Sage, 2005) 58.

[226] See also Thain, 'Letter' (above n 209); and Thain and Christie, 'Treasury Power' (above n 83) 4.

[227] Manin (above n 157) 140.

[228] Ibid, 149.

[229] C Adams, 'Ussher Aims to Give City a Whitehall Voice' *Financial Times* (30 July 2007) 3. Ms Ussher became the Director of Demos, an influential think tank, in 2010.

[230] P Routledge, *Gordon Brown: The Biography* (London, Simon and Schuster, 1998) 297. See also H Rumbelow, P Webster and J Harding, 'Man Who Stepped into Limelight on the Darkest of All Mondays' *Times* (22 September 2007) 6.

[231] HM Treasury, *Meeting the Aspirations of the British People: 2007 Pre-Budget Report and Comprehensive Spending Review October 2007* (Cm 7227, 2007); M Wolf, 'Diligent, Dull and Politically Defensive' *Financial Times* (10 October 2007) 10; D Strauss, 'Short, Measured and No Word of Prudence' *Financial Times* (10 October 2007) 2; and S Brittan, 'The Tragedy of the Pre-Budget Report' *Financial Times* (12 October 2007) 17.

[232] Editorial, *Financial Times* (20 December 2007) 12; G Parker, 'A Firefighter under Fire' *Financial Times* (22–23 September 2007) 11; Rumbelow, Webster and Harding (above n 230); Porter and Reece (above n 221); and L Barber, J Blitz and C Giles, 'Stability is Darling's Watchword' *Financial Times* (4 July 2007) 3.

[233] Dorey (above n 225) 74–78; and A King, *The British Constitution* (Oxford, Oxford University Press, 2007) 233. Ed Balls subsequently became an MP and Economic Secretary to the Treasury.

[234] WH Greenleaf, *The British Political Tradition, Volume Three: A Much Governed Nation, Part I* (London, Methuen, 1987) 250.

finance ministry.[235] 'The Treasury', Peter Hennessy wrote in 1990, 'is about money, and money is a mighty weapon of power . . . Knowledge, too, is power, and the Treasury has a window into every ministry and departmental activity across Whitehall'.[236] He would have had even greater reason to reiterate these words in 2010, as the Treasury supervised a highly contentious round of public spending cuts.

Prudence was often associated with Gordon Brown, yet as I explained in chapter two, the prudence of Machiavelli tended not to be related to that of Brown the Chancellor.[237] This was surprising, because commentators often tended to associate him with Machiavellian characteristics. Thus, while David Marquand wrote of the latter's 'often infuriating caution',[238] Jackie Ashley commented in 2007 that 'simply to say Brown is cautious won't do. He's bold, too';[239] and Suzanne Moore extolled Mr Brown's 'sheer nous, cunning, cleverness, realpolitik, whatever you want to call it'.[240] The non-association was the more surprising, since there is an intellectual heritage of Machiavellism in rationalist Scottish thought. It was thus no objection to the invocation of Machiavellian prudence to say that Brown was a 'son of the Manse',[241] nor to point to his 'deep moral convictions'.[242] HCG Matthew, describing the strategy of one of Mr Brown's one-time predecessors, talked about Gladstone's *virtù*.[243] Gladstone, indeed, for David Marquand, became a point of intellectual comparison with Mr Brown in 2007.[244] Finally and most importantly, it was no objection to this argument to identify the latter's prudence with that described by Adam Smith in his *Theory of Moral Sentiments*.[245] In 2004, Mr Brown himself associated prudence, as Simon Lee pointed out, with Adam Smith.[246] Gordon Brown used Smith's prudence, however, to describe an ideal human characteristic,[247] not necessarily – as with Machiavelli – an actual mode of behaviour. I claim that political prudence is as essential to corporation tax

[235] P Stephens, 'The Treasury under Labour' in A Seldon (ed), *The Blair Effect* (London, Little Brown, 2001) 185. Hence Tony Blair's apparent plan to split it: P Wintour, 'No 10 Strategy Unit, Headed by Birt, Wanted Brown to go to Foreign Office' *Guardian* (9 May 2007) 1. On the pre-Gordon Brown Treasury, see C Thain and M Wright, *The Treasury and Whitehall: The Planning and Control of Public Expenditure, 1976–1993* (Oxford, Clarendon Press, 1995).

[236] P Hennessy, *Whitehall* (London, Fontana, 1990) 394.

[237] J Snape, 'Corporation Tax Reform: Politics and Public Law' (2007) *British Tax Review* 374, 392.

[238] D Marquand, 'The Creator' *New Statesman* (24 September 2007) 36.

[239] J Ashley, 'Glimpses of the Real Gordon' *Guardian G2* (30 May 2007) 4.

[240] S Moore, 'Group Hug' *New Statesman* (24 September 2007) 43. See also S Richards, *Whatever it Takes: The Real Story of Gordon Brown and New Labour* (London, Fourth Estate, 2010) 118.

[241] Naughtie (above n 219) 5 and 188.

[242] W Keegan, *The Prudence of Mr Gordon Brown* (Chichester, John Wiley, 2003) 128.

[243] Matthew, *Gladstone: 1875–1898* (above n 183) 237.

[244] Marquand, 'The Creator' (above n 238) 36. See also C Thain and R Christie, 'A New-Look Treasury under its New Boss: Mr Brown' *Parliamentary Brief* (February 2008), available from http://www.treasuryproject.org (accessed 21 February 2008) 21.

[245] A Smith, *The Theory of Moral Sentiments* [1759/1790], RP Hanley (ed) (London, Penguin, 2009) 250–56.

[246] S Lee, *Best for Britain? The Politics and Legacy of Gordon Brown* (Oxford, Oneworld, 2007) 45.

[247] Ibid.

legislation as to any other area of public policy. Mr Brown, as Chancellor, showed himself to be its virtuosic if controversial exponent. George Osborne, if less obviously Machiavellian, has nonetheless seemed to have clear traits of the Machiavellian prudence. George Parker in March 2011 reported the views of one of the Chancellor's associates, to the effect that Mr Osborne was 'the most calculating person' that the associate 'had ever met'. Not only that, but according to colleagues, Mr Osborne was 'also the minister "for looking round corners"', having an uncanny ability to 'see the political fallout from any decision better than anyone'.[248] George Osborne's 2010 institution of both the Office for Budget Responsibility and the Office of Tax Simplification should perhaps be seen in a comparably prudential, virtuosic light.

The politicisation of corporation tax issues, something to which the discussion turns in chapter four, has made the prudential qualities of Treasury ministers[249] more important than they might have been even a decade ago. To emphasise this requirement is not, however, to diminish the importance of Treasury senior civil servants, since, irrespective of Gordon Brown's allegedly 'Stalinistic' tendencies,[250] it is to be presumed that at the Chancellor's elbow, at the scene of crucial decisions, has been the prudential voice of a team of the Treasury's most gifted public servants and special advisers. There has, of course, been much unease about the 'politicisation' of the civil service,[251] given the need to ensure the accountability of individuals employed under the royal prerogative.[252] After all, like ministers, civil servants exercise the powers of the Crown,[253] although, unlike ministers, Parliament does not hold civil servants 'to constitutional account'.[254] So there may be good grounds for concern, especially since management properly understood is but an aspect of the art and science of government, and it is management rather than administration as such that characterises the role of Thain's 'official' or 'permanent Treasury', as part of the contemporary civil service.[255] The point is indeed illustrated better by the Treasury than by any other department of government.

[248] G Parker, 'Osborne's Long Game' *FT Weekend Magazine* (19/20 March 2011) 15, 16 and 18.

[249] Currently, and setting aside those mentioned in the text above, these are: Danny Alexander (Chief Secretary to the Treasury); Mark Hoban (Financial Secretary to the Treasury); David Gauke (Exchequer Secretary to the Treasury); and Justine Greening (Economic Secretary to the Treasury).

[250] N Timmins, '"Stalinist" Brown, by Ex-cabinet Secretary' *Financial Times* (20 March 2007) 1; R Watts, 'Chancellor "Ruthlessly Rejected" Warnings on Pensions' *Sunday Telegraph* (8 April 2007) 2.

[251] R Peston, *Brown's Britain* (London, Short Books 2005) 110; and R Rhodes, 'The Civil Service' in Seldon (ed) (above n 235) 97, 102 and 106.

[252] See generally, *A Draft Civil Service Bill: A Consultation Document: Presented to Parliament by the Minister for the Cabinet Office by Command of Her Majesty, November 2004* (Cm 6373, 2004); and N Timmins, 'Draft Bill on Civil Service Finally Published' *Financial Times* (16 November 2004) 4.

[253] Tomkins, *Public Law* (above n 41) 61.

[254] Ibid, 77.

[255] Rhodes, 'The Civil Service' (above n 251); C Thain, 'Treasury Rules OK? The Further Evolution of a British Institution' (2004) 6 *British Journal of Politics and International Relations* 123, 124; Thain and Christie, 'Treasury Power' (above n 83) 3; N Macpherson, 'Evolution of the Modern Treasury' ESRC Seminar, All Souls College, Oxford (9 December 2009), available at http://www.treasuryproject.org/NickMac.pdf (accessed 17 July 2011). Ussher and Walford stress the momentous nature of the 1994 Fundamental Expenditure Review, instigated by the then Chief

Of all the buildings visible from the London Eye, the Treasury building is an especially powerful symbol of governance values that are traceable, in one form or another, to the development of neoliberal ideas in the second half of the twentieth century.[256] Returning to the Treasury in 2004, the commentator Anthony Sampson noted how a corporate boardroom ambience had replaced the curving corridors and peeling linoleum of former days.[257] Emblematic of this managerial approach is the person of Nick Macpherson, Permanent Secretary to the Treasury since August 2005 and successor to Sir Gus O'Donnell,[258] who was responsible for the O'Donnell Report of 2004,[259] which resulted in the merging of the former Revenue Departments – the Inland Revenue and Customs and Excise[260] – as well as the introduction of a new Budget, Tax and Welfare Directorate in the Treasury, now headed up by Edward Troup, which was originally designed to ensure closer liaison with the new HMRC.[261] Responsibility for corporation tax reform has thus been shared between the Treasury and HMRC,[262] the former having had, under Gordon Brown, specialist corporation tax expertise on a panel of US-style special advisers, called the Council of Economic Advisors. Equally, HMRC has had a designated group of public servants specialising in corporation tax, who were originally intended to liaise closely with the Treasury but whose capacity to do so seems to have become considerably reduced by the end of the Labour administration in 2010.[263] This, despite the fact that HMRC's 2010–11 Business Plan not only demonstrates a clear intention to deal sensitively with business taxation but is, in its style and layout, entirely conformed to the values and objectives of a government department in a neoliberal governance structure.[264] Although much criticism was levelled at HMRC around three years ago, over

Secretary to the Treasury, Michael Portillo, in shaping the Treasury of today: Ussher and Walford (above n 213) 23 and 72. See also *Fundamental Review of HM Treasury's Running Costs: A Report to the Chancellor of the Exchequer by Sir Colin Southgate et al* (London, HMSO, 1994) 86.

256 R Barker, *Political Ideas in Modern Britain* (London, Methuen, 1978) 190. Note the shelved Fulton report of the 1960s: Lord Fulton (Chairman), *The Civil Service, Vol 1: Report of the Committee 1966–68* (Cmnd 3638, 1968) esp ch 5. On Fulton, see, eg, Keith Dowding, *The Civil Service* (London, Routledge, 1995) 20; K Theakston, *The Civil Service since 1945* (Oxford, Blackwell, 1995) 88; and Thain, 'Treasury Rules OK?' (ibid) 128.

257 Sampson, *Who Runs This Place?* (above n 8) 126. See also A Sampson, *Anatomy of Britain Today* (London, Hodder and Stoughton, 1965) 291.

258 S Cameron, 'Mandarin Dynasty' *FT Magazine* (8–9 April 2006) 16.

259 HM Treasury (G O'Donnell, chair), *Financing Britain's Future: Review of the Revenue Departments* (Cm 6163, 2004), available at http://webarchive.nationalarchives.gov.uk/+/http://www.hm-treasury.gov.uk/media/3/2/odonnell_fore_ch1_245%5b1%5d.pdf (accessed 9 June 2011).

260 See generally, Treasury Committee, *10th Report: Inland Revenue Matters* (HC 2002–03, 834) 3.

261 Judge (above n 16) 158; HM Treasury, *HM Treasury Annual Report and Accounts 2008–09* (HC 2006–07, 518) 110; C Giles, 'Treasury to Retain Key Role, Darling Insists' *Financial Times* (16 January 2008) 2; and HMRC, *Departmental Report 2009: HM Revenue & Customs* (Cm 7107, 2009) 25 and 65.

262 Commissioners for Revenue and Customs Act (CRCA) 2005 s 1(1).

263 Wales, 'Commentary' (above n 65) 1305; Bowler (above n 97) 6; and Ussher and Walford (above n 213) 45–47.

264 HM Revenue and Customs, *Delivering our Vision: Business Plan 2010–11* (2010), available at http://www.hmrc.gov.uk/about/bus-plan-2010-11.pdf (accessed 9 June 2011).

operational matters such as the loss of taxpayer data, and although the Treasury Committee has recently found 'a disengaged workforce with poor morale' within HMRC,[265] this has not specifically involved corporate taxation.[266] Nonetheless, so far as policymaking is concerned, Christopher Wales, a member of the Council of Economic Advisers from 1997 to 2003, regrets its concentration ever more tightly in the Treasury, the loss of grassroots policymaking experience located in the former Inland Revenue and the absence of an Office of Tax Analysis, along US lines.[267]

The need for prudence, whether that of elected ministers or of unelected officials, is intrinsic to the circumstances in which political institutions operate. This brings the discussion to a point of fundamental importance: the continuing pre-eminence of the political institutions whose buildings are visible from the London Eye over those whose buildings are not, namely those of the European Union. Arguments that Great Britain has somehow ceded sovereignty to a supranational authority are misconceived, both because of the vision of sovereignty rehearsed above[268] and because, as Helen Thompson has pointed out, '[t]he Commission, except in competition policy, can only issue regulations and directives on the basis of decisions made in the Council [of the EU], and its right to initiate legislation is mediated through the largest member states.'[269] Even the Court of Justice of the EU may not, in reality, pose a serious threat to national sovereignty. This is because, despite the European Court's energy in ensuring that corporate tax law is consistent with the 'fundamental freedoms' of the European Treaties,[270] tax remains a matter of national competence. Moreover, as Thompson says, 'the administration of EU laws remains dependent on national judiciaries',[271] and even the European Court has itself begun to show a sensitivity to the dangers to the European enterprise that would be presented by too rigid an adherence to its more uncompromising corporate taxa-

[265] Treasury Committee, *7th Report: Administration and Expenditure of the Chancellor's Departments 2008–09* (HC 2009–10, 156) 32.

[266] *Civil Service Capability Reviews: Capability Review of HM Treasury*, available at http://www.civilservice.gov.uk/Assets/Capability_Review_HMT_tcm6-1064.pdf (accessed 13 July 2011); N Timmins, 'Need to Rebuild Trust after Data Loss' *Financial Times* (18 December 2007) 3; C Wales, 'The Implications of the O'Donnell Review for the Making of Tax Policy in the UK' (2004) *British Tax Review* 543, esp 544 and 557; R Christie, 'Continuity and Change' (2008) 3 *The Treasury under New Labour Project Bulletin* 10, available at http://www.treasuryproject.org (accessed 9 June 2011).

[267] Wales, 'Commentary' (above n 65) 1305–6.

[268] M Loughlin, *Sword and Scales: An Examination of the Relationship between Law and Politics* (Oxford, Hart Publishing, 2000) 147. See also N Walker, 'Post-Constituent Constitutionalism? The Case of the European Union' in Loughlin and Walker (eds) (above n 209) 247.

[269] H Thompson, 'The Modern State and its Adversaries' (2006) 41 *Government and Opposition* 23. See also C Turpin and A Tomkins, *British Government and the Constitution: Text and Materials*, 6th edn (Cambridge, Cambridge University Press, 2007) 16; and Marsh and Rhodes (above n 90) 259.

[270] Eg, S Kingston, 'A Light in the Darkness: Recent Developments in the ECJ's Direct Tax Jurisprudence' (2007) 44 *Common Market Law Review* 1321.

[271] Thompson (above n 269) 37, citing JHH Weiler, 'A Quiet Revolution: The European Court of Justice and its Interlocutors' (1994) 26(4) *Comparative Political Studies* 510.

tion precedents.[272] This study does not therefore envisage a governance structure of which the EU institutions form either the apex or the base.[273] What it conceives of instead is Britain as a sovereign state, albeit with competences limited by European law and the General Agreement on Tariffs and Trade (GATT) 1994, whose *capacity* is enhanced rather than depleted by membership of the European Union or WTO.[274]

This is a return to the second of the strands of the chapter referred to above. In such a world, *fortuna* appears in several guises. On the one hand, given the Treasury's role, she represents the vicissitudes of the markets or the threats of multinationals to leave the national jurisdiction. On the other, she represents the unknowable summed up in Timothy Lyons's reiteration of Melchior Wathelet's rhetorical and despairing question: 'What will the ECJ decide tomorrow?'[275] Despite the 'legal' nature of the latter question, its very 'unpredictability' makes it disconcertingly similar to the former one. Only the ability to move quickly, to think quickly, to prevent these unknowns from deflecting the overall policy[276] – in short, to behave *prudentially* – is enough to deal with them. Sovereignty is, after all, a 'generative' conception.[277]

Given the necessity for prudence, it is contended that, given the Treasury's need for effectiveness in reaching its twin goals of 'Raising Trend Growth' and 'Promoting Fairness and Opportunity for All',[278] the idea that informs all of the values at play is 'reason of state'.[279] This point is developed in chapter five; it is central to the idea that institutions must be effective in order for them to generate trust and confidence. For the moment, we can note that what shapes these values is not morality as such but the 'advancement of the public interest',[280] as that is defined and shaped by ideology, perhaps, but certainly by the ideologically motivated sovereign. This might seem a case of 'double standards', but it is not that. There are only, as Crick says, two sets of standards: one applicable to the private sphere, the other applicable to the 'political realm'[281] – the latter, as Loughlin tells us, being the field of operation of political jurisprudence,[282] of which taxation law is so important a part.

[272] Case C-446/03 *Marks and Spencer plc v Halsey (HMIT)* [2006] 1 CMLR 18; and *Cadbury Schweppes v CIR* (above n 79). See also Snape (above n 237) 388.

[273] R Baldwin and M Cave, *Understanding Regulation: Theory, Strategy and Practice* (Oxford, Oxford University Press, 1999) ch 12.

[274] Loughlin, *The Idea of Public Law* (above n 10) 94.

[275] T Lyons, 'What Will the ECJ Decide Tomorrow?' (2006) *British Tax Review* 399.

[276] J Gray, 'Maggie's Gift to Gordon' *New Statesman* (24 September 2007) 47.

[277] M Wolf, 'Does Globalisation Render States Impotent?' (2000) *British Tax Review* 537. See also above n 110.

[278] HM Treasury, *Annual Report and Accounts 2008–09* (above n 261).

[279] Loughlin, *The Idea of Public Law* (above n 10) 148.

[280] G Brown, 'Advancing the Public Interest' in W Stevenson (ed), *Gordon Brown: Moving Britain Forward: Selected Speeches 1997–2006* (London, Bloomsbury, 2006) 136.

[281] Crick (above n 218) 66.

[282] Loughlin, *The Idea of Public Law* (above n 10) 43.

VI. POLICY NETWORKS

Gazing out from the London Eye at the panorama described at the beginning of the chapter, the signs of policy networks are, as has been suggested, everywhere apparent. Corporation tax reform, in common with other areas of public policy, is so much a matter of involving policy networks that the role and values of such bodies fall to be interpreted next.

It is important to be clear, however, about exactly the kind of organisation that I am here seeking to pinpoint. It is not, as discussed in the previous section, the totality of the relevant Departments of State, the Treasury and HMRC; nor is it, as discussed in the third section of the chapter, some monolithic notion of the corporate sector as a whole. It is rather those individuals or groups of individuals who 'mediate' in the development of corporation tax reform proposals, those who deliberate on the 'concerns of business' when reforms are proposed: civil servants from the Treasury and from HMRC; lawyers; accountants; academics; members of think tanks; journalists; and coalitions of producers, including the CBI and ad hoc groups of corporate treasurers. The importance of these networks, as Stoker has pointed out, is not only that they are in a position to 'interpret and lead public debate' but also that they can influence policy, in some cases requiring a united front from their members to 'nudge' the government in one direction more than another.

For me, the best starting point for interpreting the role of policy networks is again Manin's dissection of the 'principles of representative government'. Manin is not concerned to offer a complete theory of the principles and values of interest groups in Britain's system of representative democracy. What he is concerned with, however, is the role of extra-parliamentary political discussion in such a system. Whatever influence the corporate sector may exert in the corporate ambience of Whitehall is mediated by this extra-parliamentary debate. It is in this context that policy networks fall to be considered. Explanation and interpretation of their role has fallen to Rod Rhodes and David Marsh, in a penetrating and enduringly persuasive analysis.[283] In this section of the chapter, elements of each analysis will be used to cast light on the other.

Given the involvement in policy networks of civil servants, the context of the debate is the accountability of the Crown and its servants. There is, as discussed above, no political accountability for civil servants, nor, as we shall see, are they subject to any legal accountability by way of judicial review. Instead, their position, as individuals employed under the royal prerogative, is governed by a case-law 'vicariousness' principle, by a number of executive measures falling

[283] Marsh and Rhodes (above n 90). See also Judge (above n 16) 106; and Dorey (above n 225) ch 5. For an overview of other approaches, see Peters, *Institutional Theory in Political Science* (above n 11) ch 7, esp 128–29. But see H Pemberton, 'Policy Networks and Policy Learning: UK Economic Policy in the 1960s and 1970s' (2000) 78 *Public Administration* 772.

outside parliamentary scrutiny[284] and by some narrowly targeted statutory provisions. Under the rather pragmatic *Carltona* principle,[285] a decision of a civil servant is 'of course, the decision of the minister'[286] – Minister and civil servant being regarded as 'legally indistinguishable parts of a single unit, the Government Department, united together in the service of the Crown'.[287] The executive measures include, most importantly, the 1995 Civil Service Order in Council[288] and the Civil Service Code;[289] but none of them are subject to judicial or Parliamentary scrutiny.[290] Finally, following the enactment in 2010 of the Constitutional Reform and Governance Act, a new Civil Service Commission has jurisdiction to ensure that 'civil servants . . . carry out their duties in accordance with the core Civil Service values of integrity, honesty, objectivity and impartiality'.[291] Although these statutory developments mark a cultural change, they are also indicative of continuing unease concerning the accountability of civil servants.

With such accountability problems firmly in mind, Rhodes and Marsh offer an interpretation of government/interest group relations that is different from both 'corporatist' and 'pluralist' models.[292] In keeping with the objectives of the study, their approach is strongly interpretative, emphasising the roles of interest groups in different policy areas[293] and looking for 'aggregations of interests'.[294] In the corporation tax debate, Rhodes and Marsh would accordingly distinguish between a 'producer network' (such as the CBI or the British Bankers' Association (BBA), most notably) and 'professional networks' (such as the Law Society, think tanks such as the Institute for Fiscal Studies (IFS) or the CIOT).[295] To the latter they would also add, presumably, the small group of financial journalists who have long followed the gradual politicisation of corporate taxation, most notably Vanessa Houlder of the *Financial Times*.[296] What the distinction serves to illustrate is the 'relative stability' of the professional network, as against that of the producer; the considerable reliance of the Treasury and HMRC on the former 'to get the technical detail right'[297], for instance, in rela-

[284] Tomkins, *Public Law* (above n 41) 76.
[285] *Carltona Ltd v Commissioners of Works and Others* [1943] 2 All ER 560 (EWCA).
[286] Ibid, 563B (Lord Greene MR).
[287] Tomkins, *Public Law* (above n 41) 85.
[288] Available at http://www.civilservicecommissioners.org (accessed 2 September 2010).
[289] Ibid.
[290] Tomkins, *Public Law* (above n 41) 77.
[291] Constitutional Reform and Governance Act 2010 s 9 and Explanatory Notes, available at http://www.opsi.gov.uk (accessed 2 September 2010).
[292] RAW Rhodes and D Marsh, 'Policy Networks in British Politics: A Critique of Existing Approaches' in Marsh and Rhodes (above n 90) 1–26. See also Pierre and Peters (above n 26) 33.
[293] Marsh and Rhodes (above n 90) 4.
[294] Ibid, 9.
[295] Standing Committee A (23 May 2006) HC vol 446 col 321 (Brooks Newmark).
[296] Who, as LexisNexis Tax Writer of the Year 2007, has rightly been valued by the relevant policy network. Wales's global comments about 'standards of journalism on taxation issues' seem to overlook Houlder's contribution: Wales, 'Commentary' (above n 65) 1301.
[297] M Gammie, 'The Process of Fiscal Reform in the United Kingdom' (1989) *British Tax Review* 252, 253.

tion to the incorporation, by reference, of international GAAP into the corporation tax code; and the tendency of both to further their own economic interests. Rather interesting in this latter context are the *Financial Times* journalists covering corporate tax reform, since they have ceased – as Manin might predict – to take a partisan approach and instead have concentrated on reporting and reflecting the debate.[298] Marsh and Rhodes's new categorisation also, however, highlights a stark contrast with the issue networks,[299] such as the Tax Justice Network (TJN), UK Uncut, Christian Aid and the (very different) Taxpayers' Alliance.[300] What characterises these latter four is that, albeit in very different ways, their activities are directed at influencing public opinion, having 'little or no access to government'.[301]

Given that in Rhodes and Marsh's analysis, 'economic and professional interests dominate' the policy community, they also point to the limited variety of participants in professional and producer communities. Thus, although the trades unions tend not to contribute to policy debates, other names in the professional community tend to recur: among law firms, Slaughter and May, commenting on the importance of EU factors in shaping the course of corporation tax reform, and McGrigors, on the accounting aspects of trade profit calculations,[302] to take just two examples. Likewise, among 'professional services' firms, we tend to find PricewaterhouseCoopers, Deloitte and KPMG commenting on the impact of EU developments. As for the producer networks, no one would deny the monolithic status of the CBI, ready as Jonathan Guthrie has written, to comment if necessary on 'raindrops racing down a window pane'[303] but especially on corporate tax rates and on the complexity of tax legislation.[304] The 'economic and/or professional interests' of these groups, focussing recurrently on corporation tax simplification, contrast rather vividly with the corporation tax fairness issues raised by those such as the accountant Mr Richard Murphy and, latterly, the academic Sol Picciotto.[305]

Reference to the contributions of Mr Murphy and Professor Picciotto reminds us of the aspect of personal interactions in what Marsh and Rhodes take to be a second dimension of policy networks: 'integration'.[306] Within the corporation tax policy community (which Professor Tiley calls 'tax folk'),[307] the same

[298] Manin (above n 157) 228 and 232. A worry about taxation coverage in, eg, the *Daily Telegraph* is that – though often very acute – it tends to present taxation issues polemically, as sources of anxiety to those directly affected, rather than as part of a dispassionate examination of the policy issues.

[299] Marsh and Rhodes (above n 90) 254.

[300] Http://www.taxpayersalliance.com (accessed 9 June 2011).

[301] Marsh and Rhodes (above n 90) 256.

[302] J Collins and D Dixon, 'Open and Shut Case?' *Tax Journal* (9 April 2007) 6.

[303] J Guthrie, 'Tax Treatment of Private Equity? Don't Ask' *Financial Times* (26 April 2007) 15.

[304] Houlder, 'Rules Getting "More and More Complicated"' (above n 105).

[305] R Murphy and S Picciotto, 'Letter' *Financial Times* (27 September 2007) 14. See also R Murphy and J Christensen, 'Letter' *Financial Times* (12 March 2004) 18.

[306] Marsh and Rhodes (above n 90) 251.

[307] Tiley, *Revenue Law* (above n 48) 62 (6th edn, 66).

lawyers' names recur: Stephen Edge of Slaughter and May; Malcolm Gammie, QC, of the tax bar; and Edward Troup, already referred to.

Among the accountants, perhaps especially prominent have been: John Whiting, formerly of PricewaterhouseCoopers;[308] Loughlin Hickey of KPMG; and John Cullinane of Deloitte. Indeed, one of the first acts of the Coalition has been to establish a Tax Professionals Forum, of which Mr Gammie, as eminent tax counsel, is a member. All of these are participants in an almost constant and, as mentioned in chapter two, sophisticated public discussion of the direction in which corporation tax reform is going. They are characterised by their longevity as participants in the debate, by – with the possible exception of Stephen Edge – their commitment to a somewhat Diceyan ideal of corporation tax law and by values, immanent to their extensive writing, well assimilated to the broad policy objectives that corporation tax reform is seeking to attain. Mr Gammie, an acerbic commentator with a formidable grasp of the technical tax issues, is characteristic. His views on 'the rule of law' are essentially Diceyan,[309] and his evidence to the House of Lords Select Committee on Economic Affairs has reflected his long held frustration at the lack of progress on 'rational' tax simplification. Take, for instance, Mr Gammie's comments on the 2007 decision to abolish capital allowances for expenditure on industrial buildings,[310] which the Government had justified on tax simplification grounds:

> Chairman [Lord Wakeham]: Could I just finish on this with one pretty simple question. If the Chancellor [Gordon Brown] were sitting where you are sitting and we said, 'Come on, tell us about this simplification, because we ain't heard too much that has been impressive so far about simplification' What answer would he give? Why does he think what he has done is simplification?
>
> Mr Gammie: To the extent that he has removed allowances for buildings, he has simplified the system. There will be a degree of repealed legislation. As I say, companies will no longer have to do all the calculations.
>
> . . .
>
> Chairman: That is the main simplification.
>
> Mr Gammie: That seems to me to be the main simplification.[311]

The fundamental similarity of the Diceyan approach of tax professionals, which Mr Gammie once summed up in the idea that it did not matter what Parliament provided for, so long as it was clear about its intentions,[312] nonetheless leads them to accept and work with the legislative outcomes, however flawed they may find them. With such a united front on the corporation tax

[308] Now Tax Director of the Office of Tax Simplification.

[309] M Gammie, 'Tax Avoidance and the Rule of Law: A Perspective from the United Kingdom' in GS Cooper (ed), *Tax Avoidance and the Rule of Law* (Amsterdam, IBFD Publications, 1997) 185.

[310] FA 2007 s 36.

[311] Select Committee on Economic Affairs, *4th Report: The Finance Bill 2007, Volume II: Evidence* (HL 2006–07, 121-II) 5.

[312] Gammie, 'The Process of Fiscal Reform' (above n 297) 254.

policy, it is unsurprising that the chief role of the TJN is the undermining of the tax policy community position. One illustration is Mr Murphy's attempt in the BBC's *File on Four* programme to move the discussion on transfer pricing away from a preoccupation with 'anti-avoidance' to the effect of Great Britain's transfer pricing provisions on the economies of developing countries.[313]

So the corporation tax reform policy community has a tightly integrated and fairly constant membership. It also has, as the evidence would lead us to infer, considerable intellectual and economic resources. Writing of policy communities in general, Marsh and Rhodes contrast what they see as the 'relationship of exchange'[314] that subsists between a policy community and the relevant department of the government, and the contrasting inability of issue networks to offer any expertise that the government is interested in acquiring. For indeed, the 'special codes' on corporate finance[315], which are a fundamental component of the corporation tax code, represent an almost astonishing assimilation of professional expertise to the legislative function, born no doubt of many a congenial meeting over coffee and biscuits in Whitehall. In a similar spirit, reforming the rules on controlled foreign companies resulted under Labour in the formation of a working-group of producers, including Xerox, IBM and Rolls-Royce.[316] When the Coalition came to power in 2010, this idea was almost immediately reinstated and developed, with the establishment of the Business Forum on Tax and Competitiveness already referred to, as well as with the creation in the winter of 2010–11 of a Corporate Tax Reform Liaison Committee. Membership of the former includes delegates from Diageo, Vodafone Group, Royal Dutch Shell and GlaxoSmithKline; the latter includes members from BP, AstraZeneca, GE and Tesco. Ambitious proposals capable of addressing the wide disparities between the tax revenues of developed and developing countries,[317] as revealed by the *File on Four* report on transfer pricing, does not seem to be on the agenda of either body.

The relative lack of financial resources on the issue network side is reflected in its non-hierarchical organisation. By contrast, as Marsh and Rhodes have suggested, policy communities such as the CBI are hierarchical and as such are able to 'deliver [their] members'. More than that, the Law Society and the ICAEW are each in a position to discipline and exclude certain or other of their membership. The lack of resources suffered by issue networks may not endure, however. Environmental policy is perhaps the classic example of an area in which arguments once spoken to electorates over the heads of governments have gained some salience in the counsels of policy communities. The same may yet

[313] BBC Radio 4, 'Companies "Looting" a Continent' *BBC File on Four* (29 July 2007), available at http://news.bbc.co.uk/1/hi/programmes/file_on_4/6908997.stm (accessed 9 June 2011).

[314] Marsh and Rhodes (above n 90) 251.

[315] CTA 2009 pts 5, 6 ('loan relationships' and 'relationships treated as loan relationships etc') and pt 7 ('derivative contracts').

[316] Http://www.hm-treasury.gov.uk/controlled_foreign_companies.htm (accessed 24 August 2010).

[317] BJ Arnold and MJ McIntyre, *International Tax Primer*, 2nd edn (The Hague, Kluwer, 2002) 4.

happen with corporation tax reform, especially in its international setting. However, this currently seems – at the very least – unlikely.

A criticism that might be made of the foregoing discussion is that, whatever it might rightly say about the respective positions of policy network members, it gives undue prominence to the TJN, an organisation whose salience is primarily web- and media-based and whose public persona has been – until Picciotto recently took up his pen – substantially confined to a single individual. The point would possibly be well made. The TJN is almost unique as an issue network in this policy area, however, and unlike, possibly, the Taxpayers' Alliance, it has a position widely divergent from the government, as well as, again by comparison with the Taxpayers' Alliance, few if any powerful backers.

Indeed, it is in relation to power that Marsh and Rhodes have found a fourth dimension common to policy communities and issue networks. The involvement in the corporation tax reform debate of bodies such as the TJN, whilst it has the potential to lift corporation tax reform to a political significance comparable to that of, say, climate change, is hampered by the fact that, as Marsh and Rhodes have pointed out, the participation of members in such networks can only ever be a 'zero-sum game', since the TJN and other issue networks have disparate powers, which reflect their 'unequal resources' and the 'unequal access' of their members.[318] With the corporation tax reform policy community, however, there is 'a balance of power among members':[319] although the arguments of the CIOT or the Law Society may dominate, and although both may on particular issues prevail over the government or vice versa, their constructive engagement is almost by definition a positive-sum game, since that is why the community is found to exist in the first place. This point was illustrated by a warning from KPMG, issued through an article of Houlder's in the *Financial Times*,[320] that business's failure to engage with the arguments raised by the Treasury and HMRC in a 2007 consultation paper on overseas profits[321] would likely result in a highly disadvantageous settlement as regarded the corporate sector interests concerned.[322]

For the moment, the biggest challenge to trust and confidence that policy networks – especially policy communities – seem to present is that of inadequate accountability. It means that the Treasury and HMRC are competent to develop by self-regulation. Indeed, policy networks are a fine example of how, '[i]n the absence of both political and legal oversight and accountability, the Crown-as-executive is left free to develop and to transform itself, unsupervised

[318] Marsh and Rhodes (above n 90) 251.

[319] Ibid.

[320] V Houlder, 'Sweeping Reforms in Corporate Taxation Proposed' *Financial Times* (22 June 2007) 2; and V Houlder, 'Warning to Groups over Tax Reform Debate' *Financial Times* (20 July 2007) 3.

[321] HM Treasury and HMRC, *Taxation of the Foreign Profits of Companies: A Discussion Document* (2007).

[322] But see V Houlder, 'Foreign Profits Tax Reform Fear' *Financial Times* (5 October 2007) 2.

and unconstrained'.[323] When governance is seen as a matter of 'self-organizing networks', says Rhodes, the challenge to 'governability' is that 'the networks become autonomous and resist central guidance'.[324] The facts that the Coalition's new Business Forum and Corporate Tax Reform Liaison Committee are closely corralled within the Treasury and that great efforts have been made to ensure the transparency of their deliberations will not reassure everyone as to the autonomy issue. All governments are torn between using the sheer levels of expertise available and managing the dangers to trust and confidence that such unaccountable advisers may bring with them.

VII. THE JUDICIARY

The role of the judges in the reform of corporation tax is, in a number of respects, an anomalous one. Although the judges of the specialist Upper Tribunal are people who have made distinguished careers in the tax law arena,[325] most of the more senior judges charged with interpreting corporation tax legislation were not, in their days as advocates, specialist tax lawyers.[326] Whether, as Professor Tiley has implied,[327] this is to be regretted is a matter for debate, but it has meant that historically, the attention of judges in corporation tax cases – as in other tax cases – has been focussed on the general issues of principle raised. The establishment of the specialist tax chamber of the Upper Tribunal, by contrast, strongly underlines the public law dimension of taxation. Moreover, although particular judges – Lord Brightman,[328] for example, and in another age, Lords Radcliffe and Diplock[329] – have contributed in various capacities to the debate on the specifics of tax reform, the judiciary have not generally been involved in the ex ante discussion of corporation tax proposals. Instead, the role of judges has been carefully confined to the more restricted one of statutory interpretation and may yet involve considering individual enacted provisions in hearings for judicial review.

[323] Tomkins, *Public Law* (above n 41) 77.

[324] RAW Rhodes, 'The New Governance: Governing without Government' (1996) 44 *Political Studies* 652, 667.

[325] Eg, Mr Gammie himself, a deputy judge of the Upper Tribunal and previously a special commissioner since 2002; Graham Aaronson, QC, counsel for the taxpayer in, eg, *Barclays Mercantile Business Finance Ltd v Mawson (HMIT)* [2004] UKHL 51; [2005] STC 1, has also sat as a special commissioner. Mr Aaronson chairs the new GAAR study group. See above n 92.

[326] Lord Walker of Gestingthorpe was, however, and he has therefore customarily been allocated to revenue appeals: B Dickson, 'The Processing of Appeals in the House of Lords' (2007) 123 *Law Quarterly Review* 571, 589.

[327] J Tiley, 'One Way of Improving the Judges: Law Clerks?' (2000) *British Tax Review* 133.

[328] D Hope, 'Voices from the Past: The Law Lords' Contribution to the Legislative Process' (2007) 123 *Law Quarterly Review* 547, 562 and 570 on Lord Brightman's extensive contribution to legislative debate (not only on tax matters). See also Joint Committee on Tax Simplification Bills, *1st Report: Capital Allowances Bill: Minutes of Evidence, 31 January 2001* (HC 2000–01, 175-II).

[329] K Diplock, 'The Courts as Legislators' in BW Harvey (ed), *The Lawyer and Justice* (London, Sweet and Maxwell, 1978) 263; Lord Radcliffe (Chair), *Royal Commission on the Taxation of Profits and Income: Final Report* (Cmd 9474, 1955); and R Stevens, *The English Judges: Their Role in the Changing Constitution* (Oxford, Hart Publishing, 2005) 29.

In one sense puzzling but in others deeply revealing of the tensions in the historical role of the higher judiciary is the distance of the Royal Courts of Justice from Westminster, as well as the presence in Parliament Square of the Supreme Court of the United Kingdom.[330] The panorama viewed from the London Eye is such as to make the contradictions implied extremely apparent. The role of judges in matters of taxation has always been unusually sensitive. In reliance, possibly, on Bacon's idea of the 'lions under the throne'[331] and facing a Parliament looking for 'redress of grievances' as the price of granting taxation to the Crown, Charles I tried to rely on the royal prerogative to levy taxation.[332] As might possibly be inferred from Tomkins' essay on the topic,[333] this has been at the forefront of judges' minds in their closing off the opportunities for challenging tax legislation under human rights legislation.[334] In between these two historical junctures is a body of case law dating from the late nineteenth century and especially from 1978.[335] What we have in this period, as Roger Kerridge has said, is a notable judicial effort to give meaning to often obscurely directed and drafted legislative provisions, while at the same time avoiding the kinds of constitutional controversies to which reference has just been made.[336] 'On the whole', as Kerridge has concluded, the judges, in deploying a kind of intuition, 'are to be congratulated'.[337] David Robertson, in his essay on the now iconic income tax case of *Pepper v Hart*,[338] has written instead of a broad 'discretion' then exercised in the House of Lords,[339] but he cannot take this much further than to explain the exercise of this discretion in terms of a rather selective judicial use of Parliamentary papers.[340] Dicey himself, to be sure, had remarkably little to say about the constitutional position of the judiciary.[341]

[330] Constitutional Reform Act 2005 ss 23–60, since 30 September 2009; and D Woodhouse, 'The Constitutional and Political Implications of a United Kingdom Supreme Court' (2004) 24(1–2) *Legal Studies* 134.

[331] F Bacon, 'Of Judicature' [1612] in J Pitcher (ed), *The Essays* (London, Penguin, 1985) 222 invoking the lions under King Solomon's throne (3 Kings, x, 19–20).

[332] WJ Jones, *Politics and the Bench: The Judges and the Origins of the English Civil War* (London, George Allen and Unwin, 1971).

[333] A Tomkins, *Our Republican Constitution* (Oxford, Hart Publishing, 2005) 67–87.

[334] Eg, *NAP Holdings UK Ltd v United Kingdom* (1996) 22 EHRR Comm Supp CD 114; App No 13013/87, *Wasa Liv Ömsesidigt, Fërsäkringsbolaget Valands Pensionsstiftelse and a Group of Approximately 15,000 Individuals v Sweden* (1988) 58 ECHRDR 163. On the sensitivity of the judicial/Crown relationship in tax, see Lord Woolf, 'Tax and Judicial Review' (1993) *British Tax Review* 219.

[335] Ie, the date of the first reported corporation tax appeal: *Willingale (HM Inspector of Taxes) v International Commercial Bank Ltd* (1978) 52 TC 242 was decided in February 1978.

[336] Kerridge [2003] BTR 257.

[337] Ibid, 260.

[338] *Pepper (Inspector of Taxes) v Hart* [1993] AC 593.

[339] D Robertson, *Judicial Discretion in the House of Lords* (Oxford, Clarendon Press, 1998). See also D Pannick, *Judges* (Oxford, Oxford University Press, 1987) 10.

[340] Robertson (ibid) 160. See also S Sedley, 'Judicial Discretion in the House of Lords: Book Review' (1999) *Cambridge Law Journal* 627, 628.

[341] AV Dicey, *Introduction to the Study of the Law of the Constitution* [1885], ECS Wade (ed) (London, Macmillan, 1965) 60 and 410.

What is proposed here is an analysis of the judicial role in corporation tax appeals as a concrete instance of judges carrying out a complementary role to that carried out by the Treasury and by the legislature, in the particular area of corporation tax reform. The judges are, in other words, engaging in the political practice of statutory interpretation, and they are doing so in a manner that reflects the Hobbesian truth[342] that, as Tomkins puts it, 'the judiciary derives its constitutional power ultimately from that of the Crown'.[343] Senior judges, he points out – like Cabinet ministers – are Privy Councillors,[344] and '[t]he judicial oath of allegiance is to the Crown – not to the constitution, not to the people, and certainly not to Parliament – but to the Crown.'[345] The truth of this is no doubt the historical reason for the attitude of circumspect submission assumed in DC Potter's conclusion on *Sharkey v Wernher* that had it not been made by the House of Lords, he would have concluded that the decision was wrong.[346] It is also apparent, however, in the tendency of judges as late as the 1980s to refer to the taxpayer, not as such, but as 'the subject'.[347] More recently, as the enterprise of the European Union and its implications have become better understood, and especially with the advent of the Human Rights Act 1998, the language of 'state' and 'subject' has been suppressed. However, as will shortly become apparent, the political approach that it reflects has come to be reasserted, albeit with much greater subtlety and to different effect than in former times. The attitude of the contemporary judiciary to taxation statutes is no less prudential, though manifested in different circumstances, than that in *IRC v Duke of Westminster*.[348]

I can illustrate this first broad point by reference to examples dealing with corporation tax avoidance schemes and with the calculation of trade profits for corporation tax purposes: *Barclays Mercantile v Mawson*[349] and *Revenue and Customs Commissioners v William Grant and Sons*.[350] Each of these cases, among the last corporation tax decisions of the House of Lords before the transfer of its jurisdiction to the Supreme Court of the United Kingdom, involve contributions by judges whose approach can be seen, in the sense discussed

[342] Hobbes (above n 20) 158 (pt 2 ch 23). See Loughlin, *The Idea of Public Law* (above n 10) 152.

[343] Tomkins, *Public Law* (above n 41) 54, discussing *Proclamations* (1607) 77 ER 1352; *Prohibitions del Roy* (1611) 77 ER 1342; and *In re* M [1994] 1 AC 377. See Loughlin, *Foundations of Public Law* (above n 10) 223; and JAG Griffith, *The Politics of the Judiciary*, 5th edn (London, Fontana, 1997) esp ch 9.

[344] Tomkins, *Public Law* (above n 41) 53.

[345] Ibid.

[346] Reflections on *Sharkey v Wernher* [(1955) 36 TC 275] (1964) *British Tax Review* 438, 439.

[347] Eg, *van den Berghs Ltd v Clark (HMIT)* [1935] AC 431, 439 (Lord Macmillan); *Hochstrasser (HMIT) v Mayes* [1960] AC 376, 389 (Viscount Simonds); and *WT Ramsay Ltd v IRC* [1982] AC 300, 323C, E (Lord Wilberforce).

[348] *CIR v His Grace the Duke of Westminster* [1936] AC 1; Stevens (above n 329) 23; and A Likhovski, 'Tax Law and Public Opinion: Explaining *IRC v Duke of Westminster*' in J Tiley (ed), *Studies in the History of Tax Law: Volume 2* (Oxford, Hart Publishing, 2007) 183.

[349] *Barclays v Mawson* (above n 325).

[350] *CRC v William Grant and Sons Distillers Ltd*; *Small (HMIT) v Mars UK Ltd* [2007] UKHL 15; [2007] STC 680.

elsewhere in this study, as prudential, on the particular issue and at the particular historical convergence in question. At the time of writing, there were only two corporate tax decisions of the Supreme Court, neither of which illuminates the present discussion, so these older examples remain highly apposite.[351] Other examples, reflecting the fact that Britain retains its competence in taxation matters, are discussed below in chapter four. In each case, the judges are enhancing Britain's tax sovereignty by finding a 'true' or 'right' interpretation, by a prudential method.

In the later case, the judgment in which was handed down on 28 March 2007, the question, to which the judicial committee gave an affirmative answer, was the highly 'technical' one of whether the amount of depreciation deducted in calculating a company's trading profits for accounting purposes should exclude depreciation of trading stock. If so, the company's taxable profits for the period would be reduced; if not, they would be increased. It was a classic example of the old question of how far 'profits per accounts' should be aligned with taxable profit for corporation tax purposes. Of the two speeches delivered by their Lordships, the one that attracted the greater degree of comment was that of the mercurially talented former senior Law Lord, Lord Hoffmann.[352] He took a quintessentially prudential approach, which left various members of the corporation tax policy community reeling,[353] before, in a considered note, Graeme MacDonald recognised the elegance of the solution, although without describing it as 'prudential'.[354]

Indeed, viewed in Loughlin's prism of political jurisprudence as a political practice, certain aspects of Lord Hoffmann's speech have a significance different from that ascribed by MacDonald in his extremely useful note. Thus, although, as MacDonald commented, 'many [people] were hoping for some guidance from their Lordships [on] the relationship between accounting practice and the law in computing taxable profits', Lord Hoffmann wisely avoided fulfilling this hope. It was the first time that the House of Lords had considered international accounting standards, and full discussion at that point might not have been entirely helpful. Not only might it have closed off future possibilities, but it might have drawn attention to the IASB's influence on the corporation tax base, as on the question of whether, in the light of this, the GAAP deviations referred to in what is now section 46(1) of the Corporation Tax Act 2009 were adequate to safeguard the public interest. Secondly, consistent with the delicate constitu-

[351] See n 1.

[352] *CRC v William Grant* (above n 350) 683a–688a. Lord Hoffmann retired in April 2009, his place being filled by Lord Collins. He is a member of the GAAR study group. See above n 92; and N Tait, 'Influential Rulings and Modern Attitudes in Court Win Plaudits' *Financial Times Innovative Lawyers Report 2007* (6 July 2007) 12.

[353] Collins and Dixon (above n 302); and M Parry-Wingfield, 'Depreciation in Stock: Where Next?' *Tax Journal* (28 May 2007) 13.

[354] G MacDonald, '*Revenue and Customs Commissioners v William Grant and Sons Distillers Ltd* and *Small (Inspector of Taxes) v Mars (UK) Ltd*: Accountancy Practice and the Computation of Profit' [2007] *British Tax Review* 366.

tionality of the judiciary's role in tax cases, Lord Hoffmann endorsed the comments of Sir John Pennycuick V-C in *Odeon Associated Theatres v Jones*[355] and of Nolan LJ in *Gallagher v Jones*[356] that there was no room for 'judge made' rules on GAAP issues.[357] Any modifications of GAAP had thus to be made by statute, not by the judges. This ensured that, so far as possible, the House of Lords judges were avoiding superimposing their own will on that of Parliament. Whether, as MacDonald wondered, the judiciary will ever retreat from this position, is a question of prudence – not accountants' prudence,[358] but the political prudence discussed above. They may do so; they may not. It depends on the context in which the question comes to be considered next time round.

If the point decided in *William Grant* suggests a prudential approach to public law issues in an area which might at first sight be thought of as merely technical, *Barclays Mercantile v Mawson*, decided on 25 November 2004, evinced prudence in a more obviously political area: corporation tax avoidance. Here, the question was whether capital allowances were available to a finance lessor, Barclays Mercantile, that had incurred expenditure in a complicated series of financing arrangements, the purpose of which – in Professor Tiley's comments on the decision – had not been, as such, to avoid tax, but 'to ensure the bank [Barclays] met the capital adequacy rules laid down by Britain's banking regulatory authorities'.[359] In an answer that, whilst technical, had a strong element of policy, their Lordships held that capital allowances were available in such circumstances.

Just as *William Grant* was a classic case on the calculation of trading profits, *Barclays Mercantile* might have seemed to be a classic tax avoidance case. In declining to treat it as such and in thereby clarifying the application of the *Ramsay* principle, their Lordships took a highly prudential course. This feature of the decision, and hence its public law importance, did not figure in commentaries on the case, however. Professor Tiley, for instance, commended the quality of the decision and, like MacDonald on *William Grant*, described its prudential aspects without actually characterising them in such terms. He liked the way their Lordships eschewed a 'detailed analysis of the existing case law',[360] since 'the principles . . . [were] now clear'. All that was necessary, instead, was to read the statute: 'first [said Lord Nicholls] . . . decide, on a purposive construction, exactly what transaction will answer to the statutory description and secondly, . . . decide whether the transaction in question does so'.[361] Professor Tiley wondered whether

355 *Odeon Associated Theatres Ltd v Jones (Inspector of Taxes)* [1971] 2 All ER 407, 414a–b.

356 *Gallagher v Jones (Inspector of Taxes)* and *Threlfall v Jones (Inspector of Taxes)* [1993] STC 537, 560c-d.

357 *CRC v William Grant* (above n 350) 685f.

358 See Accounting Standards Board, *Statement of Principles for Financial Reporting*, available at http://www.frc.org.uk/documents/pagemanager/asb/Statement%20-%20Statement%20of%20Principles%20for%20Financial%20Reporting.pdf (accessed 13 July 2011) paras 3.18–3.20.

359 J Tiley, 'Barclays and Scottish Provident: Avoidance and Highest Courts; Less Chaos but more Uncertainty' (2005) *British Tax Review* 273, 274.

360 Ibid, 277.

361 *Barclays v Mawson* (above n 325) 13b.

the House of Lords was nudging Parliament towards a GAAR, since as a result of the decision, it may be that what we had was 'all the disadvantages of the uncertainty of a GAAR without the protection of an advance rulings system, the one thing that makes a GAAR for some workable'.[362] Finally, he praised their Lordships for reformulating the legal position in a single speech,[363] in response to the request from Barclays' counsel 'on behalf of the profession' for 'definitive guidance'.[364] All of these well-made comments were nonetheless characteristic of a technical tax lawyer rather than of one with broader public law concerns. They did not emphasise what was perhaps the most important public law point: a judicial deference at the highest level to the will of Parliament.

Though the precise contexts were different, both *William Grant* and *Barclays Mercantile* were cases on statutory interpretation. Indeed, the bigger of the two Supreme Court corporate tax decisions thus far, *HMRC v DCC Holdings (UK) Ltd*,[365] was also presented as a case on statutory interpretation. There is also the question, however, of how prudence might shape the response of the judiciary to the judicial review of taxation statutes. This is, in Tomkins' terms, legal rather than political accountability and, in the present context, would tend to rely on the illegality ground famously enunciated by Lord Diplock in 1984.[366] Thus far, no corporation tax provision has been considered in a judicial review case, but as yet unsuccessful applications in relation to other taxes[367] indicate that it remains a real possibility. The feasibility of a challenge to a corporation tax provision by judicial review, arising through non-compliance with GATT 1994, the European Treaties or the European Convention on Human Rights, is certainly a constraint on ministers and civil servants when deciding to take reform measures forward.[368] Suffice it to say that judicial review could certainly be used for holding the Treasury to account ex post. What, given the absence of a Civil Service Act, is not possible is the judicial review of the actions and decisions of civil servants, since there is as yet no 'framework of law' against which to test them.[369]

362 Tiley, 'Barclays and Scottish Provident' (above n 359) 280. Professor Tiley is a member of the new GAAR study group. See above n 92.

363 Ibid, 277.

364 *Barclays v Mawson* (above n 325) 11b.

365 Above n 1.

366 *Council of Civil Service Unions and Others v Minister for the Civil Service* [1985] 1 AC 374, 410F. See also Woolf (above n 334).

367 *R (on the Application of Professional Contractors Group Ltd and Others) v IRC* [2001] EWHC Admin 236, [2001] STC 629 (Burton J), [2001] EWCA Civ 1945, [2002] STC 165 (CA); *R (on the Application of British Aggregates Association and Others) v CCE* [2002] EWHC 926 (Admin), [2002] 2 CMLR 51 (Moses J); and *Federation of Tour Operators and Others v HM Treasury and Others* [2007] EWHC 2062 (Admin), [2007] UKHRR 1210 (Stanley Burnton J).

368 Note the unsuccessful challenge, subsequently referred to the European Court of Justice (ECJ) under TFEU Art 267 (ex-Art 234 EC), in *R v HM Treasury, ex parte Daily Mail and General Trust plc* [1987] STC 157 (Macpherson J); and Case 81/87 *R v HM Treasury and Inland Revenue Commissioners, ex parte Daily Mail and General Trust plc* [1988] STC 787 (notice of motion for order of mandamus).

369 Tomkins, *Public Law* (above n 41) 77.

Opinions are sharply divided on the legitimacy of accountability through judicial review. Annabelle Lever considers it to be necessary to protect potentially disadvantaged groups;[370] Jeremy Waldron has argued that it is 'democratically illegitimate'.[371] Either way, the day of a successful challenge to corporation tax legislation must be near, not least because it looks more effective than political accountability. However, we need, as Tomkins says, to guard against the assumptions that 'no constitutional problem is solved unless or until it is judicially solved, and that there is no constitutional problem that cannot be successfully solved by the judiciary'.[372] Political accountability is more easily squared with the idea of a sovereign state than is the legal accountability provided by the judges.

VIII. SOME INTERIM OBSERVATIONS

The conclusion of my discussion of the contribution of judges is an appropriate point to reflect on the links between the argument so far, as well as on the substance of the argument I shall be making in chapter four.

What I have proposed is that the effectiveness of the institutional ordering of corporation tax reform depends on two intersecting tensions. Each of these is a general feature of governance in Britain, and each too reveals policy assumptions specific to the policy area.

The more salient of these tensions is that between the state's sovereignty, on the one hand, and the effects of economic globalisation, on the other. In other words, these are the tensions between the government and the multinationals. Less prominent in debate, however, is the tension in Britain's constitutional arrangements between the Crown, as represented by the Treasury and HMRC, and Parliament. In this chapter, which has largely been concerned with the ex post scrutiny of corporation tax reform, I have depicted the tension between Crown and Parliament as being one of perspective. The Treasury must look forward, using all of its prudential skills to confront and manage the contingencies of an uncertain world; Parliament, however, with the benefit of hindsight, must use all of its Members' analytical skills, all of its powers of compulsion, to reconstruct the effects that the Treasury's policies have produced and, where appropriate, to alert Treasury ministers to areas where the latter's conduct of policy is creating unforeseen and undesirable consequences. Experience shows that the Treasury has, over the last decade and a half, been somewhat more effective in its constitutional task than has the select committee system.

Indeed, it is in the weaknesses of the arrangements that I have just discussed that the implications of the other main tension, between the corporate sector

370 A Lever, 'Is Judicial Review Undemocratic?' (2007) *Public Law* 280.

371 J Waldron, 'The Core of the Case against Judicial Review' (2006) 115 *Yale Law Journal* 1346.

372 Tomkins, *Public Law* (above n 41) 210. See also D Goldberg QC, 'Between the Taxpayer and the Executive: Law's Inadequacy, Democracy's Failure?' (1996) *British Tax Review* 9.

and the government, are most keenly feared. People worry that because of a combination of the economic might of the corporate sector and shortcomings in parliamentary accountability, the cumulative effect of apparently prudential decisions by Treasury ministers is not the promotion of a coherent public interest but the furtherance of the narrow self-interests of multinational groups. Such, with a welter of examples, has been the longstanding argument of George Monbiot.[373] In the next chapter, I would therefore like to interrogate these concerns, but in the particular context of the process by which corporation tax reform proposals are initiated, reach maturity and finally become law. How can we analyse what the public interest in corporation tax reform might be? Does it matter where reform proposals come from? Does the breadth and depth of the policy deliberations, in an area so marked by technical difficulty and political tension, really matter? These and other questions form the subject matter of chapter four, which seeks to complement the discussion in this chapter by analysing the ex ante scrutiny of corporate tax reform.

A significant element in what has gone before, besides the deconstruction of the tensions between corporations and the state, between Crown and Parliament, has been the interrogation of the contribution to these tensions of the respective objectives and values of, on the one hand, policy networks and, on the other, the judiciary. In chapter four, against the background of the issues uncovered in chapter three, I shall reflect, to some extent at least, on the role of policy networks in some salient corporation tax reform measures. I shall also briefly recall how the judiciary's role in this process might be said to have supplemented these policy developments.

Finally, I should reiterate that the interpretation pursued in these pages is driven by the notion of public law – including taxation law – as a political practice, the dominant method of which is political prudence. This does not necessarily mean that the categories of taxation law and tax politics collapse into one. What it does mean, however, is that the latter provides an intellectual context for the former. The methods of corporate tax legislation should be prudential ones, but not all political prudence is a matter of public law. Values are shaped and prioritised in particular policy contexts both by public law and by the prudential logic of effectiveness. So the prudential qualities of those who shape the on-going project of corporation tax reform are all-important.

[373] See generally, G Monbiot, *Captive State: The Corporate Takeover of Britain* (London, Macmillan, 2000).

4

The Process of Reform

IT IS ONE thing, as the expression goes, to ask readers to imagine the vista presented from the London Eye; it is quite another to offer a convincing interpretation of the interactions of the different institutions in the making of corporation tax policy and law. Yet that is what the present chapter seeks to do. Chapter three analysed the objectives and values with which various institutions and groups approach the problems of corporation tax reform. The aim of that discussion was to demonstrate how far the institutional ordering might contribute to the augmentation of trust and confidence in the government in the corporate tax arena.

John Locke in the late seventeenth century wrote that a government has power over 'the society' only 'with this express or tacit trust, that it shall be employed for their good'.[1] This chapter analyses the extent to which the government's management of the various groups and institutions in the reform process might augment that trust. If created, such trust is not easily destroyed. Locke continued: 'Revolutions happen not upon every little mismanagement in public affairs. Great mistakes in the ruling part, many wrong and inconvenient laws, and all the slips of human frailty, will be born [*sic*] by the people without mutiny or murmur'.[2] The challenge presented by the need to augment confidence and trust is common to all attempts in law and politics to consolidate power in the policymaking process.

Imagine that it were possible, in some Dickensian flight of fancy, to eavesdrop on the proceedings of the various institutional personnel and policy communities discussed in the previous chapter. In a Whitehall lecture theatre, we might find, as did a reporter from the *Financial Times* newspaper one spring morning in 2006, the head of the home civil service giving a motivational talk to new recruits on the intrinsically worthwhile nature of a job that involves furthering the public interest rather than helping companies to avoid their corporate tax responsibilities.[3] Close by, we might listen in on a meeting of senior public servants from the Treasury and HM Revenue and Customs (HMRC) with various practitioners, deliberating over the specifics of a new legislative measure. Across

[1] J Locke, *Two Treatises of Government* and *A Letter Concerning Toleration* [1690/1689], I Shapiro (ed) (New Haven, Yale University Press, 2003) 176.

[2] Ibid, 199; and B Manin, *The Principles of Representative Government* (Cambridge, Cambridge University Press, 1997) 126.

[3] S Cameron, 'Mandarin Dynasty' *FT Magazine* (8/9 April 2006) 16.

the street, in the Palace of Westminster, the House of Commons might be debating a statutory anti-avoidance provision, while in the Middlesex Guildhall, the Supreme Court justices might be handing down a judgment in a corporation tax case. Meanwhile, across the River Thames, in a glass and steel building of the City of London, a group of tax specialists from one of the large City professional services firms might be assessing the Government's Code of Conduct on unacceptable tax avoidance[4] with the senior management of a merchant bank.

None of this is to suggest that tax avoidance and its regulation is the sole – or even most important – preoccupation of corporate tax reform. Indeed, as I shall show, broader fairness issues, as well as questions of efficiency, have some greater or lesser part to play. What this flight of fancy does emphasise, however, is the idea that at any given time, individual reform proposals will be at different stages of development. There is no single process of reform but, instead, various incremental measures,[5] in support of a broader set of policy objectives. Neither is there an all-embracing policy decision but, instead, numerous choices made at different institutional levels.[6]

Chapter three depicted institutional, group and even individual objectives and values. In the course of introducing the material, I remarked on the so-called 'new institutionalism' of authors such as March and Olsen; Tsebelis and Money; and Weaver and Rockman – noting that, if used as an 'organising perspective', as suggested by David Judge, aspects of this new institutionalism might help us to interpret the mutual interaction of institutions in the reform process. The main strands of the discussion in chapter three, however, concerned the ways in which the values and functions of governmental institutions and those of the corporate sector might differ; how, given the sovereign status of the Crown-in-Parliament, it is the Westminster institutions rather than those of the European Union that are sovereign; how, following Martin Loughlin, sovereignty is not merely a legal but a 'relational' concept; and how, albeit with significant reservations, the functions and values of the different institutions involved are indeed such as to inspire trust and confidence in their respective spheres.

Chapter three was therefore about the question of what institutions bring to the reform process: interests, skill, a variable ability to hold the government to account and so on. The present chapter is about the interaction of these institutions, on sample corporation tax topics, in the actual process of reform. However, just as chapter three was concerned with institutional safeguards and

[4] See, eg, Ed Balls, then Economic Secretary to the Treasury, speaking about the tax avoidance industry: Public Bill Committee (HC vol 460 col 215) (17 May 2007); V Houlder, 'Revenue Study Explores Roots of Aggressive Tax Planning' *Financial Times* (30 July 2007) 3; and V Houlder, G Parker and M Murphy, 'Big Banks Meet Tax Code of Conduct Deadline' *Financial Times* (1 December 2010) 2.

[5] See Dawn Primarolo, then Paymaster General, speaking to Standing Committee A: Hansard HC vol 421 col 114 (11 May 2004).

[6] C Wales, 'The Implications of the O'Donnell Review for the Making of Tax Policy in the UK' (2004) *British Tax Review* 543, 550.

the political tensions that make them effective, so chapter four is devoted to the ways in which the government's approach to reform, as well as the procedural categories within which reform takes place, add to or detract from the trust and confidence necessary to sovereignty. The focus of chapter three, as mentioned in its closing pages, was the ex post dissection of prudential reasoning: the present chapter is about ex ante scrutiny, and the strengths and limitations of the processes within which that scrutiny takes place.

Students of public policy will be aware of the sheer range of theoretical possibilities that such an undertaking as this one can open up.[7] Indeed, new institutionalism, a highly diluted version of which plays a subsidiary role in this study, sets out to offer such insights. In Wayne Parsons' words, each of the distinct variants of new institutionalism supplies:

> . . . a different window or insight into how institutions shape the way in which decision-making takes place – and, especially in the case of economic institutionalism, how institutions ought to be arranged so as to ensure that they function 'efficiently'.[8]

Suggesting an alternative arrangement of institutions is not, as will be appreciated, a significant objective of my study. However, what I am concerned with, especially here, is the consolidation of power. How, in other words, the institutions, processes and outcomes of corporate tax reform augment rather than undermine Britain's corporate tax sovereignty. Everywhere, my emphasis is on power as constituent power.[9] Not on power as a kind of grim coercion, but as something energising, something enabling, born of a mutual confidence and trust between governors and governed. Such, ultimately, is my reason for rejecting an analysis of the reform process based on some version of Niklas Luhmann's systems theory. It is true that Loughlin suggested in 1992 that Luhmann's 'sociological theory of law' might assist in 'revitalising' the 'functionalist style' of public law scholarship.[10] By 2003, however, in propounding his 'pure theory of public law', Loughlin had at least postponed that possibility, relegating Luhmann's contribution to a single point of interpretation.[11] His reasons, which of course might only be provisional, are nonetheless not hard to decipher. Although Luhmann can explain why a potentially very wide range of policy

[7] W Parsons, *Public Policy: An Introduction to the Theory and Practice of Policy Analysis* (Cheltenham, Edward Elgar, 1995) 247. Colin Thain and Ross Christie choose Theodore Lowi's four-dimensional analysis: see C Thain and R Christie, 'Treasury Power: Past, Present and Future', presented at JUC PAC Conference (Belfast, 3–5 September 2007), available at http://colinthain.com/images/pub_uploads/pacpaper.pdf (accessed 5 July 2011); and TJ Lowi, 'Four Systems of Policy, Politics, and Choice' (1972) 32 *Public Administration Review* 298.

[8] Parsons (ibid) 324.

[9] M Loughlin, 'Constituent Power Subverted: From English Constitutional Argument to British Constitutional Practice' in M Loughlin and N Walker (eds), *The Paradox of Constitutionalism: Constituent Power and Constitutional Form* (Oxford, Oxford University Press, 2007) 27.

[10] See above ch 2. See also M Loughlin, 'The Functionalist Style in Public Law' (2005) 55 *University of Toronto Law Journal* 361, 402.

[11] M Loughlin, *The Idea of Public Law* (Oxford, Oxford University Press, 2003) 97n. Systems theory is mentioned only briefly in Loughlin's latest work: M Loughlin, *Foundations of Public Law* (Oxford, Oxford University Press, 2010) 464.

alternatives is in fact narrowed down, he does so through the obscure idea of expectations being 'normatively' but not 'cognitively' closed.[12] Without denying the possibility that this can illuminate the role of law in certain public policy areas, the view taken in these pages is that this does not allow for placing the central public law practice, prudential decision-making, at the forefront of the discussion.

Secondly, although, through the orderly 'structural couplings' for which Luhmann's theory provides, political influences, no less than other outside influences, may play their part, the central contention of my study is not the truism that corporation tax law is shaped by normative expectations, but that the theory and values that it embodies are conditioned by the nature and scope of the political or ideological consensus at a particular time. The durability of that consensus, the so-called neoliberal 'Washington Consensus',[13] has no doubt been undermined by the economic events of the last three or four years, but – so far, at least – its essential elements remain.

Thirdly, between 1992 and 2010, Loughlin's thought has become increasingly preoccupied with the role of public law in the formation and augmentation of the idea of constituent power, or political sovereignty: in the old theorist's evocative words, the 'power to model a state'.[14] So my study is concerned, too, with investigating the role of a particular species of public law – corporation tax law – in contributing to modelling the British state. The role of corporation tax must indeed be an extremely important one, not just in terms of the revenue raised by the tax but of the system's ability to encourage foreign direct investment and in the manifest capacity of corporation tax reform to command the heights of public policy debate.[15]

Finally, although I do not think it appropriate to characterise Luhmann's contribution as mere 'metaphor' (a possibility suggested by the editor of *Lloyd*[16]), his systems theory has to be rejected on the historical and interpretative grounds that I have emphasised so greatly throughout. What I am concerned with here is not a generic system[17] but rather a unique combination of national factors at work in a specific historical context.

[12] MDA Freeman (ed), *Lloyd's Introduction to Jurisprudence*, 7th edn (London, Sweet and Maxwell, 2001) 701.

[13] MB Steger and RK Roy, *Neoliberalism: A Very Short Introduction* (Oxford, Oxford University Press, 2010) 19.

[14] Loughlin, 'Constituent Power Subverted (above n 9).

[15] Eg, V Houlder, 'Fright Could Turn to Flight as Tax Regime Gets Tighter' *Financial Times* (23 December 2005) 4; V Houlder, 'Companies Anchored to Tax Regime in Spite of Discontent' *Financial Times* (20 June 2006) 3; V Houlder, 'HSBC Says Tax Regime May Force It to Move' *Financial Times* (6 October 2006) 3; J Eaglesham, 'CBI Warns of Multinational Exodus' *Financial Times* (10 October 2006) 4; V Houlder, 'A Charm Offensive from the Taxman' *Financial Times* (17 November 2006) 3; and V Houlder, 'Trouble to Avoid' *Financial Times* (7 February 2011) 9.

[16] Freeman (above n 12).

[17] N Luhmann, *Law as a Social System*, F Kastner, R Nobles, D Schiff and R Ziegert (eds) (Oxford, Oxford University Press, 2004) ch 12; and M King and C Thornhill, *Niklas Luhmann's Theory of Politics and Law* (Basingstoke, Palgrave Macmillan, 2003) 209.

So it is, therefore, that in the present chapter I seek to add a further dimension to the discussion in chapter three, and in a similar vein. I set out to present, as someone once put it, another 'view of the cathedral'[18] – or at least of the doings of those people whose working lives are spent in the buildings so visible from the London Eye. Four similar strands to those that ran through chapter three run through the present chapter, although to a distinct purpose.

First, the significance of the state's pre-eminence, or more specifically, the pre-eminence of its representative – the Crown-in-Parliament – in the policymaking process is transformed. It becomes, not the government's obligation to account for the success or failure of its activities to a small group of Parliamentary Select Committees, but its right of legislative initiative,[19] in this case, in the corporation tax field. Within the logic of Britain's representative democracy, unlike in the direct democracy of ancient Athens,[20] this power of initiative is unique in the state. Its exercise or non-exercise under the discretions conferred by the prerogative power calls for the qualities of prudence already discussed. Prudence dictates that, in initiating reform measures, account be taken of the possibility that the decisions surrounding a particular move will be scrutinised in due course by the Treasury Committee.

Secondly, in chapter three, the importance of the sovereign status of the Crown-in-Parliament was seen as its continuing pre-eminence over the institutions of the European Union: in tax matters especially, Westminster, not Brussels, is still the focal point of British government. Thus, as regards policy issues arising out of the interaction between Britain's corporate tax system and the principles of European law, the real questions are not ones of sovereignty but of jurisdiction and competence. A similar point applies in the present chapter. It is that, in taking the legislative initiative with particular reforms, the government has first to consider its competence to act in that way. This issue needs to be taken into account, not just by the government in initiating policy, but by Parliament, especially when amendments are sought for legislative proposals.

The third of the strands running through chapter three was how the government's sovereignty is more than a question of its competence to act. Equally importantly, sovereignty in taxation is a question of capacity. It depends, as I have emphasised, on the quality of the relationship between state and non-state actors involved in corporation tax reform. This point remains valid in chapter four. The generation of trust and confidence is no less essential to the ex post scrutiny of policy than it is to the making of policy in the first place. Therefore, although in chapter three, generating trust and confidence depended on the prudential qualities of Treasury ministers and on an effective system of ex post

[18] See JM Black, 'An Economic Analysis of Regulation: One View of the Cathedral' (1996) 16 *Oxford Journal of Legal Studies* 699.

[19] Thain and Christie, 'Treasury Power' (above n 7) 7 and 16 (referring to an interview with Lord Turnbull, former Permanent Secretary to the Treasury (1998–2003). See also N Timmins, '"Stalinist" Brown, by Ex-cabinet Secretary' *Financial Times* (20 March 2007) 1; and C Giles, 'Treasury to Retain Key Role, Darling Insists' *Financial Times* (16 January 2008) 2.

[20] Manin (above n 2) 15.

accountability, in chapter four it becomes a matter of how the government consolidates its capacity in tabling and developing reform initiatives. The fourth major strand in the chapter is therefore the extent to which the process of reform augments or detracts from trust and confidence in corporate tax policy. The need to take action, or indeed not to do so, is dictated by a prudential practice, something that may require greater or lower levels of consultation, less or more pre-emptive action. Getting the balance wrong involves not just 'losing the support of business'[21] but, given the purpose of corporation tax reform, damaging Britain's prospects for economic growth.

I. PROCESSES AND INTERACTIONS

This chapter is therefore about the interactions of state and non-state actors over the reform of corporate tax in Great Britain's developed representative democracy. While acknowledging the difficulties of unravelling the two, we are concerned here with the effectiveness of the reform process, rather than the functions of the institutions themselves.

One characteristic of the particular policy area is an unusually high level of technical detail. For this reason, the first part of the discussion elaborates on the distinction between the technical and the political originally set up in chapter two. Working up this difference demonstrates how the interactions of corporate tax technicalities with politics, policy and reform are conditioned by the idiosyncrasies of Britain's representative institutions. The logic of these institutions is effectiveness and, through this, their ability to inspire some degree of trust and confidence in the measures that the government takes.

It is thus that, just as the discussion of the institutions in chapter three differed from a Sheffield school approach, so also does my main emphasis in the present chapter. Chris Hilson's work, which provided an important inspiration for the present study, concentrates on what he calls 'ex ante accountability'.[22] My endorsement of this expression is reflected in its use in these pages. What it is crucial to appreciate, however, is that ex ante accountability is put to work here in a somewhat different way from that in which Hilson uses the term. Accountability,[23] in Hilson's portrayal of a specific area of social regulation, is

[21] Eg, J Eaglesham and J Guthrie, 'Business on Attack after Concessions' *Financial Times* (25 January 2008) 4; J Willman and J Eaglesham, 'A Wilting Relationship: Fiscal Fumbles Leave Business Feeling Less Enamoured of Labour' *Financial Times* (28 January 2008) 9; J Willman, 'Ears and Eyes in Business for No 10' *Financial Times* (8 February 2008) 3; and G Parker, 'Labour Unease over Darling Reforms' *Financial Times* 12 February 2008 2. But see J Eaglesham, 'Chancellor Rebuffs Pleas for Delay' *Financial Times* (14 February 2008) 2; J Eaglesham, 'CBI Launches Savage Attack on Treasury' *Financial Times* (27 February 2008) 2; and J Willman, 'Rock and Tax Wobble City's Financial Crown' *Financial Times* (29 February 2008) 2.

[22] C Hilson, *Regulating Pollution: A UK and EC Perspective* (Oxford, Hart Publishing, 2000) 57.

[23] R Mulgan, ' "Accountability": An Ever-Expanding Concept?' (2000) 78 *Public Administration* 555.

the key legitimating characteristic of the system.[24] I am arguing that ex ante accountability is indeed an important feature of corporate tax reform, but that its legitimating capacity depends on a true understanding of its proper function. Such an understanding relies in turn on an appreciation of the systemic strengths and weaknesses incident to involving the corporate sector in governance through New Public Management.

Responsibility for corporation tax, as a major direct tax, was historically that of the Inland Revenue, since its sister department, Customs and Excise, was in charge of indirect taxes. Both departments were subordinate to the Treasury, and since the early 1980s, both had been reformed along lines suggested by the neoliberal ideology gaining ground at that time, and latterly by New Public Management.[25] The key objective of these reforms might be described as the attainment of what Dennis Frampton called the 'administrative virtue' of increased efficiency; to this end, public servants staffing the Inland Revenue were encouraged to have a 'better business focus'.[26] This process of increasing efficiency went through a number of stages, including Raynerism, the Financial Management Initiative, Next Steps[27] and Gershonisation.[28] Most importantly, by the early 1990s, the then 63,000 staff of the Inland Revenue were being reorganised along the Next Steps contours of New Public Management.[29] This is almost exactly the same period as that in which the reforms discussed in this study have been taking shape, and the 'business focus' that they created may help to explain the enthusiasm with which the departments have pursued them. Whether this approach also led, ultimately, to subsequent failures of management in the Inland Revenue,[30] especially under its last permanent Chairman, Sir Nicholas Montagu, does not need to be examined here. What does need to be stressed, however, is that the Labour Government's reaction was to commission the O'Donnell Report of 2004,[31] which resulted in the amalgamation of the two old Departments in the new and somewhat ill-starred HMRC.[32] Crucial, too, is the perception that the politics of corporate taxation are characterised by the commercial culture that these developments engendered.

[24] Hilson (above n 22) 57 and ch 5.

[25] Eg, OE Hughes, *Public Management and Administration: An Introduction*, 2nd edn (London, Macmillan, 1998); and Steger and Roy (above n 13) 13.

[26] D Frampton, *Practical Tax Administration* (Bath, Fiscal Publications, 1993) 58.

[27] D Richards and MJ Smith, *Governance and Public Policy in the UK* (Oxford, Oxford University Press, 2002) 104. See also Frampton (ibid) ch 4.

[28] R Peston, *Brown's Britain* (London, Short Books, 2005) 150.

[29] G Drewry, 'The New Public Management' in J Jowell and D Oliver (eds), *The Changing Constitution*, 4th edn (Oxford, Oxford University Press, 2000) 177.

[30] Treasury Committee, *10th Report: Inland Revenue Matters* (HC 2002–03, 834).

[31] G O'Donnell (Chair), *Financing Britain's Future: Review of the Revenue Departments* (Cm 6163, 2004).

[32] Eg, V Houlder, 'Penalty-Based Revenue under Attack' *Financial Times* (20 November 2007) 2; V Houlder, 'Security Breach a Sign of Deep-Rooted Problems' *Financial Times* (21 November 2007) 2; and J Burns and J Eaglesham, 'Police to End Hunt for Lost Data CDs' *Financial Times* (14 December 2007) 2. See generally the Commissioners for Revenue and Customs Act 2005.

The disciples of New Public Management, and indeed Gus O'Donnell himself, premised distinctive roles for the state's apparatus, on the one hand, and for the corporate sector, on the other.[33] This has meant, as regards corporate taxation, a greater involvement of business in making public policy than was the case, say, in the early 1980s. My discussion in chapter three examined the arguments around the proposition that corporate tax reform is just another case of the domination of Britain's political institutions by multinationals and by fund managers based in the City of London. In the second part of what follows, I seek to analyse the consequences of my conclusion that the dominant neoliberal ideology has in fact shaped some identity of interest between the government and these groups. The institutions of British government are quite capable of achieving this outcome, despite – or perhaps because of – their historic purpose of promoting 'the worldly interests of the majority and preventing vested minority interests from capturing control of the legislative process'.[34] I therefore focus on the importance of the concept of the public interest, or national interest, to the government's role in tax matters, and on the ideological nature of the interest concept itself.

The problematic aspect of the ideology involved is that economic growth can be combined with social justice, that efficiency and fairness can go hand in hand. This is the essence of the neoliberalism to which reference has already been made. That corporation tax reform has a decisive part to play in promoting this vision has been emphasised by Labour and Coalition administrations on many occasions. Whilst the point has not so far been fully developed in the literature, especially in relation to issues such as tax avoidance, it is nonetheless crucially important in making sense of corporate tax policy.

An emphasis on the ideological nature of the public, or national, interest and on its importance in understanding the study's subject matter has two main implications. First, it helps us to isolate the relevance of economics, as well as particular strands of economic thought. In a sense, the only values running through corporate tax legislation are economic ones, corporation tax having evolved as a form of economic regulation. But this does not necessitate a public choice or other economistic view of the motives, much less the outcomes, of the actions of the individuals and institutions involved.[35] I gave brief reasons for this in chapter one. It is not simply that public choice is the province of the political economist rather than the lawyer. It is rather that, although a public

[33] C Hood, *Explaining Economic Policy Reversals* (Buckingham, Open University Press, 1994) ch 7, esp 130.

[34] J Israel, *A Revolution of the Mind: Radical Enlightenment and the Intellectual Origins of Modern Democracy* (Princeton, Princeton University Press, 2010) viii and 89–90; and Loughlin, *Foundations of Public Law* (above n 11) 171.

[35] AL Hillman, *Public Finance and Public Policy: Responsibilities and Limitations of Government* (Cambridge, Cambridge University Press, 2003) ch 6; RA Musgrave and PB Musgrave, *Public Finance in Theory and Practice*, 5th edn (New York, McGraw-Hill, 1989) ch 7; and J Tiley, *Revenue Law*, 5th edn (Oxford, Hart 2005) 15 (6th edn, 15).

choice analysis may offer powerful insights,[36] revealing various forms of 'rent-seeking behaviour' from politicians and public servants alike,[37] its relevance does not seem borne out by the facts of British corporate tax policymaking over the last decade and a half. Moreover, as shown by Timothy Besley, himself a contributor to the Mirrlees review, a stringent public choice analysis may present too stark an alternative to the economic assumptions that it is designed to counter, neglecting in particular the possibilities for institutional safeguards against rent-seeking and for ensuring the selection of capable individuals to serve in government.[38] Those assumptions are, of course, those of welfare economics, the idea that a well-motivated government can promote social welfare objectives through the pursuit of optimal policies.[39] Furthermore, as discussed in chapter two, an express aim of this study is to place the particular brand of political economy embodied by the optimal taxation approach of the Mirrlees review within a broader context. This is not to denigrate the economic analysis; nor does it obviate the idea that economics might have a role in other areas of policy.[40] It is simply to say that further analysis of the public law background would help to illuminate the issues Mirrlees raises.

Stressing the ideological nature of the public, or national, interest also provides a clue to analysing the kind of power being managed in the reform process. It is no part of my argument to depict power relations as involving certain narratives that have proved so enduring in Western political writing. Thus, for instance, I am not suggesting that the process of corporate tax reform is an illustration of 'the power of organised interests',[41] as corporatist theories would suggest;[42] or of technocrats, since my argument is specifically that, whatever levels of technical expertise are involved, corporation tax reform raises important political issues;[43] or even of elites, as C Wright Mills suggested in the United States of the 1950s[44] and as Hywel Williams has argued in relation to the Britain

[36] Parsons (above n 7) 307.

[37] T Besley, *Principled Agents? The Political Economy of Good Government* (Oxford, Oxford University Press, 2006) 1; and A Kaletsky, *Capitalism 4.0: The Birth of a New Economy* (London, Bloomsbury, 2010) 194.

[38] Besley (ibid) ch 1; and J Alt, I Preston and L Sibieta, 'The Political Economy of Tax Policy' in Adam, Besley et al (eds), *Dimensions of Tax Design: The Mirrlees Review* (Oxford, Oxford University Press, 2010) 1204.

[39] Besley (above n 37) 20–24.

[40] Parsons (above n 7) 306–23; R Baldwin and M Cave, *Understanding Regulation: Theory, Strategy, and Practice* (Oxford, Oxford University Press, 1999) 21; and CD Foster and FJ Plowden, *The State Under Stress: Can the Hollow State be Good Government?* (Buckingham, Open University Press, 1996) 33.

[41] Parsons (above n 7) 257.

[42] On corporatism, see W Grant, *Economic Policy in Britain* (Basingstoke, Palgrave, 2002) 219; and J Pierre and BG Peters, *Governance, Politics and the State* (Basingstoke, Macmillan, 2000) 34 and 80.

[43] Parsons (above n 7) 265. See also CM Radaelli, *Technocracy in the European Union* (London, Longman, 1999) 111.

[44] CW Mills, *The Power Elite* (New York, Oxford University Press, 1959); S Lukes, *Power: A Radical View*, 2nd edn (Basingstoke, Palgrave Macmillan, 2005) 66and 76; and Parsons (above n 7) 265.

of the twenty-first century.[45] The reason is that all three, as well as any neo-Marxist position we might adopt, would portray power as a kind of domination.[46] Throughout the study, I have been very careful to avoid that suggestion. Instead, as already stated, I seek to portray the policymaking process in corporate taxation as involving the augmentation of constituent power, via the prudent manipulation of values generated within an ideological consensus.

It is true that corporation tax reform has a strong technical dimension. Nevertheless, the political dimension of corporate taxation is no less salient. Constituent power is about, in the famous Hobbesian distinction, enablement rather than domination.[47] So, in trying to make sense of corporate tax reform, my question is essentially this: How is it that, despite criticism of the length and complexity of the corporation tax code, the tax seems to work? How does it continue to raise considerable receipts?[48] How is it that there is at best only questionable evidence that it either discourages inward investment or promotes capital flight?[49] Prudent decision-making seems to be the answer: welcoming the participation of but eschewing domination by technically well-informed groups, by those affected and by lobbyists.

In case this response may seem naive, consider the following points. We should not expect the practices of politics to be very edifying. Economic growth is now the dominant component of the neoliberal ideological consensus.[50] The non-consensual views of such as George Monbiot[51] and Colin Leys[52] may suggest different ways of practising both politics and economics, but they are ideological challenges to the consensus.[53] Though they are acute, they are not my primary concern. Corporation tax reform needs to be judged by its economic effects within a consensus of neoliberalism.

All of these points are intended to pave the way for the analysis in sections V to VIII below. The argument in chapter three was that the institutions within

[45] H Williams, *Britain's Power Elites: The Rebirth of a Ruling Class* (London, Constable, 2006) 217.

[46] A Stewart, *Theories of Power and Domination: The Politics of Empowerment in Late Modernity* (London, Sage, 2001) 46.

[47] T Hobbes, *Leviathan* [1651], M Oakeshott (ed) (Oxford, Basil Blackwell, 1955) 56 (pt 1 ch 10); and MA Wenman, 'Power' in I MacKenzie (ed), *Political Concepts: A Reader and Guide* (Edinburgh, Edinburgh University Press, 2005) 371.

[48] Corporation tax receipts are notoriously volatile, eg: V Houlder, 'Treasury Weighs Up Loss of Tax Revenue' *Financial Times* (19 September 2008) 7; and D Pimlott, 'Tax Receipts Ease Public Borrowing' *Financial Times* (20 August 2010) 3.

[49] Ipsos MORI, *UK Corporate Taxation and International Competitiveness* (London, CBI, 2006) Appendix Section 2; Houlder, 'Companies Anchored to Tax Regime' (above n 15); Eaglesham, 'CBI Warns of Multinational Exodus' (above n 15); Houlder, 'A Charm Offensive from the Taxman' (above n 15); J Willman, 'Business Relieved Its Voice is Heard at Last' *Financial Times* (23 March 2007) 3; and V Houlder, 'CBI Team to Assess Corporate Tax Risks' *Financial Times* (14 May 2007) 3.

[50] Eg, J Schwarzmantel, *Ideology and Politics* (London, Sage, 2008) 42.

[51] G Monbiot, *Captive State: The Corporate Takeover of Britain* (London, Macmillan, 2000).

[52] C Leys, *Market-Driven Politics: Neoliberal Democracy and the Public Interest* (London, Verso, 2001).

[53] L Murphy and T Nagel, *The Myth of Ownership* (Oxford, Oxford University Press, 2000) 173.

which corporation tax reform is effected are ordered so as to provide the government with a certain freedom of action. Such action is subject to close ex post scrutiny by Parliament, a scrutiny that is rather successful overall, although it shines rather an intermittent beam on the taxation of companies. The object of the scrutiny arrangements is to allow Parliament to hold the Crown-in-Parliament to account. Having examined the political and ideological settings, I go on therefore to apply this institutional logic to the reform process. I do so by taking up the division of tax policymaking that, basing himself on O'Donnell,[54] Christopher Wales, a long-serving member of Gordon Brown's Council of Economic Advisers,[55] suggested in a 2004 paper: 'initiation', 'development', 'presentation' and 'delivery'.[56] This division is elaborated, where appropriate, to reflect the similar but more detailed dissections proposed in the Coalition's so-called 'New Approach'[57] to tax policy (NATP) of June 2010, and in its 'Corporate Tax Road Map' (CTRM) of November the same year.[58]

Wales' 2004 paper is only one contribution to a significant literature on tax policy that has appeared during the last decade. In section IV, I offer a brief critical overview of this material, since there is good reason to think that aspects of it have shaped both the New Approach and the Corporate Tax Road Map. Dr Wales's 2004 paper remains uniquely valuable, however, given its basis in personal experience. I should emphasise also that each one of Wales' four stages involves delicate judgments: in appraising reform proposals; in timing and scoping consultation; in determining the nature and detail of explanatory material; and in issuing practical guidance on any new measures. In a word, although Wales does not express it thus, the government must employ different ways of behaving prudently.

In sections V through VIII below, I analyse in some detail what this has entailed in practice. Suffice it to say that although the fourfold division of the process tends to mask the point, the crucial stage is that part of the development phase involving detailed parliamentary debate of Finance Bill clauses. This is the sacral point at which, by historical necessity, tax legislation is approved by Parliament. It is what early modern theorists thought of as the ancient, unwritten, practical wisdom of the British system. True it is that debate may be short; that consultation may have been brief or even non-existent; that MPs are not, in the main, tax professionals. Within the logic of the system, however, none of these points is as important as the mere fact that the clauses of the Finance Bill have been consented to, having been argumentatively scrutinised by the democratically elected representatives of the people. By way of illustration,

[54] O'Donnell (above n 31).

[55] D Lipsey, *The Secret Treasury* (London, Viking, 2000) 46.

[56] Wales, 'The Implications of the O'Donnell Review' (above n 6) 549.

[57] HM Treasury and HMRC, *Tax Policymaking: A New Approach* (June 2010), available at http://www.hm-treasury.gov.uk/d/junebudget_tax_policy_making.pdf (accessed 18 June 2011).

[58] HM Treasury and HMRC, *Corporate Tax Reform: Delivering a More Competitive System* (November 2010), available at http://www.hm-treasury.gov.uk/d/corporate_tax_reform_complete_document.pdf (accessed 30 November 2010).

I offer historical examples relating to increased consultation on legislation. Each of these examples relates to enhancing the efficiency and fairness of the corporate tax system. Plainly, augmenting trust and confidence in corporate tax reform is more complex – and more widespread – than a casual reader of the newspapers or the professional journals might imagine.

Allowing for the choices involved, including the rejection of a systems theory approach, it is now necessary to develop two aspects of the discussion originally introduced in chapter two: the political implications of corporation tax reform; and, within the practice of managing those implications, the question of the nature and scope of the public interest, or national interest, in the reform process.

II. THE POLITICAL DIMENSION OF CORPORATION TAX REFORM

In chapter two, I maintained that the reform of corporate taxation had over recent years been transformed from an essentially technocratic enterprise into a largely political one. By way of a preliminary explanation, my discussion sought to characterise the main political issue in terms of whether government policy causes capital flight. What energised the incipient conflict was the economists' conception of a struggle among states for the 'scarce resource' of capital.[59] Multinationals leaving the jurisdiction, fund managers getting frightened off, foreign direct investment petering out – all these are the spectres of the neoliberal imagination. But there are other, lesser political issues, too. Hence, I would argue that traces of skilfully averted conflict are to be found, for example, in the special code on the tax treatment of corporate lending and borrowing, the so-called loan relationships code.[60] Alongside these greater or lesser tensions, I contend that there is nonetheless an important deliberative aspect to corporation tax reform, one that involves the policy networks discussed in chapter three.

I would now like to broaden and deepen those preliminary points in two interrelated ways: first, by analysing how, over the last 15 years or so, the incremental process of corporate tax reform has involved an idiosyncratic brand of politics; and, secondly, by demonstrating how that process has drawn in elements of both politics and policy, one never quite gaining ascendancy over the other. I attempt also to relate this latter part of the interpretation back to the idea of political economy that I advocated in chapter one, this being the discipline with which corporate tax reform has historically been most closely associated. Taken together, these analyses aim to explicate the pressures shaping the issues in the rest of the discussion.

[59] AJ Auerbach, MP Devereux and H Simpson, 'Taxing Corporate Income' in Adam, Besley et al (eds) (above n 38) 837 and 856.

[60] Corporation Tax Act (CTA) 2009 ss 292–476 (formerly Finance Act (FA) 1996 pt IV ch II). See also the discussion of the alignment of accounting and tax below, ss V and VI.

My argument is that analysing the relationship between politics and policy is crucial to an appreciation of the role of the public interest, or national interest, idea within the reform of corporate taxation, and of the relationship between the four stages of the reform process already introduced. I contend that what unifies the four stages is the government's need to augment Britain's sovereignty in corporate tax matters through prudential decision-making, sovereignty being understood as the promotion of the public, or national, interest by concerted and effective action.

A. Politics and Corporate Taxation

It will be recalled from chapter two that approaches to politics may be thought of in one of two main ways: either as calculation or as deliberation. The former, which sees political issues as questions of expedient ratiocination, is an unedifying emblem of modernity.[61] It conceives of politics as the art, or possibly as the science, of government. It is conflictual, realistic, materialistic; and its association with Machiavelli marks it out as being concerned with the management of power. The latter approach, which envisages political issues as matters of communitarian deliberation, was originally a creation of ancient Greek philosophy. Rooted in Aristotle, it is essentially consensual and idealistic, concerned with promoting a conception of the common good.[62]

This dichotomy between expedient calculation and deliberative communitarianism is doubtless over-simplistic. Even so, it produces useful categories. Machiavelli has adherents in our contemporary world, not philosophers perhaps so much as people who want to get things done. Jonathan Powell's recent book provides a current if worrying example, based on his experience as Tony Blair's chief of staff.[63] Aristotle, too, has had eminent spiritual descendants, notably John Locke (in some senses), Immanuel Kant, Michael Oakeshott, John Rawls, Ronald Dworkin, Jürgen Habermas and Michael Sandel. Moreover, as discussed in chapter two, certain thinkers, such as Adam Smith[64] and, in our own day, Amartya Sen, do not fit easily into either category.

So the basic point that I would like to make about the political aspect of corporate tax reform is that, since it has elements both of calculation and of deliberation, it may best be understood in terms of Smith's and Sen's middle way.

[61] TV McAllister, *Revolt against Modernity: Leo Strauss, Eric Voegelin, and the Search for a Postliberal Order* (Lawrence, University Press of Kansas, 1997).

[62] EO Eriksen and J Weigård, *Understanding Habermas: Communicative Action and Deliberative Democracy* (London, Continuum, 2003) 7; and J Elster (ed), *Deliberative Democracy* (Cambridge, Cambridge University Press, 1998).

[63] J Powell, *The New Machiavelli: How to Wield Power in the Modern World* (London, Bodley Head, 2010). See also above ch 2.

[64] A Smith, *The Wealth of Nations, Books I–III* [1776], AS Skinner (ed) (London, Penguin, 1999) 232, 356 and 358; A Smith, *The Wealth of Nations, Books IV–V* [1776], AS Skinner (ed) (London, Penguin, 1999) 108 and 197 ('general interest', 'general good'); and G Himmelfarb, *The Roads to Modernity: The British, French and American Enlightenments* (London, Vintage, 2008) 56.

The civilised assumptions that run through Claudio Radaelli's 1997 and 2003 studies of the European Commission's approach to corporate tax policy[65] mark them out as deliberative works. What makes them rather unconvincing as interpretations, however, is their tendency to understate the potential conflict in this area. Even if this factor seemed relatively unimportant when the studies appeared, it has been underlined since, as aggressive national interests have predominated in Europe.[66] In Britain, where the institutional context of corporation tax is that of the tensions anatomised in chapter three, the two studies seem even less convincing. However, given the contribution of policy networks to corporate tax reform, the deliberative approach can nonetheless offer useful insights. Indeed, the Coalition's New Approach combines these elements of calculation and deliberation. Consultation is essential, David Gauke, the Exchequer Secretary to the Treasury, has said, but so too is the 'flexibility to make changes to the tax system'.[67] Deliberation will be the norm, in other words, but bold action might also be necessary.[68]

All of the interactions discussed in this study, between state and corporate sector, and between the corporate sector and the rest of society, imply a constant possibility of conflict. If we reflect on the five dilemmas of corporation tax governance discussed in chapter three, the truth of this point is plain. The involvement of bodies outside the Westminster and Whitehall institutions, such as the European Commission, the Court of Justice of the EU and the International Accounting Standards Board (IASB), invites the ever-present prospect of conflict over competences, if not over capacity. Influential opinion-formers in the media and in special interest groups operate in a way that suggests the constant possibility of sections of the corporate sector being ready to enlist in a struggle against the government, especially in the event of some serious failure of corporate tax policy. Even drawing business networks into policy development creates the constant possibility of disputes over the inclusion of some professional or producer networks to the exclusion of others. And underneath all of this, as it were, is the 'ground bass' of the struggle for that most mobile of resources: capital.

With each of these factors in contention, the politics of corporate tax reform must necessarily have a strong element of calculation. That said, much of the debate around these factors also has a deliberative dimension. A number of

[65] CM Radaelli, *The Politics of Corporate Taxation in the European Union: Knowledge and International Policy Agendas* (London, Routledge, 1997); and CM Radaelli, 'The Political Economy of EU Direct Tax Policy' in A Lymer and D Salter (eds), *Contemporary Issues in Taxation Research* (Aldershot, Ashgate Publishing, 2003) 145.

[66] P Stevens, 'Europe is Unravelling in a Tangle of National Interests' *Financial Times* (30 April 2010) 13.

[67] HM Treasury and HMRC, *Tax Policymaking: A New Approach* (above n 57) 3.

[68] Ibid. See also HMRC, *Tax Policymaking: Draft Protocol on Announcements Outside Scheduled Fiscal Events* (9 December 2010), available at http://www.hmrc.gov.uk/budget-updates/autumn-tax/tax-policy-other-6655.htm (accessed 22 March 2011); HM Treasury PN68/10, *Government Announces Tax Avoidance Clampdown* (6 December 2010), available at http://www.hm-treasury.gov.uk/press_68_10.htm (accessed 8 January 2011); and G Parker and V Houlder, 'Osborne Adopts "Robin Hood" Tactics' *Financial Times* (22 March 2011) 10.

aspects of corporation tax policy have been the subject of lengthy consultation: controlled foreign companies (CFCs) legislation, originally designed to prevent the deferral of corporation tax on the overseas income of offshore subsidiaries; the taxation of intellectual property rights; and the taxation of overseas branches, to name just three examples.

If a combination of calculation and deliberation is one feature of the politics of corporate tax reform, a preoccupation with the need to address a perceived reality, as distinct from the attainment of an ideal, is present too. Should the conclusions of the Mirrlees review be quietly ignored, as many fear, then this will be why. Deliberation tends to assume a normative mode of thinking rather than a functionalist one: its concern is with matters as they ought to be rather than as they are. Deliberative systems of thought may point us towards a better way of living, but they are unlikely by themselves – so it is argued – to be able to help us understand the conflictual reality of programmes of legislative reform as convincingly as the calculating, realistic ones of Machiavelli, Thomas Hobbes and GWF Hegel. For the purposes of the present study, we really do need to have some such appreciation of the hold of this rein on our imaginations. It explains why, for instance, the Coalition's New Approach gives consultation and deliberation pride of place, whilst reserving the right to abridge it or dispense with it in appropriate circumstances. It underlines the fact that consultation may itself be used, not with a view to the attainment of some general good, but in a calculating and prudential way to promote the public, or national, interest.

Calculation and deliberation, idealism and realism, all then form aspects of the politics of corporate tax reform. So, too, however, does another factor, to be elaborated on in the next section: the promotion of the public, or national, interest. The whole point of deliberation is to ascertain which side of the argument helps to promote the common good, the establishment of the just society. In the politics of calculation, however, whilst expressions such as 'the common good' are sometimes used, more frequent is the employment of its significantly different cognate, 'the public interest' or 'the public good'.[69] These latter are expressions whose focus is not, as such, the establishment of the just society, but the building up of a powerful state,[70] the state being understood not simply as the apparatus of government but in the three dimensions listed in chapter two.

[69] But note the related concept of non-excludable public goods or common goods: D Hume, *A Treatise of Human Nature* [1739], LA Selby-Bigge and PH Nidditch (eds), 2nd edn (Oxford, Clarendon Press, 1978) 539; Smith, *The Wealth of Nations, Books IV–V* (above n 64) 279, 297 and 310. See Murphy and Nagel (above n 53) 86ff; M Wolf, *Why Globalization Works* (London, Yale, 2005) 61; O'Donnell (above n 31) 93; R Hardin, *David Hume: Moral and Political Theorist* (Oxford, Oxford University Press, 2007) 77–78 and 121–23; and H Kiesling, *Taxation and Public Goods: A Welfare-Economic Critique of Tax Policy Analysis* (Ann Arbor, University of Michigan Press, 1992) 9–12.

[70] H Arendt, *The Human Condition*, 2nd edn (Chicago, University of Chicago Press, 1998) 182; N Machiavelli, *The Discourses* [1517], B Crick, LJ Walker and B Richardson (eds and trans) (London, Penguin, 2003) 100–38; and Q Skinner, *Machiavelli* (Oxford, Oxford University Press, 1981) 54–55 and 58–67.

For reasons I shall examine, it is the concept of the national interest that seems to encapsulate the goal of corporate tax reform better than does the common good. Again, this seems to be understated in Radaelli's nonetheless elegant and scholarly accounts.

Fourthly, just as the tradition of politics-as-calculation emphasises the building up of the powerful state, the deliberative and communitarian one tends to presuppose the state's existence.[71] If corporation tax revenues, unstable though they are, are so crucial to Britain's continued security that their loss or significant diminution would threaten the British state, the Machiavellian emphasis, as an interpretation, may be all the more telling. This is, for sure, a point that Radaelli is compelled to recognise when he admits the tendency of one state to try to encroach on the tax base of another.[72]

Thus it is that the politics of corporate tax reform owe something to the Aristotelian tradition but are formed mainly by the calculating Machiavellian balancing of ends and means. Such is a hybrid conception of politics within which sometimes deliberation, sometimes calculation, is pre-eminent, according to what the prudence of a particular situation requires. This art – or science – of government by ratiocination is no doubt an ancient feature of representative government in Britain.[73] An emphasis on deliberation, within the pattern of calculation, is a much more recent phenomenon. The Corporate Tax Road Map, in line with the New Approach, undertook to make a strong version of the hybrid a 'cornerstone' of the Coalition's 'engagement strategy'.[74] A somewhat weaker version, relying heavily on calculation but with some deliberative aspects, characterised the approach both of Labour and of the Conservative administration that left office in 1997. Indeed, the Labour government had signalled an approach foreshadowing the Corporate Tax Road Map in February 2010.[75] In the rest of the chapter, I hope to show how thoroughly this hybrid conception – this statecraft – has been embedded in Britain's corporate tax policy process.

B. Politics, Policy and Corporate Tax Reform

Politics and policy are close bedfellows. The foundation of the Coalition's New Approach has been the claim that good politics means having a clear policy. The Corporate Tax Road Map was intended to lend substance to this proposition. The crucial point is that, even when intended to promote stability, a policy can never simply be about the deployment of technical knowledge. Since policy is so close to politics, prudential judgment is no less essential to one than to the

[71] A Gamble, *Politics and Fate* (Cambridge, Polity, 2000) 4.
[72] Radaelli, 'The Political Economy of EU Direct Tax Policy' (above n 65) 148.
[73] Loughlin, *The Idea of Public Law* (above n 11) 151.
[74] HM Treasury and HMRC, *Corporate Tax Reform* (above n 58) 19.
[75] HM Treasury, *Tax Framework for Business: Document for Consultation* (February 2010).

other. Tax reform is so delicate a policy area that prudence must necessarily gain a special importance. Ministers from parties that are steeped in the prudential traditions of British government are obviously aware of this point. Still, it might be useful to spell out certain features of the relationship between politics and policy.

Making a distinction between the two words is one usage for which English is apparently unusual among European languages.[76] Indeed, the configuration of the present discussion assumes that there might be important differences to reveal as between corporation tax policy and the politics of corporation tax. Contemporary English-language commentators, generally speaking, use politics and policy in somewhat different senses.[77] Within the Coalition's New Approach and the Corporate Tax Road Map, no mention is made of politics, but policy is omnipresent. Hugh Heclo, writing about the distinction between the two, has observed that policy seems to be used to describe a phenomenon lesser than 'general social movements' but greater than particular decisions, the latter being the proper sphere of politics.[78]

If neoliberal ideology constitutes the general social movement from which corporate tax reform draws inspiration, then corporate tax policy represents the deployment of that ideology in a particular economic context. It is thus that the practice of political economy can truly be regarded as an aspect of politics.[79] Moreover, since within this context, there is a consensus that taxes affect behaviour,[80] and since it has not thus far proved possible to strip back the tax system to the minimalist Hayekian system described in chapter one, any serious tax reform must have some substantive end in view.[81] If calculation and deliberation are the stuff of politics as governance, policymaking is the goal-oriented activity that informs those activities.[82] 'To have a policy [writes Wayne Parsons] is to have rational reasons or arguments which contain both a claim to an understanding of a problem and a solution'.[83]

The conception of corporate tax policy, together with policy more generally, as the embodiment of a rational overall objective, reveals the particular historical association of policy with the centuries-old concept of police. We are accustomed to associate this latter word exclusively with law enforcement officers, but as mentioned in chapter two, it long denoted a crucial aspect of governmental capacity, the 'actual ability' of government 'to control the disposition of

[76] Parsons (above n 7) 13–14.

[77] Eg, J Blitz, 'This is More about Politics than Policy' *Financial Times* (12 July 2007) 2.

[78] HH Heclo, 'Review Article: Policy Analysis' (1972) 2 *British Journal of Political Science* 83, 84.

[79] See above ch 1.

[80] J Mirrlees, S Adam, T Besley et al, *Tax by Design* (Oxford, Oxford University Press, 2011) 1 (pre-publication draft chapters available at http://www.ifs.org.uk/mirrleesReview/design (accessed 30 November 2010)).

[81] M Oakeshott, 'Rationalism in Politics' [1962] in T Fuller (ed), *Rationalism in Politics and Other Essays*, 2nd edn (Indianapolis, Liberty Fund, 1991) 5, 27.

[82] Parsons (above n 7) 13.

[83] Ibid, 15; and JR King, 'Debt and Equity Financing' in P Shome (ed), *Tax Policy Handbook* (Washington, DC, IMF, 1995) 158–61.

things'.[84] In the German states of the eighteenth century, so Loughlin relates, police became the subject matter of the 'administrative technology' of Cameralism, a political science premised on the idea that 'the welfare of the state is the highest law'.[85] Cameralism was a science of politics or policy rather than of economics,[86] and public revenue was at its core.[87] It could be that Adam Smith's maxims of taxation are ultimately traceable to that science, and this in turn could be why, later on, John Stuart Mill did not think taxation should strictly be part of a pure academic study of political economy.[88] Although towards the end of the eighteenth century, the latter came to replace Cameralism,[89] policy continued to be preoccupied with enhancing 'economic performance and trade';[90] it might involve deliberation, but crucially, it always required calculations; and its calculations were about assessing 'possible future risk' – or, as Jeremy Bentham put it, about the application of 'expedients . . . *before-hand*'.[91]

It is this last feature that identifies the idea of policy as the government's exercise of its absolute prerogative to govern[92] and that shrouds policymaking with its arcane aura. It also accounts for the oxymoronic quality of political economy referred to in chapter one. Indeed, this idea of policy as calculating, as being something other than law, has a double further significance: it underscores the fact that no distinction can legitimately be drawn between regulatory and other taxes,[93] and it is why the government's choice of corporate tax policies, unlike the mechanisms of its implementation, is not justiciable in administrative law.[94]

In the light of this history, Arthur Smithies was clearly justified in observing that '[n]obody has attained political maturity who does not understand that policy is politics'. He went on, pointedly, to say that this was something economists were especially prone to overlook.[95] Developing a policy, and then maintaining it, is thus an essentially prudential activity – quick, clever reactions, ones that weigh ends and means, might be necessary to keep a policy vision alive.[96] So

[84] Loughlin, *Foundations of Public Law* (above n 11) 407.

[85] Ibid, 418.

[86] Ibid, 417.

[87] Ibid, 418.

[88] S Collini, D Winch and J Burrow, *That Noble Science of Politics: A Study in Nineteenth-Century Intellectual History* (Cambridge, Cambridge University Press, 1983) 139.

[89] Loughlin, *Foundations of Public Law* (above n 11) 421.

[90] Ibid.

[91] Ibid 425, quoting J Bentham, *An Introduction to the Principles of Morals and Legislation* [1781], JH Burns and HLA Hart (eds) (Oxford, Clarendon Press, 1996) 201.

[92] Loughlin, *Foundations of Public Law* (above n 11) 379 and 423; and *Bates's* case (1606) 2 St Tr 371, 388–91.

[93] ERA Seligman, *Essays in Taxation*, 9th edn (London, Macmillan, 1923) 406.

[94] Loughlin, *Foundations of Public Law* (above n 11) 431.

[95] A Smithies, 'Memorial: Joseph Alois Schumpeter, 1883–1950' (1950) 40(4) *American Economic Review* 628, 644; and C Wales, 'Commentary [on Alt, Preston and Sibieta (above n 38)]' in Adam, Besley et al (eds) (above n 38) 1300 and 1304.

[96] Parsons (above n 7) 42; and Loughlin, *The Idea of Public Law* (above n 11) 151.

to speak is not to deny the Mirrlees review's contention that '[e]conomics is the right place to start when thinking about the fundamentals of tax design'.[97] It is merely to emphasise that Mirrlees acknowledges that economics is only the starting point. '[T]echnical knowledge is never self-complete', as Oakeshott wrote, and it is therefore no substitute for 'a genuine, concrete knowledge of the permanent interests and direction of movement of a society'.[98] This partly accounts for the argument that economics should, though long detached from politics, nonetheless be seen as part of it.

So, good politics is about keeping a policy on track, and a policy, even in the economic sphere, requires the application of prudential reasoning. Reform, in turn, is a species of policymaking.[99] Indeed, the vastness of the tax reform literature[100] no doubt owes something to the fact that all public policy issues involving taxation are, in an important sense, concerned with tax reform rather than 'tax design'.[101] Some of the specific accomplishments of corporate tax reform will be discussed both in this chapter and in chapter five. Here, I would simply note four distinct though interrelated points.

First, it is necessary to stress that corporate tax reform is incremental and often reactive in nature. Responding prudentially to successive European Court decisions has thus been a more important part of the practical reality[102] than advancing the European Commission's plans for a common consolidated corporate tax base (CCCTB).[103] So incremental has the reform been indeed that, although many would date the policy vision to a consultation document of July 2001,[104] the case seems rather stronger for harking back to the earliest systematic corporation tax consultation, that of 1989, on foreign exchange (FOREX) gains and losses.[105] Secondly, reform is by its very nature never finished, a point that has been underlined by Joel Slemrod.[106] Thirdly, whilst all reform is difficult to manage, tax

[97] Mirrlees, Adam, Besley et al (above n 80) 2.

[98] Oakeshott (above n 81) 17 and 27.

[99] See Shome (ed) (above n 83).

[100] S James and C Nobes, *The Economics of Taxation: Principles, Policy and Practice*, 7th edn (Harlow, Financial Times/Prentice Hall, 2000) 285–87; Radaelli, *The Politics of Corporate Taxation in the EU* (above n 65) 55; and V Thuronyi (ed), *Tax Law Design and Drafting* (Washington, DC, IMF, 1996).

[101] Murphy and Nagel (above n 53) 128; and M Feldstein, 'On the Theory of Tax Reform' (1976) 6 *Journal of Public Economics* 77, 90–98.

[102] F Vanistendael, 'The Role of the European Court of Justice as the Supreme Judge in Tax Cases' (1996) *EC Tax Review* 114, esp 122.

[103] V Houlder and N Tait, 'European Corporate Tax Plans under Fire' *Financial Times* (7 February 2011) 5; Commission (EU), 'Proposal for a Council Directive on a Common Consolidated Corporate Tax Base (CCCTB)' COM (2011) 121/4, 16 March 2011, available at http://ec.europa.eu/taxation_customs/resources/documents/taxation/company_tax/common_tax_base/com_2011_121_en.pdf (accessed 11 June 2011).

[104] HM Treasury and Inland Revenue, *Large Business Taxation: HM Government's Strategy and Corporate Tax Reforms* (2001).

[105] Inland Revenue, *Tax Treatment of Foreign Exchange Gains and Losses: A Consultative Document* (1989).

[106] J Slemrod, 'The Economic Impact of the Tax Reform Act of 1986' in J Slemrod (ed), *Do Taxes Matter? The Impact of the Tax Reform Act of 1986* (Cambridge, MA, MIT Press, 1990) 1, quoted in Radaelli, *The Politics of Corporate Taxation in the EU* (above n 65) 55.

reform is perhaps especially so: as Machiavelli himself wrote, '[o]ne should bear in mind that there is nothing more difficult to execute, nor more dubious of success, nor more dangerous to administer, than to introduce new political orders'.[107] Finally, it is at least arguable that describing this incremental process as one of reform may be misleading. Some people, unconsciously perhaps, harbour a Burkean idea of reform as a process that retains something of the subject matter's 'true' substance.[108] Others think of it as a bottom-up reworking of the subject matter. This is the fork in the road that we are just now passing.

What Gordon Brown attempted, as I shall show, was a radical reworking of the nature and purposes of corporate taxation. David Gauke, his Coalition successor, announced a somewhat Burkean rediscovery of aspects of Nigel Lawson's corporation tax reforms of the 1980s.[109] This divergence of purpose is something to which I turn next.

III. THE PUBLIC, OR NATIONAL, INTEREST IN CORPORATE TAX REFORM

If to govern well is to legislate in the public interest, or the national interest, the big question is how that objective has been formulated. When corporate tax policy is discussed, it is usually in terms of what business wants rather than what the public interest requires.[110] I referred at the beginning of the study to the suspicions, not least among politicians, that the former kind of discussion generates. So it is important to have some clear conception of the national interest in corporate tax reform, something that goes beyond simply giving in to business demands or amorally guessing how much of the total tax take should come from the corporate sector. One reason for this is that, given the ideas of politics, policy and public law already embraced, such a conception is essential to the interpretation of corporation tax legislation as public law. Another is that the very idea of the public,[111] or national, interest in tax policy signifies an ideological position, not least because of what it says about the relative roles of state and corporate sector. Still another reason is that, for most of the last decade and a half, corporation tax has been put to work in the service of a highly distinctive

[107] N Machiavelli, *The Prince* [1532], P Bondanella (ed and trans) (Oxford, Oxford University Press, 2005) 22.

[108] E Burke, 'A Letter to a Noble Lord' in I Kramnick (ed), *The Portable Edmund Burke* (New York, Penguin Books, 1999) 213 and 218; and FP Canavan, *The Political Reason of Edmund Burke* (Durham, NC, Duke University Press, 1960) 177.

[109] David Gauke MP (Exchequer Secretary to the Treasury), 'Check against Delivery', speech presented at the Centre for Business Taxation, Oxford University (2 July 2010), available at http://www.hm-treasury.gov.uk/speech_xst_020710.htm (accessed 19 June 2011).

[110] But see, eg, Case C-324/00 *Lankhorst-Hohorst GmbH v Finanzamt Steinfurt* [2003] STC 607, 627a-b; and COM (2007) 785 final, *The application of anti-abuse measures in the area of direct taxation – within the EU and in relation to third countries*, 10 December 2007 2, 3.

[111] C Webber and A Wildavsky, *A History of Taxation and Expenditure in the Western World* (New York, Simon and Schuster, 1986) 142, 296 and 356.

form of ideology. Unusually, this was developed and articulated very fully in the published writings of a serving politician. What Gordon Brown brought to corporate tax policy, especially in his period as Chancellor from 1997 to 2007, was immediately challenged in May 2010 by the Coalition's similar but less firmly articulated notion of the national interest.

A. The Public, or National, Interest and the Common Good

'Let the welfare of the people be the first of laws', the Ciceronian maxim, was introduced in chapter two: *salus populi suprema lex esto*.[112] These, the words with which Locke inscribed his famous work on government, are, so Loughlin explains, the cornerstone of the police power, of the arcane skill of policy, of the prerogative of rule.[113] A muted version of them, albeit in the context of foreign policy, appears in the Coalition Agreement of 12 May 2010.[114] The words will be familiar to David Hartnett, the Permanent Secretary for Tax at HMRC, who is reported to be an enthusiast of the Roman advocate.[115]

Yet the *salus populi* formulation is laden with ambiguity.[116] What 'the welfare of the people' might amount to is inextricably bound up in what we take the state to be for.[117] Oakeshott's irreconcilable and omnipresent tension between the state as an enterprise association and as a civil association, troubles us when we bring the ambiguity of the people's welfare to mind. That ambiguity, so far as corporate tax policy is concerned, colours the various conceptions of the public, or national, interest. If, as I contend throughout this study, the purpose of corporation tax policy is to promote the public interest,[118] it is important to reflect briefly on what the idea of the public, or national, interest might imply that other, apparently similar concepts, such as 'the common interest' and especially the common good, may not.

The first point we can make, although the usage is not absolutely consistent, is that the public interest is perhaps more closely identified with the idea of politics as calculation than with politics as deliberation. The latter tends to talk about the common good or the common interest,[119] rather than about the public

[112] See above ch 2; and B Barry, *Political Argument: A Reissue with a New Introduction* (Berkeley, University of California Press, 1990) 187–89 and 224–25.

[113] Loughlin, *Foundations of Public Law* (above n 11) 387.

[114] Cabinet Office, *The Coalition: Our Programme for Government* ['Coalition Agreement' hereafter] (2010) 7, available at http://www.cabinetoffice.gov.uk/news/coalition-documents (accessed 5 March 2011).

[115] S Cameron, 'Supertaxman Can't Avoid the Leakers' *Financial Times* (22 December 2010) 11.

[116] See above ch 2 (p 34).

[117] Loughlin, *Foundations of Public Law* (above n 11) 158–64.

[118] App No 21319/93 *National and Provincial Building Society and Others v UK* [1997] STC 1466 (ECtHR); and Arendt (above n 70). Similarly, see Stewart (above n 46) 36.

[119] J-J Rousseau, 'Discourse on Political Economy' in C Betts (trans and ed), *Discourse on Political Economy and The Social Contract* [1755/1762] (Oxford, Oxford University Press, 1994) 63; and JS Mill, 'Considerations on Representative Government' in J Gray (ed), *On Liberty and Other Essays* (Oxford, Oxford University Press, 1991) 255.

interest, the public good, the 'general interest' or the national interest.[120] Hannah Arendt has drawn attention to the fact that St Thomas Aquinas, shaping Christian thought in Aristotelian terms, recognised not a political realm as such, but the common spiritual and material needs of human beings.[121] Within the Aquinian tradition, John Finnis has described the common good as:

> . . . a set of conditions which enables the members of a community to attain for themselves reasonable objectives, or to realise reasonably for themselves the value(s), for the sake of which they have reason to collaborate with each other (positively and/or negatively) in a community.[122]

But Finnis then glosses somewhat when he goes on to say that '[t]he common good is a frequent or at least a justified meaning of the phrases "the general welfare"[123] or "the public interest".'[124] John Rawls, too, though expressly and avowedly not writing in the Aquinian tradition of Aristotelian thought, wrote that the common good consists of 'certain general conditions that are in an appropriate sense equally to everyone's advantage'.[125]

Machiavelli, by contrast, although he was not entirely consistent, thought in terms of the public good and the public interest.[126] Hobbes, too, since explicitly bringing out the role of the state, rejected the idea that the people had 'any agreed notion about what is good . . . [advocating] some agency, some impartial arbitrator or impartial judge, to decide what is in the common good',[127] and in doing so, he talked about the 'good of the people'.[128] In the famous judicial decision from the first century of the English state, one that still forms the basis of the contemporary purposive approach to statutory interpretation,[129] Sir Edward Coke reported the Exchequer barons to have characterised the legislative purpose as *pro bono publico* rather than *pro bono communi*.[130] Likewise, Samuel Pufendorf, the Enlightenment natural law jurist, held that laws were to there to make sure that the conduct of citizens served 'to preserve and promote the public good'.[131] For Pufendorf, writes Loughlin, the public sphere was 'the sphere of ethics and politics, the world of civil government exercised in the pursuit of social peace'.[132] Someone who, like Gordon Brown, writes consistently of 'the

[120] Barry (above n 112) 203.
[121] Arendt (above n 70) 35.
[122] J Finnis, *Natural Law and Natural Rights* (Oxford, Clarendon Press, 1980) 155.
[123] Murphy and Nagel (above n 53).
[124] Finnis (above n 122) 156.
[125] Ibid, 217.
[126] Skinner, *Machiavelli* (above n 70) 85.
[127] J Rawls, *Lectures on the History of Political Philosophy*, S Freeman (ed) (Cambridge, MA, Belknap Press, 2007) 84.
[128] Loughlin, *The Idea of Public Law* (above n 11) 141.
[129] Tiley (above n 35) 52–57 (6th edn, 56–60); and Public Bill Committee, Hansard HC vol 421 col 217 (17 May 2007, Ed Balls).
[130] *Heydon's* Case (1584) 76 ER 637; Barry (above n 112) 202; and Locke (above n 1) 173.
[131] S Pufendorf, *On the Duty of Man and Citizen* [1682], J Tully (ed) (Cambridge, Cambridge University Press, 1991) 133; and Loughlin, *Foundations of Public Law* (above n 11) 78.
[132] Loughlin, *Foundations of Public Law* (above n 11) 81.

public interest' is therefore emphasising the role of the state to promote a particular idea of the people's welfare.

The second point is that the idea of the public, or national, interest is more realistic than that of the common good; it is more interpretatively useful here, since it is more consonant with the idea of representative government. The concept of the common good, as it underplays the role of the state, is more attuned to the idea of politics as deliberation. This is not to say that a political discussion cannot take place in a deliberative mode, only that in reality many political decisions are taken by the few, on behalf of the many, without wider deliberation. This is reflected in the point that Machiavelli's prudence is the prudence of the virtuous sovereign. In the Aristotelian tradition, whilst prudence, as a cardinal virtue, is an important quality in shaping the common good, it is not the province of government alone, but of every human being.[133] Jean-Jacques Rousseau, who abominated representative government, wrote with surprising consistency of 'the common interest', something that he equated with 'the general will'.[134] So, if, like Mr Brown, you write of the public interest, you are not merely emphasising the state's role in policy. You are, too, assuming that a considerable administrative discretion vests in the institutions of representative government.

Thirdly, the common good, of course, is proper to the common good of mankind. It does not, in other words, necessarily relate to one state rather than another.[135] The public interest, by contrast, is an interest in the building up of a powerful state, one that can hold its own, economically, politically and militarily, against other states. That is one reason why the use of the term 'public interest' has historically been closely aligned with the expression 'national interest'. George Osborne, who described the promised direct loans to Ireland in November 2010 as being in Britain's national interest, did so both because of the levels of Britain's trade with the latter and because of the vulnerability of the British banking sector 'to a further downturn in the Irish economy'.[136] So, again, a politician who uses either of these terms is making a statement about maintaining the standing of one nation state as against the others. Gordon Brown accordingly described the return of the 'unambiguously pro-business' Lord Mandelson to the Labour Government in October 2008 as being 'in the national interest', at a time of particular crisis in the British economy.[137]

Fourthly, the public interest, unlike the common good, has a recognised place in the welfare economics literature, one that has informed the neoliberal economic

[133] *Catechism of the Catholic Church*, rev edn (London, Geoffrey Chapman, 1999) 400.

[134] Loughlin, *Foundations of Public Law* (above n 11) 117.

[135] Ibid, 30n, 348 and 416–19; and B Jordan, *The Common Good: Citizenship, Morality and Self-Interest* (Oxford, Basil Blackwell, 1989) 174–84.

[136] N Hume, 'Why It Is in the National Interest to be Neighbourly' *Financial Times* (21 November 2010) 25.

[137] G Parker, 'Mandelson Recall is "in National Interest"' *Financial Times* (4–5 October 2008) 2; and Anonymous, 'Mandelson Rises from Political Dead: Return of New Labour's Spin-Doctor is an Audacious Bet (Editorial)' *Financial Times* (4–5 October 2008) 14.

policies of both Labour and Coalition governments since 1997.[138] This was made clear over 30 years earlier by Richard Musgrave, who wrote that welfare economics is what economists 'have to say about "the public interest"'.[139] To stress this point, as Besley has explained, is not to play on words. The claim that a particular policy is in the public interest specifically draws attention to that policy rather than to some wider state of affairs. Besley explains how Kenneth Arrow asserted the economic impossibility of 'a scientific foundation for social welfare and hence for notions of common good'.[140] Likewise, others argued 'that there are too many competing notions of the good for an idea of *common* good to make sense'.[141] 'Pareto efficiency' could only be regarded as providing a 'very weak and ambiguous idea of the common good'.[142] Welfare economists therefore tend to focus on individual policies, such as taxation or the environment, as being 'optimal' and thus 'in the public interest.[143] Welfare economics is, in other words, about 'correcting for' economic inefficiencies, which can of course include 'spillover costs' – most obviously pollution[144] – but also 'spillover benefits', such as technical innovation.

The welfare economics model, 'one of the crowning achievements of twentieth-century economics',[145] has a long and illustrious pedigree, including Alfred Pigou and two economists familiar by now from this study, James Meade and James Mirrlees.[146] The idea of spillover benefits were crucial to Labour's ideology of the public interest as the advancement of economic growth[147] combined with 'societal fairness'. What welfare economics therefore provides is a sophisticated basis for mapping the possibilities for the exercise of the police power in terms of political economy. The public interest, in welfare economics, is therefore an attempt to reconcile private interests in relation to particular policies[148] by formalising the 'trade-off' between efficiency and equity.[149]

[138] Kiesling (above n 69). See also HM Treasury, *Reforming Britain's Economic and Financial Policy: Towards Greater Economic Stability*, E Balls and G O'Donnell (eds) (Basingstoke, Palgrave, 2002); and HM Treasury, *Microeconomic Reform in Britain: Delivering Opportunities for All*, E Balls, J Grice and G O'Donnell (eds) (Basingstoke, Palgrave Macmillan, 2004).

[139] RA Musgrave, 'The Public Interest: Efficiency in the Creation and Maintenance of Material Welfare' in CJ Friedrich (ed), *Nomos V: The Public Interest* (New York, Atherton Press, 1962) 107; and Murphy and Nagel (above n 53) 136.

[140] Besley (above n 37) 21.

[141] Ibid.

[142] Ibid, 22; and Kaletsky (above n 37) 160.

[143] Besley (above n 37) 24.

[144] HM Treasury and Inland Revenue, *Large Business Taxation* (above n 104) para 1.17; and Balls, Grice and O'Donnell (eds) (above n 138) 10.

[145] Besley (above n 37) 25.

[146] Ibid, 20.

[147] D Coyle, *The Soulful Science: What Economists Really Do and Why it Matters* (Princeton, Princeton University Press 2007) 51; Murphy and Nagel (above n 53) 50; and J Slemrod and J Bakija, *Taxing Ourselves: A Citizen's Guide to the Debate over Taxes*, 3rd edn (Cambridge, MA, MIT Press, 2004) 114.

[148] D Slater and F Tonkiss, *Market Society: Markets and Modern Social Theory* (Cambridge, Polity Press, 2001) 41; and Himmelfarb (above n 64) ch 2.

[149] AB Atkinson and JE Stiglitz, *Lectures on Public Economics* (London, McGraw-Hill, 1980).

B. The Ideological Nature of the Public, or National, Interest

It is therefore one of the central arguments of this study that what sustained corporation tax reform, especially in the decade after 1997, was its role in the advancement of a particular conception of the public interest. The role of corporation tax in promoting a subtly different idea of the national interest, under the Coalition, was announced by David Gauke at a conference in Oxford soon after the May 2010 General Election.[150] Gordon Brown and his close advisers had set out Labour's conception of tax and the public interest in great detail. Indeed, in some respects, it had even been enshrined in public law.[151] The Coalition has been careful to eschew so prescriptive an approach.

Gordon Brown had referred fairly consistently to the public interest, rather than to the common good or the national interest, throughout his period as Chancellor. This is no doubt one reason why his Coalition successors have tended to refer instead, though more sparingly, to the national interest. Presumably, the consistent contrast between Labour's repeated and prescriptive use of the one expression and the Coalition's intermittent, non-prescriptive use of the other is calculated to signify an ideological difference of a kind long thought dead. The difference between the two expressions, indeed, is essentially one of emphasis: 'public' might be taken to stress the role of government as the nation's delegate; 'national', by contrast, might be intended to emphasise the British people's own role as a political unity.[152] The shift in emphasis encapsulates, perhaps, the difference between the leaden, statist emphasis of Mr Brown's 'Stronger and Fairer Britain'[153] and David Cameron's rather incoherent 'Big Society'.[154] Although one would look in vain for the expression 'national interest' in the Coalition's New Approach, or even in the Corporate Tax Road Map, Mr Osborne did nonetheless offer the national interest as the fundamental justification for the policies contained in both the Budget[155] and the Comprehensive Spending Review of 2010.[156]

Chancellor Brown's firmly articulated expression of the public interest – his ideology – attempted to blend 'enterprise' with 'fairness'.[157] His emphasis on fairness, in the sense of equality of opportunity, was indeed a token of the

[150] Gauke (above n 109).

[151] Troup, E, 'Finance Act Notes: Fiscal Stability – Sections 155 and 156' (1998) *British Tax Review* 490, discussing both FA 1998 s 155 and HM Treasury, *Equipping Britain for Our Long-Term Future: Financial Statement and Budget Report July 1997* (HC 1997–98, 85).

[152] Loughlin, *Foundations of Public Law* (above n 11) 226n, quoting Carl Schmitt.

[153] HM Treasury, *Prudent for a Purpose: Working for a Stronger and Fairer Britain: Economic and Fiscal Strategy Report and Financial Statement and Budget Report, March 2000* (HC 1999–2000, 346).

[154] G Parker, E Jacobs and J Pickard, 'A Quiet Rebellion' *Financial Times* (12–13 February 2011) 11.

[155] M Wolf, 'Two Brave Gambles in a Huge Fiscal Tightening' *Financial Times* (23 June 2010) 20.

[156] H Mulholland and N Watt, 'Spending Review 2010: George Osborne Announces Extra £7bn of Welfare Cuts' *Guardian* (20 October 2010), available at http://www.guardian.co.uk/politics/2010/oct/20/spending-review-2010-osborne-cuts (accessed 19 June 2011).

[157] Balls, Grice and O'Donnell (eds) (above n 138) 6.

centrality of his ideology to his politics.[158] 'Prudence . . . for a purpose' might almost, indeed, have been a slogan of an Oakeshottian enterprise association. Although, notoriously, equality of outcome became ever wider in the years 1997–2010,[159] it is clearly within this framework that the Labour contribution to the incremental process[160] of corporate tax reform must be understood. Thus, in a 2003 speech, Mr Brown emphasised the close interrelationship of efficiency and 'social justice' and characterised business tax reform as supporting business.[161] What clearly concerned him, as a matter of ideology,[162] was cementing a certain identity of interest between state and corporate sector:

> Britain has a unique opportunity to be, once again, a beacon to the world, advancing enterprise and fairness together – a dynamic, vibrant economy that is the first economy in the new era of globalisation to match flexibility with fairness and, in doing so, to attain the high levels of growth and employment that are the best route to prosperity for all.[163]

Since this passage was concerned with building a 'modern economy', it set out some of the key intersections in the ideological debate over the public interest in corporation tax reform. First, it embodied a clear desire to put British interests first:[164] '[t]he way forward is mutual recognition of national practices[,] not harmonised regulations; and tax competition[,] not tax harmonisation'.[165] This was an approach that, as I shall show, has permeated the interaction of corporate tax reform with the fundamental freedoms of European law. Secondly, in its reference to 'high levels of growth',[166] the speech underlined Mr Brown's ideological espousal of the 'post-neoclassical endogenous growth theory'[167] that had gained ground since the 1980s. The impact of this theory on the values immanent to the changing corporation tax code will be discussed in chapter five. For the moment, it is sufficient to note that in macroeconomic terms,[168] Labour's approach involved reducing inflation before achieving full employ-

[158] Loughlin, *Foundations of Public Law* (above n 11) 198.

[159] But see Wales, 'Commentary' (above n 95) 1308.

[160] Standing Committee A, Hansard HC vol 421 col 114 (11 May 2004, Dawn Primarolo).

[161] W Stevenson (ed), *Gordon Brown: Moving Britain Forward – Selected Speeches, 1997–2006* (London, Bloomsbury, 2006) 119.

[162] Thain and Christie, 'Treasury Power' (above n 7) 11.

[163] Stevenson (ed) (above n 161) 135; and Murphy and Nagel (above n 53) 181, whose ideology is remarkably similar.

[164] But see Murphy and Nagel (above n 53) 198 n 7; and the Coalition Agreement (above n 114) 20.

[165] Stevenson (ed) (above n 161) 118; Standing Committee A, Hansard HC vol 421 col 112 (11 May 2004, Dawn Primarolo); and K Ussher, *The Spectre of Tax Harmonisation* (London, Centre for European Reform, 2000) 47.

[166] Note the 1944 White Paper on the independence of the Bank of England (referred to in Stevenson (ed) (above n 161) 91).

[167] Coyle (above n 147) 48; and D Coates, *Models of Capitalism: Growth and Stagnation in the Modern Era* (Cambridge, Polity Press, 2000) 48 and 265.

[168] (As redefined) Balls and O'Donnell (eds) (above n 138) ch 1; Balls, Grice and O'Donnell (eds) (above n 138) ch 1. See also N Lawson, 'Changing the Consensus' in H Davies (ed), *The Chancellors' Tales* (Cambridge, Polity, 2006) viii, 113 and 115.

ment, while in microeconomic terms,[169] it entailed attempting to use the corporation tax system to encourage, for instance, investment in research and development.[170] These were archetypal neoliberal objectives.[171] A subtly different but fundamentally similar aim was suggested in the Corporate Tax Road Map's elliptical statement that the Government's 'objective' was to have 'a more competitive tax system'.[172] But this was against the background of the 2007–09 financial crisis, a corporation tax system remodelled by Labour and the Coalition's conviction that a competitive – that is, stripped-back – tax system was crucial 'to creating the best possible environment for a private sector led economic recovery'.[173]

Ideological conflict, in terms of differing perceptions of the public interest, was also a feature of Gordon Brown's approach. This third observation accounts for Mr Brown's emphasis on fairness and on the pairing of 'high levels . . . [of] employment' with economic growth. All debates about corporation tax reform, especially as they relate to corporation tax avoidance, are about differing conceptions of the requirements of fairness and its prioritisation relative to some version of efficiency. The Coalition has been working through the implications of this reality; its demands gave the Labour administration almost constant trouble. Philip Gillett, speaking in 2006, was right to regard anti-avoidance measures as involving a political calculation,[174] since they are fundamentally about a government's ability to strike the right balance between the values of fairness and efficiency. He would probably, too, have acknowledged that such measures have no other jurisprudential reality: there is no legalistic way of testing whether and when an anti-avoidance measure is a step too far. So far as companies affected are concerned, views on such measures are a matter of personal ideologies about the role of the state in promoting fairness,[175] while, as regards the government, their introduction is simply a matter of tricky political judgment. These are issues to which I shall return in chapter five.

IV. PUBLISHED MATERIAL ON THE REFORM PROCESS

Having treated at some length of both the politics and ideology of corporate tax reform, I pause briefly to comment on the literature devoted to the policy-making process. As mentioned in the introductory part of the chapter, this literature has mushroomed in recent years. In general, it appears at once more insightful in some respects and less so in others than might be anticipated.

[169] C Thain and R Christie, 'A New-Look Treasury under its New Boss: Mr Brown' *Parliamentary Brief* (February 2008) 21, available at http://www.treasuryproject.org (accessed 21 February 2008).

[170] Coyle (above n 147) 48.

[171] Steger and Roy (above n 13) 11–15.

[172] HM Treasury and HMRC, *Corporate Tax Reform* (above n 58) 19.

[173] HM Treasury and HMRC, *Tax Policymaking: A New Approach* (above n 57) 3.

[174] V Houlder, 'Victory is Sweet but Result could be Bitter' *Financial Times* (13 September 2006) 3.

[175] G Niemeyer, 'Public Interest and Private Utility' in Friedrich (ed) (above n 139) 1.

Technical taxation arguments are on the whole made with great clarity, and this aspect of matters has been given fresh impetus by the two-stage publication of the Mirrlees review conclusions in 2010 and 2011.[176] The constitutional, political and policy arguments, even in Mirrlees, are less clear, however, with the result that corporate tax reform arguments can sometimes have an air of unreality about them.

Two contributions to the debate on the process of corporate tax policymaking have gained a pioneering status in recent years. One of them is the 2004 paper already referred to[177] in which Christopher Wales shaped a critical discussion of the corporation tax policy process around the four stages of initiation, development, presentation and delivery. He has reflected further on his conclusions in a journal note[178] and in a short contribution to Mirrlees.[179] The other pioneering document is an austere discussion paper produced by a working party under Sir Alan Budd's chairmanship[180] and published in 2003 by the Institute for Fiscal Studies (IFS).[181] I shall refer to this IFS document in conjunction with a 2010 paper by Tracey Bowler[182] from the same source, which underlines and elaborates various points in the IFS contribution. These have in turn been taken up by Paul Johnson in his 2011 contribution to the IFS's Green Budget,[183] the IFS's annual assessment of the state of the British economy.

The two pioneering documents – the Christopher Wales paper and the IFS document – are quite different from each other. The value of the former, as already indicated, is that it sets out the public views of a long-serving member of Gordon Brown's Council of Economic Advisers.[184] Indeed, the extent of Wales' influence on corporate tax policy under Labour is shown by the fact that when he was still a City accountant,[185] it was to his offices that Ed Balls wended his way early on the morning of Labour's General Election victory in 1997. The importance of the IFS document is that the working party consisted of a distinguished group of tax practitioners, including Malcolm Gammie, QC, Edward Troup and John Whiting, as well as several academics and Parliamentarians.

[176] Adam, Besley et al (eds) (above n 38); and Mirrlees, Adam, Besley et al (above n 80).

[177] Wales, 'The Implications of the O'Donnell Review' (above n 6).

[178] CJ Wales, 'The Making of Tax Policy in the Post-O'Donnell World: Can the HMT-HMRC "Policy Partnership" Meet the Challenge?' (2009) *British Tax Review* 245.

[179] Wales, 'Commentary' (above n 95) 1300.

[180] Provost of Queen's College, Oxford, Sir Alan Budd, was head of HM Government Economic Service and Chief Economic Adviser to the Treasury from 1991 to 1997. He was the first chair of the Office for Fiscal Responsibility in 2010.

[181] Tax Law Review Committee, *Making Tax Law: Report of a Working Party on the Institutional Processes for the Parliamentary Scrutiny of Tax Proposals and for the Enactment of Tax Legislation chaired by Sir Alan Budd* (London, Institute for Fiscal Studies, 2003).

[182] T Bowler, 'Tax Policymaking in the UK', Tax Law Review Committee (TLRC) Discussion Paper No 8 (London, Institute for Fiscal Studies, 2010).

[183] P Johnson, 'Defining a Tax Strategy' in M Brewer, C Emmerson and H Miller (eds), *The IFS Green Budget: February 2011* (London, IFS, 2011) 207.

[184] Thain and Christie, 'Treasury Power' (above n 7) 12.

[185] H Pym and N Kochan, *Gordon Brown: The First Year in Power* (London, Bloomsbury, 1998) 44. See also Lipsey (above n 55) 126 for Christopher Wales's contribution.

That said, the text of the IFS document does seem to reflect particularly clearly the long held views of the first of the three.[186] It goes without saying that both discussions are extremely valuable in the present context:[187] the Wales paper because it reflects on the findings of the 2004 O'Donnell Report as they relate to tax policymaking; the IFS document because it sets out the considered views of some of those practitioners who have been most closely involved with corporate tax reform. I should remind the reader that James Alt, Ian Preston and Luke Sibieta's chapter on 'The Political Economy of Tax Policy' in the Mirrlees review,[188] discussed in chapter one, contains a discussion of the policymaking process. Valuable as it is, however, I do not foreground Alt, Preston and Sibieta's contribution, given the sense in which I employ the term 'political economy' and my earlier observations on the proper sphere of the legal commentator.

One of the ways in which the pioneering documents seem less incisive than might be anticipated is in the way they relate corporate tax reform to the institutions and processes of Britain's representative democracy. Anatole Kaletsky has written that the conditions created by the financial crisis have necessitated an understanding of the nature and purpose of representative institutions.[189] The IFS document, however, proceeds on certain questionable assumptions about the role of Parliament in the legislative process,[190] especially as regards the nature and scope of legislative debate. These assumptions, as I shall demonstrate, disclose some misapprehension about Britain's constitutional arrangements, not least as regards the proper role of the House of Lords in tax policy. Likewise, although the Wales paper has particular strengths, it also has certain weaknesses, some of which it shares with the IFS document. Overall, in both discussions, there is less emphasis on how we reached the present situation than on how matters could be improved for the future. Making proposals about the latter is much easier than patiently engaging with the former.[191] Peter Riddell's criticism of Alt, Preston and Sibieta's contribution to Mirrlees may be too severe,[192] but I would agree with his general point that, in common with the Wales paper and the IFS document, it understates the importance of historical experience in the debate about tax reform.

Over the rest of the chapter, I seek to show how each of the four policy stages has illustrated different aspects of corporate tax policy and politics. It will be

[186] Mr Gammie was the working party's secretary. (The list appears in Tax Law Review Committee (above n 181) v.)

[187] But A Robinson and C Sandford, *Tax Policy-Making in the United Kingdom: A Study of Rationality, Ideology and Politics* (London, Heinemann, 1983); M Rush, 'Influencing the 1986 Budget' in M Rush (ed), *Parliament and Pressure Politics* (Oxford, Clarendon Press, 1990); BG Peters, *The Politics of Taxation: A Comparative Perspective* (Oxford, Blackwell, 1991); and Hood (above n 33) ch 6.

[188] Alt, Preston and Sibieta (above n 38).

[189] Kaletsky (above n 37) 276.

[190] Tax Law Review Committee (above n 181) para 3.5.

[191] Oakeshott (above n 81) 8.

[192] P Riddell, 'Commentary [on Alt, Preston and Sibieta (above n 38)]' in Adam, Besley et al (eds) (above n 38) 1280.

recalled that, in his paper, Christopher Wales identifies the first such stage as 'policy initiation'.

V. INITIATING REFORM MEASURES

Setting a particular reform measure in motion is necessarily an arcane endeavour. I am not just thinking here of the confidential discussions between government ministers and between ministers and civil servants. Discreet soundings, taken from interested parties outside government, are also quite usual.[193] My earlier comments on the nature of representative institutions, as well as on the roots of policy in the prerogative, should make none of this surprising. I therefore start by assessing what we can infer from the somewhat occluded policy initiation stage. Given the long view taken over the whole study, I cast the net wide over the last 15 years or so. I then consider how three specific sets of corporate tax reforms, as initiated over that period, illustrate these inferences. My object is to demonstrate how each embodies a judgment about the prudent promotion of an ideology of the public, or national, interest. Finally, I reflect further on what each of these viewpoints tells us about the relative importance of technical knowledge to prudential policy initiation, as well as on the significance of the Coalition's plans to ensure that policy initiatives are subject to strategic oversight.

A. Uncovering the Arcanum

The fact that in Britain's representative democracy it is the government alone that has the prerogative to initiate policy[194] places a particularly heavy accent on the coherence and consistency of corporation tax policy choices. Christopher Wales has written:

> Policy initiation requires a particular blend of skills and knowledge. It requires an understanding of macro and micro-economic policy[195] and the key elements that underpin the Government's strategy. It requires a deep understanding of the tax system, an understanding of how the system functions and where it is dysfunctional; and it requires an appreciation of how policy change might be engineered to reduce the risks that change itself can create.[196]

The need for extreme sensitivity in policy initiation is underlined all the more forcefully by four further factors. First, the system places absolute discretion over the initiation of policy in the hands of ministers of the Crown, there being

[193] Wales, 'The Implications of the O'Donnell Review' (above n 6) 549.
[194] Tax Law Review Committee (above n 181) para 6.3; and L Beighton, 'Tax Policy and Management: The Role of the Inland Revenue' (1987) 8 *Fiscal Studies* 1, 5.
[195] See Balls and O'Donnell (eds) (above n 138); and Balls, Grice and O'Donnell (eds) (above n 138).
[196] Wales, 'The Implications of the O'Donnell Review' (above n 6) 549.

no doctrine of mandate and recall in a representative system, and, as the Coalition quickly demonstrated, no binding electoral pledges in the British system.[197] It is this discretionary dimension to Britain's governance arrangements that Stein Ringen quite rightly regards as momentous: in combination with a large Parliamentary majority, it enabled Labour to legislate before 2007 on a wide range of tax and other public policy issues, seemingly oblivious to the economic dangers from the financial sector.[198] The same factors had facilitated the Conservative Administration's radical public policy measures in the 1980s, measures that included sweeping corporate tax reforms.[199] It was that Administration's activities that prompted the Sheffield school's search for 'rule of law values' in Britain's constitution.[200]

Secondly, it is perfectly legitimate in a representative government for the choice of one reform proposal rather than another to lie with the relevant minister, on the advice of her civil servants and policy advisers, and for that decision to be made behind closed doors.[201] This applies both to big 'strategic policy' choices and to smaller decisions involved in 'policy maintenance',[202] although, as Christopher Wales has perceptively stated, '[t]he corporate tax reform programme is a prime example of strategic policy that has swept up a range of maintenance issues'.[203]

Thirdly, although the leaders of the Parliamentary Labour Party have a wide competence to decide on priorities between different public policy options[204] and although Coalition ministers were careful not to bind themselves to particular corporate tax measures, some degree of self-limitation may itself be prudent. Thus, on taking office in 2010, the Coalition committed itself to adhering to the broad principles set out in the New Approach and in the Corporate Tax Road Map.[205] Besides promoting the principles of simplicity and stability within the corporation tax code itself,[206] the New Approach undertook to 'publish more tax legislation in draft, to allow for pre-legislative scrutiny', as well as to 'improve supporting documentation accompanying tax changes'.[207] Likewise, the Corporate Tax Road Map contained a five-year reform programme, as well as an undertaking both to 'ensure [that] significant reforms . . . [were] designed

[197] Manin (above n 2) 163.

[198] S Ringen, *The Economic Consequences of Mr. Brown: How a Strong Government was Defeated by a Weak System of Governance* (Oxford, Bardwell, 2009).

[199] See below ch 5.

[200] I Harden and N Lewis, *The Noble Lie: The British Constitution and the Rule of Law* (London, Hutchinson, 1986).

[201] Manin (above n 2) 167; S Brittan, 'The Pitfalls of Confidential Advice' *Financial Times* (5 March 2010) 15. See Loughlin, *The Idea of Public Law* (above n 11) 83; and Loughlin, *Foundations of Public Law* (above n 11) 264 and 267.

[202] O'Donnell (above n 31) 95.

[203] Wales, 'The Implications of the O'Donnell Review' (above n 6) 549.

[204] Manin (above n 2) 214.

[205] HM Treasury and HMRC, *Tax Policymaking: A New Approach* (above n 57); HM Treasury and HMRC, *Corporate Tax Reform* (above n 58); and Wales, 'Commentary' (above n 95) 1307.

[206] See below ch 5.

[207] HM Treasury and HMRC, *Tax Policymaking: A New Approach* (above n 57) 15.

and planned effectively with fewer small changes' and to conduct 'extensive and timely consultation with business'.[208] Consistent with their nature, each was explicitly subject to unforeseen contingencies. That said, one felt that the likelihood of such events materialising was diminished by the somewhat limited objectives to which the Coalition policy aspired.

Fourthly, we should note the fact that, as Dr Wales has pointed out, one of the consequences of the merger of the Inland Revenue and Customs and Excise was that the 'strategic policy advice' of civil servants has been 'single-sourced':[209] 'A future Chancellor may well regret having had her sources of advice narrowed to such an extent'.[210] Returning to this subject in 2009, Wales suspected that his argument had been vindicated by what he saw as the lack of consistency and coherence in the Budgets taking place in the interim.[211] Since this period followed his departure from the Treasury, one wonders whether, had Christopher Wales stayed, subsequent corporate tax reform debates would have been less troubled by the absence of a strategic approach.

In the light of these observations, and appreciating the need for the prudent promotion of the public, or national, interest, we may reflect on the three corporate tax initiatives outlined earlier.

B. Three Public, or National, Interest Initiatives

I explained in chapters one and two that discussions of corporate tax reform embody two key political values: efficiency and fairness. Contrasting prioritisations of these values reflect slightly different perceptions of the national, or public, interest. Three reform initiatives of the past decade and a half illustrate this point well: first, the closer alignment of commercial profits with taxable profits, which is an issue of efficiency; secondly, the reshaping of the mechanisms for determining and collecting the tax due, also an efficiency measure; and thirdly, conforming corporation tax law to the provisions of the European Treaties, a trickier objective than the other two because of delicate trade-offs between the two dominant values.

Of the three policy initiatives, the most longstanding has probably been the ever-closer alignment of profits measurement tax purposes, with their measurement for purposes of either UK generally accepted accounting practice (GAAP)

[208] HM Treasury and HMRC, *Corporate Tax Reform* (above n 58) 15

[209] Wales, 'The Implications of the O'Donnell Review' (above n 6) 556. And so, apparently, it came to pass: V Houlder, 'Treasury Hands Compound Political Errors' *Financial Times* (11 February 2008) 3. See also Beighton (above n 194) 2.

[210] Wales, 'The Implications of the O'Donnell Review' (above n 6) 556; and Wales, 'Commentary' (above n 95) 1305.

[211] Wales, 'The Making of Tax Policy in the Post-O'Donnell World' (above n 178) 245; K Ussher and I Walford, *National Treasure* (London, Demos, 2011) 45; and C Giles, 'Treasury Culture Needs Shake-Up, Says Demos Study' *Financial Times* (8 March 2011) 2.

or international accounting standards (IASs).[212] Although the alignment process has encompassed a number of areas – not merely the use of GAAP/IASs as a means of calculating taxable profits, but also the development of special codes on corporate finance and on the treatment of intangibles – the strength of each initiative was its consistency with successive governments' broadly neoliberal outlook. Thus, the 1993 Finance Act introduced a new corporation tax code for the treatment of profits and losses arising on a company's foreign exchange (FOREX) transactions. This was followed in 1994 with new rules for the taxation of financial instruments and then, in Finance Act 1996, with the loan relationships code. Although the tenor of these 'distinct but overlapping, independent but interdependent', separate but integrated,[213] codes was largely to assimilate corporation tax and GAAP, they also removed, in the areas to which they applied, the time-honoured direct tax distinction between income and capital. Not even the use of GAAP in computing trading profits, under what was then Schedule D, Case I – an area that had seen some notable case law[214] – had had so radical an effect. I shall return to this point in chapter five: at present, however, it is sufficient to note, as David Southern has, that the three special codes on corporate finance fundamentally altered the nature of the corporate tax base, or at least a substantial part of it.[215]

Deemed a success, if a qualified one, by the practising legal and accounting professions, the special codes were nonetheless significantly remodelled in 2002, becoming, in the process, two. As Ruth Kelly, then the Economic Secretary to the Treasury, explained at the Committee Stage of that year's Finance Bill, '[a]lthough all three regimes were thought radical in their time, they . . . suffered from two main problems: complexity and lack of fairness'.[216] Remodelled though the special codes were, the basic idea of the alignment of tax law with GAAP remained; consistent with this, Finance Act 2002 also saw the broad assimilation of the tax and accounting treatments of intellectual property and other intangibles.

Whatever the temptations to act differently, there was in all of these cases a commitment to the neutral taxation of corporate finance within open markets. For example, in its 2002 reaffirmation of the Conservatives' approach of 1993–96, Labour acknowledged not only that the pre-1996 corporation tax treatment of

[212] CTA 2009 s 46(1) (formerly FA 1998 s 42(1)); and CTA 2010 s 1127 (formerly FA 2004 s 50(1)). For background, see Organisation for Economic Co-operation and Development (OECD), *The Relationship between Taxation and Financial Reporting: Income Tax Accounting* (Paris, OECD, 1987) 12.

[213] D Southern, *Taxation of Corporate Debt, Foreign Exchange and Derivative Contracts*, 7th edn (London, Lexis Nexis, 2004) 2.

[214] Eg, *Herbert Smith v Honour* (1999) 72 TC 130 (Lloyd J) paras 11–32; 15; *CRC v William Grant and Sons Distillers Ltd*; *Small (HMIT) v Mars UK Ltd* [2007] UKHL 15, [2007] STC 680; and the contributions to the special issue of the *British Tax Review* entitled *Accounting Standards and Taxable Profits*: (1995) *British Tax Review* 433–510.

[215] Southern, *Taxation of Corporate Debt, Foreign Exchange and Derivative Contracts* (above n 213) 2.

[216] Standing Committee F, Hansard HC vol 386 col 318 (11 June 2002).

corporate debt had been anomalous[217] and full of avoidance opportunities,[218] but that there had previously been no serviceable tax law on FOREX[219] or financial instruments.[220] In doing so, Labour did not dissent from leaving the vacuum to be filled by GAAP/IAS, which already had conceptual frameworks for such items.[221] Specifically, the 2002 reaffirmation of the loan relationships code reflected an ideological commitment to the continued facilitation of the 'gilt strips' market[222] and, more importantly, to the Private Finance Initiative (PFI),[223] something that Gordon Brown had always affirmed to be in the public interest.[224]

Initiation, or reaffirmation, of the policy in each of these cases was the prudent course, not least because a barely noted effect of the loan relationships code had been a broadening out of the corporate tax base.[225] Unwise and impractical, given Labour's commitment to open markets, would have been the suggestion, which was actually referred to at the Committee Stage of the FOREX code in 1993,[226] that a 'Tobin tax'[227] would be the appropriate means of taxing transactions in currencies. It was not that such an innovation would have been bad in itself: there were, in fact, arguments for it under an economic policy designed to tackle spill-over costs.[228] It was simply that it would not then have

[217] D Southern, 'Big Bang for Bonds' *Tax Journal* (23 November 1995) 6; N Doran and A Greenbank, 'Be Vigilant on Tax Reforms' *The Times* (11 April 1996); E Keeling, 'Taxing Foreign Exchange Gains and Losses: Past Doubts and Future "Solutions"' (1995) *British Tax Review* 122, 122; and J Freedman, 'The Role of Realisation: Accounting, Company Law and Taxation' in P Thorell (ed), *The Influence of Corporate Law and Accounting Principles in Determining Taxable Income* (London, Kluwer Law, 1997) 29, 43.

[218] Eg, Income and Corporation Taxes Act (ICTA) 1988 s 74(1)(m); ICTA 1988 s 337(2)(b); ICTA 1988 s 337(3) (*Cairns v MacDiarmid* [1983] STC 178); ICTA 1988 s 338 (*Wilcock v Frigate Investments Ltd* [1982] STC 198; *Macniven (HMIT) v Westmoreland Investments* [2001] UKHL 6, [2001] 2 WLR 377); Taxation of Chargeable Gains Act (TCGA) 1992 ss 251, 253 and 254 (*Cleveley's Investment Trust Co v IRC* (1971) 47 TC 300; *Aberdeen Construction Group Ltd v IRC* [1977] STC 302; *WT Ramsay Ltd v IRC* [1979] STC 582, 587 (Templeman LJ)).

[219] J Pagan 'Foreign Exchange Gains and Losses' (1993) *British Tax Review* 276.

[220] Freshfields, 'Taxation of Financial Instruments' (1991) 5 *Corporate Briefing* 284; and S Cook, 'The Taxation of Financial Instruments: New Rules' (1993) *British Tax Review* 429. See generally, AC Warren, Jr, 'Commentary: Financial Contract Innovation and Income Tax Policy' (1993) 107 *Harvard Law Review* 460; JS Alworth, 'Taxation and Integrated Financial Markets: The Challenges of Derivatives and Other Financial Innovations' (1998) 5 *International Tax and Public Finance* 507; and D Southern, 'The Taxation of Derivatives' (1998) *British Tax Review* 348.

[221] Eg, D Southern, *Tolley's Taxation of Corporate Debt and Financial Instruments*, 2nd edn (Croydon, Tolley Publishing, 1998) ch 13.

[222] D Hole, 'The Taxation of Gilts and Bonds' (1995) *British Tax Review* 511.

[223] Inland Revenue, *The Taxation of Gilts and Bonds: A Consultative Document* (London, Board of Inland Revenue, 1995) 7.

[224] Stevenson (ed) (above n 161) 167. But see AM Pollock, D Price and S Player, 'An Examination of the UK Treasury's Evidence Base for Cost and Time Overrun Data in UK Value-for-Money Policy and Appraisal' *Public Money and Management* (April 2007) 1.

[225] Southern, *Taxation of Corporate Debt, Foreign Exchange and Derivative Contracts* (above n 213) 7.

[226] Standing Committee A, Hansard HC vol 224 cols 11–12 (18 May 1993, Alistair Darling).

[227] I Kaul, I Grunberg and M ul Haq, 'Overview' in M ul Haq, I Kaul and I Grunberg (eds), *The Tobin Tax: Coping With Financial Volatility* (New York, Oxford University Press, 1996) 1.

[228] R Kelly, 'Taxing the Speculator: The Route to Forex Stability', Fabian Society Discussion Paper No 15 (London, 1993) 18; Leys (above n 52) 27; and B Eichengreen, 'Conclusion: The Tobin Tax: What Have We Learned?' in ul Haq, Kaul and Grunberg (eds) (above n 227) 273, 279.

been seen as consistent with Labour's developing ideology of the public interest. It should be remembered, too, that, even as late as 2010, Mr Brown was promoting, not a unilateral, but a multilateral version of the Tobin tax idea.[229]

If aligning accounting and taxation treatments of profits was a prudential response, not only to more open financial markets but also to the need to encourage private finance for public infrastructure projects, then a similar rationale was behind the strengthening of mechanisms for the assessment and collection of corporation tax. Just as open markets and a reduced state have been hallmarks of neoliberalism, so too have stronger tax enforcement measures. Indeed, Manfred Steger and Ravi Roy have pointed out that the 'effective enforcement' of tax liabilities was specifically part of the Washington Consensus' 'global framework for "proper" economic development'.[230] Accordingly, the main innovation here was the introduction, 'in relation to accounting periods ending on or after [1 July 1999]', of corporation tax self-assessment (CTSA). The particular wisdom of introducing CTSA in Finance Act 1998 was that the bringing-in of quarterly interim payments of tax could be taken as the quid pro quo for the abolition of what by the late 1990s had become the much resented advance corporation tax (ACT). This 'up-front' payment of tax had been a key feature of the corporate tax landscape since 1972.[231] Because there was a cap on the amount of ACT that could be set against 'mainstream corporation tax',[232] and because overseas tax on foreign dividends had to be relieved before ACT,[233] many companies by the time of its abolition were carrying 'ACT mountains'. So, whilst it was a risky strategy to begin a process of introducing interim corporation tax payments, under CTSA, it was obviously the right one.[234] Not only was criticism reasonably muted[235] – the problem of so-called 'shadow ACT' possibly apart[236] – but CTSA has remained one of the more stable components of the corporation tax code ever since.[237]

[229] J Snape, 'Tax and the City: The UK's Proposals for a Bank Levy' in JR LaBrosse, R Olivares-Caminal and D Singh (eds), *Managing Risk in the Financial System* (Cheltenham, Edward Elgar, 2011). But see G Brown, *Beyond the Crash: Overcoming the First Crisis of Globalisation* (London, Simon and Schuster, 2010) 107.

[230] Steger and Roy (above n 13) 19.

[231] FA 1972 ss 84–92; HM Treasury, *Reform of Corporation Tax: Presented to Parliament by the Chancellor of the Exchequer* (Cmnd 4630, 1971); Select Committee on Corporation Tax, *Report, Together with Minutes of Evidence, Appendices and Index* (HC 1970–71, 622). The Select Committee's membership included David Marquand.

[232] ICTA 1988 s 239(2) (FA 1972 s 85(2)).

[233] ICTA 1988 s 797(4)(a); and C Whitehouse, L Watson, L Narain and N Lee, *Revenue Law: Principles and Practice*, 18th edn (Croydon, Butterworths Tolley, 2000) para 33.44. The problem had been mitigated by FA 1994 s 138 and sch 16, but it was still a real one: Whitehouse, Watson, Narain and Lee (above), paras 33.46–33.70.

[234] Given the impact on pensions of the withdrawal of 'payable' ACT credits, it was also an illustration of how, in a contest between efficiency and fairness, efficiency tends to win.

[235] Lipsey (above n 55) 130.

[236] C Whitehouse, L Narain, L Watson and N Lee, *Revenue Law: Principles and Practice*, 19th edn (Croydon, Tolley Lexis Nexis, 2001) paras 33.76–33.100.

[237] J Watterston, *Core Tax Annuals: Corporation Tax 2010/11* (Haywards Heath, Bloomsbury Professional, 2010) ch 2.

Generally speaking, the initiation of policy in areas such as the two just discussed was straightforward. Aligning tax and accounting and strengthening the tax base were the kind of technical measures that lend themselves well to the initiation of tax policy by a Treasury minister deliberating in private with her civil servants. Both were long-term projects, easily conforming to an ethos of greater efficiency in markets, and as such their rationale could easily be parsed. The same cannot necessarily be said, however, for initiatives taken in response to or in anticipation of international – and especially European – legal developments. It is tempting to assume that, given the unique status of taxation as a prerogative of the state, the government has had a free hand over corporate tax policy. However, Great Britain's status as an EU Member State, as well as its membership – along with the European Union itself – of the World Trade Organization (WTO), has meant that to do so is misleading. Until recently, each organisation was a somewhat understated factor in Britain's corporate tax capacity. And whilst the WTO's influence has perhaps yet to be felt, the impact of the European Treaties' fundamental freedoms on corporation tax law has been growing ever more apparent. Critical attention, once focussed on the apparent inability of the Commission to move beyond a handful of legislative measures on corporate tax,[238] shifted to the role of the European Court in holding certain longstanding elements of corporation tax law to fall foul of various Treaty provisions, most often those on freedom of establishment.

There is a winding path of European Court jurisprudence, four milestones on which have included the following: in 1998, a ruling as contrary to what are now Articles 49 and 54 of the Treaty on the Functioning of the European Union (TFEU),[239] domestic legislation restricting entitlement to consortium relief to holding companies whose business consisted wholly or mainly in the holding of shares in 90 per cent British-resident subsidiaries;[240] in 2001, the striking-down, for the same reason, of the disqualification of a British-resident subsidiary of a non-resident holding company from making a group income election;[241] in 2005, a decision that Articles 49 and 54 ruled out the restriction of group relief to British-resident groups;[242] and, in 2006, a decision that the same treaty articles also precluded the maintenance in its then form of the Britain's CFC regime.[243] When not overtaken by separate developments, each of these rulings has required the government to make appropriate changes to British law. The latter

[238] BJM Terra and PJ Wattel, *European Tax Law*, 4th edn (The Hague, Kluwer Law, 2005) chs 9–16.

[239] Formerly arts 43 and 48 EC.

[240] Case C-264/96 *Imperial Chemical Industries plc v Colmer* [1998] 3 CMLR 293 (now CTA 2010 s 107).

[241] Case C-397/98 *Metallgesellschaft Ltd and Others v CIR* [2001] ECR I-1727. Group income elections were abolished when ACT was abolished by FA 1998.

[242] Case C-446/03 *Marks and Spencer plc v Halsey* [2006] 1 CMLR 18, [2006] EWHC 811, [2006] STC 1235 (Park J); affirmed by [2007] EWCA Civ 117, [2007] 2 CMLR 21 (now CTA 2010 ss 111–28).

[243] Case C-196/04 *Cadbury Schweppes plc v IRC* [2007] 1 CMLR 2 (now FA 2007 s 48 and sch 15).

two have, moreover, in time precipitated the Coalition's endorsement of a greater territoriality in corporate taxation,[244] as reflected in recent consultations. In the short term, the 2005 decision on losses also necessitated prudential, but pragmatic, measures to prevent deals in 'overseas losses', following the European Court's decision in *Marks and Spencer*.[245]

The reason why the initial ministerial decision in each of the European law areas is so sensitive is that each involved a trade-off between efficiency and fairness. Efficiency issues were engaged because, insofar as the impugned British legislation is concerned, a cost was imposed on the companies involved. Fairness was engaged, at the domestic level, by the need to ensure that companies continued to pay appropriate levels of corporation tax, as well as by the need to protect Britain's tax base relative to those of other EU Member States. Whatever initial decision a minister made on these priorities quickly gained its own momentum as draft legislation was put out for consultation.

C. Ensuring Prudent Decisions

Each of the three areas just discussed has involved subtly different kinds of prudence. Since practical wisdom cannot be reduced to a formula,[246] they illustrate very well the circumstantial limitations on ambitious plans for reform. They show, too, how the Wales paper and the IFS document may understate the crucial role of politics and experience in assessing the feasibility of change.

However, if a lack of context is a drawback of the two pioneering documents, a countervailing insight is their recognition of the relative roles of expertise and debate in policy initiation. This point touches on issues to be developed in the next section, about Parliament's role in the reform process. Its importance here is what it implies about the key role of expertise from the beginning. Although I would not necessarily agree with the central proposition of the IFS document that Parliament should have greater resources and more time to scrutinise tax legislation earlier,[247] I would endorse the argument that making legislative proposals is a matter for government experts in consultation with those affected. The need for strong expertise in tax policymaking is also a constant refrain in the Wales paper.[248] It has gained increased stridency because, as interviews reported by Alt, Preston and Sibieta confirm, there are increased concerns that the post-O'Donnell structure left the links between the Treasury and HMRC weakened.[249] In addition, as Bowler has reported, the new structure resulted in a

[244] HM Treasury and HMRC, *Corporate Tax Reform* (above n 58) 13; and above ch 2.

[245] *Marks and Spencer plc v Halsey* (above n 242), discussed in J Snape, 'Corporation Tax Reform: Politics and Public Law' (2007) *British Tax Review* 374, 398.

[246] Oakeshott (above n 81) 14.

[247] Tax Law Review Committee (above n 181) para 1.4.

[248] Wales, 'The Implications of the O'Donnell Review' (above n 6) 551 and 559.

[249] Alt, Preston and Sibieta (above n 38) 1214–15.

decline of the status of HMRC's 'technical knowledge' at the Treasury.[250] It is worrying because all that representative government requires is for legislative proposals to be subjected to 'argumentative scrutiny'.[251] Ill-considered reform proposals cannot therefore be allowed to gain their own momentum.

Stressing the importance of technical input does not, as is sometimes claimed, amount to government by technocracy.[252] It is simply a factor of the need for prudence. The government, as the initiator of corporate tax legislation, knows that its actions will be subject to 'the retrospective judgment' of the electorate, and this awareness should figure in ministers' tax policy counsels.[253] As Manin has said, 'Prudence dictates . . . [that the government act] now in preparation for that day of popular judgment',[254] and the apparent 'aptitude' of the responsible minister 'for making good decisions'[255] is all-important. It is rational for the government to get robust technical advice on such technical matters at the earliest stage possible.[256]

It would be fair to say that the Coalition has not offered specific reassurances on the liaison between the Treasury and HMRC.[257] This may undermine the strategic oversight intended to be provided by the Corporate Tax Reform Liaison Committee and the various ad hoc working groups referred to in the Corporate Tax Road Map,[258] each of which have been gathered within the Treasury. Certainly, Mr Gauke's decision not to limit the tax deductibility of interest payments,[259] as well as his proposal for an eventual 8 (later 5.75) per cent tax rate on finance companies otherwise caught by CFC regime legislation,[260] met with some sceptical responses, largely because of the confidentiality behind the decisions,[261] and despite the reasons for those decisions being set out in the relevant policy documentation.

[250] Bowler (above n 182) 8.
[251] Manin (above n 2) 191.
[252] F Fischer, *Technocracy and the Politics of Expertise* (London, Sage, 1990) 21–26; and CM Radaelli, *Technocracy in the European Union* (London, Longman, 1999) 149 (sets 'technocracy' in opposition to 'democracy').
[253] Manin (above n 2) 181.
[254] Ibid, 237.
[255] Ibid, 221.
[256] Lord Turnbull, Permanent Secretary to the Treasury, 1998–2002. See Timmins, '"Stalinist" Brown' (above n 19)); Thain and Christie, 'Treasury Power' (above n 7) 12; and Alt, Preston and Sibieta (above n 38) 1210.
[257] Ussher and Walford (above n 211).
[258] HM Treasury and HMRC, *Corporate Tax Reform* (above n 58) 20.
[259] Ibid, 14.
[260] Ibid, 32; and V Houlder, 'Tax Base Changes Seek to Tempt Back Multinationals' *Financial Times* (24 March 2011) 7.
[261] Anonymous, 'In the Back: Tax Avoidance: Haven sent' *Private Eye*, No 1277 (10–23 December 2010) 28; Anonymous, 'Street of Shame' *Private Eye*, No 1279 (7–20 January 2011) 7; BBC Radio 4, *The Report* (30 December 2010), details available at http://www.bbc.co.uk/Radio4 (accessed 21 February 2011) .

VI. DEVELOPING THE MEASURES

Having gone so far, it is useful to reiterate the basis of the interaction of Crown and Parliament in the process of corporate tax reform. Hobbes's point, it will be recalled, was that Leviathan – in our day, the United Kingdom of Great Britain and Northern Ireland – is something above and beyond the people. It is the '*mortal god*, to which we owe under the *immortal God*, our peace and defence',[262] and the government is its representative. It is not Parliament as such that is the sovereign but the government, and the government is the Crown-in-Parliament.[263] All of this is apparent from the close analysis to which Loughlin has subjected the historical material, especially Hobbes.[264] The sovereign's capacity to act depends on the quality of the relationship between it and the governed. That relationship, which is called sovereignty, subsists so long as the government continues to make prudent decisions in the public, or the national, interest. Such decisions do not always have to be effective. However, when accounts come to be rendered, they have to stand up as having been the most prudent decisions, taken in the national interest, at the relevant time. It is not therefore the people who are the sovereign, except when they re-elect or dismiss the government at a periodic General Election.[265] In legislating on tax policy, the government is exercising its prerogative of police. Parliament's function, as mentioned in chapter two, is either to give or to withhold its consent to the exercise of that power.[266]

It might be wondered why it is necessary to underscore these points now. The reason is that they help to give shape and significance to the development stage of corporation tax reform proposals, especially as regards the true role of Parliament in the process. Since the IFS document concentrates on only one aspect of the development stage, that of Parliamentary scrutiny, admittedly with some regard to the importance of consultation on legislative proposals, we need to turn to Dr Wales's characterisation of the second-stage elements. Wales characterises the development stage as that of the widest scope, since it is made up of 'the entire process of translating the [policy] vision into law'.[267] It was this width of scope that, under Labour, made this stage relatively volatile. The Coalition has attempted to stabilise it in the Corporate Tax Road Map, by setting out a timetable of measures for 2010 to 2014.[268]

262 Hobbes (above n 47) 112 (pt 2 ch 17).
263 Ibid.
264 Loughlin, *The Idea of Public Law* (above n 11).
265 Manin (above n 2) 234.
266 Loughlin, *Foundations of Public Law* (above n 11) 381.
267 Wales, 'The Implications of the O'Donnell Review' (above n 6) 549.
268 HM Treasury and HMRC, *Corporate Tax Reform* (above n 58) 17.

A. The Importance of Knowledge

Given my own preoccupations, the development stage is about how the prudence of an initial decision to proceed with a particular course of action needs to be replicated in that of public servants, either working alone or in co-operation with Treasury ministers. As someone with considerable experience of the demands on the individuals involved,[269] Dr Wales's points are particularly important, and it is necessary to analyse the most relevant ones rather closely. Before doing so, however, I must emphasise the link between the prudence of politicians and officials in managing tax proposals in our time, and the prudence of the architects of the institutional ordering within which they operate. Baron de Montesquieu in the 1740s described the English system of government as a 'fine system', one that 'was found in the forests'[270] – the forests 'of *Germania*, that is', rejoins Manin, '. . . which had also given birth to "Gothic" customs and the feudal system'.[271] The English system has what in early modernity was called 'the Gothic prudence':[272] a strength born of experience and of history, and with a logic of its own. There have been changes since the eighteenth century, to be sure, but – as chapter three showed – the British system is still fundamentally that which was created in the bloodshed of the seventeenth and early eighteenth centuries.[273]

These points are not merely quaint or eccentric. They provide the logic by which the feasibility of all proposals, including those of the IFS and of Christopher Wales, must be judged. Without a strong sense of history, we cannot make sense of Treasury policy, as Thain and Christie have emphasised.[274] This point is especially applicable perhaps to the proposals in the IFS document, which lack a certain historical sensitivity. It also applies to Dr Wales's, however, since, although his analysis of the Treasury's role and the functions of the old Revenue Departments reflects a keen awareness of how that part of the government works, his discussion of the role of Parliament embodies certain preconceptions that appear too in the IFS document.

For Christopher Wales, the development stage has a particular aura, and it makes exacting and specific demands, especially on expertise. I do not want to set up a black-and-white contrast between his paper and the IFS document, but there is, it seems to me, an insightfulness and a truth about this part of Dr Wales's discussion, which makes parts of the IFS document seem at best naïve

[269] Lipsey (above n 55) 126.

[270] Baron de Montesquieu, *The Spirit of the Laws* [1748], T Nugent (trans) (New York, Hafner Publishing, 1949) 161.

[271] Manin (above n 2) 90.

[272] Ibid, quoting J Harrington, 'The Prerogative of Popular Government' [1658] in JGA Pocock (ed), *The Political Works of James Harrington* (Cambridge, Cambridge University Press, 1977) 389, 477.

[273] Either – or both – 1688 or 1707 (the date of the Act of Union) can be seen as Britain's 'constitutive moment'. See Loughlin, *Foundations of Public Law* (above n 11) 261–62.

[274] Thain and Christie, 'Treasury Power' (above n 7).

and at worst, ideologically highly charged. Dr Wales first identifies the importance of discussions between senior Treasury and HMRC civil servants and Treasury ministers about translating the ideological vision into policy materials.[275] It is to be inferred that there is some overlap, some inter-fertilisation here, with the policy initiation stage, although in Dr Wales's classification, this first part of the development stage makes particular demands, both on the ministers involved and especially on the officials. The demands on civil servants become particularly prominent in what Dr Wales identifies as 'the iterative process with the ministerial team to consider how the proposals fit with the Government's broader policy objectives'.[276] The key passage is as follows:

> [T]he policy development process requires a very broad range of skills. It requires an understanding that spans the vision and the detail; to identify how the vision can be made to work within the framework of the existing system and to see where further change will be needed to allow the old and the new to work effectively together. It requires the skills of the analysts and statisticians to take the detailed proposals and assess their effect on behaviour and yield and, of course, a system that traps the necessary information and allows it to be manipulated to identify and quantify the effects of change.[277]

These points are substantially restated in Christopher Wales's contribution to the Mirrlees review.[278] It is convenient, though, to stick with this extract from 2004 and to stress that every part of it demands our closest attention. This is not only because it demonstrates an analytical subtlety far beyond the somewhat box-like assumptions on which the IFS document relies. It is unnecessary to highlight, but we should certainly note Dr Wales's encapsulation of the Machiavellian calculation in emphasising the need for skills that can comprehend the 'vision' and 'the detail'. What the opening words of the extract disclose, however, is more than this, since Dr Wales writes of 'the vision' and its being put to work within the existing system.

Although Samuel Brittan and others might want to be spared 'the vision thing',[279] Christopher Wales emphasises, in a way that is almost completely absent from the IFS discussion, the fact that what is undertaken here is the use of the corporation tax system to bring about a specific, democratically sanctioned conception of the public, or national, interest. Supreme technical ability is needed to achieve this, but it is a political, not a technocratic, project. It is about harnessing a mass of technical material to an agreed political end. This point is drawn out particularly strikingly where Dr Wales stresses the importance of technical skill in making 'the vision' work within the 'existing system' and seeing where further change will be needed.

275 D Healey, 'Why the Treasury is so Difficult' in Davies (ed) (above n 168) 53.
276 Wales, 'The Implications of the O'Donnell Review' (above n 6) 550.
277 Ibid.
278 Wales, 'Commentary' (above n 95).
279 S Brittan, 'Please Spare Us This Vision Thing' *Financial Times* (23 November 2007) 15.

Building on Labour's ideological construct of the public interest, chapter five will demonstrate in detail how deeply corporation tax has been imprinted with the ambitiousness of Labour's plans for it. Nowhere was this felt more acutely than in relation to Labour's hedging around of reform measures with anti-avoidance provisions. Policymaking in this area was taken very seriously and most often done in secret, without prior consultation.[280] 'The Government', said Ruth Kelly in the speech already referred to, was 'determined to remove avoidance opportunities as far as possible, so that all companies pay their fair share of tax and compete on a level playing field'.[281]

If the alignment of tax and accounting in the special codes on corporate finance was designed to 'fine tune' the way in which the corporation tax base is defined, then these anti-avoidance provisions were designed to prevent the tax base so defined from being manipulated in ways considered to be unacceptable. This may be the reason why Dr Wales refers to the 'effect' of policies 'on behaviour'. The special codes therefore themselves contained a broad 'general anti-avoidance rule', the well-known 'paragraph 13', which disallowed deductions attributable to so-called 'unallowable purposes'. However, of arguably much more general significance were successive anti-avoidance provisions, in generally quite separate areas, introduced in 2003, 2004 and 2005. In 2003, measures were introduced that were designed to limit corporation tax deductions for contributions to employee trusts, and Finance Act 2004 extended pre-existing legislation on transfer pricing to transactions entered into between British-resident companies. The essence of the transfer pricing provisions, which take in measures on thin capitalisation, is to require British-resident companies to enter into transactions with connected British companies on an 'arm's length' basis. Sections 306 to 319 of Finance Act 2004 also famously imposed mandatory notification requirements on the promoters of 'tax avoidance schemes', the results of which led directly to the introduction in Finance Act 2006 of four targeted anti-avoidance rules designed to prevent corporation tax avoidance through the unacceptable 'creation and use of corporate capital losses'. These measures, to which I return in chapter five, were further strengthened in Finance Act 2007. The acceptability of such measures over the long term, as the Coalition has tried to learn, depends on the care with which they are explained, argued, adjusted and justified,[282] as well as on the number and range – cumulatively speaking – of the measures involved. Suffice it to say that Labour's efforts in this direction, though inspired by fairness, were highly controversial.

Making 'the vision' work within 'the existing system' is something rather poorly understood by those who comment on tax reform in general and on the need for simplicity in the system in particular. This is not simply a matter of issues such as the formal constraints on competence imposed by the General

[280] J Isaac, 'Development of Tax Policy Formulation and Presentation: A Retrospect' (2006) *British Tax Review* 222, 223.

[281] Standing Committee F, Hansard HC vol 386 col 319 (11 June 2002).

[282] Isaac (above n 280).

Agreement on Tariffs and Trade (GATT) 1994/WTO and/or European law. One of many memorable points made by Murphy and Nagel in *The Myth of Ownership*[283] (and one to which we shall return) is that tax policy is never about 'tax design'; it is always about reform, because it always has to take account of the existing system. In placing emphasis on the history, this study seeks to reflect an understanding of this insight. What Murphy and Nagel do not say, however, is that reform creates avoidance opportunities, something that has encouraged governments to hold back from large-scale reform of their tax systems.[284] Secondly, to the extent that radical political change must for all these good reasons be accommodated within existing institutional and conceptual structures, 'complexity' is inevitable. Only lack of change, lack of intervention, makes things simple. This is why simplification arguments have often come from neoliberals on the libertarian Right.[285]

In relation to the foregoing extract from Dr Wales's paper, we might finally draw attention, again harking back to Murphy and Nagel, to the emphasis in the last part of the extract on the importance of information in weighing ends and means. Murphy and Nagel rightly speak, in an engaging phrase, of 'large empirical uncertainties about the economic consequences of [the] different choices'[286] involved in tax policymaking. That is not, however, to deny the importance of such information as there is. This strand is drawn out by Dr Wales in his reference to 'the skills of the analysts and statisticians',[287] whose projections are the basis of political calculation. John McEldowney has written persuasively about the contribution to the development of public law of 'the statistical movement',[288] and we may note in passing the link between 'political arithmetick'[289] and political economy on which rests, in a sense, the whole matter of the present study. It is in this part of the corporation tax policy development process, in the weighing of ends and means, however, that statistical work comes into its own.

[283] Murphy and Nagel (above n 53).

[284] Tiley (above n 35) 16 (6th edn, 16).

[285] G Howe, 'Reform of Taxation Machinery' (1977) *British Tax Review* 97; G Howe, 'Simplicity and Stability: The Politics of Tax Policy' (2001) *British Tax Review* 113; G Howe, 'Can 364 Economists all be Wrong?' in Davies (ed) (above n 168) 76, esp 101; and Steger and Roy (above n 13) 19–20 and passim.

[286] Murphy and Nagel (above n 53) 4.

[287] Cabinet Office, *The 46th Civil Service Yearbook* (2007) 233–35.

[288] JF McEldowney, *Public Law*, 3rd edn (London, Sweet and Maxwell 2002) paras 8-058a–8-067; and JF McEldowney and S McEldowney, *Environmental Law and Regulation* (London, Blackstone Press, 2001) 21–23. See generally, W Petty, 'A Treatise of Taxes & Contributions' in CH Hull (ed), *The Economic Writings of Sir William Petty*: together with the *Observations upon the Bills of Mortality* more probably by Captain John Graunt [1662], 2 vols (New York, AM Kelley, 1963 and 1964) I 1.

[289] JGA Pocock, *The Machiavellian Moment: Florentine Political Thought and the Atlantic Republican Tradition* (Princeton, Princeton University Press, 1975) 425n.

B. Consultation and Deliberation

The end towards which statistical information and modelling techniques and, indeed, political prudence are directed, of course, is effectiveness. All the corporate tax reform proposals in the world are nothing if they do not work towards the realisation of the vision of the public, or national, interest that the governing party has put before the electorate. Christopher Wales's reference to making 'the old and the new . . . work effectively together' is what encapsulates the significance of the remaining elements in policy development. These are the importance of effective parliamentary liaison and, rather less prominent in Wales than in the IFS document, consultation. There could be little argument about the importance of effective liaison, in other words, with the need for Treasury and HMRC to work effectively with parliamentary counsel 'to ensure that the legislation, when enacted, will achieve the policy intent'.[290] Neither would anyone be likely to dispute the importance of successfully 'handling of the Parliamentary process itself' or 'the provision of support for ministers in the House'.[291] However, each of the two areas does give rise to issues of discussion, which I would like to defer until I consider the role of Parliament in the development stage. As to consultation, however, this does require some close consideration at this point. There are two reasons for this. First, the relativity of its importance to effectiveness, and secondly, its significance as a place where the governance dilemmas already examined[292] are played out.

A commitment to consultation is certainly accorded prominence in the Coalition's Corporate Tax Road Map.[293] The Road Map was in fact published alongside details of the three longstanding consultations already referred to: on CFCs, on the taxation of overseas branches and on the taxation of intellectual property rights. This is no doubt proof positive of Christopher Wales' comment in 2009 that 'the culture of consultation has become well embedded among the tax policy teams'.[294] To the extent that this is so, it is something of a tribute to the personal commitment of Malcolm Gammie. To illustrate this, I think it is worth giving a flavour of the changes to consultation that have taken place over about 20 years.

There had certainly been consultation processes[295] – even before the introduction of the FOREX legislation in Finance Act 1993 – but, as Mr Gammie pointed out in an influential 1988 lecture, 'draft legislation . . . [had] not [been]

[290] Wales, 'The Implications of the O'Donnell Review' (above n 6) 550.

[291] Ibid.

[292] See above ch 3.

[293] HM Treasury and HMRC, *Corporate Tax Reform* (above n 58) 19; and Ussher and Walford (above n 211) 51–54.

[294] Wales, 'The Making of Tax Policy in the Post-O'Donnell World' (above n 178) 245.

[295] M Gammie, *The Enactment of Tax Legislation: An Analysis of the Consultative Process and the Finance Acts 1979 to 1987* (London, Law Society of England and Wales, 1988).

produced, often because the timetable for change . . . [was] too short'.[296] The FOREX legislation marked something of a departure in this respect. Consultation on the way in which FOREX gains and losses should be treated for tax purposes, the result of which was the Finance Act 1993 rules, had begun four years before, within a year of Mr Gammie's lecture. Consultation on the tax treatment of 'swap' fees began the same year. 1991 saw the publication of a consultative document on financial instruments,[297] the result of which were the provisions included in Finance Act 1994. And on a brisk morning in November 1995,[298] practitioners – or, more accurately, one suspects, their trainees and out-door clerks' – waited outside Somerset House for the distribution of copies of *The Taxation of Gilts and Bonds: A Consultative Document*,[299] the deliberations on which led in turn to the loan relationships code in Finance Act 1996. In fact, even the 2002 remodelling of the special codes discussed above was preceded by at least four separate discussion documents.

A second example of this more extensive approach to consultation might be the series of documents that eventually led to the 2004 extension of the transfer pricing and thin capitalisation rules. The process began in August 2002, with a consultation document[300] canvassing views on the corporation tax treatment of capital assets, both as to the possibility of assimilating capital and income gains, along the lines of the special codes on corporate finance, and abolishing the concept of capital allowances; the removal of the distinction between trading and investment companies;[301] and – a radical suggestion at that stage – the 'rationalisation' of the 'Schedular' system itself. The 2002 document, which, so the government reported, had attracted in excess of 150 written replies,[302] was followed by a further document almost exactly a year later. This requested further comments on a narrower range of issues than those in the paper of 2002, albeit in the same three areas. However, the government also announced its intentions with regard to the reform of transfer pricing and thin capitalisation and requested views on those areas too. To this document, the government received 147 'substantive written responses',[303] and in a technical note of December 2003, it published draft legislation on the two areas that it was at that

[296] M Gammie, 'The Process of Fiscal Reform in the United Kingdom' (1989) *British Tax Review* 252, 256. The 1965 introduction of corporation tax was with virtually no consultation: Hansard HC cols 1322–24 (8 December 1964).

[297] Inland Revenue, *Financial Instruments: The Tax Treatment of Financial Instruments for Managing Interest Rate Risk* (London, Board of Inland Revenue, 1991).

[298] R Ballard and B Staveley, 'New Relationships: Part 1' *Tax Journal* (7 December 1995) 4.

[299] Inland Revenue, *The Taxation of Gilts and Bonds* (above n 223).

[300] HM Treasury and Inland Revenue, *Reform of Corporation Tax: A Consultation Document* (London, Inland Revenue, 2002).

[301] Eg, N Lee (ed), *Revenue Law: Principles and Practice*, 24th edn (Haywards Heath, Tottel, 2006) paras 41.22, 41.47–41.49, ch 48 and para 41.71.

[302] HM Treasury and Inland Revenue, *Corporation Tax Reform: A Consultation Document* (London, Inland Revenue, 2003) 1.

[303] Inland Revenue, *Corporation Tax Reform: The Next Steps (Inland Revenue Technical Note, December 2003)* (London, Inland Revenue, 2003) para 1.2.

time inclined to carry forward: transfer pricing and thin capitalisation, as well as changes to the rules for the deduction of management expenses. Drafted in 'the modern style developed by the Tax Law Rewrite project', these clauses became, without significant amendment, the Finance Act 2004 provisions mentioned above. In relation to the other matters raised for consultation in the 2002 document, a December 2004 technical note brought forward draft clauses to replace the corporation tax Schedules with a single set of rules for a company's 'operating business'. The third proposal made in 2002, namely reforming the corporation tax treatment of capital assets, was put on hold, and as matters turned out, the 'operating business' concept did not make it to either of the Finance Acts of 2005. Ironically, although capital allowances reform was taken up again in 2007, a significant part of this, the abolition of industrial buildings allowances, was effected without warning,[304] consultation being confined to a set of proposals designed to reduce 'the distortive impact' of such allowances.

Christopher Wales does not focus on the importance of consultation, although he does acknowledge the special nature of the 'presentational skills' involved in 'a formal process of public consultation'.[305] Mr Gammie, whose views seem to be deeply embedded in the findings of the IFS document, does do so, however, and in the process evinces a slight change of position from his earlier work on the importance of consultation. The IFS document promulgates the view that the emphasis on consultation places Parliament too far back in the process, and proposals are too far down the line by the time they reach the House of Commons.[306] With respect, this seems to betray a fundamental misunderstanding of the constitutional role of Parliament. The IFS document laments most of all a lack of 'uniformity' in the consultation process,[307] but in a slightly obscure passage, it also concedes that consultation periods and forms need to be 'tailored'.[308] We shall return to the constitutional misunderstanding presently. But there seems also to be a failure to appreciate that the only reason for consultation is prudence, the need to make provisions work effectively, and that effectiveness might actually require less consultation in some cases, and more in others.

The former point, which is related to the governance issue to be discussed in a moment, is in a way acknowledged within the document, because the IFS is interested in making tax legislation work better, although with insufficient emphasis on its political purpose. The latter point, however, is elided. Given that the watchword is prudence – how best to attain the political end – the reform project in question might not be such as to lend itself to consultation. If

[304] A necessarily unattributable story circulating among practitioners at the time was that, in a meeting between Gordon Brown and his advisers, it had been found that the abolition of the allowances would raise an amount of revenue roughly equal to a shortfall that needed to be met elsewhere. Industrial buildings allowances therefore bit the dust.

[305] Inland Revenue, *Corporation Tax Reform: The Next Steps* (above n 303).

[306] Tax Law Review Committee (above n 181) para 4.5.

[307] Ibid, para 3.3.

[308] Ibid, paras 3.4 and 5.2.

we consider the issues raised by the process of aligning tax with accounts, or indeed by the introduction of CTSA, what is prudent is the building up of a broad base of support over a long period of time, in an atmosphere of as much transparency as supports the public interest.[309] Each of the initiatives in these two areas have been successful,[310] and this broad, deep form of consultation, being prudent in the circumstances, has worked. In other cases, however, especially those involving anti-avoidance measures, the activities that the government seeks to curtail will be the province of opportunists, for whom transparency would merely make matters easier. In such cases, prudence declares for no consultation, effectiveness requiring swift action.

Not all cases are easy to judge, however. One good illustration, albeit not from the corporate tax arena, is the 2008 abolition of the 10p income tax rate.[311] Another might be the unexpected 1997 changes to the taxation of company distributions,[312] especially as those changes impacted on pension funds, something that returned to haunt Gordon Brown in the 2010 General Election campaign.[313] The Corporate Tax Road Map, specifically its claim that consultation should be the norm, has signalled a determination to avoid this sort of policy reversal, whereby, as Wales says, 'proposals . . . have been subject to major change during the process between announcement and enactment'.[314] It remains to be seen whether, in publishing not only the Road Map itself but within it a timetable of reform in which draft legislation is normally published at set stages, the Coalition has been over-ambitious. The New Approach, in accordance with the 2008 Howe report,[315] suggested a convention, under which most tax law changes would take effect only three months after their announcement and would be accompanied by draft legislation.[316]

Failing to match the length and depth of consultation to the prudential requirements of the situation is only part of the way in which the discussion in the IFS document is skewed. Prudence has a part to play in another area, although it is a slightly different one. I have touched briefly on this point at the end of the previous section. The consultation stage, I would suggest, is the point at which the five governance dilemmas discussed in chapter three come into play. The reasoning in an individual case might go as follows. The Treasury might

309 Lipsey (above n 55) 88.

310 C Giles, 'Master of Illusion's Debt Vanishing Act' *Financial Times* (21 October 2005) 3.

311 G Parker, 'Brown Weakened by 10p Tax Climbdown' *Financial Times* (24 April 2008) 1.

312 FA 1998 s 31 and sch 3; W Keegan, *The Prudence of Mr Gordon Brown* (Chichester, John Wiley, 2003) 140, 194 and 260; and Peston (above n 28) 101.

313 J Greenwood, 'Defuse Your Pensions "Time Bomb"' *Daily Telegraph* (2 April 2010), available at http://www.telegraph.co.uk/finance/personalfinance/pensions/7546765/Defuse-your-pensions-time-bomb.html (accessed 20 June 2011). See further, C Sanger, 'Corporate Tax Road Map' (2011) *British Tax Review* 2, 5 (retrospective abolition of industrial buildings allowances).

314 Wales, 'The Making of Tax Policy in the Post-O'Donnell World' (above n 178) 246; and Mirrlees, Adam and Besley et al (above n 80) 8.

315 Lord Howe (Chair), *Making Taxes Simpler: The Final Report of a Working Party Chaired by Lord Howe of Aberavon* (London, Conservative Party, 2008) 1.

316 HM Treasury and HMRC, *Tax Policymaking: A New Approach* (above n 57) 8; and Ussher and Walford (above n 211) 44.

approve of what, say, the IASB has to say about profits measurement, and it might be convenient to translate it into tax law; but the informed electorate might not approve if they knew the influence of this non-elected, relatively unaccountable body. The matter probably will not become important, provided there is no risk, and there is unlikely to be if the government legislates to modify the IASB's rules where necessary.[317] The Treasury might, in the process of adopting this solution, become over-reliant on the accountancy profession, but if it listens to them, the Treasury might gain their influential support. To do so, the Treasury will have to work within a policy network – but, again, in a relatively low-risk policy area, so the unaccountability of some of the individuals involved is probably not overly important. There is some risk, nonetheless, that any added technical complexity might discredit the policy, but in an already complex area, this is unlikely to make much difference. At each stage, as Manin might infer, the questions are: Is the decision taken the most prudent of those available? And is it demonstrably in the public, or national, interest? If not, on either count, and there are adverse consequences, the government's credibility will be affected. Such must be the considerations going through the mind of the minister signing a – usually very brief – regulatory impact assessment, once the process of consultation on corporation tax reform measures is complete.

I have deliberately chosen a neutral and hypothetical example to make my previous point, but this issue could become ever more present with the involvement in strategic oversight of the Corporate Tax Reform Liaison Committee. Not only is its membership far from uncontroversial, but it may be that the apparently prudential idea of publicising its deliberations is not enough to dispel lingering doubts about the nature and extent of its influence in shaping the public, or national, interest.[318]

C. The Consent of Parliament

The part of the development stage to which Christopher Wales gives the least detailed consideration, and one that the O'Donnell Report did not consider, forms the subject matter of what is a relatively weak part of Dr Wales's otherwise robust analysis. This is Wales' discussion of the role of Parliament in corporate tax reform. Much more consideration is given to this in the IFS document. However, I would disagree with both analyses on this point, and for generally similar reasons. The yardstick of strength or weakness here is not the prudence of today's decision-makers, nor yet of some exogenous norm, but the prudence of the ages: the prudence that was found 'in the forests of Germania'.

Before exploring this issue in detail, we should refer to the fact that Dr Wales places much more emphasis than does the IFS on the contribution of effective

[317] CTA 2009 s 46(1) (formerly FA 1998 s 42(1)).

[318] HM Treasury and HMRC, *Corporate Tax Reform* (above n 58) 20.

mutual understanding and close co-operation between officials in the relevant department and parliamentary counsel,[319] both in terms of the drafting of instructions to counsel and their interpretation.[320] The IFS has nothing complimentary to say about the drafting of tax legislation. Secondly, Dr Wales obliquely pays tribute to the accumulated experience, by 2004, of Labour's Treasury ministers.[321] The IFS makes no mention of them. But anyone who has read the contributions to Standing (or latterly, Public Bill) Committee debates by the ministers involved – Labour or Coalition – would be impressed by the intellectual grasp of people who do not always have legal training,[322] and on the effectiveness of the public servants briefing them.

The first of the ways in which both Christopher Wales's contribution and that of the IFS seem to underestimate the constitutional theory is in relation to the 'effective [Parliamentary] scrutiny' of legislation. Dr Wales thinks it is 'weak';[323] the IFS, furthermore, claims that 'the House of Commons fails to scrutinise the rules (if not the levels) of taxation in any real sense at all'.[324] Within the logic of the system, it has to be said that neither comment is justified. It is not simply the fact that in each Parliamentary session for the last decade many columns of Hansard have been devoted to Finance Bill debate.[325] It is, more importantly, that representative democracy requires only that legislative proposals be subject to 'argumentative scrutiny'.[326] More fully, what representative democracy insists on is that 'no measure can be adopted unless a majority deems it *justified* after argumentative scrutiny'.[327] Although the IFS deprecates both the nature and the scope of argument in the Commons, not to say the 'scrutiny', involved, Dr Wales obviously regards Finance Bill debates as a significant challenge to the ministers and public servants involved, because he earlier emphasises the gruelling nature of the exchanges:

[319] T Daintith and A Page, *The Executive in the Constitution: Structure, Autonomy and Internal Control* (Oxford, Oxford University Press, 1999) 221; and Cabinet Office, *The 46th Civil Service Yearbook* (above n 287) 237.

[320] Wales, 'The Implications of the O'Donnell Review' (above n 6) 557.

[321] Ibid, 560; and Thain and Christie, *Parliamentary Brief* (above n 169).

[322] David Gauke is a former City solicitor. The Treasury ministers who were 'sacked' in 2007 when Gordon Brown took office as Prime Minister had considerable combined experience, all having been long-serving in their roles. Dawn Primarolo, in Lipsey's words (above n 55), 'a former left-winger who looks and sounds like a faintly flustered Sunday-school teacher', was nonetheless a 'safe pair of hands' (25) and 'bore the bulk of the burden' of 'tax responsibilities' (126) as Paymaster General throughout most of the period covered by this study.

[323] Wales, 'The Implications of the O'Donnell Review' (above n 6) 563.

[324] Tax Law Review Committee (above n 181) para 2.4.

[325] Statistics on the length of standing committee debates on FBs in Hansard are striking: FB 1997, 9 sittings, 509 cols; F(No 2)B 1998, 23 sittings, 1063 cols; FB 1999, 19 sittings, 787 cols; FB 2000, 26 sittings, 1051 cols; FB 2001, 7 sittings, 221 cols; FB 2002, 16 sittings, 579 cols; FB 2003, 15 sittings, 633 cols; FB 2004, 21 sittings, 777 cols; FB 2005, 8 sittings, 319 cols; F(No 2)B 2005, 21 sittings, 785 cols; FB 2007, 14 sittings, 525 cols. It would not therefore be correct to say that there is no scrutiny of FB clauses. See also Riddell (above n 192) 1290.

[326] Manin (above n 2) 191.

[327] Ibid.

> In our Parliament's confrontational process, the officials involved [namely, civil servants advising ministers] need to be able to identify the issues that the Opposition are likely to target and prepare and provide appropriate briefing and support . . . [T]his is a matter of linking policy objectives to detail. Technical analysis on its own is not sufficient and neither is pure policy advice.[328]

As has Manin said, the seventeenth- and eighteenth-century 'English aristocrats and French lawyers'[329] who invented representative government 'certainly did not confuse a parliament with a learned society'.[330] Occasionally, it is true, debate seems somewhat perfunctory, but often (such as in the case of the Standing Committee debate on the Finance Bill 1998 measures on CTSA)[331] this is explained by the context (there, the continuing legislative euphoria following the 1997 landslide election victory). More frequently, as in the case of the Standing Committee proceedings on the second 2005 Finance Bill[332] clauses on the intra-Community surrender of group losses, both the knowledge and engagement of the participants rather impresses.[333] More of a problem, little underscored in the literature, is the use of the 'guillotine' to curtail debate,[334] but the institution itself recognises this as an expedient, which is why the occasions on which the 'guillotine' is used are carefully minuted.[335]

The crux of the matter appears, as Manin has pointed out, in the following words of Emmanuel Joseph Sieyes, who explains why the will of the majority in Parliament is an expression of the public interest:

> Without doubt the general interest[336] is nothing if it is not the interest of someone: it is that particular interest that is common to the greatest number of voters. From this comes the necessity of the competition of opinions.[337]

The point only needs to be read for its importance to be clear. 'Public decision' is the result of 'trial by discussion', plus 'majority consent'.[338] So the national interest and the public interest are closely correspondent ideas. For Manin, this means:

[328] Wales, 'The Implications of the O'Donnell Review' (above n 6) 550.

[329] Manin (above n 2) 234.

[330] Ibid, 190.

[331] Standing Committee E, Hansard HC vol 332 cols 704–12 (9 June 1998).

[332] F(No 2)B 2005 became FA 2006.

[333] Standing Committee A, Hansard HC vol 446 cols 159–79 (16 May 2006).

[334] Standing Orders (SOs) Nos 83, 83A–83I; W McKay et al (eds), *Erskine May's Treatise on The Law, Privileges, Proceedings and Usage of Parliament*, 23rd edn (London, LexisNexis UK, 2004) (hereafter 'Erskine May') 466; and I Ferrier, 'Tax Editor's Notes (July/August)' (2003) *Conveyancer and Property Lawyer* 346.

[335] House of Commons Information Office Factsheet P10, *Programming of Government Bills* (London, UK Parliament, 2004), available at http://www.parliament.uk/factsheets (accessed 20 June 2011).

[336] See above nn 119 and 120; and accompanying text.

[337] EJ Sieyes, *Vues sur les moyens d'exécution dont les représentants de la France pourront disposer en 1789* (Paris, anonymous publisher, 1789) 92, quoted in Manin (above n 2) 188. See also Burke (above n 108) 156, also cited in Manin (above n 2) 187n).

[338] Manin (above n 2) 190.

> (1) parliamentary debate does not constitute a disinterested activity, oriented solely by the search for the truth, but a process that aims to identify the interest common to the greatest number,[339] and (2) the general interest, unlike Rousseau's 'general will',[340] does not transcend particular interests and is not of a different nature than them.[341]

To similar effect had been the conclusion of John Locke in the seventeenth century,[342] and Jeremy Waldron in the twentieth.[343] If the idea of the sanctity of argumentative scrutiny indeed reflects the logic of the system, then few of the arguments put forward by the IFS seem relevant: that the House of Commons lacks the time to scrutinise Finance Bills adequately; that it lacks the 'inclination' to do so; and – most perversely – that it lacks the requisite 'expertise'.[344] If it is objected, even in the face of so many pages of Hansard devoted to debating corporation tax reform proposals, that scrutiny is nonetheless inadequate, it is necessary to turn only to John Stuart Mill. Mill, in Manin's analysis,

> . . . suggested that propositions of laws [*sic*] be drafted by a commission of experts appointed by the Crown and then brought before Parliament only for discussion and approval. He even went so far as to deny Parliament the right to amend the commission's propositions in the course of discussion. Mill wrote: '[The bill] once framed, however, Parliament should have no power to alter the measure, but only to pass or reject it; or, if partially disapproved of, remit it back to the Commission for reconsideration.' According to Mill, the principal function of the debating body should be to grant or withhold 'the final seal of national assent' after a public exchange of arguments, not to conceive and formulate legislative measures.[345]

This obviously contrasts with the IFS's disapproval of legislative proposals being brought before Parliament as 'faits accomplis',[346] and it sits ill, too, with its rather dogmatic assertion that 'consultation is not and should not become a substitute for Parliamentary scrutiny'.[347] It does, however, fit well with the kind of debate referred to above, on the surrender of losses between EU Member States, as well as the *Marks and Spencer* litigation that had just been before Park J in the Chancery Division.[348] There, Mark Hoban made a carefully analytical and measured contribution to the debate; and even the Opposition backbench disagreement on the point of principle,[349] as led by one David Gauke,

339 See Arendt (above n 70) on the significance of 'inter-est'; and Barry (above n 112) ch 10.

340 For Rousseau, 'the general will' was 'the first principle of the public economy and the fundamental rule of government': J-J Rousseau, *Discourse on Political Economy and The Social Contract* [1755/1762], C Betts (trans and ed) (Oxford, Oxford University Press, 1994) 9 (in 'Discourse on Political Economy') 73. Rousseau deplored (England's) representative government (127).

341 Manin (above n 2) 188n.

342 Ibid, 189n, quoting Locke (above n 1) 142.

343 J Waldron, *The Dignity of Legislation* (Cambridge, Cambridge University Press, 1999) ch 4.

344 See Wales, 'The Implications of the O'Donnell Review' (above n 6) 563; and Isaac (above n 280) 224. But it is the fact of having been elected, not expertise, that qualifies an MP to legislate.

345 Manin (above n 2) 191, quoting Mill (above n 119) 280 and 283.

346 Tax Law Review Committee (above n 181) para 3.8.

347 Ibid, para 3.9.

348 Snape, 'Corporation Tax Reform' (above n 245) 399.

349 Ibid, 395–96.

was a vivid illustration of the 'argumentative scrutiny' that representative democracy requires.[350]

That first group of arguments mounted by both Dr Wales and the IFS is about the nature and extent of parliamentary scrutiny. Both go on to argue that each aspect would be facilitated by the allocation of greater resources to this aspect. Dr Wales advocates the introduction of an 'adaptation' of the US Congressional Budget Office, which provides Congress with 'the objective, timely, non-partisan analyses needed for economic and budget decisions',[351] suggesting that 'it would surely improve the process of scrutiny that tax proposals undergo in Parliament'.[352] Somewhat less ambitiously, the IFS argues for more resources, including the institution of a new select committee and a 'team' to work on 'tax structure'.[353] There is, however, an historical and logical objection to these superficially sensible suggestions. Unlike the US Congress, 'Parliament is not the forum of public discussion. Each party is grouped around a leading figure, and each parliamentary party votes in a disciplined manner in support of its leader.'[354] In short, therefore, sensible as it sounds, this suggestion ignores the significance of the still crucial concept of party discipline. Nonetheless, circumstances may by now have so changed as to suggest that its advantages outweigh the disadvantages, and it is not subject to the same a priori objections as some other suggestions about the reform process. Whether the formation of the 2010 Coalition is a factor of such change remains to be seen, especially if voting patterns shift following any introduction of the alternative vote system for electing MPs.[355]

If, on this historical and interpretative basis, Dr Wales and the IFS are wrong on each of the foregoing questions, then perhaps a third argument, somewhat common to both, might stand further analysis. Dr Wales offers the idea that the House of Lords could perhaps undertake 'a greater level of scrutiny' of Finance Bills, arguing that 'the problem of a lack of effective scrutiny of tax law proposals in the Commons has been compounded by the convention that the House of Lords has a very limited role in relation to Finance Bills'.[356] On this point, the IFS is rather more cautious: it suggests that a joint committee of Lords and Commons 'would not infringe the current prerogatives of the House of Commons in tax

[350] Standing Committee A, Hansard HC vol 446 cols 159–79 (May 16 2006).

[351] Wales, 'The Implications of the O'Donnell Review' (above n 6) 563, quoting the Congressional Budget Office's Mission Statement, available at http://www.4uth.gov.ua/usa/english/politics/legbranc/agencies/cbo.html (18 July 2011).

[352] Wales, 'The Implications of the O'Donnell Review' (above n 6) 564; and Ussher and Walford (above n 211) 40–41.

[353] Tax Law Review Committee (above n 181) paras 1.4, 6.2 and 7.6.

[354] Manin (above n 2) 231.

[355] M Wolf, 'Why We Should Choose the Alternative Vote' *Financial Times* (25 February 2011) 15; B Johnson, 'AV Was a Last Gasp from Brown's Bunker – And It's a Gigantic Fraud' *Daily Telegraph* (28 February 2011) 22; and J Pickard, 'More than 100 Labour MPs Defy Miliband on Alternative Vote' *Financial Times* (17 March 2011) 6.

[356] Wales, 'The Implications of the O'Donnell Review' (above n 6) 564.

legislation'[357] but goes on to suggest that, even if such a committee was constituted solely from the House of Commons, this 'would not prevent the House of Lords establishing its own Committee on Taxation'.[358] The problem, however, is that the House of Lords is not elected.[359] Election – that is, representation – is the quid pro quo for taxation, not taxation expertise.

In this light, it is encouraging that the rather obfuscatorily named House of Lords Select Committee on Economic Affairs has encountered difficulties in enlisting co-operation from officials on tax matters, and rather surprising that Dr Wales should find this state of affairs so unsatisfactory.[360] He may be right that 'a reformed House of Lords might be in a position to make a stronger claim',[361] but this too would depend on the Lords being an elected representative assembly.[362] Furthermore, it is a little disingenuous for the IFS to suggest that the taxation subcommittee of the House of Lords Select Committee on Economic Affairs might provide some kind of antecedent for its proposed committee.[363] The Lords Committee, as its name suggests, is a Select Committee and as such is concerned only with the ex post scrutiny of tax legislation.

Christopher Wales puts one other argument that we might put aside, if did it not illustrate so well Loughlin's point that sovereignty is not competence alone, but constituent power – competence enlarged by capacity. Although he does not make it a large part of his argument, Dr Wales makes the point:

> [I]n the last twenty years, there have been very few Finance Bills that meet all the requirements of the definition as [*sic*] a money bill.[364] So, in reality, if the House of Lords had wanted to intervene in Finance Bill debates, it would probably have been able to do so.[365]

Even allowing that the premise were true, readers who have followed the argument of this study so far will appreciate that precisely the opposite is the case. In *theory*, the House of Lords might have been able to intervene. In 'reality', any such intervention might have precipitated the abolition of the Chamber.

What I find so strange in both the Wales and the IFS accounts is that both betray a fundamental unwillingness to entrust tax legislation to the House of Commons, and a commensurate willingness – without any obvious basis,

[357] Tax Law Review Committee (above n 181) para 6.3.

[358] Ibid, para 6.5.

[359] Except in the limited sense provided for by the House of Lords Act 1999: Ministry of Justice, *The Governance of Britain* (Cm 7170, 2007) 41; and J Eaglesham, 'Lords Reform Slips off Labour Priorities' *Financial Times* (20 July 2007) 2.

[360] Wales, 'The Implications of the O'Donnell Review' (above n 6) 564.

[361] Ibid.

[362] Ministry of Justice (above n 359) 42; and E Rigby, 'Lords Reform could See Elected Senators by 2015' *Financial Times* (10 March 2011) 3.

[363] Tax Law Review Committee (above n 181) para 6.5.

[364] Parliament Act 1911 (as amended by Parliament Act 1949) s 1(2). See also P Jackson and P Leopold (eds), *O Hood Phillips & Jackson: Constitutional and Administrative Law*, 8th edn (London, Sweet and Maxwell, 2001) para 8-034; and Erskine May (above n 334) 928.

[365] Wales, 'The Implications of the O'Donnell Review' (above n 6) 564.

especially not an historical one – to enlist the help of the House of Lords.[366] This, combined with the Lords' difficulties in establishing a legitimate claim to interfere, not just in corporate taxation matters but in tax matters generally, would explain both Mr Gammie's demeanour, already noted, before the Lords' Economic Affairs Committee, as well as the Committee's own fulsome appreciation of his contribution to their deliberations.[367] Distinguished and influential as Mr Gammie deservedly is, it is difficult to understand the foundations of his sympathies on this question. The same comment applies to Christopher Wales's views on the Lords' role. Regrettably, too, it applies to the Chartered Institute of Taxation's 2010 report on the tax legislative process, where it is stated that the exclusion of the House of Lords from the making of tax law is one of a number of 'restrictive parliamentary protocols', and unfortunate given 'the expertise of peers' in these matters.[368] What we see in the debates on the Finance Bills is democracy in action – or more accurately and rather significantly – representative democracy in action. The right of elected representatives of the people to argue about matters of taxation applies even, perhaps especially, to corporate taxation.

VII. PRESENTATION OF REFORM MEASURES

With the conclusions of the previous section in mind, it is possible to make some relatively brief comments on Dr Wales's own rather concise treatment of the third and fourth stages of the reform process. '[A] significant omission' from the O'Donnell Report was its failure, in Dr Wales's view, to identify 'policy presentation as an important part of the [reform] process'.[369] In practice, the presentation of reform measures, allowing (as it does) for 'a more detailed engagement between officials and those affected by the new policy', has been a common feature of the reform process 'over the last few years'.[370]

Perceptively, Christopher Wales portrays both what was once the Pre-Budget Report (PBR) and is now the Autumn Statement, and indeed the Budget Report itself, not as part of the legislative process but as part of the political process of presenting reform proposals to the electorate.[371] It is certainly possible to infer that one effect of combining successive announcements of increases in economic growth with publishing decisions on corporate tax reform has been that the former has energised the latter. In other words, that the combined announce-

[366] See Anonymous, 'Called to Ordure' *Private Eye*, No 1281 (4–17 February 2011) 8, on the 'filibustering' of what became the Parliamentary Voting System and Constituencies Act 2011.

[367] Select Committee on Economic Affairs, *4th Report: The Finance Bill 2007, Volume II: Evidence* (HL 2006–07, 121) 5.

[368] Chartered Institute of Taxation, *The Making of Tax Law: Proposals for Reform from the Chartered Institute of Taxation* (June 2010) 4; and Ussher and Walford (above n 211) 39.

[369] Wales, 'The Implications of the O'Donnell Review' (above n 6) 548.

[370] Ibid, 550.

[371] Ibid; and Lipsey (above n 55) ch 7 (esp 120 and 130).

ments on either occasion are a crucial way of building up the government's capacity in relation to taxation policy. Whilst the IFS document takes the PBR as the start of the legislative process,[372] Dr Wales's analysis of its significance as a presentational one therefore seems the more persuasive. It also, somewhat paradoxically, squares with the more general idea that Parliament is not 'a learned society'.[373] Dr Wales is surely right, too, in his premise as to the administrative significance of the presentation stage.

In terms of the requirements of representative government, confronting the electorate with the legislation itself has a crucial importance. Manin regards the interaction of Parliament with the world outside as being a function of whether our current system is viewed primarily as a 'party democracy' or as an 'audience democracy'.[374] If the former, then there is a sense in which the law is 'handed down' to the people most closely affected by the reform measure in question. If the latter, then '[t]he extra-parliamentary voice of the people . . . [is] made . . . more peaceful and rendered commonplace',[375] and there is a sense in which it is 'passed across the table'. As already suggested, Britain's system now has features of both 'party democracy' and 'audience democracy', and much may depend on the potential for conflict suggested by the measures in question. Measures combatting tax avoidance, especially when previously unannounced, fall into the former category, with matters relating to the alignment of tax and accounts falling into the latter. It would be tempting to push the point too far, but as will become apparent in the next chapter, to the extent that anti-avoidance measures purport to further a particular and contentious concept of fairness, they bear the hallmark of party democracy – one that is held up for inspection by a constituency more used to being treated with a degree of respect.

In either case, judging what prudence requires, in terms of 'a more detailed engagement between officials and [taxpayers]' or 'ministerial visits and speeches'[376] is clearly of crucial importance. It may be a prudence of a lesser scope, involving conversation and dialogue, but it too has the objective of advancing the public, or national, interest.

VIII. DELIVERY OF THE MEASURES

With this final stage in the evolution of corporate tax reform measures, the spotlight falls, in administrative terms, exclusively on the contribution of the junior Department to the Treasury, HMRC. We are here edging towards the parameters of the study, but we can nonetheless comment usefully on one or two aspects.

372 Tax Law Review Committee (above n 181) para 4.1.
373 Manin (above n 2) 190.
374 See above ch 3.
375 Manin (above n 2) 231.
376 Wales, 'The Implications of the O'Donnell Review' (above n 6) 550.

This is an experiential and practical stage,[377] the chief element being 'the issue of detailed guidance for taxpayers and the revenue department's own network'.[378] It is therefore where the increased publication of technical materials comes into its own, but it may also involve, as Dr Wales mentions, 'audit and investigation' in the case of new anti-avoidance measures.[379] Furthering the national, or public, interest, as sanctioned by Parliament, can indeed be the only justification for time spent in audit or in settling the HMRC guidance documents, without which, it is to be suspected, the system would not work. It still involves management though and, with this, a certain prudence, since it entails engaging with the practising tax profession.

Delivery involves myriad prudential calculations about the priorities and interests of professional society (who, after all, have mortgages and school fees to pay),[380] as well as the standing of the legal and accountancy professions in society. The former is the subject of a considerable literature; the taxation context of the latter is beginning to be noted.[381] Tax professionals' expertise is at one and the same time useful to the Department and mystifying to people in general. This was one reason why, for example, the *Guardian* newspaper's flawed reporting of the tax avoidance industry in 2009 met with such a critical response from tax professionals.[382] The professionals themselves, though widely regarded with some wariness, are valued by those who understand what they do. These factors together are the raw materials of the government's prudential calculations.

We might finally note that although this fourth stage is largely the province of HMRC, the judiciary's role in interpreting and applying corporate tax legislation to specific cases can most usefully be considered in this light. The importance of judicial prudence in this area has already been discussed in detail.[383] Indeed, I have analysed elsewhere the crucial role of such prudence in sustaining a consistent vision of the public, or national, interest in particular, rare cases. These cases include those where the European Court – but not, at the relevant time, Parliament – has had an opportunity to intervene.[384] There is no need here

[377] Ibid, 551.

[378] Ibid.

[379] Ibid.

[380] H Perkin, *The Rise of Professional Society: England since 1880* (London, Routledge, 1989) 457 and 461 (1960s to 1980s); and H Perkin, *The Third Revolution: Professional Elites in the Modern World* (London, Routledge, 1996) 210 (of the 1990s). See generally, R Sennett, *The Corrosion of Character: The Personal Consequences of Work in the New Capitalism* (New York, WW Norton, 1998) ch 3, esp 52; and J Schmidt, *Disciplined Minds* (Oxford, Rowman and Littlefield, 2000) ch 13.

[381] E Stary, 'The March of the Tax Profession' (2006) *British Tax Review* 249.

[382] Eg, A Goodall, 'Tax Avoidance under Scrutiny' *Tax Journal* (23 February 2009) 5; A Goodall, 'Knowledge Gap Hinders Debate' *Tax Journal* (2 March 2009) 10; R Maas, 'The Great Tax Avoidance "Debate"' *Tax Journal* (16 March 2009) 9; and N Shaxson, *Treasure Islands: Tax Havens and the Men Who Stole the World* (London, Bodley Head, 2011) 276.

[383] See above ch 3.

[384] Snape, 'Corporation Tax Reform' (above n 245) 399.

to rehearse the details of *William Grant*[385] or *Barclays Mercantile*[386] in the House of Lords or *Marks and Spencer* before Park J[387] or the Court of Appeal.[388] The Court of Appeal's 'reading in' of statutory language in the *Vodafone 2* case regarding CFCs is a particularly striking example.[389] What each decision demonstrates, however, is a clear grasp – on the judges' part no less than that of the government – to make prudent decisions in the public, or national, interest, in 'delivering' tax policy in particular areas.

IX. SOME CONNECTIONS

We are now at the stage of the analysis of theory and values in the reform of corporation tax where we can make some important interpretative connections. Specifically, it is possible to overlay chapter three's examination of institutional claims to trust and confidence with aspects of the current chapter's discussion of how the process of reforming corporation tax may inspire these essential elements of sovereignty in the corporation tax context.

Just as the physical manifestations of the institutions involved in corporation tax reform might present themselves vividly to interested observers, especially in the spring sunshine, so the ways in which they interact in the reform process remain, by comparison, rather dark. Various, generic explanations are possible, an obvious one being a Luhmannian systems theory analysis. In the preceding pages, however, I have sought to find the thread of an historically informed interpretation, based on the idea of corporation tax law as a species of 'political jurisprudence'.[390] From such a perspective, it has been essential to uncover what the 'political' element in the reform of corporation tax might be. This chapter has sought to characterise that element as, in a word, 'conflict', or at least as the constant potential for conflict; and following Loughlin, the policymaking process has been portrayed as being, to a very high degree, a demanding process of managing conflict, in the intellectual tradition of Hobbes and of Machiavelli. And it has done so in the context of a range of reform initiatives over the last 15 years or so. It is thus that, in examining the values immanent to the corporation tax base, in chapter five we may expect to find, as mentioned in chapter two, signs of conflict averted – in the very textures of the corporation tax code itself. It is thus, too, as chapter five explains, that we can expect to find values, not of a distinctively legal nature (except to the extent that they live within the rules and exceptions embodied in the corporation tax code itself), but of a political kind, in the sense delineated above.

[385] *CRC v William Grant and Sons*; *Small (HMIT) v Mars* (above n 214).

[386] *Barclays Mercantile Business Finance Ltd v Mawson (HMIT)* [2004] UKHL 51, [2005] STC 1.

[387] *Marks and Spencer v Halsey* (above n 242) (Park J).

[388] [2007] EWCA Civ 117, [2007] 2 CMLR 21. For the subsequent history in the lower courts, see Watterston (above n 237) 338–41.

[389] *Vodafone 2 v HMRC* [2009] EWCA 446, [2010] Ch 77.

[390] Loughlin, *The Idea of Public Law* (above n 11) 134.

If we can expect the corporation tax base to be characterised by the skilful prioritisation of political values, we can anticipate, too, that it will embody a particular vision, or visions, of the public interest. Chapter four has sought to show that, understated as it is in debates on corporation tax reform, the importance of the public interest is heavily underscored by the present study's conception of corporation tax law as a type of political practice, as that term is applied to public law in general in Loughlin's functionalist account of what public law involves. Chapter five will therefore illustrate in cumulative fashion how the corporation tax base embodies a particular ideology of the relationship between state and corporate sector. Taken together, chapters four and five demonstrate tellingly how, within the kind of functionalist critique undertaken in this study, public law can embody no public, or national, interest separate from political choices. Whilst it is certainly possible to argue that things should not be falling out in this way, it cannot sensibly be contended that the existing state of affairs represents a domination of government by the corporate sector. There is not, in any sensible interpretative sense, a 'corporate takeover of Britain'. What there is, instead, is an ideological consensus in which strong economic growth is a core element, perhaps the main element, of the public, or national, interest.

The truth of the ideas that the shape of the corporation tax base represents conscious political choices and that it is a reasonably accurate depiction of the contribution of the corporate sector to Britain's representative democracy is illustrated both by the stages of the reform process analysed in the current chapter and by the values disclosed by the corporation tax code itself. This is because the four stages described by Christopher Wales, as well as their prudential management, embody an idea of the appropriate role of corporate taxation within Britain's representative democracy.

Imagine a watercolour picture painted onto a sheet of paper and built up in stages by the use of washes of colour. Detailed over the insights offered in chapter three, and in order to build up an image of the corporation tax system of which chapter five forms the final layer, chapter four has sought to depict exactly why it is that despite political controversies, the system still has the capacity to inspire a high degree of trust and confidence. It is therefore quite misleading to opine, as William E Simon once did, that 'the nation should have a tax system which looks like someone designed it on purpose'.[391] There is not one purpose, but many; and they are worthy of respect as the outcomes of conscious political choices, of prudential decisions in a complex world.

[391] DF Bradford et al, *Blueprints for Basic Tax Reform*, 2nd edn (Arlington, Tax Analysts, 1984) 1.

5

The Evolving Corporation Tax Base

AT THE END of the preceding stage of the discussion, I asked readers to imagine each chapter as if it were a wash of colour, progressively yielding an ever fuller interpretation of the material. Each stage should have added some greater light or shade, some subtler, more delicately etched detail, to an ever more finished picture. This fifth chapter, which forms the imaginary painting's top layer, is concerned with the theory and values immanent to the corporation tax base, or the corporation tax code, at the time of writing (April 2011). In this part of the discussion, we move from the public law ordering of institutions and processes to the public law outcomes.[1] By way of reminder, I use the deceptively tidy expression 'the corporation tax code' to refer to both statutory and non-statutory material on corporation tax.[2]

Characterised in this way, these two terms – the 'code' and the 'base' – although capable of evoking rather different associations, are alike in at least one significant respect: since the corporation tax base – including what is and what is not taxed – is constructed by the legislative code, the theory and values immanent to one will correspond to those immanent to the other. However, without relying on an explicit distinction between substance and form, there is considerable merit in concentrating for certain purposes on the code, on the form taken by the constitutive elements of corporation tax. This is because much discussion of the reform of the tax has concentrated on the volume, on the changeability and on the extreme complexity of corporation tax legislation.

Whilst readers are urged to engage with the pictorial element in the discussion, such an intellectual embrace should be mindful of one crucial point: the fleetingness of the picture presented. The discussion in chapter four has illustrated how, following the logic of prudential government, much corporation tax reform is reactive. Here in chapter five, it is necessary to bring out the fast-moving, electronic and often 'closed' nature of the economic activities the aggregate gains on which the system seeks to tax.[3] All relevant commentaries

[1] T Besley, *Principled Agents? The Political Economy of Good Government* (Oxford, Oxford University Press, 2006) 21. See above pp 7 and 19.

[2] See above ch 2. The legislation is consolidated annually in, eg, A Redston (conslt ed), *Tolley's Yellow Tax Handbook 2010–11*, 51st edn (London, LexisNexis, 2010).

[3] See generally above ch 1; AJ Auerbach, MP Devereux and H Simpson, 'Taxing Corporate Income' in S Adam, T Besley et al (eds), *Dimensions of Tax Design: The Mirrlees Review* (Oxford, Oxford University Press, 2010) 871; K Messere, F de Kam and C Heady, *Tax Policy: Theory and*

give prominence to the speed of financial markets in general and the pace of change in the City of London's markets in particular.[4] It is the work of moments, for instance, for Layna Mosley's Goldman Sachs-based bond trader or the fund manager working at Fidelity, sitting in front of her computer screen, to allocate investments to one jurisdiction rather than to another.[5] Not only that, but she has a range of financial instruments at her disposal for hedging against investment risks.[6] More generally, we know that multinational corporations have the capability, if commercial considerations so dictate, to move operations relatively quickly from one country to another, and they, too, can hedge against currency and interest rate risks. Thus, in looking for the theory and values immanent to the corporation tax code, we need to be mindful of the dimension of impermanence, occasioned by the need to respond to a rapidly changing financial and commercial reality. Indeed, it is possible to assert with some cogency that a tax that relies so fundamentally on concepts of residence, source and profits is uniquely vulnerable in a world of instantaneous, or at least very rapid, investment decisions – and largely without exchange controls.[7]

If impermanence is, paradoxically, the one constant feature of the corporation tax code, so too is what the code says about how taxation legislation consolidates political power – that is, sovereignty – in this particular area of public policy. An important question in what follows is therefore how, despite the charges of change and of complexity, corporation tax legislation remains effective; and what are the ways in which, for the most part, it continues to command trust and confidence from those affected by it? Equally important are the ways in which certain features of the code tend to undermine that trust and confidence. Recent debates on corporation tax reform have understandably tended to focus on the latter rather than on the former. Since taking office in May 2010, the Coalition Government has been quick, in a changed political climate, to look for ways of augmenting the former and mitigating the latter.

Practice in OECD Countries (Oxford, Oxford University Press, 2003) 115; and SR Bond, 'Levelling Up or Levelling Down? Some Reflections on the ACE and CBIT Proposals, and the Future of the Corporate Tax Base' in S Cnossen (ed), *Taxing Capital Income in the European Union: Issues and Options for Reform* (Oxford, Oxford University Press, 2000) 161 and 172.

[4] Eg, M Buckle and J Thompson, *The UK Financial System: Theory and Practice*, 4th edn (Manchester, Manchester University Press, 2004) 149; WM Clarke, *How the City of London Works: An Introduction to its Financial Markets*, 6th edn (London, Sweet and Maxwell, 2004) 12 and 120; D Kynaston, *The City of London, Vol IV: A Club No More, 1945–2000* (London, Chatto and Windus, 2001) ch 22; R Roberts, *The City: A Guide to London's Global Financial Centre* (London, Profile, 2004) ch 3; and WE Scheuerman, *Liberal Democracy and the Social Acceleration of Time* (London, Johns Hopkins University Press, 2004) 5 and 159.

[5] L Mosley, *Global Capital and National Governments* (Cambridge, Cambridge University Press, 2003) 25.

[6] Buckle and Thompson (above n 4) chs 13 and 14; Clarke (above n 4) ch 13; and Roberts (above n 4) 73.

[7] HM Treasury, *Reforming Britain's Economic and Financial Policy: Towards Greater Economic Stability*, E Balls and G O'Donnell (eds) (Basingstoke, Palgrave, 2002) 35; and Bond (above n 3) 171–72.

What chapter four depicted was the on-going, dynamic interaction of the institutions whose functions, objectives and values had been discussed in chapter three. Shaping the discussion in this way has allowed the emergence of some important, evolving conclusions about the way that power – constituent power – is consolidated within this system of taxation. First, the tensions between the corporate sector and the government have been managed in the context of successive administrations whose general ideologies place a high premium on the importance of the corporate sector in promoting the public, or national, interest and whose commercial success is *in itself* part of that interest. Chapter four afforded various examples of this process. One example was Labour's refusal after 1997 to reshape the foreign exchange (FOREX) rules to reflect the idea of the Tobin tax, a possibility that Alistair Darling had himself alluded to in Opposition when the accounting-based 1993 Finance Bill provisions reached the Committee Stage. A more recent example was the Coalition's refusal in November 2010 to alter the generous rules on the deductibility of corporate borrowing costs, even in the wake of the 2007–09 financial crisis.[8] The current chapter, in offering a snapshot of the main values in the corporation tax code at a particular historical juncture, shows how the neoliberal ideology illustrated by both examples is embedded in the code as a whole, as well as how the politically contentious mixture of efficiency and fairness significantly contributes to dissatisfaction with it.

Secondly, chapters three and four have moreover shown that the premium placed on the co-operation of the corporate sector has underlined the managerial, that is to say, the governance, dimension to the government's approach to corporation tax reform. Statecraft of this kind, combining calculation and deliberation, has been well illustrated by the use of policy communities to take the reform process forward. Chapter five seeks to show how, within the corporation tax code itself, there is much evidence of this managerial approach. A major example, already referred to in various connections, is the use of accounting terminology and concepts in the drafting of the special codes on the tax treatment of corporate finance.

Thirdly, chapters three and four have shown that, although this governing ideology and this managerial approach each present certain challenges to the structure of Britain's representative institutions, they also display to advantage the historical strengths of those institutions. Despite the gaps in the possibilities for bringing responsible individuals before the House of Commons Treasury Committee and despite the intermittent beam that the Committee has hitherto been able to bring to bear on corporation tax, the Committee did signal in 2010 its intention to concentrate far more extensively on the latter.[9] Furthermore, as

[8] HM Treasury and HMRC, *Corporate Tax Reform: Delivering a More Competitive System* (London, 2010) (hereafter 'Corporate Tax Road Map' or 'CTRM'), available at http://www.hm-treasury.gov.uk (accessed 30 November 2010) 14. Regarding the CTRM and this document, see above ch 2 n 8.

[9] Treasury Committee, *Letter from the Chairman to the Exchequer Secretary regarding Tax Policy* (4 November 2010), available at http://www.parliament.uk (accessed 20 December 2010).

chapter four has shown, the debate on individual reform measures is both fuller and, within the logic of the institutional structure of representative government in Britain, more effective than some commentators may lead us to believe.

My task in chapter five therefore is to analyse the theory of and the main values immanent to the corporation tax code produced by the institutions and the processes analysed earlier in the study. The theory is, as ever, about effectiveness – about prudence. Although much has been said on different aspects of this already, we shall build later on, on one or two points, as they relate to the theory. For the moment, I briefly return to the immanent values.

It will be recalled from chapters one and two that the present study accepts that certain values – namely efficiency and fairness – are immanent to corporation tax law. They are political, not rule of law values; and they are to be discerned by close examination of the legislative texts and policy documents, bringing to bear a sense of historical awareness, an acute sense of what is coherent, what is non-contradictory and what is consistent. This is Martin Loughlin's critical method, based on Isaiah Berlin,[10] and it is traceable ultimately to the immanent critique of GWF Hegel.[11] Loughlin has written:

> Immanent critique stems from a philosophical idealism which tries to examine experience in a coherent and comprehensive manner in order to reveal the logic and rationality immanent in this experience. . . [T]ruth always lies ahead; at any moment it is immanent but never realised.[12]

We are looking therefore for how the practice of corporation tax law, as embodied in the corporation tax code and given the overwhelming need for effectiveness, shapes and prioritises, in particular situations, the values immanent to this area of law. As Loughlin has stated elsewhere, we are therefore developing an 'explanatory framework', with a view to revealing 'the value of assumptions, the causal relations and the dominant features' of corporation tax law as a political practice.[13]

Different aspects of the same four strands as those that occurred in previous chapters therefore appear in chapter five. Thus, rather than the government's liability to account for the success or failure of its corporation tax reform measures, and instead of the government's right of legislative initiative, we are concerned with how and how far the corporation tax code reflects the state's pre-eminence. Secondly, we are interested, not in the formal constraints on corporation tax reform spelt out in the European Treaties, but in how the cor-

[10] I Berlin, 'Does Political Theory Still Exist?' in H Hardy and R Hausheer (eds), *The Proper Study of Mankind: An Anthology of Essays* (London, Pimlico, 1998) 59 and 76.

[11] D Knowles, *Hegel and the Philosophy of Right* (London, Routledge 2002) 71; M Loughlin, 'Review Article' (1988) 51 *Modern Law Review* 531, 533, quoting Berlin (ibid) 76; and M Loughlin, *Foundations of Public Law* (Oxford, Oxford University Press, 2010) 154.

[12] Loughlin, 'Review Article' (ibid), quoting Hegel's *Philosophy of History*. This is different, Loughlin points out, from the 'immanent critique' developed by the Frankfurt school (535–36).

[13] M Loughlin, *Public Law and Political Theory* (Oxford, Clarendon Press, 1992) 35; and M Loughlin, 'Theory and Values in Public Law: An Interpretation' (2005) *Public Law* 48, 59.

poration tax code and its accompanying policy statements reveal an intergovernmentalist[14] view of the relationship of Britain's corporation tax base with those of the rest of Europe, and also with those of the Organisation for Economic Co-operation and Development (OECD) and the General Agreement on Tariffs and Trade (GATT) 1994/World Trade Organization (WTO) members. Thirdly, we are concerned, not with how the processes of reform augment or detract from confidence in the tax, but with the role of the code in mediating the relationship between the government and the corporate sector, and possibly with society more widely. The final strand in the discussion is therefore the extent to which the form and content of the corporation tax code militates in favour of or against its effectiveness.

I. ECONOMICS, REALISM AND POLITICS

The aim of the current chapter is to develop the implications of the idea that it is the public law status of the corporation tax code that dictates its constant propensity for change, its complexity and the prioritisation of the political values within it. Given the nature and role of public law as 'a set of practices concerned with the establishment, maintenance and regulation of the activity of governing the state',[15] whose 'even-handedness' helps to 'create intimacy, shape identity, generate trust, and strengthen allegiance',[16] it would indeed be surprising if corporation tax law did not respond to the commercial and financial developments sketched out above.[17] It is the contention of this study that much, if not most of the scholarly writing on corporation tax fails, for one reason or another, to take sufficient account of this point. Some reference was made to this state of affairs in chapter two above, where it was contended that theoretical discussion of corporation tax tends to lack a context outside economics.

To redress the imbalance somewhat, this chapter unfolds in a sequence designed to illustrate the importance of the public law nature of the corporation tax code, the implications of this for the code's complexity and instability, and the consequences of its public law nature for the values that the corporation

[14] AS Milward, *The European Rescue of the Nation-State*, 2nd edn (London, Routledge 2000) ch 1; J Snape, 'Corporation Tax Reform: Politics and Public Law' (2007) *British Tax Review* 374; M Cini, 'Intergovernmentalism' in M Cini (ed), *European Union Politics* (Oxford, Oxford University Press, 2003) 93; Standing Committee A (16 May 2006) HC vol 446, col 166 (Mark Hoban) and col 167 (Rob Marris); and M Rifkind, 'In Some Areas, Sovereignty Should Be Shared in Europe' *Financial Times* (13 December 2006) 15.

[15] Loughlin, 'Theory and Values in Public Law' (above n 13) 58.

[16] M Loughlin, 'Constitutional Law: The Third Order of the Political' in N Bamforth and P Leyland (eds), *Public Law in a Multi-Layered Constitution* (Oxford, Hart Publishing, 2003) 40.

[17] Public Bill Committee (17 May 2007) HC vol 446, col 216 (Ed Balls, then Economic Secretary to the Treasury); and G Brown, 'Foreword' in HM Treasury and Inland Revenue, *Large Business Taxation: HM Government's Strategy and Corporate Tax Reforms: A Consultation Document* (2001).

tax code embodies, as well as their prioritisation in particular areas. It is therefore important to be clear, both about the nature of the economics learning on corporation tax and about the strengths and limitations that it presents for the issues under consideration.

The first point to be made about the economic analysis of corporate taxation is that it has long had a strongly normative character. This comment might seem surprising to economists of taxation. James and Nobes, for example, in their classic study, say when discussing fairness in taxation that economists 'are inclined to leave the definition of equity to others', since they 'are trained from an early age to steer clear of normative arguments'.[18] Two points can be made about this claim. First, it does not necessarily set up normativism in disjunction with functionalism, as does the present study. It simply seeks to establish descriptive, value-free credentials for James and Nobes' own investigation. James and Nobes may not have thought through the possible range of connotations of the term that they are invoking. The idea of normativism, in other words, seems to be used somewhat loosely within the economics discourse.[19] This is not a disparaging comment, since the possibility of characterising arguments as one or other depends on the contexts in which they appear. Secondly and more importantly, there are grounds for believing that, try as they might, economists do think in normative terms when they write about taxation.[20] Normativism in the study of public law, and as used in this study, is 'rooted in a belief in the ideal of the separation of powers and in the need to subordinate government to law'.[21] In economics, normativism is a complimentary enterprise.

One of the chief advocates of normativism in both disciplines was Friedrich von Hayek.[22] In economics, Gunnar Myrdal associated normativism with the making of unwarranted assumptions about what taxation should and should not seek to achieve.[23] Myrdal's work,[24] though not recent, continues to be highly relevant to explicating these distinctions.[25] The normative assumptions are unwarranted in the sense that they have been neither tested by ideological struggle nor based on intense empirical observation of the incidence of taxes.[26] What they have in common with the normative tradition in public law is that they

[18] S James and C Nobes, *The Economics of Taxation: Principles, Policy and Practice*, 7th edn (Harlow, Financial Times Prentice Hall, 2000) 78.

[19] Eg, A Kaletsky, *Capitalism 4.0: The Birth of a New Economy* (London, Bloomsbury, 2010) 326.

[20] L Murphy and T Nagel, *The Myth of Ownership* (Oxford, Oxford University Press, 2000) 136.

[21] Loughlin, *Public Law and Political Theory* (above n 13) 60 and 144.

[22] MB Steger and RK Roy, *Neoliberalism: A Very Short Introduction* (Oxford, Oxford University Press, 2010).

[23] G Myrdal, *The Political Element in the Development of Economic Theory*, P Streeten (trans) (London, Routledge and Kegan Paul, 1953) ch 7.

[24] H Arendt, *The Human Condition*, 2nd edn (Chicago, University of Chicago Press, 1998) 44n; and JA Schumpeter, *History of Economic Analysis*, EB Schumpeter (ed) (London, George Allen and Unwin, 1954) 1173.

[25] DM Hausman and MS McPherson, *Economic Analysis and Moral Philosophy* (Cambridge, Cambridge University Press, 1996) 211–20.

[26] Myrdal (above n 23) 185–86; and A Greenspan, *The Age of Turbulence: Adventures in a New World* (London, Allen Lane, 2007) 262.

clearly separate economics from both the politics and the law disciplines, and they close off a more profound, distinctively political debate, about what the tax system is actually *for*.[27] Timothy Besley encapsulates this normative approach to economics in terms of a preoccupation with institutional design and fiscal constraint.[28] In Besley's portrayal, it is associated with the public choice theory of James Buchanan and with the idea of political economy as the analysis of politics using economic tools.[29]

The use of 'optimal taxation' theory in the Mirrlees review of 2010 and 2011[30] marks something of a departure from a normative approach. Optimal taxation, says Mirrlees, 'is a methodology for designing tax systems to achieve the best outcome given the constraints faced by the government', and so as to balance the value of efficiency with fairness, it 'begins by clarifying the objectives of policy and identifying the constraints upon policy'.[31] Optimal is what 'best achieves the objectives whilst satisfying the constraints'. Whilst it is a distinctively welfare economics approach rather than a strictly normative one, Mirrlees is still problematic, because it specifically disavows matters of political judgment while urging a rational approach to tax policy.[32] Mirrlees tells policy-makers what the best tax policy is to achieve a particular result: 'tax by design'. It cannot, obviously, tell politicians when and how to translate that policy into action. It is therefore important to recognise both the strengths and weaknesses of the Mirrlees review.

In 1978 and 1982 respectively, the Meade Committee[33] and the authors of the Green Paper on corporation tax reform[34] each wondered whether bringing in a 'flow-of-funds' corporation tax would make taxing corporate profits more neutral. Again in 1991, the Institute for Fiscal Studies (IFS)[35] suggested improving neutrality by making an 'allowance for corporate equity' (an ACE)[36] in the taxation of corporate profits.[37] The ACE, which would eliminate the tax advantage of the deductibility of borrowing costs, continues to be the principal corporate

[27] J Tiley, *Revenue Law*, 5th edn (Oxford, Hart Publishing, 2005) 815–23 (6th edn, 833–41).

[28] Besley (above n 1) 20.

[29] Ibid, 21–23; D Coyle, *The Soulful Science: What Economists Really Do and Why it Matters* (Princeton, Princeton University Press, 2007) 205–8; and Kaletsky (above n 19) 194.

[30] Adam, Besley et al (eds) (above n 3); J Mirrlees, S Adam, T Besley et al, *Tax by Design* (Oxford, Oxford University Press, 2011) ch 2 (pre-publication draft chapters available at http://www.ifs.org.uk/mirrleesReview/design (accessed 30 November 2010)).

[31] Mirrlees, Adam and Besley et al (ibid) 19.

[32] Ibid, 5.

[33] JE Meade (ed), *The Structure and Reform of Direct Taxation: Report of a Committee Chaired by Professor JE Meade* (London, George Allen and Unwin, 1978) ch 12.

[34] *Corporation Tax: Presented to Parliament by the Chancellor of the Exchequer by Command of Her Majesty* (Green Paper, Cmnd 8456, 1982) ch 7.

[35] Institute for Fiscal Studies (IFS) Capital Taxes Group, 'Equity for Companies: A Corporation Tax for the 1990s', IFS Commentary No 26 (London, 1991); and M Devereux and H Freeman, 'A General Neutral Profits Tax' (1991) 12(3) *Fiscal Studies* 1.

[36] JR King, 'Debt and Equity Financing' in P Shome (ed), *Tax Policy Handbook* (Washington, DC, IMF, 1995) 161; and generally, Bond (above n 3).

[37] Bond (above n 3) 164–69.

tax recommendation of Mirrlees in 2011.[38] Still, its adoption seems unlikely, given the terms of the Coalition Government's Corporate Tax Road Map (CTRM) of 2010[39] and David Gauke's comments about the tax treatment of corporate debt. In the same vein is the European Commission's consideration of the advantages of a 'common consolidated corporate tax base' (CCCTB) for Europe.[40] Intellectual feats though all of these approaches are, they do not help us to interpret the process of corporation tax reform. At the very most, they tend to betray the ideological stance of their progenitors, a point to which we return below. The conclusion must be that normativism cannot help us with interpreting corporate tax reform, and by definition optimal taxation theory alone does not profess to elucidate the political and public law dimensions of corporate tax reform.

The second point that might be made about the economic analysis of corporation tax is the lack of realism implied by the preceding comments. This is a charge that can certainly not be levelled against the interpretative turn in political writing. It is impossible to illustrate this point more vividly than by reference, not to academic writing, but to the rich and illuminating memoirs of Nigel Lawson,[41] the Chancellor of the Exchequer in the early years of the Thatcher administration, who had been responsible for commissioning the 1982 Green Paper referred to above. He describes how, whilst admiring the intellectual beauty of its recommendations, he had contemplated with horror the political consequences of proceeding down that line:

> We [Lawson and Arthur, later Lord, Cockfield][42] looked into the theoretically attractive switch from an income tax to an expenditure tax system, and had a long session with Professor James Meade, its foremost exponent, but (in my view rightly) shrank from the upheaval and practical problems that would have been involved.[43]

Lord Lawson's attitude – that of an extremely successful practitioner of politics as calculation – is here thrown vividly into relief by the deliberative mind-set of the particular economist, a mentality that Baroness Thatcher resented where she found it among members of the Whitehall civil service.[44] There is no need to elaborate further on this here; suffice it to say that insofar as

[38] Mirrlees, Adam and Besley et al (above n 30) 30–32.

[39] CTRM (above n 8) 14; and C Sanger, 'Corporate Tax Road Map' (2011) *British Tax Review* 2, 8.

[40] V Houlder and N Tait, 'European Corporate Tax Plans under Fire' *Financial Times* (7 February 2011) 5.

[41] P Riddell, 'Commentary' in Adam, Besley et al (eds) (above n 3) 1280 and 1284.

[42] Lord Cockfield was a distinguished official and Commissioner of Inland Revenue between 1951–52; he eventually became an EC Commissioner, before quarrelling with Margaret Thatcher: N Lawson, *The View from No 11: Memoirs of a Tory Radical* (London, Bantam Press, 1992) 17, 22, 31, 35–36, 336 and 894–98; and M Thatcher, *The Downing Street Years* (London, HarperCollins, 1993) 547.

[43] Lawson (ibid) 17 and 344–45; and M Gammie, 'Has Nigel Lawson Really Reformed Business Taxation?' (1984) *Fiscal Studies* 82.

[44] Thatcher (above n 42) 46 (although Baroness Thatcher does not herself identify this mindset as 'Aristotelian').

they pinpoint the gulf '[b]etween the idea [a]nd the reality',[45] the cleavage between the deliberative and the calculating conceptions of politics,[46] Nigel Lawson's comments remain as relevant today as they were in the 1980s. Lord Lawson is still commended for the clarity of his thinking and for his prudence. Mirrlees revealed in 2010 that Meade's plans would quickly have been overtaken by economic globalisation, especially transfer pricing issues,[47] while David Gauke has described Nigel Lawson as 'a great tax reformer'.[48]

The third point that we can make about economics writing is that, as an enterprise of political economy, the very technicality of corporation tax reform tends to remove its difficulties from public deliberation, despite the fact that, as shown in chapter four, the most important corporation tax issues are eminently political. To the extent that corporation tax reform thereby becomes the province of experts, of technocrats, it is a neat illustration of the range and importance of the issues that, given the involvement of policy networks and the vagaries of the Select Committee system, are outside effective parliamentary scrutiny. It is not necessary to develop this point here, since the accountability issues raised have already been discussed. All that it is necessary to affirm at this stage is that the inaccessibility of the policy material, together with its insidiously influential qualities, can hardly be regarded as a positive contribution to prudential governance. Mirrlees sees this as being the main significance of corporate taxation's legendary complexity, and Alt, Preston and Sibieta pinpoint the occluded nature of corporation tax reform as making it 'especially vulnerable to lobbying'.[49]

My final point is linked to the normative pull of much traditional economics writing on corporation tax. It is also, so far as it draws in questions of legislative simplicity, relevant to the concerns about complexity, instability and the rule of law discussed below. This is partly what Jürgen Habermas seems to be getting at in saying that once policy issues become identified with political economy, 'the category of law [loses] its central role in theoretical analysis'.[50] Although this may serve as a lament for scholars whose 'home discipline' is law, it is much more important than this, for two reasons: first, it means that the usefulness of the economics literature for lawyers is diminished by its understatement of the crucial importance of law; and secondly, on a related point, it involves assumptions about the nature of law and of legal studies, which, in the light of trends in public law scholarship, are increasingly unjustifiable.

[45] Cf TS Eliot, 'The Hollow Men' in *Collected Poems, 1909–1962* (London, Faber and Faber, 1974) 91.

[46] Eg, M Loughlin, *The Idea of Public Law* (Oxford, Oxford University Press, 2003) 34n.

[47] Auerbach, Devereux and Simpson (above n 3) 838.

[48] David Gauke MP (Exchequer Secretary to the Treasury), 'Check against Delivery' Speech at the Centre for Business Taxation, Oxford University (2 July 2010), available at http://www.hm-treasury.gov.uk/speech_xst_020710.htm (accessed 2 March 2011).

[49] Mirrlees, Adam and Besley et al (above n 30) 21; and J Alt, I Preston and L Sibieta, 'The Political Economy of Tax Policy' in S Adam, T Besley et al (eds), *Dimensions of Tax Design: The Mirrlees Review* (Oxford, Oxford University Press, 2010).

[50] J Habermas, *Between Facts and Norms*, W Rehg (trans) (Cambridge, Polity Press, 1997) 45.

Aspects of each of these four points inform the developing discussion in the present chapter. Our attention turns first to the expansion, in the light of these comments, of elements of the theory of public law as it relates to corporate taxation. This is a fuller examination of why the values of the corporation tax code are political values, as well as why and how the code must be analysed as a manifestation of a 'political practice'. The discussion is illustrated by reference to a number of cases in which the public law nature of the judicial technique in tax law cases has been in evidence. The issues are related to and shaped by the governance issues raised in chapter three and the portrayal of the political dimension to corporation tax reform offered in chapter four. What is sought is to stress the theory of effectiveness, as well as the paramount status of prudential reasoning.

From an elaboration of the public law nature of the corporation tax code in the first part of the chapter, the second part moves to a consideration of the implications of this characterisation of corporation tax law for what is ubiquitously but inaccurately referred to as the rule, not of men, but of law.[51] My contention is that much of the debate on corporation tax reform misses the significance of legitimate divergences of opinion on the nature and consequences of the rule of law,[52] and it misses the implications of this for complexity in the code, as well as for perceptions of its instability. Unless we move beyond these out-dated and unrealistic, Hayekian preconceptions, I argue, we shall never properly be able to understand what is going on, nor assess the viability of routes to improvement.

The foregoing lays the groundwork for the extended discussion of the values immanent to the changing corporation tax code in section IV below. This consists of extended and complementary analyses of the values of efficiency and fairness. What vision of each of these terms does the code embody? How far are these values and their prioritisation a reflection of the institutions and processes discussed in chapters three and four? What are the strengths and weaknesses of the concepts thus deployed? Why, despite everything, do they seem in reality, just now, to be fairly robust? As a basis for shedding light on these issues, in the rest of section IV there is an extended discussion of the importance of a theory of effectiveness in giving shape and content to the values themselves.

I continue, therefore, by building outwards the implications of the idea of corporation tax as public law, with the aims suggested above firmly in mind.

II. FURTHER IMPLICATIONS OF CORPORATION TAX AS PUBLIC LAW

Previous chapters have emphasised that, properly understood, corporation tax law is to be seen as a form of public law. The truth of this contention is appar-

[51] Loughlin, *Foundations of Public Law* (above n 11) 132, 312n.

[52] Eg, *Deutsche Morgan Grenfell Group plc v IRC and A-G* [2006] UKHL 49, [2007] STC 1, 41h–42c (Lord Walker of Gestingthorpe).

ent, not only from the fact that taxation in general is the exercise of one of the most fundamental 'prerogatives of the state',[53] but also from the essentially political nature of the issues with which it has, as a 'practice of politics', to contend. In the next several pages, I seek to justify the importance of this argument in understanding the textures of the corporation tax code itself, especially in the light of the nineteenth- and twentieth-century hostility of English lawyers[54] and political philosophers[55] to any distinction between public and private law. In making out this justification, I follow Loughlin's discussion of public law 'method',[56] reflecting on the specific implications of that method for the reform of corporation tax law.

First and foremost, the corporation tax code is more than a highly detailed and extremely complicated collection of what Loughlin refers to as 'the edicts of the supreme authority in the state'.[57] It is that, of course, since, as was mentioned above, it is, like all effective British tax legislation, a manifestation of the pre-eminence of the state and its representative, the Crown-in-Parliament, that is, the government. 'Juridification'[58] – what Loughlin, drawing on Habermas, calls 'the tendency to conceptualise extensive spheres of public life in legal terms'[59] – will not help us to see what this extra dimension might be, since it underestimates 'the social dimension' of the 'normative authority'[60] contained within the highly detailed prescriptions of the code. Neither, Loughlin would argue, will certain reactions to juridification, namely the liberal normativism of Habermas and of Dworkin,[61] help us to identify this additional quality. Each of these, for different reasons, underestimates the distinctiveness of public law and is 'unable to supply critical standards against which governmental action is to be measured'.[62] It is, we may infer, the Aristotelian impetus behind Habermas and Dworkin that so limits their interpretative potential when confronted with legislation such as the corporation tax code.[63] Instead, the code must be analysed for what it is, as 'an aspect of political practice', part of the 'third order of

[53] *Ferrazzini v Italy* [2001] STC 1314. But see *N Ali and S Begum and Others v CCE* [2002] VATDT No 17681.

[54] AV Dicey, *Introduction to the Study of the Law of the Constitution* [1885], ECS Wade (ed), 10th edn (London, Macmillan, 1965) 202–3; and Lord Hewart of Bury, *The New Despotism* (London, Ernest Benn, 1929) chs 3 and 4.

[55] M Oakeshott, *On Human Conduct* (Oxford, Clarendon Press, 1975) 151.

[56] Loughlin, *The Idea of Public Law* (above n 46) ch 8.

[57] Ibid, 131.

[58] Ibid.

[59] Ibid.

[60] Ibid.

[61] But see J Freedman, 'Defining Taxpayer Responsibility: In Support of a General Anti-avoidance Principle' (2004) *British Tax Review* 332. Professor Freedman is a member of the new GAAR study group: HM Treasury, 'Details of Avoidance Study Group Set Out', Press Release 04/11 (14 January 2011), available at http://www.hm-treasury.gov.uk (accessed 21 January 2011).

[62] Loughlin, *The Idea of Public Law* (above n 46) 132.

[63] But see JF Avery Jones, 'Tax Law: Rules or Principles?' (1996) *British Tax Review* 580; and J Prebble, 'Should Tax Legislation be Written from a Principles and Purpose Point of View or a Precise and Detailed Point of View?' (1998) *British Tax Review* 112.

the political'.[64] The corporation tax code is an expression, in other words, of the government's sovereignty, its tax sovereignty – the term being used, not in the sense of competence only, but in its fullest, 'generative'[65] sense: sovereignty as 'capacity', as constituent power. Viewed thus, at any one stage in its development, the corporation tax code marks out with great precision the exercise of the sovereign power of the government in taxing corporate income.

Secondly,[66] the corporation tax code must, in the light of the foregoing, be viewed as 'political jurisprudence'.[67] This might seem worrying, as it might suggest few, if any, limitations on what the code might come to contain. This is the 'paradox' to which Loughlin, finding its origins in Jean Bodin,[68] attaches fundamental weight, however: 'it is precisely because limits are disabling, that they are enabling';[69] or to put it another way, 'authority is enhanced when competence is limited'.[70] Loughlin draws strength from Stephen Holmes's analogy with grammar – grammatical rules enable greater clarity of expression, not less. Thus, if we look at the corporation tax code as a whole, we can draw at least three related conclusions about its status as 'political jurisprudence'.

First, especially as it consists of primary legislation, which has been tested in the fora analysed in chapter four (namely expert discussion in policy communities and 'argumentative scrutiny' by elected representatives of the people), it reflects the enabling power of constraint or, perhaps, restraint: '[P]rohibition on taxation without consultation' is specifically identified by Holmes as a hallmark of the enabling power of institutional restraint.[71] We can, without doing violence to the idea, read 'consultation' here as encompassing not only the consultation of Parliament but the consultation of experts prior to the Parliamentary stage. That is why Malcolm Gammie was absolutely right to focus on the absence of proper consultation as a major problem with tax measures of the 1980s. Secondly, however, we can draw contrasting conclusions about those parts of the code that result from the conferring on the Treasury of wide delegated powers or measures that, even though they appear in primary legislation, were not subject to full consultation before Parliament argued over them, in circumstances such that it would have been prudent so to do. The 1965 introduction of corporation tax itself provides interesting material for consideration, so far as this last point is concerned. Would it have been more prudent for the Labour Administration to have consulted widely on its introduction,[72] or

[64] Hence my claim that the more important corporation tax rules and values may be regarded as part of constitutional law: Snape (above n 14) 379.

[65] See above ch 1.

[66] I am here following the structure of Loughlin's argument on 'method': Loughlin, *The Idea of Public Law* (above n 46) 134.

[67] Ibid.

[68] Ibid, 137.

[69] Ibid.

[70] Ibid, 138.

[71] Quoted ibid, 137.

[72] Ibid.

was the prudent course the calculating and decisive one that was actually taken?[73] Difficult as it is to reconstruct the circumstances of the decision,[74] it is interesting to note that we are fast approaching the point at which every major structural feature of the 1965 tax has been reconstructed, albeit over four decades. Thirdly, although this is a point to which we return later in the chapter, with the code viewed as political jurisprudence, the complicated and detailed plethora of reliefs and exemptions begins to look as though they reflect what is politically possible – and desirable – in the furtherance of government policy.

Bearing in mind the conception of the corporation tax code as political jurisprudence, we can consider further the assumptions about the nature of law and the purpose of law that the code therefore embodies.[75] First, it is an idea of law explicitly as a means of 'advancing the public interest'.[76] Full discussion of how the code seeks to do this is reserved to the last section of the chapter. For the moment, it is enough to recall the discussion of the public, or national, interest in chapter four, especially the ideas that the promotion of policies in the public interest will be ideological; that the pursuit of an ideology is an entirely legitimate objective for law; and that much of the disagreement about the pros and cons of corporation tax reform fails to take proper account of this point. Secondly, the code enshrines an idea of law as what is created by the state, that is, by 'those forms and institutions that establish and regulate the exercise of governmental authority',[77] and which create 'conditions for maintaining state authority'.[78] The corporation tax code is thus the creation of the person differentiated from other persons because it is instituted 'precisely for the purpose of creating law'; of an established set of procedures, which help to create trust and security;[79] and, as Bodin says, of the state's unique and nearly fundamental prerogative, the right to raise taxes.

We can say, therefore, even before we begin to look for the values immanent to the code, that the corporation tax code is a precise indicator of the boundaries at any one time of the sovereign power of the state to tax corporate income. Secondly, as such, the code is an example of political jurisprudence, drawing strength, paradoxically, from the constraints under which it constantly evolves. Thirdly, as political jurisprudence, it is designed to further the public, or national, interest, as that idea is conceived of by 'the government of the day'.[80] Fourthly, it has been promulgated through established channels, a point the full

[73] Finance Bill 1965 was debated on the floor of the House: I Ferrier, 'Tax Editor's Notes (July/August)' (2003) *Conveyancer and Property Lawyer* 346.

[74] But see Kynaston (above n 4) 300, 304, 307 and 311; and R Holt, *Second Amongst Equals: Chancellors of the Exchequer since the Second World War* (London, Profile Books, 2002) 14–15.

[75] I am here still following Loughlin, *The Idea of Public Law* (above n 46) 140.

[76] Ibid, 140–41, although Loughlin does not use the expression 'the public interest'.

[77] Ibid, 141.

[78] Ibid.

[79] Ibid, 142.

[80] M Gammie, 'The Process of Fiscal Reform in the United Kingdom' (1989) *British Tax Review* 252, 253.

significance of which will become apparent when I consider the code's relationship with 'the rule of law'. Finally, the code represents the unique and basic power of the state, the power of levying taxes. This leaves for consideration the relevance of the final component in Loughlin's depiction of public law method: the technique of public law that the corporation tax code illustrates.[81] In this study, I shall avoid detailed consideration of a possible fifth stage in the method, which is the code's relationship with an ethic of distributive justice.[82] It is not simply that the corporation tax code is a monumental example of economic regulation. More fundamentally, it is that the political conditions managed by the code, as well as, within them, the economic conditions,[83] are themselves the basis of a 'moral life'[84] mapped out for us in the historical terms of modernity that Loughlin, for one, has described in detail.[85] We here put aside the idea of the primacy of morality in Rawls and in Dworkin on the basis that misunderstands the reality of politics shaped by that historical legacy.[86]

This final point about the nature of the corporation tax code, what it says about the techniques of public law, is its role in managing that 'brokenness',[87] that potential for conflict that throughout the study has been taken to characterise 'the concept of the political'. In chapter four, this was related to the potential for conflict that arises out of the five dilemmas of governance identified in chapter three. These are potential conflicts between the government and the corporate sector; between the government and other EU Member States and institutions; and between conflicting interests within the corporate sector itself. Since there is 'no authoritative morality' through which these conflicts or potential conflicts can be resolved – neither Dworkin nor Rawls is in a position to help much here – we cannot expect to find either moral values or a moral ordering of values within the code. Instead, we find that the theory running through the code is reason of state,[88] and its method is prudence,[89] albeit in juristic form. Given the objectives and values of the institutions discussed in chapter three, as well as the logic of the reform process itself, as discussed in chapter four, neither point should be in any way surprising.

The idea of reason of state being the reasoning at work in the corporation tax code[90] may strike readers as un-British.[91] Yet, as Loughlin shows, reason of state is the underlying idea of one of the foundational documents of British government, the Bill of Rights of 1689. The ban on 'the levying of money for or

[81] Loughlin, *The Idea of Public Law* (above n 46) 148–52.
[82] See above ch 2.
[83] C Schmitt, *The Concept of the Political*, G Schwab (trans) (Chicago, University of Chicago Press, 1996) 88 (L Strauss' note).
[84] Loughlin, *The Idea of Public Law* (above n 46) 145.
[85] Loughlin, *Foundations of Public Law* (above n 11) esp 408–16.
[86] Loughlin, *The Idea of Public Law* (above n 46) 147.
[87] Ibid, 148.
[88] Ibid, 139–40.
[89] Ibid, 149.
[90] Ibid, 151.
[91] *Deutsche Morgan Grenfell* (above n 52).

to the use of the Crown by pretence of prerogative without grant of Parliament' is itself a prudential one. This predisposition to prudence runs through not just the corporation tax code itself but also, as indicated in chapter three, the way in which the judiciary, also obliged to be prudent, interpret its injunctions, sometimes disingenuously perhaps or even in ignorance of the label. The juristic prudence of the code is the subject matter of the next part of the discussion and, by extension, the rest of the chapter as well.

At the level of judicial activity, we may note the following points. First, the existence of the well-known exclusion of the securing of the 'payment of taxes or other contributions' from the right to possession of property under the European Convention on Human Rights (ECHR), Protocol 1, Article 1, reinforces the prudential nature of judicial reasoning in cases that might involve challenges to reform measures;[92] however, even if some future case were to fall outside the exception, Loughlin's notion of rights as the 'positivisation' of 'political claims'[93] would mean that the reasoning would still have to be of a prudential kind, since human rights adjudication itself involves ruling on political norms.[94] Falling outside the exception in Protocol 1, Article 1 is not an escape from the political into a reassuringly certain realm of law. Secondly, European judges seem much better at understanding the public law nature of the taxation function than are certain of their English counterparts.[95] Thirdly, although the outer limits of the public law nature of taxation need still to be fully charted,[96] cases clearly of a public law nature show much evidence of judges using a prudential technique.[97] Finally, as recent cases on claiming repayment of tax paid under a mistake of law and on the nature of interest awards illustrate, a prudential approach may require the application of principles of private law, especially where the amounts in question can be quantified.[98] These cases might possibly be regarded as contributing to marking out the boundaries of the public law of taxation. The better view, it is argued, is that the use of private law principles is

[92] See generally, App No 13013/87, *Wasa Liv Ömsesidigt, Fërsäkringsbolaget Valands Pensionsstiftelse and Others v Sweden* (1988) 58 ECHRDR 163; App No 21319/93, *National and Provincial Building Society and Others v UK* [1997] STC 1466 (ECtHR) (civil claim originating in tax as a civil right within ECHR, Art 6); and *Eagerpath Ltd v Edwards (HMIT)* [2001] STC 26.

[93] Loughlin, *The Idea of Public Law* (above n 46) 125 and 130.

[94] Ibid, 162.

[95] But see *Ferrazzini v Italy* [2001] STC 1314 (ECtHR); and App No 73053/01, *Jussila v Finland* (2006) 9 ITL Rep 662, alongside *N Ali and S Begum and Others v CCE* [2002] VATDT No 17681 (S Oliver, QC (Chairman)) [2002] STI 1675.

[96] Lord Woolf, 'Tax and Judicial Review' (1993) *British Tax Review* 219; I Saunders, *Taxation: Judicial Review and Other Remedies* (Chichester, John Wiley, 1996) 103–6 and 153–55; M Elliott (ed), *Beatson, Matthews and Elliott's Administrative Law Text and Materials*, 3rd edn (Oxford University Press, Oxford, 2005); and Loughlin, *Foundations of Public Law* (above n 11) 445–48.

[97] Case C-446/03 *Marks and Spencer plc v Halsey (HMIT)* [2006] 1 CMLR 18, [2006] EWHC 811, [2006] STC 1235 (Park J); affd [2007] EWCA Civ 117, [2007] 2 CMLR 21; *CRC v William Grant and Sons Distillers Ltd*; *Small (HMIT) v Mars UK Ltd* [2007] UKHL 15, [2007] STC 680; and *Barclays Mercantile Business Finance Ltd v Mawson (HMIT)* [2004] UKHL 51, [2005] STC 1.

[98] *Deutsche Morgan Grenfell* (above n 52); and *Sempra Metals Ltd (Formerly Metallgesellschaft Ltd) v IRC and Another* [2007] UKHL 34, [2007] 3 WLR 354.

itself a prudential response to a public law problem,[99] since it tends to augment trust and confidence, not merely in the judiciary but also in the 'creditworthiness' of the state itself.[100]

III. COMPLEXITY AND INSTABILITY IN THE CORPORATION TAX CODE

If the characterisation of the corporation tax code in the terms just invoked is maintainable, then there are important consequences for the significance of current political debates over the complexity and the instability of the code. The Corporate Tax Road Map affirmed the commitment to address these issues made in the Coalition Government's New Approach to tax policy of June 2010.[101] Indeed, the establishment of the Office of Tax Simplification has been a testimony to one part of the commitment.[102] It seems likely, however, that this will merely rouse these debates to renewed vigour, since they were rumbling on even before the period covered by this study. Such debates tend to be framed by reference to 'the rule of law', so we next need to consider what the implications of the rule of law, if any, may be for the idea of the corporation tax code as political jurisprudence.

John Cullinane, writing in the *Financial Times* in April 2006, set out the key elements of the current debate with particular clarity.[103] His contribution, though brief, merits serious consideration, since it appeared in what has become one of the leading fora for tax policy, and it came from the pen of a leading member of the corporation tax policy community.[104] Mr Cullinane's 'hammering on the doors of representative government', to adapt Bernard Manin's phraseology, was thus apt to carry particular resonance. The corporation tax code,[105] he wrote, was 'complicated', for instance because there were still many exceptions to the alignment of tax with accounts; it was 'unclear', since among the exceptions to the alignment were research and development allowances and reliefs,[106] and these were notoriously difficult to apply to individual cases; and,

[99] Ie, in that it applies principles of positive, civil private law: Loughlin, *Foundations of Public Law* (above n 11) 4–5; and see above ch 2.

[100] Eg, *John Entick v Nathan Carrington and Others* (1765) 95 ER 807 KB.

[101] CTRM (above n 8) 15; and HM Treasury and HMRC, *Tax Policymaking: A New Approach* (above n 8) 7 and 10.

[102] See above ch 3; and Office of Tax Simplification, *Small Business Tax Review: March 2011* (London, HM Treasury, 2011), available at http://www.hm-treasury.gov.uk/ots (accessed 16 March 2011). Note the background pressure, which had been building for some time, eg: The Law Society, *Tax: Good Governance and Better Law Making: A Manifesto for Improving Tax Law* (March 2010) 3, available at http://www.lawsociety.org.uk/aboutlawsociety/influencinglaw (accessed 22 March 2011).

[103] J Cullinane, 'Chaos Theory in Corporate Decisions and Tax' *Financial Times* (20 April 2006) 11; and J Cullinane, 'Rule of Law' *Taxation* (11 May 2006) 147.

[104] Mr Cullinane was at the time of writing the article deputy president of the Chartered Institute of Taxation (CIOT) and later became its president.

[105] In fact, Mr Cullinane refers to 'tax' in general, but it is clear from the context that corporation tax is intended.

[106] See text to nn 230–32 below.

finally, the code, like its counterparts in other jurisdictions, was subject to frequent and often retrospective change.

What was wrong with each of these tendencies, wrote Mr Cullinane, was that they ran counter to the rule of law, the 'idea' of which was that 'people and businesses know where they stand and can make decisions accordingly'.[107] What was needed was a 'return' to the rule of law, something which would, he argued, have very specific consequences for the corporation tax code: further marrying of 'taxable profits' with 'profits per accounts'; assessing more accurately the costs that businesses will have to bear in order to comply with reforms to the code, which would include, presumably, reducing its complexity; and finally, 'keeping the rules as stable and comprehensive as possible'.

If the view of the corporation tax code presented in this study commends itself to readers, it will be apparent that, while Mr Cullinane's conclusions might be maintainable, his reasoning is somewhat controversial. This is because the characteristics that he attributes to the rule of law are at best contentious and because his conclusions are nonetheless supportable within a conception of corporation tax law as a 'political practice', as 'political jurisprudence'. The second part of this statement is discussed under sub-sections B and C below. What it is necessary to consider next, however (in A), is the contentious nature of the rule of law.

A. The Rule of Law

Judith Shklar,[108] the elegance of whose argument was somewhat underestimated both by Brian Tamanaha[109] and by the late Lord Bingham,[110] has traced the modern conception of the rule of law to Baron de Montesquieu. So located, its significance for this study is in the well-established institutions and processes through which corporate taxation law in Britain is created.[111] The historical and interpretative nature of Shklar's analysis makes it essential to a functionalist interpretation of the corporation tax code as political jurisprudence.

Montesquieu, says Shklar, provides the rule of law with its later historical signification as 'the rule of institutions', the earlier fatally circumscribed and much-abused one being Aristotle's 'rule of reason'.[112] Cullinane's aspirations for

[107] Cullinane, 'Chaos Theory' (above n 103).

[108] Shklar, who died in 1992, was a powerful commentator on the relationship of politics and law.

[109] BZ Tamanaha, *On the Rule of Law: History, Politics, Theory* (Cambridge, Cambridge University Press, 2004) 59.

[110] Lord Bingham, 'The Rule of Law' (2007) *Cambridge Law Journal* 67; and T Bingham, *The Rule of Law* (London, Allen Lane, 2010).

[111] J Shklar, 'Political Theory and the Rule of Law' in AC Hutchinson and P Monahan (eds), *The Rule of Law: Ideal or Ideology?* (Toronto, Carswell, 1987) 1.

[112] Ibid, 5; and Aristotle, *The Nicomachean Ethics* [350 bc], JAK Thomson, H Tredennick and J Barnes (eds) (London, Penguin, 2004) 187–89 and 215–16, quoted in M Loughlin, *Sword and Scales: An Examination of the Relationship between Law and Politics* (Oxford, Hart Publishing, 2000) 69–71 and 183–84.

the corporation tax code coincide with neither of these, but with Lon Fuller's post-Hayekian,[113] Aristotle-twisting view of the rule of law: Fuller maintains that, in accordance with the rule of law, law must be inter alia 'clear', 'enduring' and 'promulgated'.[114]As Shklar says, acidly, 'as a legal ideal for us there is little either to accept or reject in this conventional list of lawyerly aspirations'.[115] Although Fuller does not say in what kind of society such characteristics might obtain,[116] they could be compatible even with a 'repressive and irrational government'.[117] What Montesquieu provides is an analysis of the concept as protection from 'the fear of violence, the insecurity of arbitrary government and the discrimination of injustice'.[118] In describing the English system of the eighteenth century, Montesquieu conceived of the rule of law as a means of ensuring via institutional controls the personal security of individuals.[119] As EP Thompson concluded,[120] 'England was not [in the eighteenth century] a gulag society[,] and its political classes had to some degree shackled themselves'.[121] That was the method of prudence[122] – the foundation of the very system, analysed in chapters three and four, which is, in our own days, producing the corporation tax code.[123]

If this is right, the significance of the rule of law to the corporation tax code is simply that it is the product of those institutions and processes discussed in previous chapters. This has already been identified as a characteristic of political jurisprudence earlier in the chapter. What it means is that the corporation tax code, in all its instability and complexity, is a vivid illustration of Loughlin's point, closely aligned to Shklar's (via Montesquieu) that the rule of law in this system means no more and no less than the rule of institutions: 'that authority can only be wielded through recognized legal forms and that the legal machinery of the state exists to ensure the compliance of office-holders with these forms'.[124]

So if Cullinane is wrong about the premises but supportable, possibly, in his conclusions, what is the true significance of complexity and instability in the corporation tax code itself?

[113] Shklar (above n 111) 7 ('no social end in view').

[114] LL Fuller, *The Morality of Law*, rev edn (London, Yale University Press, 1969) 46, regarding the eight 'desiderata that make up the internal morality of the law' (81).

[115] Shklar (above n 111) 13.

[116] Shklar describes Fuller's notion of the 'rule of law' as 'political and historical fantasizing': ibid, 14.

[117] Ibid, 13.

[118] Ibid, 16; and Baron de Montesquieu, *The Spirit of the Laws*, T Nugent (trans) (New York, Hafner Publishing, 1949) 151.

[119] Shklar (above n 111) 4.

[120] EP Thompson, *Whigs and Hunters: The Origin of the Black Act* (London, Penguin, 1990) 258–69.

[121] Shklar (above n 111) 5.

[122] G Savile, 'The Character of a Trimmer' [1688] in MN Brown (ed), *The Works of George Savile Marquis of Halifax*, vol 1 (Oxford, Clarendon Press, 1989) 33.

[123] Loughlin, *Sword and Scales* (above n 112) 183–85.

[124] Loughlin, *The Idea of Public Law* (above n 46) 132. This might be what Lord Bingham in his 2007 article (above n 110) was saying, albeit indirectly, in reference to the Constitutional Reform Act 2005.

B. Complexity

John Cullinane has pinpointed the complexity of the corporation tax code as one of its most undesirable characteristics[125] and grounds this argument in the requirements of a version of the rule of law. Are we therefore to conclude, with John Tiley in 2005, that the corporation tax code, along with the rest of British taxation law, is merely a 'shambles',[126] or does its complexity denote something more? When Professor Tiley wrote these words, only two of the eventual four Tax Law Rewrite Acts applicable to corporation tax had actually been passed. What is more, although the Rewrite had modernised the language used in tax legislation, the concepts that the legislation contained remained intricate and highly abstract. Most significantly, the Rewrite was halted before the intricate statutory provisions on corporate chargeable gains had been rewritten. Understandably, therefore, much of the Coalition's policy documentation has focussed on the need for simplicity.[127] A report sponsored by the Confederation of British Industry (CBI), published in 2006, referred to the perception on the part of its members of levels of complexity that were thereunto undreamt of.[128] These political debates have ascribed the significance of complexity, not to a breach of the rule of law, but to international competitiveness issues, although as Martin Wolf[129] and Samuel Brittan[130] would insist, this is properly to be regarded as 'competitiveness' not between states but between individual firms headquartered in different states. What I maintain is that, given the institutional and procedural background and given the status of corporation tax law as public law, such complexity is unavoidable.[131] The most we can say is that it can be more or less prudently managed.

[125] Cf *Great Western Railway Company v Bater (Surveyor of Taxes)* (1922) 8 TC 231, 255 (Lord Wrenbury); *Wankie Colliery Co v IRC* [1922] 2 AC 51, 71 (Lord Carson); CK Allen, *Law in the Making*, 7th edn (Oxford, Clarendon Press, 1964) 484–85; H Monroe, QC, *Intolerable Inquisition? Reflections on the Law of Tax* (London, Stevens, 1981) 23–24; and M Parry-Wingfield, 'The Chicken or the Egg?' (2000) *British Tax Reform* 597, 598. On the vaunted need for simplicity, see, eg, Meade (ed) (above n 33) 18–21.

[126] Tiley, *Revenue Law*, 5th edn (above n 27) 49 (removed from the 6th edn in deference to the Tax Law Rewrite).

[127] V Houlder, '"Confusion Layered on Complexity" with Growth of Legislation' *Financial Times* (24 March 2006) 2; 'Memorandum submitted by the Institute of Chartered Accountants in England and Wales' in Treasury Committee, *5th Report. The 2007 Budget, Volume II: Oral and Written Evidence* HC (2006–07) 389-II pp Ev 61, Ev 62; and V Houlder, 'Tax System Grows More Complicated' *Financial Times* (11 December 2009) 4. For a brief discussion of the Rewrite project, see ch 1, s II above.

[128] Ipsos MORI, *UK Corporate Taxation and International Competitiveness* (London, CBI, 2006) 2.

[129] M Wolf, *Why Globalization Works* (London, Yale University Press, 2005) 80–81.

[130] S Brittan, '"Competitiveness" Rears Its Ugly Head' *Financial Times* (31 August 2007) 11.

[131] DL Paul, 'The Sources of Tax Complexity: How Much Simplicity Can Fundamental Tax Reform Achieve?' (1997) 76 *North Carolina Law Review* 151; and Public Bill Committee (17 May 2007) HC vol 460 col 215 (Ed Balls, then Economic Secretary to the Treasury).

With complexity, we are not talking about the sheer technical intricacy of issues that thereby become difficult to relate to the democratic process,[132] nor about the 'complexity' of complexity science.[133] We are talking instead about the complexity that has often resulted from the need to make corporation tax legislation effective.[134] The complexity of all tax legislation arises from the prudential need to make difficult decisions and careful distinctions between situations.[135] Three types of distinction have a particularly important part to play in the corporation tax code. First, there is the need to devise provisions suitable for a wide range of different service industries, as diverse as banking and life assurance.[136] Secondly, there is the need to maintain fairness in the system by combating tax avoidance, a process that needs to address the difficulties exacerbated by the historically literal approach of judges to the difficulties of interpreting parts of the corporation tax code.[137] Thirdly, there is the need prudently to address the legitimate concerns of interest groups over corporation tax reform measures, particularly within the corporate sector.[138] It may be, for example, that that was the essential problem with the capital allowances simplification in relation to industrial buildings: the replacement of the complexity of effectiveness with a relatively new phenomenon, the simplicity of ineffectiveness. Perhaps this was what Oliver Wendell Holmes really meant when he said, 'I do not care about the simplicity that lies this side of complexity'.[139] Christopher Wales would seem to think so: 'taxation has to be as complicated as the subject matter demands [and] . . . should be aimed at an expert audience'.[140]

The logic of the statutory response to each of these three areas of difficulty has been prudence – that is, juristic prudence. Such a reading of the suggestions in the tax simplification literature may put the current complexity of the

[132] D Zolo, *Democracy and Complexity: A Realist Approach*, D McKie (trans) (Cambridge, Polity Press, 1992); and J Bohman, *Public Deliberation: Pluralism, Complexity, and Democracy* (Cambridge, MA, MIT Press, 1996).

[133] E McMillan, *Complexity, Organizations and Change* (London, Routledge 2004) 25–28.

[134] But see Standing Committee A (11 May 2004) HC vol 421 cols 118–19 (Dawn Primarolo, then Paymaster General). Effectiveness is 'glossed' in Tax Law Review Committee, *Making Tax Law: Report of a Working Party on the Institutional Processes for the Parliamentary Scrutiny of Tax Proposals and for the Enactment of Tax Legislation chaired by Sir Alan Budd* (London, Institute for Fiscal Studies, 2003) para 8.2.

[135] J Prebble, 'Why is Tax Law Incomprehensible?' (1994) *British Tax Review* 380; and J Slemrod and J Bakija, *Taxing Ourselves: A Citizen's Guide to the Debate over Taxes*, 3rd edn (Cambridge, MA, MIT Press, 2004) 163–72. On the importance of casuistry when state-building, see Loughlin, *The Idea of Public Law* (above n 46) 131 and 152.

[136] Monroe (above n 125) 23; G Moffat, *Trusts Law: Text and Materials*, 5th edn (Cambridge, Cambridge University Press, 2009) 98–99; and Sanger, 'Corporate Tax Road Map' (above n 39) 4. On the life assurance industry, see HM Treasury, *Microeconomic Reform in Britain: Delivering Opportunities for All*, E Balls, J Grice and G O'Donnell (eds) (Basingstoke, Palgrave Macmillan, 2004) 278.

[137] Monroe (above n 125) 32.

[138] Ibid, 31 and 34.

[139] Quoted in D Southern, 'Big Bang for Bonds' *Tax Journal* (23 November 1995) 6.

[140] CJ Wales, 'The Making of Tax Policy in the Post-O'Donnell World: Can the HMT-HMRC "Policy Partnership" Meet the Challenge?' (2009) *British Tax Review* 245, 248.

corporation tax code, as well as the feasibility of the proposed solutions,[141] in a more realistic perspective. What is ironic is that the prudential nature of the now shelved Tax Law Rewrite may have been undermined, both by the rewritten legislation itself, which tended to be less telescoped than the original, and by a temporary impression of vastness created by the operation of the rewritten personal income tax legislation alongside the older corporation tax legislation subsequently rewritten in the 2009 and 2010 Rewrite Acts.[142]

C. Instability

Of the criticisms made by Mr Cullinane, among many other people, the charge of instability in the corporation tax code needs particularly careful consideration. Again, we need to decide what its significance is, once we have excluded it from the conception of the rule of law chosen as relevant to the present study.

The first, perhaps the most important point is the need to highlight the long-standing, almost instinctive hold on the Western imagination that the idea of stability has. John Pocock relates how, once the reality of a post-classical city republic had emerged in fifteenth-century Italy, writers like Machiavelli fell to wondering how, having come into existence, such an institution might meet its end.[143] Keeping the ship of state afloat and on course was as important to its constituent policies as to the enterprise of the state as a whole. Some proximate sense of stability, it is suggested, pervades discussions on the need for stability in laws. When Gordon Brown as Chancellor talked hubristically about 'economic stability', this was the kind of imagery that he seemed to invoke. In this pre 2007–09 worldview, tax had an important role in economic stabilisation.[144]

[141] Most importantly, the shelved Tax Law Rewrite. See FA 1995 s 160 (a 'one-off' measure only); and Inland Revenue, *The Path to Tax Simplification: A Background Paper* (1995). See generally, D Salter, 'Pre-Parliamentary Procedure, Consultation and the Tax Law Rewrite' (1997) 16 *Civil Justice Quarterly* 294; D Salter, 'Towards a Parliamentary Procedure for the Tax Law Rewrite' (1998) 19 *Statute Law Review* 65; and V Houlder, 'Experts Attack Rewrite of Arcane Legislation' *Financial Times* (25 February 2008) 4.

[142] Houlder, 'Confusion Layered on Complexity' (above n 127); V Houlder, 'Britain Remains Competitive on Tax Even as Law Book Expands' *Financial Times* (8 November 2006) 4; V Houlder, 'Fewer Tax Laws as Treasury Reacts to Criticism' *Financial Times* (15 August 2007) 3, citing the following numbers as the 'average number' of pages in FBs since the early 1980s: '153 in 1980–84; 209 in 1985–89; 266 in 1990–94; 312 in 1995–99 and 463 in 2000–07'; HM Treasury, *Meeting the Aspirations of the British People: 2007 Pre-Budget Report and Comprehensive Spending Review* (Cm 7227, 2007) paras 4.49–4.53; and M Gammie, 'Tax Simplification' in R Chote, C Emmerson, D Miles and J Shaw (eds), *The IFS Green Budget: January 2008* (London, Institute for Fiscal Studies, 2007) 260–67.

[143] JGA Pocock, *The Machiavellian Moment: Florentine Political Thought and the Atlantic Republican Tradition* (Princeton, Princeton University Press, 1975) 99–103.

[144] RA Musgrave, *The Theory of Public Finance: A Study in Public Economy* (New York, McGraw-Hill Book Company, 1959) 5–6; RA Musgrave and PB Musgrave, *Public Finance in Theory and Practice*, 5th edn (New York, McGraw-Hill, 1989) 11–13; HM Treasury and Inland Revenue, *Corporation Tax Reform: A Consultation Document* (London, Inland Revenue, 2003) para 1.11; and M Keen, A Klemm, V Perry, 'Tax and the Crisis' (2010) 31(1) *Fiscal Studies* 43.

In artificially unpicking economic from legal considerations, however, we need to distinguish carefully between a concrete notion of the role of taxation in general in economic stabilisation[145] and more imaginative notions of the city on the sea. Brief reference has already been made to Edward Troup's contemporary critique of the 1998 *Code for Fiscal Stability*. In the course of his commentary, he commended the then newly elected Labour Administration for its formal commitment to 'the worthy, if slightly Calvinistic aims of "transparency, stability, responsibility, fairness and efficiency"'.[146] However, Mr Troup was careful to emphasise that, despite its name, the Code related to 'the formulation and implementation of – (a) fiscal policy, and (b) policy for the management of the National Debt'.[147] It was about 'government borrowing (ie, the excess of spending over taxation)' – in other words, not about tax levels per se, and certainly not about the stability of tax legislation.[148] Without mentioning the practice of political prudence, Mr Troup nonetheless acknowledged that no government would commit itself to stasis in this way. As the Treasury Committee acknowledged in 2011, tax legislation must by its very nature change and evolve.[149] The question is whether this means that the corporation tax code is inherently unstable.

It is true that stability is an important element in prudential governance. We can see this from Hobbes's acceptance that the purpose of the 'art and science of government' is men's desire 'with all their hearts, to conform themselves into one firm and lasting edifice',[150] with the penalty of failure (a lack of prudential legislation) being destruction:

> [F]or want, both of the art of making fit laws, to square their actions by, and also of humility, and patience, to suffer the rude and cumbersome points of their present greatness to be taken off, they[151] cannot without the help of a very able architect, be compiled into any other than a crazy building, such as hardly lasting out their own time, must assuredly fall upon the heads of their posterity.[152]

Loughlin provides a powerful analysis of this key passage in his latest work.[153] Hobbes is speaking here not only of the ordering of the state but also of the particular laws it creates; and given the scope of public law discussed in chapter two, we may conclude that prudential reasoning is the essential means of framing such

[145] EN (Lord) Plowden (Chair), *Control of Public Expenditure* (Cmnd 1432, 1961) para 10; and James and Nobes (above n 18) ch 6.

[146] FA 1998 s 155(2); and HM Treasury, *The Code for Fiscal Stability* (1998), available at http://archive.treasury.gov.uk/budget/1998/cfs.pdf (accessed 8 July 2011).

[147] FA 1998 s 155(1).

[148] E Troup, 'Finance Act Notes: Fiscal Stability – Sections 155 and 156' (1998) *British Tax Review* 490, 491.

[149] Treasury Committee, *8th Report: Principles of Tax Policy* (HC 2010–11, 753).

[150] T Hobbes, *Leviathan* [1651], M Oakeshott (ed) (Oxford, Basil Blackwell, 1955) 210 (pt 2 ch 29), quoted in Loughlin, *The Idea of Public Law* (above n 46) 140–41.

[151] Ie, 'men . . . at last weary of irregular jostling, and hewing one another . . .': Hobbes (ibid).

[152] Hobbes (above n 150) 210 (pt 2 ch 29), quoted in Loughlin, *The Idea of Public Law* (above n 46) 140–41.

[153] Loughlin, *Foundations of Public Law* (above n 11) 281–82.

laws. Stability is a prudential quality, no doubt. There was a recognition of this in the commitment to 'stability of direction in legislation' over the long term, in Labour's corporation tax policy documents.[154] Not only is it, of course, reiterated in the New Approach and the Corporate Tax Road Map, but the power of the concept provides the whole impetus for what those documents say.[155] Given an objective of economic growth, prudential law-making will require stability in laws to encourage investment.[156] Hence, Mr Cullinane is right to advocate 'keeping the rules as stable . . . as possible', but the reason is prudence, rather than the rule of law. The use of the phrase 'stable . . . as possible' indeed acknowledges that absolute stability may not always be realisable. A Conservative MP spoke well in pointing out, when the provisions of the 'loan relationships' code were under consideration in Standing Committee in February 1996, that tax law was subject to 'evolutionary development': 'It is constantly necessary to revise, amend, improve and bring up to date the corpus of tax law'.[157]

None of this is to understate the economic importance of stability.[158] Plainly, it is crucial, and Mr Cullinane was right to emphasise it; it is just that his reason is not the real reason. Whether people appeal to one or other of the prudence or rule of law justifications depends on how worried they are by executive – that is, administrative – discretion. Framing the discussion in terms of the rule of law reflects the traditional normativist concern with the separation of powers referred to above.[159] Framing it in terms of prudential use of executive or policy discretion reflects a greater faith in the power of the state to shape outcomes.[160] Both views can be accommodated within a neoliberal ideological outlook. That said, the former is – as attested by the 2010 foundation of the Office of Tax Simplification – more attuned to the market liberalism of the Coalition,[161] the latter to the more statist viewpoint of Labour and the tradition of social or egalitarian liberalism.[162]

[154] Eg, HM Treasury and Inland Revenue, *Large Business Taxation* (above n 17) para 1.3; and C Sanger, 'Business Tax Policy: A Vision for the Future?' *Tax Adviser* (April 2002) 12.

[155] HM Treasury and HMRC, *Tax Policymaking: A New Approach* (2010) (hereafter 'New Approach to Tax Policy' or 'NATP'), available at http://hm-treasury.gov.uk (accessed 10 July 2010) 7–8.

[156] Meade (ed) (above n 33) 21; and HM Treasury and Inland Revenue, *Large Business Taxation* (above n 17) para 1.13.

[157] Standing Committee E (29 February 1996) HC vol 272 col 596 (Nigel Forman).

[158] Musgrave and Musgrave (above n 144) ch 30 and 531–32; James and Nobes (above n 18) ch 6; Balls and O'Donnell (eds) (above n 7) ch 1; C Thain, 'Economic Policy' in P Dunleavy, A Gamble, I Holliday and G Peele (eds), *Developments in British Politics* 6 (Basingstoke, Macmillan, 2002) 219; C Thain, 'Economic Policy' in P Dorey (ed), *Developments in British Public Policy* (Cambridge, Sage, 2005) 24; and V Houlder, 'Businesses Say Volume of Tax Changes Deters Growth' *Financial Times* (21 March 2011) 10.

[159] Loughlin, *Foundations of Public Law* (above n 11) 391–402.

[160] Ibid, 402 and 452.

[161] K Ussher and I Walford, *National Treasure* (London, Demos, 2011) 54–56. See generally, D Laws and P Marshall (eds), *The Orange Book: Reclaiming Liberalism* (London, Profile, 2004); and BBC Radio 4, *Analysis: The Orange Book – Clegg's Political Lemon?* (27 February 2011), details available at http://www.bbc.co.uk/Radio4 (accessed 18 March 2011).

[162] Steger and Roy (above n 22) 9.

I shall return to these points once I have considered the significance of a theory of effectiveness in shaping the values contained in the corporation tax code itself.

IV. THE PRIORITISATION OF POLITICAL VALUES IN THE CORPORATION TAX CODE

Readers should by this stage in the chapter be persuaded that most theoretical discussions of the current state of corporate taxation have little, if any, interpretative value. This is not, of course, to deny their normative usefulness or their undoubted intellectual rigour. What it does assert, however, is that arguments for reform that do not explicitly address the deep implications of the public law nature of the corporation tax code or that do not recognise the political significance of the code's complexity are to some greater or lesser extent inadequate, in interpretative terms. The present study is not, of course, concerned with constructing a normative theory, but it is appropriate to stress that any such theory would be much the stronger for building on robust interpretative foundations.

These points made, I am now in a position to etch in the final details of the picture that this study seeks to create. They are concerned with reality: what configuration of values have the institutions and processes discussed in previous chapters in fact created? What are the strengths and weaknesses of that structure? And how is it that such weaknesses as there are, are nonetheless outweighed, for the present at least, by the system's strengths?

I continue by referring to two roughly contemporaneous theoretical pieces that help to underline the stance taken in the study as a whole. The first is part of Loughlin's archaeological work on the origins of public law;[163] the second is from Sol Picciotto's work on the establishment of a social, economic and political context for the principles of the taxation of international business.[164]

What Loughlin is at pains to point out is that Adam Smith's *The Wealth of Nations*[165] – still, as we know, nearly always referred to in theoretical discussions of taxation[166] – is not, properly understood, to be read as laying down a series of exogenous norms about what taxes and tax systems ought or ought not do. If so, the maxims of taxation[167] would provide no clue as to the weight to be attached to one maxim relative to that to be attached to the others, either generally or in a particular case. Instead, the maxims, indeed Smith's work as a whole, should be regarded as a highly sophisticated and nuanced handbook of

[163] Loughlin, *Public Law and Political Theory* (above n 13) 5; and Loughlin, *Foundations of Public Law* (above n 11) esp 421.

[164] S Picciotto, *International Business Taxation* (London, Weidenfeld and Nicolson, 1992) 83.

[165] A Smith, *The Wealth of Nations* [1776], AS Skinner (ed) (London, Penguin, 1999).

[166] Such is Smith's intellectual stature that he is absent from Meade (1978) but included in Mirrlees, Adam and Besley et al (above n 30) 1.

[167] Smith (above n 165) Books IV–V, 418; and JS Mill, *Principles of Political Economy* and *Chapters on Socialism* [1848/1873], J Riley (ed) (Oxford, Oxford University Press, 1994) 167.

the 'science of legislation'.[168] These are the points that the legislator – the prince – needs to bear in mind, Smith is saying, if he or she is to create a tax or a tax system that will *work*.[169] It is not that taxes or tax systems that fail to reflect some or all of these principles are in some sense immoral or unfair or bad. Rather, it is simply that they will tend not to work; they will create resentment and impede the workings of the 'invisible hand', and in impeding economic growth, they will fail to raise the funds that the prince needs to create the conditions to sustain his Scottish Enlightenment conception of the public good.[170] This prudential logic of effectiveness is what, in turn, provides the 'grammar', which shapes the 'vocabulary', which the maxims of taxation contain. As Smith says, it is by the non-observance of 'some one or other' of the maxims 'that taxes are frequently so much more burdensome to the people than they are beneficial to the sovereign'.[171]

This instrumental and prudential spirit in which the maxims were laid down was well understood by John Stuart Mill in his *Principles of Political Economy*[172] and, later on, by the Whitehall civil servant Sir Josiah Stamp[173] in his remarkable *Principles of Taxation*.[174] Such an understanding is rather less apparent from Mirrlees;[175] nor was it evident from the technocratic spirit[176] of the ten 'tenets' advanced by the Institute of Chartered Accountants in England and Wales's *Pathways to Tax Reform* of 2000.[177] Something like the spirit of Smith appears, however, from the Corporate Tax Road Map. Propounding the Coalition's own five corporate tax reform principles, it envisages:

[168] Loughlin, *Public Law and Political Theory* (above n 13) 4; D Winch, 'Adam Smith's "Enduring Particular Result": A Political and Cosmopolitan Perspective' in I Hont and M Ignatieff (eds), *Wealth and Virtue: The Shaping of Political Economy in the Scottish Enlightenment* (Cambridge, Cambridge University Press, 1983) 253; and D Winch, *Adam Smith's Politics: An Essay in Historiographic Revision* (Cambridge, Cambridge University Press, 1978) esp 159.

[169] Loughlin, *Public Law and Political Theory* (above n 13); and R Porter, *Enlightenment: Britain and the Creation of the Modern World* (London, Penguin, 2000) 188.

[170] Ibid, 394–96; and D Slater and F Tonkiss, *Market Society: Markets and Modern Social Theory* (Cambridge, Polity Press, 2001) 41.

[171] Smith (above n 165) Books IV–V, 418.

[172] Mill (above n 167).

[173] Stamp was killed in an air raid in 1941: R Thomas, *The British Philosophy of Administration: A Comparison of British and American Ideas, 1900–1939* (Cambridge, Centre for Business and Public Sector Ethics, 1989) 251.

[174] J Stamp, *The Fundamental Principles of Taxation in the Light of Modern Developments* (The Newmarch Lectures for 1919) (London, Macmillan, 1921) esp ch 4; and AC Pigou, *A Study in Public Finance*, 3rd edn (London, Macmillan, 1962) 40–45, esp 43.

[175] Mirrlees, Adam and Besley et al (above n 30) 19. See also Meade (ed) (above n 33) 23, which is rather vague on what is the most important practical question; and C Sandford, *The Economics of Public Finance: An Economic Analysis of Government Expenditure and Revenue in the United Kingdom*, 4th edn (Oxford, Pergamon Press, 1992) 112, which is similarly vague on this point.

[176] M Oakeshott, 'Rationalism in Politics' [1962] in T Fuller (ed), *Rationalism in Politics and Other Essays*, 2nd edn (Indianapolis, Liberty Fund, 1991) 15–16.

[177] Institute of Chartered Accountants in England and Wales, *Towards a Better Tax System: Practical Consideration of the Ten Tenets* (London, ICAEW, 2000); Association of Chartered Certified Accountants, *Tax Principles: From Adam Smith to Barack Obama* (London, ACCA, 2009), available at http://www.accaglobal.com/pubs (accessed 22 March 2011); and Sandford (above n 175) 112.

> In practice, there will be a degree of tension between these principles. For example, the pace of change in business practices can mean that there is pressure to make quick changes to the tax system, which can affect its stability. Similarly, widespread grandfathering of existing arrangements, while improving stability, may create excessive complexity. Government and business need to debate these trade-offs openly in order to get the balance right.[178]

The need for these trade-offs, these prioritisations, is recognised, too, in the 2011 report by the Treasury Committee.[179] And it is in the prudential Smithian vein just described, although without explicit reference to Smith's maxims, that Picciotto has delineated, albeit briefly, the implications of ideas such as those just discussed, for the legitimacy of taxes and tax systems. Independently of Loughlin's interpretation of Smith but also in 1992, Picciotto drew out some strikingly similar conclusions to those of Loughlin.[180] He emphasised, as does Loughlin in relation to public law generally,[181] the point that tax law is a practical art, the 'overriding aim' of which is 'effectiveness' – an aim that will be frustrated, as it is in relation to other forms of regulation, if a system lacks 'fairness':

> Taxation is not an abstract exercise in political or economic philosophy, but a practical matter of raising state finance for the public good. The overriding aim is therefore effectiveness, which must be predicted, based on estimations of the patterns of compliance, non-compliance and avoidance. It is in this sense that the question of *legitimacy* is central to the evaluation of taxation, as well as other types of legal regulation of economic activity.[182] Legitimacy in this sense combines the interrelated issues of equity and effectiveness. To the extent that a regulatory system lacks fairness it fails in political acceptability, and will also tend to fail in effectiveness as enforcement becomes difficult and non-compliance grows. Equally, a system which has problems of enforceability and therefore of effectiveness will tend to lose political acceptability.[183]

Note the similarity to Loughlin's position here. First, although Picciotto does not relate the practical art of taxation to the 'power of practical reason' that is prudence, the idea of tax legislation as a 'practice' is surely implied. Secondly, Picciotto places the emphasis on 'effectiveness'. Unlike in the Sheffield school scheme of things, where effectiveness is presented as a rule of law value along with all the others,[184] in Picciotto's summation, as in Loughlin's 'pure theory of public law',[185] effectiveness is not merely an immanent value but the theory that shapes and prioritises such values in particular situations. Thirdly and finally, like Loughlin, Picciotto sees the significance of tax fairness not as some abso-

[178] CTRM (above n 8) 11.
[179] Treasury Committee, *8th Report* (above n 149).
[180] Picciotto (above n 164) 83.
[181] Loughlin, *The Idea of Public Law* (above n 46) esp 148–52 and 163.
[182] Murphy and Nagel (above n 20) 162: '[T]ax legislation is, in general, distinct from expenditure legislation.'
[183] Picciotto (above n 164) 83.
[184] Eg, C Hilson, *Regulating Pollution: A UK and EC Perspective* (Oxford, Hart Publishing, 2000) 127–29.
[185] Loughlin, *The Idea of Public Law* (above n 46) ch 9.

lute quality but as a value the presence of which makes a tax the more likely to succeed and the absence of which will tend to undermine its effectiveness.

The intellectual strand common to both Loughlin's portrayal of 'the science of legislation' and to Picciotto's summation of the demands of tax policy-making is the need for tax policy to be effective. This does, of course, have an administrative dimension, which is outside the scope of the study.[186] That effectiveness has to be judged by reference to what the first 'Brown Budget' (July 1997) referred to as 'the objectives of the government of the day'.[187] What shapes these objectives, as well as their relationship to a particular view of the 'public interest', has already been discussed in chapter four. The only point that I need to underscore at this late stage in the study is the analogous position of 'the prince' in Smith's world-view, and the Crown-in-Parliament in the depiction of the British constitution in the present study. Both are 'the sovereign', but the sovereignty that subsists in the relationship of government and governed depends, in the world of today, on the maintenance of trust and confidence between the two. This, in turn, depends on constantly prudential political choices. To say it is about 'trade-offs' between values, as Edward Troup expresses it,[188] gets somewhere near, but this is too mechanistic an expression for conveying what should be essentially a quicksilver ability in government.[189] What is clear, in corporation tax more perhaps than in any other area of taxation policy, is that the government's ability to make prudential decisions, to 'deserve' the trust and confidence of the electorate, is enhanced by the relatively low salience of the tax. In coolly analytical terms, it is indeed the mass of individuals that eventually bears the burden of corporation tax.[190] In politics, however, that is much less important than the fact that the tax is initially laid upon the companies themselves.[191]

Two main consequences flow from these observations, and they are of the first importance to the study as a whole. First, the values immanent to the corporation tax code at any particular moment, as well as the way in which they appear to have been prioritised, reflect not only the view of the public, or national, interest taken by the current administration, but also the public interest ideology of previous ones. Thus, we might say, do legislative codes proclaim their own histories. Secondly, it is necessary to be extremely sceptical of certain types of adverse, especially journalistic and other professional criticism of the

[186] C Wales, 'The Implications of the O'Donnell Review for the Making of Tax Policy in the UK' (2004) *British Tax Review* 543, 548.

[187] Gammie, 'The Process of Fiscal Reform' (above n 79); and *Equipping Britain for our Long-Term Future: Financial Statement and Budget Report* (HC 1997–98, 85) para 1.68.

[188] Troup (above n 148) 491.

[189] See above ch 2.

[190] J Kay, 'Talk of Raising the Corporate Burden Taxes Logic' *Financial Times* (25 October 2005) 19; J Kay and J Sen, 'The Comparative Burden of Business Taxation' (1983) 4(3) *Fiscal Studies* 23, 23; and M Gammie, 'Reforming Corporate Taxation: An Evaluation of the United States Treasury Integration Proposals and Other Corporate Tax Systems in an International Context: Part 1' (1992) *British Tax Review* 148, 149.

[191] Snape (above n 14) 403. See above pp 7 and 19.

current state of corporate taxation. When people disagree about corporation tax reform, they do so not by reference to some objective reality but by reference to their own often tacit perceptions of the national, or public, interest – that is to say, by reference to their own political or ideological viewpoints. In other words, they are arguing about the values themselves, possibly, and certainly about their prioritisation. Nowhere is this phenomenon more apparent than in relation to anti-avoidance legislation and its implications for the concept of fairness in taxation.

We can explore the implications of the propositions just advanced by unravelling the main values that are most obvious from the corporation tax code as it is currently framed: efficiency and fairness. We need to concentrate on Labour's own reforms and the reasons behind them, because the code still is shaped by these values; it will be many years before further reform has worked significantly on this state of affairs. That is why the Corporate Tax Road Map envisages the possibility of complexity perpetuated by the 'grandfathering of existing arrangements'. It may be, indeed, that despite the efforts of the Office of Tax Simplification, this combination of values remains because of the vested interests it has created. The balance between efficiency and fairness is nonetheless a crucial one. Not only do nations want to be wealthier; it is the duty of governments, if not to make them wealthier, then to create the conditions under which they can become so.[192]

The background to Labour's conception of corporate taxation is telling. Convincing Britain's electorate both of the promising nature of its ideology and of its ability to formulate and implement policies to enhance national wealth through 'credible socialism'[193] was the Labour Party's priority in 1997. By the time of the Labour landslide in the early summer of that year, the traditional party of the Left had, through a combination of miscalculation and dogmatism, been away from the 'corridors of power' for the best part of two decades.[194] 'To be socialist and at the same time credible', to repeat the aspiration voiced by Gordon Brown in a 1997 speech,[195] was Labour's solution to the party's long absence from government.[196] The implications of these ideas for tax reform were expressed thus in the July 1997 Budget report:

> It is essential that tax policy is based on clear principles. These are to encourage work, savings and investment, and fairness. A tax system should also be well designed, to meet the objectives of the government of the day,[197] without generating undesirable side effects; it must keep taxpayers' compliance costs to a minimum; it should avoid

[192] See above ch 2; and Smith (above n 165) Books IV–V, 5.

[193] See above ch 2.

[194] W Keegan, *The Prudence of Mr Gordon Brown* (Chichester, John Wiley 2003) chs 2–3.

[195] See above ch 2; and C Thain and R Christie, 'Treasury Power: Past, Present and Future', presented at JUC PAC Conference (Belfast, 3–5 September 2007), available at http://colinthain.com/images/pub_uploads/pacpaper.pdf (accessed 5 July 2011).

[196] G Brown, 'Fair Is Efficient: A Socialist Agenda for Fairness', Fabian Pamphlet 563 (Fabian Society, 1994).

[197] See above ch 4.

the less well-off bearing an unfair burden; and attention must be paid to any implications for the United Kingdom's international competitiveness.[198]

The corporation tax code, as will become apparent, became a crucial instrument in the achievement of these two objectives: 'credible' policies and 'socialist' values. Within its intricate provisions, we can trace the uneasy reconciliations that giving effect to the two objectives sometimes involved. In this part of the discussion, I shall be concentrating on the 'credibility' dimension, which for reasons also to become apparent, was in essence a question of efficiency. In the subsequent section, my emphasis will be on what we might, albeit rather crudely, think of as the 'socialist' component: the value of fairness. The untangling of the values in this way is not entirely satisfactory, since there is much interpenetration,[199] but it is nonetheless maintainable[200] and highlights the substantial differences immanent to each.

I turn next, therefore, to the values that were immanent to the corporation tax code by the end of the Labour Administration in 2010. Over time, the Coalition's corporate tax principles – 'avoiding complexity'; fairness 'across corporate tax payers'; making adaptive changes based on business conditions; '[m]aintaining stability'; and 'lowering rates while maintaining the tax base'[201] – will no doubt reshape these values significantly. For the present, they remain, so their ideological significance needs to be understood.

A. The Value of Efficiency in Corporate Taxation

That the Labour Government placed considerable emphasis on efficiency in corporate taxation was everywhere apparent in their policy documents. The fullest statement of its importance, although not the earliest, appeared in two substantial volumes,[202] in which Ed Balls[203] and Gus O'Donnell, two individuals very closely associated with corporation tax reform, set out Labour's economic policy objectives and the place of efficiency within them. The background was the distinction, already alluded to, between macroeconomic and microeconomic policy. We have already seen how, in the hands of Balls and O'Donnell, macroeconomic policy was about keeping inflation steady, at very low levels 'over the long term', to generate 'high and stable levels of growth and employment'.[204]

[198] *Equipping Britain for our Long-Term Future* (above n 187) para 1.68.

[199] Balls, Grice and O'Donnell (eds) (above n 136) 7.

[200] Ibid, 5.

[201] CTRM (above n 8) 11; and Sanger, 'Corporate Tax Road Map' (above n 39) 4.

[202] Balls and O'Donnell (eds) (above n 7); and Balls, Grice and O'Donnell (eds) (above n 136).

[203] See above ch 3; D Lipsey, *The Secret Treasury* (London, Viking, 2000) 27; and C Thain and R Christie, 'A New-Look Treasury under its New Boss: Mr Brown' *Parliamentary Brief* (February 2008) 21, available at http://www.treasuryproject.org (accessed 21 February 2008) 22.

[204] See above ch 4; and more generally, see G Brown, 'Advancing the Public Interest' in W Stevenson (ed), *Gordon Brown: Moving Britain Forward – Selected Speeches, 1997–2006* (London, Bloomsbury, 2006) 91.

With such stability as the goal of macroeconomic policy, the conditions were created under which the second and third 'pillars' of economic policy, 'tackling the supply-side barriers to growth and delivering employment and economic opportunities for all',[205] could be worked on too. Reforming corporation tax, as well as other areas of taxation, was part of the second pillar, the 'tackling' of 'supply-side barriers to growth', but it also had implications for the third. It was a key example of the post-1997 role of the Treasury as an economics ministry.[206]

Curtailing 'supply-side barriers to growth' meant, in the case of the corporation tax code, using it to assist 'firms [to] reach their full potential'[207] – that is, making the tax more efficient. However, as we shall see, this was not simply the efficiency of the fourth of Smith's taxation maxims. What we had by 2010 was a corporation tax code that had had provisions shorn from it that were seen to be inconsistent with enhancing efficiency; older provisions that were consistent with that objective retained; and new provisions introduced that were designed to enhance efficiency. The initiatives discussed in chapter four were efficiency issues in this sense. First, the alignment of tax with accounts is reflected in the large areas of the code now based on accounting practice. Secondly, the response to European and international legal developments is illustrated by those features of the code - mainly relating to the availability of reliefs within corporate groups - that reflected the single market principles of the European Treaties and GATT 1994, as well as the 'best practice' disseminated by the OECD.[208] Thirdly, action on compliance and enforcement dimensions of the tax were embodied in the rules on corporation tax self-assessment (CTSA). How each of these reflected the circumstances of their introduction and the extent to which they were consistent (or inconsistent) with their proffered objective will be addressed later in the discussion. For the moment, it is just necessary to return to Labour's policy documents on corporation tax reform and to relate the ideas they contain to economic thinking more generally.

The efficiency imperative within the code (according to Balls, Grice and O'Donnell) and the need thereby to address 'market failures' was driven by one crucial factor, already discussed at some length: the need to make markets 'work better in the public interest'.[209] As Balls, Grice and O'Donnell emphasised, 'Markets are a powerful means of advancing the public interest',[210] and this was reflected in the four 'major microeconomic goals' that they set out in what was essentially a highly detailed explanation of Labour's microeconomic policy. Two of these goals related to 'high-quality public services' delivery and to the maintaining of unprecedentedly high levels of employment. Whilst generally relevant, in the sense that the code's effectiveness impacted directly on these

[205] Balls, Grice and O'Donnell (eds) (above n 136) 5.
[206] Thain and Christie, 'Treasury Power' (above n 195) 8.
[207] Balls, Grice and O'Donnell (eds) (above n 136) 6.
[208] Eg, Organisation for Economic Co-operation and Development (OECD), *Taxing Profits in a Global Economy: Domestic and International Issues* (Paris, OECD, 1991) ch 1.
[209] Ibid, 6. See also above ch 4.
[210] OECD (above n 208).

goals, the two of most importance here were 'building a fair society', discussed below in conjunction with fairness, and what we need to consider next, 'raising the sustainable rate of UK productivity growth'.[211]

In the microeconomic goal of raising 'productivity growth', the key word was 'sustainability': the idea that it could be achieved consistently over the long term. Although this was a use of the expression 'sustainability' that environmentalists deplore, it focused attention on two key implications of the goal: the need to favour competition so as to encourage innovation and creativity and the need to eliminate market failures.

To the extent, therefore, that the corporation tax code lacked any element of protectionism in the form of tax subsidies, it reflected one aspect of efficiency. Britain's membership of the European Union and GATT 1994/WTO were major drivers for this, and we shall have occasion to return to it below. It was not merely the absence of tax subsidies that could be seen to reflect this ideal of efficiency, however. Insofar as the code promoted or at least did not undermine either access to capital or the 'free mobility of capital and labour',[212] it can also be said to have disclosed this particular vision of efficiency. Again, I shall return to this later in the discussion. Both of these manifestations of efficiency were illustrations of the government's perception that its role was 'not only to support but [to] positively enhance markets in the public interest'.[213] The ideas underlying these elements were also contained in three policy 'orientation documents', as they might be called: *Large Business Taxation: The Government's Strategy and Corporate Tax Reforms: A Consultation Document*, which appeared in July 2001;[214] *Reform of Corporation Tax: A Consultation Document*, published in August 2002;[215] and *Corporation Tax Reform: A Consultation Document*, published exactly a year later in August 2003.[216]

The 2001 document emphasised that the corporation tax code needed to contribute 'to creating the best possible location for investment', that it had to embody rates of tax that were 'as low as possible' and that it had to reflect 'the realities of the modern business environment'.[217] On this footing, '[t]he key principles for corporate tax reform' were fairness, discussed below, and 'competitiveness'.[218] Increasing efficiency enhanced competitiveness, as the document went on to make clear:

> [T]o create the best possible location for investment, the tax system should complement business competitiveness, not stifle it. This means: removing tax distortions,

[211] Ibid, 7.
[212] Ibid, 8.
[213] Ibid.
[214] HM Treasury and Inland Revenue, *Large Business Taxation* (above n 17).
[215] HM Treasury and Inland Revenue, *Reform of Corporation Tax: A Consultation Document* (London, Inland Revenue, 2002).
[216] HM Treasury and Inland Revenue, *Corporation Tax Reform* (above n 144).
[217] HM Treasury and Inland Revenue, *Large Business Taxation* (above n 17) para 1.5; and Sanger, 'Corporate Tax Road Map' (above n 39) 3.
[218] HM Treasury and Inland Revenue, *Large Business Taxation* (above n 17).

> facilitating decision-making that is driven by commercial factors, rather than by tax considerations. Businesses, not government, are best placed to judge how to operate and structure themselves.[219]

Rather than taking a doctrinaire stance, the 2001 document therefore confronted 'head-on' the fact 'that multinational businesses . . . [were] likely to increase in importance'[220] and, in an oblique reference to Nigel Lawson's corporation tax reforms of the 1980s,[221] emphasised how the world had moved on since then.[222] This being so, it was 'fair tax competition' between countries that would allow 'business to exploit real commercial opportunities'.[223] Key to this were the maintenance of 'a low-rate, broad base system' and the better alignment of commercial profits and tax profits.[224] However, it also involved the removal from the code of 'out-dated and ineffective restrictions',[225] as illustrated, for instance, by the deletion of certain restrictions on 'the transfer of assets and the use of tax losses within multinational groups'[226] and the abolition of withholding tax on interest payments.[227]

Besides removing distortions, the elimination of market failures was also detectable in the code. According to Balls, Grice and O'Donnell, these existed 'when the competitive outcome of markets . . . [was] not efficient from the point of view of the economy as a whole'.[228] In the 2001 document, the 1999 removal from the corporation tax code of the obligation to pay advance corporation tax (ACT) and its replacement by payments of corporation tax on account, under CTSA, were seen as one example of the removal of distortion,[229] while the introduction of 'a new research and development (R&D) tax credit[230] . . . aimed at encouraging innovation by large companies in recognition of the wider benefits to the economy that flow[ed] from R&D expenditure'[231] was a way to remedy a significant market failure.[232]

[219] Ibid, para 1.6.
[220] Ibid, para 1.8.
[221] Ibid.
[222] Cf L MacNeice, *Autumn Journal: A Poem* (London, Faber and Faber, 1939) 39.
[223] HM Treasury and Inland Revenue, *Large Business Taxation* (above n 17) para 1.11.
[224] Ibid, paras 1.12 and 1.14–1.15.
[225] Ibid, paras 1.12 and 1.19.
[226] Ibid, para 1.19. Now CTA 2010 ss 99, 130, 132 and 133, as amended by F(No3)A 2010 s 12 and sch 6 (ex-ICTA 1988 s 402(3A)).
[227] HM Treasury, 'Withholding Tax on International Bond Interest Abolished', News Release BN2J (21 March 2000), reprinted at (2000) *Simon's Weekly Tax Intelligence* 458–60; HM Treasury, A more competitive environment for business', Press Release (8 November 2000), reprinted at (2000) *Simon's Weekly Tax Intelligence* 1588–94; Budget Note 13/01, *Withholding Tax on Intra-UK Corporate Interest etc* (7 March 2001), reprinted at (2001) *Simon's Weekly Tax Intelligence* 442–44; FA 2001 s 85; FA 2002 s 94; and FA 2004 ss 98–106 (but now ITA 2007 s 874). See also R Bramwell, A James, M Hardwick and J Lindsay (eds), *Taxation of Companies and Company Reconstructions*, 8th edn (London, Sweet and Maxwell, 2002) s A3.10 (new law); Appendix 1.6 (old law).
[228] Balls, Grice and O'Donnell (eds) (above n 136) 8.
[229] HM Treasury and Inland Revenue, *Large Business Taxation* (above n 17) para 1.16.
[230] CTA 2009 pt 13 (formerly FA 2002 s 53 and sch 12).
[231] HM Treasury and Inland Revenue, *Large Business Taxation* (above n 17) para 1.17.
[232] Ibid (environmental incentives); S Brittan, 'A Credo for a Revived Capitalism' *Financial Times* (7 May 2010) 3; CTRM (above n 8) 55; and Sanger, 'Corporate Tax Road Map' (above n 39) 8.

It will be appreciated from all of this that a particular, highly developed idea of efficiency ran as a key value through the corporation tax code by 2010. The alignment of tax and accounting and Labour's response to European developments offer specific examples. However, before discussing them, it is important to locate these features of the code, if only briefly, in economic thinking more generally and to spell out some implications for this highly complex public law example of economic regulation.

If we try to match the idea of efficiency as just outlined with Smith's four maxims, albeit as filtered through Meade, we find mainly divergences. Smith in his fourth maxim famously related (tax) efficiency to the yield from the tax. A prince would not be prudent to impose an unprofitable tax, ie, one that required 'a great number of officers'[233] or that subjected people over-much 'to the frequent visits, and . . . odious examination of the tax-gatherers'[234] or that, in the language of Labour's policy documents, imposed an 'excess burden of taxation'.[235] An unprofitable tax of this sort would be such as to 'obstruct the industry of the people'.[236] Instead, the prince should ensure that:

> Every tax . . . be so contrived as both to take out and to keep out of the pockets of the people as little as possible, over and above what it brings into the publick treasury of the state.[237]

Allowing for the fact that the policy documents spoke of the need for corporation tax, like all taxes, to 'raise sufficient revenue for the government to fund public services and to service debt'[238] and without entering here into speculation, in an area of 'large empirical uncertainties',[239] on how far corporation tax may impose unduly high administrative costs for the government[240] and compliance costs for the corporate sector,[241] it is plain that something more significant was contained in the corporation tax code than either Smith or Meade could capture. It was true that neutrality, as an aspect of efficiency,[242] was a guiding principle of the code, since the idea that commercial – not tax – considerations should drive

[233] Smith (above n 165) Books IV–V, 416–17.
[234] Ibid, 417.
[235] James and Nobes (above n 18) 20–21.
[236] Smith (above n 165) Books IV–V, 415–18.
[237] Ibid, 417.
[238] HM Treasury and Inland Revenue, *Large Business Taxation* (above n 17) para 1.4.
[239] See above ch 4.
[240] 0.71 pence per pound (for 2005/2006), as against 0.98 pence per pound (for 2000/2001): N Lee et al (eds), *Revenue Law: Principles and Practice*, 27th edn (Haywards Heath, Bloomsbury Professional, 2009) para 1.5.
[241] Eg, C Sandford, M Godwin and P Hardwick, *Administrative and Compliance Costs of Taxation* (Bath, Fiscal Publications, 1989) 140–48 (figures for 1986–87); PricewaterhouseCoopers LLP and World Bank Group, *Paying Taxes: The Global Picture* (London, PricewaterhouseCoopers, 2006); and Houlder, 'Britain Remains Competitive' (above n 142).
[242] Neutrality is a counter to the danger of the 'excess burden of taxation': James and Nobes (above n 18) 302 and 303. See also B Bracewell-Milnes, 'A Liberal Tax Policy: Tax Neutrality and Freedom of Choice' (1976) *British Tax Review* 110.

corporate decision-making, was a Labour mantra.[243] Nonetheless, it was not a complete rationale.

What is missing from not only Smith's conception of efficiency (obviously) but also from most contemporary assessments of Labour's public interest view of corporate tax policy is an appreciation of the impact on the corporation tax code of the burgeoning in the 1980s of 'post-neoclassical endogenous growth theory'.[244] Some specific implications of this will be examined later in the discussion. For the moment, it is sufficient to note that at the pen of its main exponents, Robert Barro,[245] Robert Lucas[246] and Paul Romer,[247] it offered a way of understanding how nations get wealthier. As explained and contextualised by Diane Coyle, it went beyond Smith's classical assessment of growth as the result of the 'invisible hand' of the market[248] and beyond Robert Solow's[249] idea that 'the growth of outputs . . . [depends] on the growth of inputs, and on how effectively these inputs . . . [are] used'.[250] This is because, rather than regarding technical innovation and the increase of 'human capital' as exogenous to growth, post-neoclassical endogenous growth theory required them to be factored in, that is 'made endogenous'.[251] The idea was that human capital (according to Lucas and Barro) and 'technology and the process of innovation' (according to Romer), once 'endogenised',[252] could be shown to create positive 'spill-overs' that contributed to growth: as Coyle explained, 'the same bit of knowledge . . . [could] be used repeatedly without being used up; and one bit . . . [can become] the foundation for the next'.[253]

The obvious link to the corporation tax code was the introduction of research and development credits,[254] but as we shall see, its influence was more pervasive than that. With Gordon Brown having been taunted for it[255] and Barro himself having been satirised by the former Conservative Chancellor, Kenneth Clarke, it was hardly surprising that 'new growth theory' did not figure more prominently in discussions of corporation tax reform, even though O'Donnell and Balls expressly recognised its influence.[256]

[243] Eg, HM Treasury and Inland Revenue, *Large Business Taxation* (above n 17) para 1.6.
[244] Coyle (above n 29) ch 2.
[245] RJ Barro, 'Economic Growth in a Cross Section of Countries' (1991) 106 *Quarterly Journal of Economics* 407.
[246] RE Lucas, 'On the Mechanics of Economic Development' (1988) 22 *Journal of Monetary Economics* 3.
[247] PM Romer, 'Increasing Returns and Long-Run Growth' (1986) 94 *Journal of Political Economy* 1002.
[248] Coyle (above n 29) 39–40; and Smith (above n 165) Books IV–V, 32.
[249] RM Solow, 'A Contribution to the Theory of Economic Growth' (1956) 70 *Quarterly Journal of Economics* 65.
[250] Coyle (above n 29) 42.
[251] Ibid, 48.
[252] Ibid, 51.
[253] Ibid; and Brown, 'Fair Is Efficient' (above n 196) 21.
[254] Coyle (above n 29) 51.
[255] Lipsey (above n 203) 27.
[256] Balls and O'Donnell (eds) (above n 7) 30.

It is thus easy to see how the corporation tax code might be a scene of conflict or potential conflict. By 2010, it was not a creature of classical nor yet neoclassical political economy, as before Labour came to power it arguably had been. It had become instead an instrument of post-neoclassical political economy. It was, as such, a vast regulatory instrument, an economic instrument[257] for encouraging growth. Efficiency here was not, as such, about creating a profitable tax; it was about economic efficiency more generally – efficiency in output. The corporation tax code was a scene of conflict, therefore, because it had been put to work in the service of economic growth, as part of a project to mould and sustain output.[258] It was not simply seeking to collect the fruits of growth. Once again was the truth of Carl Schmitt's analysis being demonstrated: the political precedes and underlies the economic, and the economic energises the political.[259]

We can develop these points if we look at their implications for the alignment of tax with accounts, for Labour's engagement with developments at the European Court of Justice, and if we nod briefly in the direction of compliance and enforcement issues. Compliance and enforcement issues are not a big part of this study, but I need to include them because they underpin the others as key to the Washington Consensus on tax. Compliance and enforcement have both a classical significance – in helping to make tax profitable – and a (post-)neoclassical one, in representing the removal from the system of the distortions caused by ACT.[260] More than this, however, we need not say.

The same was not true, however, for those parts of the corporation tax code that sought to marry tax law and accounting practice, or that sought to support the neutrality of the system in European and international markets. There were at least three different strands to the alignment of tax with accounts, and their introduction in chapter four sought to isolate them as follows: the two (formerly three) 'distinct but overlapping, independent but interdependent', separate but integrated[261] special codes on corporate finance; the use in calculating trading profits of generally accepted accounting practice (GAAP); and the assimilation, in broad terms, of the taxation treatment of intangibles, including intellectual property, to their accounting treatment.

The most general of these three, the corporation tax code's co-option of GAAP in the calculation of trading profits, served as a way of putting the other two in context. The essence of what was at stake here was as follows. Generally accepted accounting practice helped to shape the corporation tax base because what is now section 1127 of the Corporation Tax Act 2010, as amended first by

[257] Eg, A Ogus, 'Corrective Taxes and Financial Impositions as Regulatory Instruments' (1998) 61 *Modern Law Review* 767.

[258] G O'Donnell (Chair), *Financing Britain's Future: Review of the Revenue Departments* (Cm 6163, 2004) 94.

[259] See above ch 4.

[260] HM Treasury and Inland Revenue, *Large Business Taxation* (above n 17) para 1.16.

[261] D Southern, *Taxation of Corporate Debt, Foreign Exchange and Derivative Contracts*, 7th edn (London, Lexis Nexis 2004) 2.

the 2004 Finance Act[262] and then by the Companies Act 2006, required trading profits to be 'computed in accordance with generally accepted accounting practice'. For the purposes of the kind of company or corporate group covered by this study, this would have been the International Accounting Standards (IASs) already encountered in the context of *Revenue and Customs Commissioners v William Grant and Sons*,[263] since these have been compulsory for listed companies since January 2005.[264] However, section 46(1) went on to provide that calculation in accordance with GAAP was 'subject to any adjustment required or authorised by law',[265] the very proviso that in *William Grant* Lord Hoffmann declined to take as giving a green light to introduce further 'judge-made rules' into the interpretation of the code.[266]

Section 46 indicates the extent to which by 2010 the corporation tax code favoured efficiency, and it invited comment on the prudence of its salience. Its attractiveness was acknowledged by Judith Freedman, who, while referring to the assumptions in the 2002 and 2003 policy documents, did not expressly make the link with new growth theory.[267] Balls, Grice and O'Donnell explicitly made the point that 'better aligning taxable and commercial profits'[268] was an important way of turning the ideal of neutrality ('that decision-making is driven by commercial factors rather than by tax considerations')[269] into reality. Professor Freedman herself pointed out elsewhere that 'aligning taxable and commercial profits' had been one of a small number of early business tax aspirations professed by Labour prior to its General Election victory in 1997.[270] The contention in the present study is that, if the depiction of the corporation tax code as public law, as a political practice, is maintainable, then it is easy to see why a number of the key arguments against alignment (including, possibly, those of Professor Freedman), have been so readily discounted in the fabric of the code itself. For instance, one objection was that using the tax system to create incentives is somehow inconsistent with aligning commercial and taxable profits.[271] That may be so, but it is clear from the policy documents that alignment was consistent with a policy that relied on incentivisation, and, moreover, all that Balls, Grice and O'Donnell argued for was 'better' alignment, not complete alignment. The system of capital allowances on plant and machin-

[262] CTA 2010 s 1127 (formerly FA 2004 s 50).

[263] *Revenue and Customs Commissioners v William Grant and Sons* [2007] UKHL 15, [2007] STC 680. See above p 94.

[264] CA 2006 ss 399(2)–399(3) and 403 (formerly CA 1985 s 227); and European Parliament and Council Regulation (EC) 1606/2002 [2002] OJ L243/1.

[265] CTA 2009 s 46(1) (formerly FA 1998 s 42(1)).

[266] See above ch 3.

[267] J Freedman, 'Aligning Taxable Profits and Accounting Profits: Accounting Standards, Legislators and Judges' (2004) 2 *eJournal of Tax Research* 71, 74.

[268] Balls, Grice and O'Donnell (eds) (above n 136) 71.

[269] Ibid, 70–71; and Sanger, 'Business Tax Policy' (above n 154) 13.

[270] J Freedman, 'Defining Taxable Profit in a Changing Accounting Environment' (1995) *British Tax Review* 434, 444.

[271] Freedman, 'Aligning Taxable Profits and Accounting Profits' (above n 267) 75.

ery, for example, had been retained, after consultation. Furthermore, if Labour regarded the corporation tax system as creating only a 'conventional' set of property rights, as is argued in the next section, one of the other main objections to alignment, its importation into the code of accountants' discretion,[272] would seem much less important. Much more compelling would be arguments from efficiency and the idea that the very fact of complete alignment would, given the function of accounts, create a major disincentive to depressing profits for tax purposes.

In considering the parts of the code devoted to intellectual property and other intangibles,[273] on the one hand, and corporate finance, on the other, it is important to recognise that, although efficiency is again to the fore, they raise important issues in addition to those raised by section 46. This is because, whilst section 46 related only to the calculation of trading profits, leaving untouched the distinction between income and capital (including capital allowances),[274] the special codes cut through it, completely assimilating capital and income.[275] As David Southern pointed out in reference to the special codes on corporate finance, in the areas to which the special codes related, the corporation tax base had been changed from profits to expenditure, as in the case of VAT.[276] The reason, as Southern trenchantly observed, was that '[a]ny measure of income requires that capital be maintained',[277] something that occurred only if an 'accounts-based approach' did not (inconsistently) try to assimilate capital to income. Efficiency was evidently seen as so important in these parts of the code that it was preferred to consistency.

Discussion of the impact of the special codes on the corporation tax base takes us back to the role of efficiency in the government's dealings with Europe. This involves an exploration of the uneasy boundary between the public interest as the furthering of economic growth (through membership of the European Union and GATT 1994/WTO[278]) and the public interest as the protection of the national tax base. The latter touches on fairness issues, and one of its specific applications, in relation to transfer pricing, is therefore discussed below. We can approach the relevant issues in stages, by moving from the limited legislative intervention by EU institutions countenanced by Britain, to the highly prudential embodiment in the corporation tax code of the consequences of the various milestone decisions of the European Court.

[272] Ibid.

[273] S Whiting, *Corporation Tax 2005/2006* (Kingston upon Thames, CCH, 2005) para 3.20.2; J Watterston, *Core Tax Annuals: Corporation Tax 2010/11* (Haywards Heath, Bloomsbury Professional, 2010) ch 11.

[274] HM Treasury and Inland Revenue, *Reform of Corporation Tax* (above n 215); and HM Treasury and Inland Revenue, *Corporation Tax Reform* (above n 144).

[275] Whiting (above n 273); and Watterston (above n 273).

[276] Southern, *Taxation of Corporate Debt* (above n 261) 2.

[277] Ibid.

[278] Cases C-21–24/72 *International Fruit Company NV v Produktschap voor Groenten en Fruit* [1975] 2 CMLR 1, para 18.

The limited legislative impact on Britain's corporation tax base of the five Directives[279] so far adopted has often been noted.[280] They are reflected in the now longstanding amendments to the corporation tax code, in the code's provisions on corporate reconstructions, intra group dividends, and interest and royalty payments.[281] Adopting the analysis used throughout the study, it can be seen that these various manifestations of EU public law[282] represent, as incorporated in the corporation tax code, the outer limits of prudent legislative endeavour on matters specifically involving European law and corporate taxation. We have to remember that the Lisbon Treaty contained no mandate for direct tax harmonisation,[283] and what energises and makes the rights and obligations spelt out in these fragmentary pieces of paper real are the successive judgments of the government as to where Britain's national interest lies, as well as the temporally limited acceptance by the British public that the government has balanced the relevant ends and means correctly. That some, especially those perhaps of a technocratic or of a quite different Aristotelian frame of mind,[284] find this disappointing[285] goes without saying. Prudence may require a new approach, in the public interest, in due course. For the moment, however, it shapes the (often rather uncomfortable) reality. The reality can be observed both at the level of the practice of politics, as in Gordon Brown's idea that the public interest was served not by tax harmonisation but by free and open – that is, fair – tax competition, and also at the level of theory, or at least at the level of those theories likely to be translated into practice. Unless even the optional adoption of the proposed common consolidated corporate tax base could convincingly be shown to serve the British national interest,[286] it had no chance of becoming a reality as far as Britain was concerned.

The legislative interventions just discussed – actual or proposed – reflected the efficiency value in the code in different ways. They tended to become and remain realities only insofar as they had assisted the government in its professed aim of using the European Union to enhance competition and promote innova-

[279] See above n 1, p xxi; BJM Terra and PJ Wattel, *European Tax Law*, 4th edn (The Hague, Kluwer Law, 2005) chs 16, 10, 9, 11, 14 and 13; P Farmer and R Lyal, *EC Tax Law* (Oxford, Clarendon Press, 1994) chs 11–16; and DW Williams, *EC Tax Law* (London, Longman, 1998).

[280] Eg, Farmer and Lyal (ibid) 246–47; and DW Williams (ibid) chs 8 and 10.

[281] Eg, TCGA 1992 ch 3 (ss 126–40G) ('Reorganisation of Share Capital, Conversion of Securities, etc').

[282] See above ch 2.

[283] Law Society, *A Guide to the Treaty of Lisbon: European Union Insight* (January 2008), available at http://www.lawsociety.org.uk/documents/downloads/guide_to_treaty_of_lisbon.pdf (accessed 9 July 2011).

[284] CM Radaelli, *The Politics of Corporate Taxation in the European Union: Knowledge and International Policy Agendas* (London, Routledge, 1997); CM Radaelli, *Technocracy in the European Union* (London, Longman, 1999); and CM Radaelli, 'The Political Economy of EU Direct Tax Policy' in A Lymer and D Salter (eds), *Contemporary Issues in Taxation Research* (Aldershot, Ashgate Publishing, 2003) 145.

[285] Eg, P Stephens, 'A Dispiriting Return to Europe's Trenches' *Financial Times* (15 January 2008) 17.

[286] See above ch 4.

tion in the push for a 'sustainable' rise in 'the rate of UK productivity growth'.[287] This was why, despite the government's wariness of the European Union, the occasional arguments made in favour of export subsidies for small manufacturers (whatever technical possibilities may arise under state aid law or WTO subsidies rules) remained thoroughly outside the mainstream of political and economic debate.[288]

It was in the context of the legislative impasse illustrated by the corporate tax Directives that the balance between efficiency and protection of the tax base, embodied in the code's responses to European Court decisions, should be considered. Whatever else may be said, there is no evidence to suggest that the European Court's activity in this area was seen in either Whitehall or Westminster as anything other than a source of apprehension and irritation. The prudential nature of the response, both of the Labour Government and of the judiciary, to the *Marks and Spencer*[289] and *Cadbury Schweppes*[290] rulings has already been referred to in chapter four. It is necessary here only to draw out two further points. First, as already suggested, the provisions of the code designed to embody European Court decisions on the European Treaties' fundamental freedoms trace a delicate boundary between efficiency and, as will be seen below, a species of fairness customarily referred to as 'inter-nation equity'. Secondly, this being so, the solutions that they embody would always be contentious, the more so since they tempered the opportunities offered by the single market with a concern for the integrity of Britain's corporate tax base, a compromise usually manifested by the prudent and studiously lawful nature of the relevant legislative conditions.[291]

The foregoing should leave us with a sense both of the dream and of the reality. Before taking up the threads of fairness, it is therefore appropriate to take stock. Efficiency, in Labour's conception of the corporation tax code, was clearly the motor of fairness. Balls, Grice and O'Donnell summed it up thus:

> [T]he Government has . . . sought to promote, on the one hand, competition, innovation and the enterprise economy, and on the other hand, a modern welfare state and world-class public services as the routes to an efficient and fair Britain in which individuals can realise their potential.[292]

[287] Balls, Grice and O'Donnell (eds) (above n 136) 8.

[288] Notoriously, the US Foreign Sales Corporation scheme (noted by R Minder and E Alden, 'WTO Rules US has Failed to Dismantle Tax Subsidy' *Financial Times* (1–2 October 2005) 7; A Beattie and R Minder, 'EU Threatens Sanctions over US Tax Breaks' *Financial Times* (14 February 2006) 6). See generally, RHC Luja, 'WTO Agreements versus the EC Fiscal Aid Regime: Impact on Direct Taxation' (1999) 27 *Intertax* 207, 212–16; and Y Brauner, 'National Report The United States' in M Lang, J Herdin and I Hofbauer (eds), *WTO and Direct Taxation* (The Hague, Kluwer Law, 2005) 727. For Britain's situation, see C Väljemark, 'National Report United Kingdom' in Lang, Herdin and Hofbauer (above) 685.

[289] Case C-446/03 *Marks and Spencer plc v Halsey (HMIT)* [2006] 1 CMLR 18.

[290] Case C-196/04 *Cadbury Schweppes plc and Another v CIR* [2007] 1 CMLR 2.

[291] Snape (above n 14) 404n.

[292] Balls, Grice and O'Donnell (eds) (above n 136) 5–6.

This, of course, was an ideology. What it suggested, however, was not simply that fairness had a political dimension, something we would expect, but that efficiency did so too.

In the context of Labour's ideology, the efficiency value embedded in the corporation tax code was not simply a technical, or technocratic, one. Were the code still to be in its pre-1993 shape,[293] such an argument might wash, but now in 2011 the code has been transformed. No, the particular idea of efficiency that it both embodies and is intended to serve is, potentially at least, highly conflictual. It was not simply the efficiency of a tax that, within the fourth of Smith's maxims, was profitable to the sovereign. Instead, it was the efficiency of what might be envisaged as an attempt to create a vast economic instrument for increasing output over the long haul. That there had been massive economic growth between 1997 and 2007 no one could seriously deny,[294] and although it was impossible to link the corporation tax code directly with that process, the informing idea of the code was certainly broadly consistent with it. The inconsistency may lie in its inevitable complexity. Conclusive judgments are difficult, but it may be that the use of the code as a regulatory instrument had made the satisfaction of Smith's fourth maxim very difficult to realise. The fact that the code seemed to work is an indication that the particular balance that it struck continued, for all its complexity, to reflect a measure of constituent power. With this in mind, we need to ask what the fairness value can be said to have added to the analysis.

B. Fairness in the Corporation Tax Code

If we read closely into the corporation tax code and compare certain provisions with the relevant policy statements of the Labour years, we find that each contains a highly particularised conception of fairness. More obviously than efficiency, fairness can be seen as one of WB Gallie's 'essentially contested concepts'[295] – in William Connolly's words, fairness describes a 'valued' state of affairs, which 'involves reference to several dimensions' and enables people 'to interpret even . . . shared values differently as new and unforeseen situations arise'.[296] Not 'radically confused' but a concept whose 'original exemplar' has an 'authority . . . acknowledged by all the contestant users of the concept',[297] fairness in the corporation tax context needs to be very carefully situated.

It is the first task of this part of the discussion to isolate the characteristics of the idea in the corporation tax context and to situate them relative to ideas of

[293] Ie, the date the FOREX rules were introduced under John Major's Conservative Government.
[294] S Brittan, 'Why This Should Be the Last "Budget"' *Financial Times* (23 March 2007) 15.
[295] WB Gallie, 'Essentially Contested Concepts' (1955–56) 56 *Aristotelian Society (Proceedings)* 167.
[296] WE Connolly, *The Terms of Political Discourse*, 3rd edn (Oxford, Blackwell, 1993) 10.
[297] Gallie (above n 295) 180; and J Rawls, *A Theory of Justice*, rev edn (Oxford, Oxford University Press, 1999).

fairness that are ubiquitous in taxation literature.[298] That this will give us a clearer sense of fairness as the second main value immanent to the code goes without saying. What it will also do, however, is enable us to reflect, as with efficiency, on how the use of the idea has been shaped by the institutions and processes discussed in previous chapters. Such conclusions as we are able to draw on this question will in turn enable us to assess the strengths and weaknesses of the fairness immanent to the corporation tax code and, as with efficiency, to suggest why, despite concerns over its complexity and its instability, the code has so far proved effective.

Throughout the period of the Labour Administration, corporation tax policy documents contained a consistent statement of the constituent elements of fairness. The tensely prepared Budget Report of July 1997[299] placed fairness in the context of the various dimensions of efficiency discussed above. As will be recalled, encouraging fairness was one of the 'clear principles' on which tax policy in general had to be based,[300] and it meant that the tax system 'should avoid the less well-off bearing an unfair burden'.[301] Recalling the discussion in chapter four above, it will be noted that these statements were clearly central to the ideology of the public interest that the incoming Labour Administration espoused.

Fairness is a value, 'essentially contested' though it may be, and it is at least as important as efficiency. Its contestedness means that how it applies to particular situations may not, however, be self-evident. Its importance was apparent from the reform documents of 2001, 2002 and 2003, already discussed in the efficiency context. In the 2001 document, the government fleshed out this earlier statement of the importance of fairness, again relative to that of efficiency. Fairness had two functions, one of which was to ensure that 'individual businesses pay their fair share of tax in relation to their commercial profits and compete on a level playing field'.[302] Stripping away the metaphor and replacing it with something like 'without unfair advantage', it becomes clear that what was fair in this context plainly involved a process of comparing a company's commercial profit level with the amount of corporation tax that it was paying and then that of comparing that tax level with other, similar companies. The other function of fairness disclosed by the 2001 document was framed explicitly in welfare economics terminology: 'to correct market failures that impose wider costs on society',[303] with corporation tax being 'the best policy instrument'[304] for this purpose. Conceived in terms of these two functions, fairness

[298] James and Nobes (above n 18) ch 5; and Musgrave (above n 144) 160.

[299] (HC 1997–98, 85) n 188; and H Pym and N Kochan, *Gordon Brown: The First Year in Power* (London, Bloomsbury, 1998) 54–58 and ch 5.

[300] (HC 1997–98, 85) n 188 para 1.68.

[301] Ibid, paras 1.66–1.69.

[302] HM Treasury and Inland Revenue, *Large Business Taxation* (above n 17) para 1.7.

[303] Ibid; and Balls, Grice and O'Donnell (eds) (above n 136) 6.

[304] HM Treasury and Inland Revenue, *Large Business Taxation* (above n 17) para 1.7; and Wales, 'The Implications of the O'Donnell Review' (above n 186) 549.

was viewed as being on a par with efficiency as a value shaping the corporation tax code. These formulae were repeated in relation to the specific reform proposals contained in the 2002 document and, by reference, in the 2003 document.[305]

For anyone familiar with the theoretical literature, these recurrent formulations of fairness present certain rather surprising features. First, they make only implicit reference to those long-established components of fairness, 'vertical equity' and 'horizontal equity'.[306] In the hands of Smith (read as argued in the earlier part of the chapter), who based his argument on Hobbes,[307] Locke and Pufendorf,[308] fairness – or 'equality' in taxation – was encapsulated by the 'benefit principle',[309] which had subsequently been taken up by Hayek[310] and rendered thus by Smith himself:

> The subjects of every state ought to contribute towards the support of the Government, as nearly as possible, in proportion to their respective abilities; that is, in proportion to the revenue which they respectively enjoy under the protection of the state.[311]

What Smith had been postulating here, of course, was the prudential need for a ruler to ensure so far as he could, not necessarily that taxpayers contribute according to their 'ability to pay',[312] but that they 'contribute in proportion to the benefit they derive from government'.[313] The benefit principle was reflected to a degree in the 2001 policy document's second 'principle', the need to 'ensure fairness between all stakeholders in the UK economy, so all sections make a fair contribution to the future of the UK',[314] but it was not as prominent as the need to combat tax avoidance. The 'brokenness' of the fairness concept, its 'essentially contested' nature, was thus easily illustrated. Even on the Left it was contested, since it was a substitution for the sharply progressive levels of personal income tax that RH Tawney had thought that fairness – or, in his word, 'equality' – required.[315] The startling contrasts that continue, after 2010, to be reported

[305] HM Treasury and Inland Revenue, *Reform of Corporation Tax* (above n 215) para 1.5; and HM Treasury and Inland Revenue, *Corporation Tax Reform* (above n 144) para 1.4.

[306] Especially Murphy and Nagel (above n 20) ch 2; and Musgrave and Musgrave (above n 144) ch 13.

[307] Hobbes, *Leviathan* (above n 150) 226 (pt 2 ch 30); and D Jackson, 'Thomas Hobbes' Theory of Taxation' (1973) 21 *Political Studies* 175, 176.

[308] ERA Seligman, *Progressive Taxation in Theory and Practice*, 2nd edn (Princeton, American Economic Association, 1908); Musgrave (above n 144) 61–68; and Murphy and Nagel (above n 20) 192–93. On Seligman, see A Mumford, *Taxing Culture: Towards a Theory of Tax Collection Law* (Aldershot, Ashgate Dartmouth, 2002) ch 3.

[309] But see J Frecknall Hughes, 'The Concept of Taxation and the Age of Enlightenment' in J Tiley (ed), *Studies in the History of Tax Law: Volume 2* (Oxford, Hart Publishing, 2007) 253, quoting DP O'Brien, *The Classical Economists* (Oxford, Clarendon Press, 1975) 241.

[310] FA Hayek, *The Constitution of Liberty* [1960], 2nd edn (London, Routledge, 2006) 315–16, quoted in Murphy and Nagel (above n 20) 192–93.

[311] Smith (above n 165) Books IV–V, 416.

[312] Mill (above n 167) 169–87. But see Pigou (above n 174) 43–44.

[313] Murphy and Nagel (above n 20) 16.

[314] HM Treasury and Inland Revenue, *Large Business Taxation* (above n 17) para 1.4.

[315] RH Tawney, *Equality*, 4th edn (London, George Allen and Unwin, 1952) 165–67.

by the IFS as to inequality in Britain ensure that the argument on the Left will continue.[316]

Secondly, the concept of fairness invoked in Labour's corporation tax policy documents suggested an idea, not of tax fairness as such, but of the role of corporation tax in creating a fairer society.[317] The discussion in chapter four illustrated how Labour viewed corporation tax reform as a means of advancing the public interest. In assessing the fairness implications of the role that Labour thereby assigned to the tax, it is argued here that the ideology that corporation tax was meant to serve owed much to the analysis of taxation in general set forth in Liam Murphy and Thomas Nagel's, *The Myth of Ownership*.[318]

When we first encountered Murphy and Nagel's work in chapter two, it was to place the accent on their notion of the 'conventionality of property' and to ascribe the work to the 'liberal normativist' tradition of Rawls and Dworkin. Here, we need to stress the work's emphasis on taxation as the key instrument in distributive justice, or in Dworkinian language, 'political morality',[319] and to show its practical realisation of a 'conventional' idea of property 'as what is created by the tax system, rather than what is disturbed or encroached on'[320] by it. Indeed, Murphy and Nagel's concluding chapter could almost have served as a normative 'blueprint' for income tax policy under the Brown chancellorship between 2000 and 2007.[321] The apparent correspondence may also have reflected something of Gordon Brown's well-known predilection for Rawls's thought[322] and for liberal American political and economic theory in general.[323] The idiosyncrasies of the reality were perhaps a neat illustration of the limitations of the political morality of Rawls and Dworkin in the real world. What we had in the corporation tax code, therefore, was a fairness that was contentious, that seemed to place a greater emphasis on anti-avoidance than on progressivity, and that relied on the conventionality of property to implement a version of societal fairness,[324] rather than tax fairness as such. Illustrations of the last of these points, including an admittedly controversial one, will be examined in a moment.

[316] M Brewer, A Goodman, M Myck, J Shaw and A Shephard (eds), *Poverty and Inequality in Britain: 2004* (London, Institute for Fiscal Studies, 2004) 9–22; M Brewer, L Sibieta and L Wren-Lewis, *Racing Away? Income Inequality and the Evolution of High Incomes* (London, Institute for Fiscal Studies, 2008); and C Giles, 'Very Rich Get Richer under Labour' *Financial Times* (18 January 2008) 3.

[317] Balls, Grice and O'Donnell (eds) (above n 136) 7.

[318] Above n 20.

[319] Murphy and Nagel (above n 20) 12.

[320] Ibid, 175.

[321] Ibid, 181–88.

[322] R Peston, *Brown's Britain* (London, Short Books, 2005) 30, which recounts Gordon Brown's fondness for Rawls's 'maximin rule': A Sen, *On Economic Inequality*, enlarged edn (Oxford, Clarendon Press, 1997) 22–23.

[323] S Lee, *Best for Britain? The Politics and Legacy of Gordon Brown* (Oxford, Oneworld, 2007) 55–56 (Sandel's 'moral limits of markets'). See also Keegan (above n 194) 12–13; Pym and Kochan (above n 299) 98 (Reich) 113 (Reich ('the Third Way') and Summers); and Stevenson (above n 204) 145, 272 (Sandel) and 84 (Greenspan).

[324] Balls, Grice and O'Donnell (eds) (above n 136) 7.

In the corporation tax policy documents of 2001–03, the conception of fairness as societal fairness, along the lines just analysed, was thus closely aligned with the curtailment of corporation tax avoidance. This was significant because, in Murphy and Nagel's account, the impact on fairness of tax avoidance was barely touched on. Part of the reason for the omission might have been that Murphy and Nagel's discussion did not specifically address corporation tax issues, and corporation tax in Britain was the area in which anti-avoidance measures had become particularly prevalent. 'Countering artificial[325] tax avoidance in the UK corporate tax environment will remain a priority',[326] the 2001 document had promised, and although similarly forthright general statements did not appear in the 2002 or 2003 documents, the importance of anti-avoidance legislation to fairness did.[327] The result of the emphasis on corporation tax anti-avoidance measures in the pursuit of fairness was that this was what, in the real world of representative institutions and corporate power, and allowing for adjustments in the name of prudence, a Rawlsian distributive justice might have looked like. While Coalition members have occasionally justified anti-avoidance measures as a quid pro quo for the reduction of tax rates generally, with Labour there was a strong sense of tax law as being there to 'mould' a fairer society, rather than as something with which the unwary might have been unfortunate enough to collide.[328]

With these points in mind, I turn to four aspects of the corporation tax code that exemplified Labour's approach to anti-avoidance as an aspect of fairness in corporation tax reform. These elements addressed four types of problem, each of which was an almost inevitable consequence of a tax that used corporate profits as its base[329] and relied greatly on the time-honoured distinction between income profits and chargeable gains.[330] The first, second and fourth measures dealt with attempts to manipulate deductions from the corporation tax base, while the third addressed attempts to allocate profits between companies in a group.

First, there was the broad 'general anti-avoidance rule', which since 2002 had been common to each of the special codes on the tax treatment of loan relationships, FOREX and financial instruments. The well-known 'paragraph 13' prevented deductions that were attributable to 'unallowable purposes', and so far as it concerned loan relationships, it stated that deductions[331] were to be disregarded to the extent that 'on a just and reasonable apportionment, [they were]

[325] Southern, *Taxation of Corporate Debt* (above n 261) 490, on the use of the expression 'fictitious or artificial transaction' in F(No 2)A 1915 s 44(3) (a criminalising measure relating to excess profits duty).

[326] HM Treasury and Inland Revenue, *Large Business Taxation* (above n 17) para 1.20.

[327] HM Treasury and Inland Revenue, *Reform of Corporation Tax* (above n 215) paras 1.5 and 1.6; and HM Treasury and Inland Revenue, *Corporation Tax Reform* (above n 144) para 1.4.

[328] Shklar (above n 111) 7; A Tomkins, 'In Defence of the Political Constitution' (2002) 22 *Oxford Journal of Legal Studies* 157; and B Dodwell, 'Budget Analysis: Corporate Tax Reform' *Tax Journal* (5 July 2010) 22, quoting George Osborne on 19 May 2010.

[329] CTA 2009 s 5(1) (formerly ICTA 1988 s 8(1)). See above pp 7 and 19.

[330] CTA 2009 ss 2, 33, 1219, 1305 and sch 1 para 273 (formerly ICTA 1988 s 6(4)(a)).

[331] CTA 2009 ss 441, 442 and 476 (formerly FA 1996 sch 9 para 13(1)).

. . . attributable to . . . [an] unallowable purpose'.[332] An 'unallowable purpose', meanwhile, was one that was 'not amongst the business or other commercial purposes of the company'.[333] This wording had a number of features that prior to its introduction had been, if not unprecedented, then certainly unusual.[334] The novelty lay in the competence of HM Revenue and Customs (HMRC) to make a 'just and reasonable apportionment' of the deductions and in the competence given to judges to define the outer limits of an 'unallowable purpose'.

The positing of the rule, as we have seen, provoked a reaction that, given the concept of fairness explained above, seemed inevitable.[335] Bramwell hinted at the difficulties of interpretation that paragraph 13 presented;[336] Ghosh and Johnson asserted that the rule had 'caused, since its inception, inevitable uncertainty and controversy';[337] and Southern considered it to be of 'limited [practical] application', given its 'inherent limitations and . . . the law of diminishing returns'.[338] A Tory backbencher, Mark Field,[339] whose early training had been as a City solicitor, neatly linked these uncertainty concerns to the idea of fairness reflected in paragraph 13, as well as to the ideological difference implied, when the rule had been confirmed and extended in 2002:

> The City of London is an important financial centre and a centre of invisible earnings for this country. I have a philosophical concern that a feeling exists that taxes must be raised, and that banks and other financial institution [sic] must go about their business ensuring that they pay a fair amount of tax; it is somehow seen as illegitimate to avoid tax and utilise the tax system. The idea that financial institutions should be willing to take everything on the chin and not use the system to their benefit is a matter of concern.[340]

In the same debate, Ruth Kelly, MP, then the Economic Secretary to the Treasury, reiterated the values underlying paragraph 13, as well as the ideological difference:

> I do not for a moment share the philosophical doubts of the hon. Member for Cities of London and Westminster about the legitimacy of raising a fair share of taxation from particular individuals or companies. I take the principled view, which I think is shared on the Labour Benches, that we should create a level playing field where everyone pays a fair share of tax. That is what the clause is designed to do.[341]

[332] CTA 2009 s 441 (formerly FA 1996 sch 9 para 13(1)).

[333] CTA 2009 s 442 (formerly FA 1996 sch 9 para 13(2)).

[334] Southern, *Taxation of Corporate Debt* (above n 261) 490–91; and D Hole, 'Finance Act Notes: Corporate and Government Debt – sections 80–105 and schedules 7–15' (1996) *British Tax Review* 347, 355–56.

[335] The original FB 1996 draft clauses, which became FA 1996 sch 9 para 13(1), referred to companies becoming parties to transactions 'otherwise than in good faith': S Edge, 'Paragraph 13: Unlucky Only for Some?' *Tax Journal* (14 December 1995) 4.

[336] Bramwell (above n 227) para A3.9.

[337] Ie, in the older J Ghosh and I Johnson, *Taxation of Loan Relationships and Derivatives* (London, Butterworths LexisNexis, 1999) para 6.31.

[338] Southern, *Taxation of Corporate Debt* (above n 261) 498.

[339] Conservative MP for the Cities of London and Westminster.

[340] Standing Committee F (11 June 2002) HC vol 386 col 323.

[341] Ibid, vol 386 col 325.

Paragraph 13 was thus one of those provisions that highlighted especially clearly both the ideology and the configuration of power immanent to the corporation tax code. The alignment of parties in the House of Commons, as well as its institutional organisation, had, in other words, given the corporation tax code a strong undertow of societal fairness. It seemed, moreover, that paragraph 13 applied this idea to loan relationships in a way that reflected a 'conventional' view of property, and tax law was thereby being put to work to mould a fairer society.

People may have disagreed about what fairness required, but that was not relevant to paragraph 13. What was relevant was that the institutions of representative democracy had accorded it a particular nature and scope and, in doing so, had recognised that property rights were 'conventional' rather than 'moral' or 'natural'.[342] That a loan relationship may not have been caught by paragraph 13 was not quite a case of being, in Walton J's aphorism, 'untaxed by concession',[343] but the conceptualisation of tax law embodied in paragraph 13 was equally not the Diceyan view of tax law implicit in the MP for London and Westminster's comments. The wording of paragraph 13 was hardly judicially tested,[344] but had the testing come, judges would have had competence to remould the property rights created by a loan relationship. The extent to which they calculated that they had the capacity so to do remained to be seen.

Deductions from the corporation tax base had been restricted, too, under an entirely separate provision, which was introduced in 2003 and applied to contributions to employee trusts. This provision was rather less well known than paragraph 13; but it highlighted an equally important point, and its existence showed that not all of the anti-avoidance measures in the code raised anti-avoidance issues as controversial as those of paragraph 13. Schedule 24 to the 2003 Finance Act[345] prevented a company from making a deduction from its profits when, without there being a receipt by the employee, the company made a contribution to an employee benefit trust (EBT).[346] In doing so, Schedule 24 removed a corporation tax avoidance opportunity by denying the company a deduction until the employee was actually paid. The corporation tax treatment of contributions to EBTs was thereby 'squared' with the situation when the employee was remunerated directly. The issue had arisen because contributions to EBTs

[342] Murphy and Nagel (above n 20) 175; and Loughlin, *The Idea of Public Law* (above n 46) ch 7 (on rights generally).

[343] *Vestey and Others v IRC* [1979] Ch 177; Public Bill Committee (17 May 2007) HC vol 460 cols 212–13 (Mark Hoban); and Chartered Institute of Taxation, *Taxed by Law, Untaxed by Concession* (London, CIOT, 2005).

[344] But see *Prudential plc v Revenue and Customs Commissioners* [2008] EWHC 1839 (Ch), [2008] STC 2820, analysed by J Ghosh, I Johnson and P Miller, *Ghosh, Johnson and Miller on the Taxation of Corporate Debt and Derivatives* (London, LexisNexis, 2010) paras C3.107 and D2.65 (discussing now repealed FA 1994, s 168A and similar wording (FA 2002 ss 83(2), 141 and sch 40)).

[345] CTA 2009 ss 1290–97 (formerly FA 2003 s 143 and sch 24).

[346] CTA 2009 ss 1291(2) and 1296(1) (formerly FA 2003 sch 24 para 9(1)) use 'employee benefit scheme', which is made to include a trust.

had previously been used to remunerate the directors of Dextra Accessories/ Phones 4U, including its founder, John Caudwell; and the Special Commissioners had held that the technique was not frustrated by section 43(11) of the Finance Act 1989.[347] Schedule 24 to the 2003 Finance Act had been the government's response to Dextra Accessories' success before the Special Commissioners, and it had pre-dated the government's subsequent successful appeal to the House of Lords.[348] Lord Hoffmann, delivering the only full speech, encapsulated the prudence of both the Law Lords' unanimous decision and the government's own legislative response:

> [T]here would be other anomalies in the construction favoured by the Special Commissioners. . . By setting up a trust such as this, the taxpayer could achieve immediate deductibility of payments into the trust and postpone indefinitely the liability of employees to tax on the emoluments for which, in part, the money was eventually applied. That would enable the purpose of section 43 to be easily frustrated.[349]

The logic of this point seems to have eluded the author of a short article in the *Tax Journal*, Jonathan Levy, who had advised the taxpayer in the litigation. He wrote of the continuing 'uncertainty' that the Law Lords' decision presented and, somewhat idiosyncratically, concluded that 'taxpayers and their advisers . . . [could not] ignore the detrimental effect that arrangements which . . . [were] perceived as being aggressive . . . [could] have on the courts'.[350] Understandable as it was, this comment was surely wide of the mark. The response of the Treasury to the Special Commissioners' decision, and the Law Lords' attitude on appeal, were each prudent responses. It was not even necessary for the judges or the Department to resort to casuistry,[351] or to adopt the kind of 'conventional' attitude to property rights discussed above. The then Paymaster General, Dawn Primarolo, using familiar imagery, spoke of Schedule 24 to the Finance Act 2003 as a 'measure [that] . . . [levelled] the playing field between employers who remunerate employees direct and those who . . . do so through third parties'.[352]

What the judges were doing in *Macdonald v Dextra Accessories* was to underline the prudence of the approach that had been taken by the government. Even the Opposition had taken this view in its tabled amendments, having concentrated on points of detail only. 'Let it be placed on the record', the Conservative MP Stephen O'Brien had said somewhat portentously, 'that there . . . [was] no attempt to undermine the major thrust of the Government's policy on anti-avoidance'.[353]

[347] Now superseded by a new FA 1989 s 43, as inserted by ITEPA 2003 sch 6 para 157.
[348] *Macdonald (HMIT) v Dextra Accessories Ltd and Others* [2005] UKHL 47, [2005] STC 1111.
[349] [2005] STC 1111, para 21.
[350] J Levy, 'Dextra, Tax Avoidance and the Courts' *Tax Journal* (25 July 2005) 9.
[351] Loughlin, *The Idea of Public Law* (above n 46) 152. On casuistry, see HP Glenn, *Legal Traditions of the World*, 2nd edn (Oxford, Oxford University Press, 2004) 352–53n. On 'casuistry' in tax law, see, eg, *IRC v Scottish and Newcastle Breweries Ltd* [1982] 1 WLR 322, 325 (Lord Wilberforce); and *Lingfield Park (1991) Ltd v Shove* [2004] EWCA Civ 391 para 4, unreported (Mummery LJ).
[352] Standing Committee B (12 June 2003) HC vol 406 col 539.
[353] Ibid, vol 406 col 542.

If the two sets of provisions discussed so far illustrate 'thick' and 'thin' approaches to fairness, the major remodelling of the transfer pricing rules in 2004 might have marked out a middle ground. The idea of these provisions was to prevent profits or losses from being allocated to different parts of domestic or multinational groups, in such a way as to enable group members to take advantage of differences in tax rates.[354] Since the measures related solely to corporate groups, they could raise fairness issues not necessarily highlighted by the two measures discussed above. The two sets of measures already discussed related to fairness as between taxpayers and groups of taxpayers. The transfer pricing rules had this function, to be sure, but they also addressed the question of fairness between states.[355] The amendments made by the 2004 Finance Act[356] to Schedule 28AA of the 1988 Income and Corporation Taxes Act combined the corporation tax thin capitalisation regime with the provisions on transfer pricing[357] and applied the expanded rules both to transactions across borders and to ones within Great Britain.[358] Subject to exceptions for 'dormant companies'[359] and 'small and medium-sized enterprises',[360] goods transferred and services provided – including loans made – between group companies were therefore treated as being in return for an 'arm's length' price.[361]

In extending the transfer-pricing rules to transactions between British-resident companies, the government had been seeking to make the rules conformable to European law.[362] Nonetheless, one of their main justifications was again that of fairness. This type of fairness was generally referred to as 'inter-nation equity',[363] but it was perhaps better thought of as being a still further implication of the benefit principle. It will be recalled that a fundamental principle of corporation tax is that non-resident companies are taxed only on the profits of a 'permanent establishment' in Britain. The non-resident is taxed in Britain, so it had once been judicially stated, because of the protection that its

[354] Tiley (above n 27) 892 (6th edn, 913).

[355] J Plender, 'Top Banks Eliminate UK Tax Liabilities' *Financial Times* (21 July 2004) 1; J Plender, 'Counting the Cost of Globalisation: How Companies Keep Tax Low and Stay within the Law' *Financial Times* (21 July 2004) 15; J Plender and M Simons, 'A Big Squeeze for Governments: How Transfer Pricing Threatens Global Tax Revenues' *Financial Times* (22 July 2004) 15; BJ Arnold and MJ McIntyre, *International Tax Primer*, 2nd edn (The Hague, Kluwer, 2002) ch 4; RS Avi-Yonah, *International Tax as International Law: An Analysis of the International Tax Regime* (Cambridge, Cambridge University Press, 2007) ch 6; Picciotto (above n 164) ch 8; and A Miller and L Oats, *Principles of International Taxation* (Haywards Heath, Tottel Publishing, 2006) ch 14.

[356] FA 2004 ss 30–37 and sch 5.

[357] TIOPA 2010 ss 152 and 154 (formerly ICTA 1988 sch 28AA paras 1A–B, 6, 7 and 14(1) (as expanded by FA 2004 ss 34–36)).

[358] TIOPA 2010 s 155 (formerly ICTA 1988 sch 28AA para 5).

[359] TIOPA 2010 s 165 (formerly ICTA 1988 sch 28AA para 5A (added by FA 2004 s 31(3))).

[360] TIOPA 2010 ss 166–67 (formerly ICTA 1988 sch 28AA, para 5B (added by FA 2004, s 31(4))).

[361] TIOPA 2010 s 147 (formerly ICTA 1988, sch 28AA, para 1(1)).

[362] Case C-524/04 *Test Claimants in the Thin Cap Group Litigation v Commissioners of Inland Revenue* [2007] 2 CMLR 31, para AG84 (Geelhoed AG).

[363] Arnold and McIntyre (above n 355) 4; and Picciotto (above n 164) 65–68 and 82–83.

British possessions received under British law.[364] When the 2004 Finance Bill was at Committee stage, the Paymaster General made a similar point: '[t]he rules are vital to ensure that business, especially multinationals, are taxed fairly in respect of their activities in the United Kingdom'.[365] Not only that, in fact, but '[t]ransfer pricing regulations and rules are about insuring and protecting the corporate tax base of this country'.[366]

This kind of fairness was not so much about the innovative shaping but rather about the protection of the public interest, or the national interest, which meant protecting Britain's tax base. The Paymaster General was clear: 'As a Minister, I am not prepared to allow the Exchequer risk that goes with . . . [permitting multinationals] to reduce taxable profits in the UK'.[367] This was, of course, an impeccably correct statement of the government's duties in the matter. The conception of fairness being played out in this part of the code was thus possibly not so much a reflection of an ideology of the public interest as an illustration of the broader duties of the government in protecting the tax base.[368] The distinction may have been a slender one, but the problem raised issues common to the European law issues discussed in chapter four. Prudential advancement of the public interest in cases involving cross-border transactions required particular vigilance against the depredations of non-residents.[369]

With the transfer pricing and thin capitalisation rules seeking to forestall the erosion of the corporation tax base by preventing the allocation of income profits among group companies, came also Labour's attempts to combat the manipulation of capital profits. This possibility had arisen because chargeable gains for an accounting period consisted of chargeable gains minus allowable losses.[370] It was met by the four 'targeted anti-avoidance rules'[371] brought in by the 2006 Finance Act[372] (and further strengthened in Finance Act 2007),[373] which were intended to block the inappropriate 'creation and use of corporate capital losses'.[374] The spur to each of these measures had been the government's

[364] *Whitney v CIR* [1926] AC 37, 54 (Lord Wrenbury).

[365] Standing Committee A (11 May 2004) HC vol 421 col 111 (Dawn Primarolo).

[366] Ibid, vol 421 col 112.

[367] Ibid, vol 421 col 120.

[368] But see BBC Radio 4, 'Companies "Looting" a Continent', *BBC File on Four* (29 July 2007), available at http://news.bbc.co.uk/1/hi/programmes/file_on_4/6908997.stm (accessed 24 August 2010).

[369] The virulence of the controversy over the income tax treatment of non-remitted income of resident but non-domiciled individuals may reflect something of this, eg: Editorial, *Financial Times* (8 February 2008) 12; and J Willman, 'Criticism of Non-Dom Tax Move Grows' *Financial Times* (9–10 February 2008) 2.

[370] TCGA 1992 s 2(2)(a).

[371] DF Williams, 'Avoidance through the Creation and Use of Capital Losses by Companies' (2006) *British Tax Review* 23, 23–24.

[372] FA 2006 was debated as F(No 2)B 2005, but the clause numbers of the Bill usefully correspond to the section numbers of FA 2006.

[373] FA 2007 s 32.

[374] FA 2006 ss 69–72 (as amended by FA 2007 ss 27 and 32), adding TCGA 1992, ss 16A and 184A–I; HM Revenue and Customs, *Avoidance through the Creation and Use of Capital Losses by Companies*, HMRC Guidance (27 July 2006), available at http://www.hmrc.gov.uk/manuals/cgmanual/attachments/capital-losses-july06.pdf (accessed 9 July 2011); HM Revenue and Customs, *Capital*

analysis of information gathered under the disclosure regime introduced in 2004.[375] The first targeted rule[376] dramatically excluded from the scope of the term 'allowable loss' any loss that accrued to a company pursuant to[377] arrangements whose purpose or main purpose was 'to secure a tax advantage'.[378] The idea with this targeted rule, as the Paymaster General explained in Standing Committee in May 2006, was to block 'tax relief for capital losses where their existence or amount . . . [had] been contrived, that is, where the losses that arise . . . [did] not reflect commercial reality'.[379]

The second and third targeted rules[380] sought to shore up what Bramwell called 'structural weaknesses'[381] in Schedule 7A to the Taxation of Chargeable Gains Act 1992, some of which had previously been evident to the Labour Administration since at least 1998.[382] The second targeted rule appeared in section 184A of the 1992 Act and restricted the buying of losses, while the third targeted rule, which appeared in section 184B of the same Act, curbed the buying of *gains*. It was the latter that illustrated the piquant sophistication of tax avoidance schemes in this area. Bramwell elaborated on the point by showing how, absent the second targeted rule, a company that owned an asset with an unrealised loss might be advised to buy a company that owned an asset with an unrealised gain, the former transferring the 'loss asset' to the latter, which would then sell both assets and set the loss against the gain for corporation tax purposes.[383] What the second and third targeted rules stated was that using losses was blocked in any case where a company was purchased mainly, or indeed wholly, 'to secure a tax advantage'.[384] That they had been successful in this was attested to by the Economic Secretary to the Treasury in the debates on the 2007 Finance Bill.[385] The second and third targeted rules were mirror images of each other, but the fourth, which appeared in sections 184G-I of the Taxation of Chargeable Gains Act 1992,[386] was quite distinct and aimed actually to shape further legislative development.

Gains Tax: Avoidance through the Creation and Use of Capital Losses, HMRC Guidance (19 July 2007), available at http://www.hmrc.gov.uk/cgt/cgt-recent-developments.pdf (accessed 9 July 2011); and Williams (above n 371) on the original FA 2006 provisions.

375 See above ch 1 on the Coalition's appointment of a working group to investigate a GAAR.

376 FA 2007 s 27 extended the first targeted rule to all chargeable persons, FA 2006 s 69 having applied only to companies.

377 TCGA 1992 s 16A (inserted by FA 2007 s 27, which repealed FA 2006 s 69 (FA 2007 s 27(6))).

378 TCGA 1992 s 16A(1)(b).

379 Standing Committee A (23 May 2006) HC vol 446 col 313 (Dawn Primarolo).

380 FA 2006 s 70.

381 Bramwell (above n 227) para D9.1.1.

382 Ie, when what was originally TCGA 1992 sch 7AA was introduced (sch 7AA repealed by FA 2006 s 70(2), which inserted TCGA 1992 s 184F(4)).

383 Bramwell (above n 227) para D9.1.4.

384 TCGA 1992 ss 184A(1)(c) and 184B(1)(c). See ibid, para D9.1.1; and Standing Committee A (23 May 2006) HC vol 446 col 332 (Dawn Primarolo).

385 Public Bill Committee (17 May 2007) HC vol 460 cols 215, 222 and 223 (Ed Balls).

386 As inserted by FA 2006 s 71.

The fourth targeted rule, innovative as it was, had been another response to information that the government had received under the disclosure regime. Briefly, if 'the main purpose'[387] of 'arrangements' into which a company entered had been to transform an income profit into a chargeable gain, so that the gain could be reduced by available losses, the use of the losses to reduce the gain was denied.[388] The novelty consisted partly in the fact that HMRC was empowered to issue a notice informing the company of the block on the deduction[389] and partly in the fact that, as already suggested and '[u]nlike the other measures being introduced as part of this package[,] this rule primarily . . . [provided] protection against *future schemes*'.[390] The main safeguard for taxpayers was that HMRC was able to 'issue the notice [only] when it [reasonably believed] . . . that the conditions of the clause [were] . . . met; [and] companies need[ed] not [to] be concerned by the provisions [of the targeted rule] unless they receive[d] a notice'.[391] An explanation was offered by the technical guidance:

> HMRC is aware that a large amount of unused capital losses is potentially available to companies, and this fact, combined with experience to date, suggest [sic] that there is likely to be increased activity in this area. This poses a significant risk not only to corporation tax on future capital gains, but also to corporation tax on companies' income profits.[392]

In line with the approach taken in this study, these safeguards may have been seen as a prudent recognition of the need for the government to augment its constituent power. Given the objective of encouraging fairness, there was a certain prudence in the four targeted rules, since they were certainly consistent, not only as between themselves but also with other anti-avoidance measures. As David Williams has pointed out, they each used 'a tax avoidance motive test', just like paragraph 13, discussed above, and like other anti-avoidance measures in the 2002 Finance Act.[393] They were examples of 'evidence-based' policymaking; they were not 'stabs in the dark'. All four targeted rules, as the Paymaster General pointed out in Standing Committee, 'result[ed] from information specifically provided under the disclosure regime and [were] specifically targeted to deal with that'.[394] They reflected, in other words, the prudence of the process analysed in chapter four, as well as a democratically sanctioned configuration of values. Given the ideology of fairness discussed above and given the public

[387] TCGA 1992 s 184G(5) (added by FA 2006 s 71(1)).
[388] TCGA 1992 s 184G(7) (added by FA 2006 s 71(1)).
[389] TCGA 1992 s 184G(6) (added by FA 2006 s 71(1)).
[390] HM Revenue and Customs, *Avoidance through the Creation and Use of Capital Losses* (above n 374) para 72; and HM Revenue and Customs, *Capital Gains Tax* (above n 374).
[391] Standing Committee A (23 May 2006) HC vol 446 col 334 (Dawn Primarolo).
[392] HM Revenue and Customs, *Avoidance through the Creation and Use of Capital Losses* (above n 374).
[393] CTA 2009 ss 690 and 691 (formerly FA 2002 sch 26 paras 23 and 24); and CTA 2009 s 864 (formerly FA 2002 sch 29 para 111).
[394] Standing Committee A (23 May 2006) HC vol 446 col 313.

interest, it is still difficult to argue with them.[395] Ministers were right to be sceptical of the kind of criticism levelled in Standing or Public Bill Committee debates. It was necessary, too, to be sceptical about allegations of uncertainty. The provisions were certainly intricate, but it was revealing that Bramwell was able to state the legal position on each of the four targeted rules with great clarity.[396]

'Between the idea/ And the reality . . .', so Eliot wrote, 'Falls the Shadow'.[397] Whether he was thinking of Hegel in writing these words or about Hegel's immanent critique, we would prefer not to say, but it might be an image for what has been attempted here. Comparing the ideal of fairness in corporation tax, as it appears from the policy documents, with the intricate reality as it has evolved is complex, yet it yields significant insights. The first of these has come from confronting the 'brokenness' of fairness as a concept. Disagreements about its application to specific situations prevail, both on the Left and between Left and Right. Although there has been a certain consensus about the need for anti-avoidance measures in each of the areas examined, simmering below the surface has been disagreement about whether the Labour Administration's approach to avoidance was itself a fair one. In opposition, the Conservatives' attack on the measures imported to the code after 1997 tended to be situated on the intersection of fairness and certainty. Most of their criticism was concerned with the 'unfairness' of companies not knowing for sure whether or not they fell within the scope of the recently introduced anti-avoidance provisions, or by invoking a form of procedural unfairness. As was evident, the code contained ambitious direct or indirect attempts to help bring about a fairer distribution of benefits and burdens in society, so Government and Opposition were often, perhaps inevitably, talking past each other when corporation tax fairness – that is, anti-avoidance – issues were raised. One consequence of this, as a National Audit Office (NAO) report of 2007[398] indicated, was that both sides (not to mention academics[399]) missed the impact of corporation tax reform on more traditional notions of 'vertical equity'[400] and 'horizontal equity'.[401]

Reporting on the NAO's findings, in August 2007, the *Financial Times* calculated that, given the availability of certain types of relief to only some areas of the corporate sector, the oil and gas industries, banks and insurance companies had had to assume a disproportionate share of the overall corporation tax

395 Ibid, 446 col 315 (Paul Goodman).

396 Bramwell (above n 227) s D9.1. Hence, possibly, the success that the government has claimed for these provisions: Public Bill Committee (17 May 2007) HC vol 460 col 223 (Ed Balls, then Economic Secretary to the Treasury).

397 Eliot (above n 45).

398 National Audit Office, *HM Revenue & Customs: Management of Large Business Corporation Tax* (HC 2006–07, 614).

399 V Houlder, 'One-Third of Biggest Businesses Pays No Tax' *Financial Times* (28 August 2007) 1: 'It is certainly surprising' (Michael Devereux, Oxford University Centre for Business Taxation).

400 Murphy and Nagel (above n 20) 13–16.

401 Ibid, 37–39.

burden.[402] Seven per cent of the 700 companies within the jurisdiction of HMRC's Large Business Service, so the *Financial Times* reported, 'paid 67 per cent of the tax [ie, due from the 700], while about 220 paid none and another 210 each paid less than £10m'.[403] Could it be that, since the unfairness has not been felt by the governing party's wider constituency, prudence had enabled its significance to be downplayed?[404] Similarly Gilbertian findings, though reshaped by dramatically altered economic circumstances, were revealed in a March 2011 report by the Oxford University Centre for Business Taxation.[405]

Secondly, a comparison of the ideal, as set out in the policy documents, and the reality, as provided for in the legislation, reveal a fundamentally different perspective as between Government and Opposition, not only as to the role of the corporation tax code but also as to the nature of corporation tax law itself. Moreover, to the extent that the attitude of the professional members of policy networks involved in this policy area reflected the Opposition view, their arguments, far from being merely technical, had a political significance. The nub of the issue was the fact that, as contended throughout this study, corporation tax reform represented, on a comprehensive scale, a harnessing of public law, not just to map out the limits of the permissible but to mould the relations between corporate sector and the state, to promote a specific ideological view of the public interest.[406] Except to the extent that it was part of the system of rule, this development was the actualisation of the functionalist tenets of public law study.[407] It follows that criticism of Labour's approach needs to be carefully weighed. Much of the criticism followed from an inability to interpret the reality[408] and an unwillingness to forsake normative intellectual positions. Thus, when the Chartered Institute of Taxation (CIOT) or the CBI criticises tax legislation for its 'complexity', their argument is valid as far as it goes. What is important, however, is to recognise it for what it is: a political position as to the role of law in the state that is fundamentally different from that in which Labour believed.[409] Criticism of complexity is not neutral, nor is it merely technical.[410]

[402] Houlder, 'One-Third of Biggest Businesses' (above n 399); and Houlder, 'Experts Attack Rewrite' (above n 141).

[403] Houlder, 'One-Third of Biggest Businesses' (above n 399).

[404] Anonymous (Private Eye editors), 'In the Back: Tax – Dodge City' *Private Eye*, No 1204 (22 February–6 March 2008) 28.

[405] V Houlder, 'Large Companies Pay Lower Rate of Corporation Tax' *Financial Times* (2 March 2011) 3, discussing MP Devereux and S Loretz, *Corporation Tax in the United Kingdom* (Oxford, Oxford University Centre for Business Taxation, 2011), available at http://www.sbs.ox.ac.uk/centres/tax (accessed 19 April 2011).

[406] Public Bill Committee (17 May 2007) HC vol 460 col 222 (Ed Balls, then Economic Secretary to the Treasury).

[407] Loughlin, *Public Law and Political Theory* (above n 13) chs 6 and 10.

[408] Public Bill Committee (17 May 2007) HC vol 460 col 224 (Mark Hoban).

[409] Eg, Tax Law Review Committee (above n 134) para 8.2.

[410] Public Bill Committee (17 May 2007) HC vol 460 cols 215–16 (Ed Balls); and Houlder,'Fewer Tax Laws' (above n 142).

It is thus that, with great respect to Philip Baker, QC,[411] who argued otherwise, there is indeed a 'principle of equality' in British tax law, possibly even a principle of fairness. It is, however, not a legal principle, much less a rule of law value, but an 'essentially contested concept'. It is fairness as conceived of in the highly specific terms discussed above, a principle of the political jurisprudence that is the corporation tax code. It is high on anti-avoidance and, as the 2007 NAO report and 2011 Oxford University reports have shown, low on traditional ideas of vertical equity and horizontal equity. The NAO and Oxford reports have demonstrated the consequences for companies. Those for individuals have been more strident – shocking even[412] – and illustrate the fact that despite the anti-avoidance provisions, prudence declares so often, not for fairness, but for efficiency. What is most important and is too often elided is the idea that the situation was one manifestation of an ideology validated, for the moment at least, by the judgment of the electorate. Its contested but not hopelessly confused nature enabled Will Hutton, who has described fairness as 'the essential handmaiden of reform', to call for a new, 'shared understanding' of how it is constituted.[413] That debate, in the context of corporation tax, is an extremely difficult one to have.

V. CONCLUDING COMMENTS

If readers have been willing to assent to the arguments developed in this study, what will have emerged is a somewhat novel and, it is hoped, a realistic interpretation of the theory and values that have been at work in corporation tax reform over the past 15 years or so. Some may, for sure, find the picture a rather disturbing one. Many, it is hoped, will see in it a persuasive depiction of a hitherto under-theorised reality. We may therefore feel some trepidation in spelling out and reflecting on the study's core conclusions. Given the complex and layered nature of the discussion, these are set out in detail in the final chapter below. We can conveniently anticipate some of them here, however.

What the corporation tax code has represented is a pattern of values that, though not perhaps ideally laid out, reflect a consensus around the imperative of economic growth, around the importance of fairness and, in the code's shifting nature and constant change, a series of more or less prudential responses to the contingencies of an uncertain world. All criticisms of the code and all

[411] P Baker, 'United Kingdom' in GTK Meussen (ed), *The Principle of Equality in European Taxation* (The Hague, Kluwer Law International, 1999) 165.

[412] Institute for Fiscal Studies (2004) and (2008) (above n 316) and subsequent reports; Giles, 'Very Rich Get Richer' (above n 316); C Giles, 'Inequality Rose under Labour, Says IFS' *Financial Times* (8 April 2010) 3; R Peston, *Who Runs Britain?* (London, Hodder and Stoughton, 2008) 3 and 7–8; and V Houlder, 'Why the Broad of Shoulder Have a Wider Range of Options' *Financial Times* (12–13 December 2009) 3.

[413] W Hutton, *Them and Us: Changing Britain – Why We Need a Fair Society* (London, Little Brown, 2010) 25, 37 and 394–95.

proposals for further reform have to take account of this much underestimated proposition.

On the basis that such a view of Britain's current system of corporation tax is correct, it has a number of rather startling – and unfashionable – implications, some of which might perhaps be expressed as follows. First, the public law nature of the corporation tax code strongly suggests the practical impossibility of a more 'durable' or less complex reality. What the Economic Secretary to the Treasury said at the Committee Stage of the 2007 Finance Bill is revealing:

> The hon. Gentleman might want to reflect a little more on the reality of tax policy-making before he gives us another of his lectures on complexity. . . [T]he global corporate tax system has become very complex. Many skilled and ingenious people are coming up with complex ways to avoid tax, and the Government must counter the resulting complexity.[414]

If this was indeed the case, then many of the simplification arguments were, as we might say, so much chaff; there is no qualitative or quantitative difference between corporation tax legislation and any other area of economic or social regulation.

Secondly, arguments about corporation tax are not merely 'political'; they are also ideological. If the former assertion springs from the political nature of the values immanent to the code, the latter arises from the ideological nature of the idea of the public, or national, interest itself. Prioritisations of efficiency and fairness, however delicate, might in truth amount to nothing less than a manifestation of the role of the state in the moulding of the public, or national, interest and of the level of the tax burden to be laid, in the first instance at least, on the corporate sector. Anti-avoidance measures will therefore provoke controversy, not just because of their tendency to increase the complexity and volume of the legislation but also because of disagreements about the role of the state in shaping the public, or national, interest. The corporate sector has traditionally been keen on the idea of efficiency in the national, or public, interest but less so on the role of fairness. Given the political consensus, it is difficult to see a way out of complexity – certainly not by conferring wide judicial discretion, and possibly not by introducing a general anti-avoidance rule either.

Thirdly, given the ideological nature of the prioritisation of efficiency and fairness, sustaining the corporation tax code is, above all, an enterprise of politics as calculation. If politics really is about governing, then corporate tax reform is about management. The world is too uncertain, London's financial markets at once too fragile and too valuable to the present ideological consensus, for matters to be otherwise.

[414] Public Bill Committee (17 May 2007) HC vol 460 col 216 (Ed Balls). This was a response to an interjection from Conservative MP Brooks Newmark.

6

Conclusions

TO MAKE SENSE of Britain's on-going reform of its corporate tax law: that was my ambitious objective at the beginning of this study. How near I have come to that goal is obviously for readers to judge. Nonetheless, I maintain that the arguments crafted in these pages enable me to close the work with at least four key conclusions.

Of these four, the first and arguably most significant is this: the fundamental requirement for critiquing this area is to render explicit the very nature of the enterprise of reforming the law of corporate taxation. My phrasing is intended to focus attention on the kind of endeavour that corporate tax reform involves. Recognising the nature of that endeavour is, however, a demanding task. It requires us to have a passable theory of the nature of corporate tax legislation as a whole.

Secondly, in order to make the nature of corporation tax reform explicit, it is necessary to focus attention on the ability of political institutions in Britain to act effectively in this area. Commentators have hitherto given much greater attention to the processes by which corporate tax law is created than to the question of how successful it has been subsequently. I have a little more to say about the latter point, but this second conclusion has very significant ramifications, as I hope to show. Thirdly, we have to appreciate exactly why it is that the way in which corporate tax law is made contributes so decisively to this effectiveness, as well as why proposals for changes to the process of reform should be treated very sceptically indeed. Fourthly, and finally, we have to recognise the good reasons why it is that the corporate tax law created in this way is so complex, and why it is apparently so unstable. In doing so, we have to accept that complexity is in no way the same as unintelligibility.

Note that none of these conclusions are statements about what the corporate tax code should or ought to contain. Instead, they embody understandings of a state of affairs as it actually seems to obtain. This kind of approach will be familiar to political economists and to political scientists. By and large, however, lawyers – and especially tax lawyers – are not used to interpretative conclusions. They are more comfortable with concrete proposals, with arguments in favour of specific solutions to previously isolated problems. However, I maintain that a plausible interpretation of what is actually going on with corporate tax reform is a key prerequisite to making specific reform proposals and judging of their feasibility.

In this final, brief chapter I would therefore like to offer some closing reflections on the four conclusions just summarised. In doing so, I aim to draw together the main elements of the whole discussion in such a way as to show how each one relates to the others. As I said at the beginning, my purpose has been not to offer solutions to specific problems but rather to throw light on important factors that those who do wish to do so cannot afford to ignore.

I. VALUES AND THEORY REVISITED

First, then, to the nature of corporate tax reform. Why, after all, should it matter that we have a theory? Why should we be bothered about what the reform is seeking to achieve? Why, indeed, should we be concerned as to the values that corporate tax law embodies? These, and many similar ones, are entirely apposite questions. Many if not most commentators confronting this troublesome area of public policy write about corporate tax reform – about aligning the accounting and taxation treatments of profits and losses, about mapping the borders of unacceptable corporation tax avoidance, for instance – without ever making these underlying questions apparent. So why not be content to do just that?

What the nature of corporate tax reform may be and what qualities corporate tax law reveal are questions that matter. And they matter for a specific reason. They force us to unpick the technicalities of particular reform proposals from the ideologies that inform them. As I argued in chapter one, most proposals for corporate tax reform assume a particular idea of the role of the tax system in a neoliberal state. Popular protest, based on highly contestable premises as it has been, challenges that assumption. It is certainly clear that arguments both ways are defined by the context of a neoliberal consensus. Recognising this, I have chosen to concentrate on corporate tax law's status as public law, in order to uncover what corporate tax law and its reform might plausibly be all about. It is not the only approach that I could have taken, nor is it the only conceivable one. But it focuses attention on the role of corporation tax law as contributing to the building of economic power and social cohesion out of incipient conflict: between government and the corporate sector, between the British state and the European Union and between Britain and other states of the world.

The public law character of corporate taxation is symbolised, as I mentioned in chapter one, by the practitioner's loose-leaf encyclopaedias that deal, for instance, with the taxation of corporate debt and derivatives or with company reconstructions. This insight owes everything to Martin Loughlin's reference to the nature of public law in general.[1] The pre-eminent example is the peerless Bramwell on the taxation of companies.[2] The intricate web of rights and duties

[1] See M Loughlin, *Public Law and Political Theory* (Oxford, Oxford University Press, 1992) 241.

[2] R Bramwell, A James et al (eds), *Taxation of Companies and Company Reconstructions*, 8th edn (London, Sweet and Maxwell, 2002).

created by the corporation tax code, as judicially explained and elaborated, is a paradigm of public law. As I argued in chapters two and five, the code is a transcription, so to speak, of the political economy of taxation into a legal substance and a legal form. Every single one of the duties and rights that the code creates denotes some value, some choice about the purpose of corporate taxation, and ultimately about the role of public finance in the right ordering of the British state. Most often, those values are fairness and efficiency – alone or in some combination.[3] But the values as embodied within the code are obviously imperfectly realised, no more than badges of sometimes shifting, sometimes concrete ideals. Fairness especially is notoriously difficult to pin down, not least because the sharpness of its meaning has been rounded and smoothed off by the omnipresence of the word in public discourse. The Coalition Government's combination of fairness and efficiency in the political notion of competitiveness, as exemplified by its Corporate Tax Road Map, has been if anything a temporary declaration in favour of a particular idea of efficiency.

How, indeed, could matters stand otherwise? As I explained in chapter five, at any given moment, the corporate tax code marks out the boundaries of what is – so far as corporate tax is concerned – politically possible. This is because, as the Scottish Enlightenment philosophers David Hume and Adam Smith well understood, the rights and duties created by statutory codes are the true indicators of the nature and qualities of a country's constitution.[4] The rule of law values of the late twentieth-century Sheffield school, which did much early on to prompt investigations of which this study is an example, have nothing like this level of interpretative force, precisely because they do not address with sufficient precision, as does Loughlin, the political and historical dimensions of public law. In the British corporate tax system, these jostling values of fairness and efficiency are a contemporary manifestation of an ethic of commercial society fashioned perhaps especially by Hume and by Smith, and often violently challenged in the subsequent rise of ideologies in the nineteenth and twentieth centuries. With these – as we should call them – neoliberal values, economic growth is everything, and the scramble for investment capital its sine qua non.

That the values of efficiency and fairness are never perfectly attained within the corporate tax code should go almost without saying. That their ideal is always, so to speak, some way off, seems inevitable. There is a 'shadow', as TS Eliot says, that falls between the 'idea' and 'the reality'.[5] Seen thus, the incremental nature of

[3] See above ch 5.

[4] See above ch 2 n 109.

[5] Cf TS Eliot, 'The Hollow Men' in *Collected Poems*, 1909–1962 (London, Faber and Faber, 1974) 91. The quotation has an interesting link with 'tax folk', although not quite the one I seek to make. Older readers will recall that Chris Whitehouse, in the last edition of *Revenue Law: Principles and Practice* to be published in his name, touchingly included the full first five lines of the poem to memorialise the passing of his co-author in that work, Elizabeth Stuart-Buttle (1952–93): C Whitehouse, P Vaines and L Narain, *Revenue Law: Principles and Practice*, 21st edn (Croydon, LexisNexis UK, 2003) preliminary matter. The quotation has been dropped from subsequent editions under different editors.

reform of corporate tax law in Britain, involving as it does the constant re-evaluation of political possibilities, remains a source of strength rather than of weakness. We live in hope of change for the better in corporate tax. Its ever-present possibility makes us constantly engage with corporate tax debate.

I would argue, therefore, that reforming corporate tax law – viewed as public law – is about governing. As such, it manifests the ability of government, whatever that ability might be, to actualise a balanced corporate tax policy free from manipulation by those who seek to exert corporate economic coercion on the life of a nation. For government, a good technique is not enough. The potential conflicts thereby engaged require political prudence, that subtle weighing of ends and means that is so repellent to those of serious cast of mind and delicate sensibilities. The more successful a government is at calculation, at promoting consistent, coherent and non-contradictory corporate tax policy towards a clear end and reconciling the sometimes disparate political values of efficiency and fairness, the greater legitimacy its legislative solutions will have.

In the spring of 2011, the overtly political value of the international competitiveness of the corporate tax system was dominant, as shown by the increasing territoriality of the British corporate tax system described in chapter two. This increased territoriality is itself a good illustration of how, given the values with which we are working, adherence to EU law, far from being a constraint on Britain's corporate tax reform, can actually be a source of strength. Making the British system more territorial is a direct consequence of several high-profile cases in the European Court of Justice on the surrender of trading losses between companies in Britain and other member states of the European Union, as well as on the validity of Britain's controlled foreign company rules.

So the first main factor that cannot, in my view, be ignored by would-be reformers is this: as a public law endeavour, the reform of corporate taxation is no more, and no less, than an important contribution to reworking the ordering of the British state in the particular context of public finance, and the burden of this reordering to be laid, in the first instance at least, on the corporate sector. Corporate tax reform is concerned with the role given to factors of efficiency and of fairness in the particular combination of territory, people and government that make up the British state. Corporation tax reform is no longer, as perhaps once it was, an adjunct to the reform of personal taxation. It is instead a place of potentially conflictual engagement between government and the internationally mobile capital and economic might of multinational corporations. To say corporate tax legislation is a form not only of administrative but also of constitutional law is not to overstate the argument. Within the neoliberal ideology, multinationals are a force for great good, as well as for something else. They are uniquely important and uniquely powerful. The state of the corporate tax code thus embodies political decisions about how we should live in a strident culture of neoliberalism.

Viewing corporate tax law as public law is to emphasise the power of a political society, through its representative government, to manage the neoliberal ideal. Thus it is that corporate tax law has become the scene of confrontation between the rival ambitions of neoliberal ideology and communitarian concern, between those who, in Oakeshott's conceptualisation, promote the state as an enterprise association and those who see it merely as a civil association.[6] To borrow a phrase from much earlier in the discussion, the significance of the reform of corporate taxation is not exhausted by the economic technicalities of the Mirrlees review.

II. WORKING TOGETHER

If treating corporate tax law as public law uncovers the values that it contains, and if it really is as significant as I have suggested, what is the importance of the institutions of government – of the reformers? Britain remains sovereign, in the sense discussed throughout the study, in tax and other areas of public policy. There can be no comprehensive European-wide corporate tax regime without Britain's full agreement, and although national tax policy is subject to the fundamental freedoms of the European Treaties, and bans on state aid, these are in any event likely to command wide acceptance in a consensus of neoliberal thought.

In chapter three, I sought to show how well equipped were Britain's political institutions to act effectively in this area. The institutions of Britain's representative government have the unique function of making corporate tax law through the process of legislating. They also, however, have the task of constructing an account of their policy initiatives. This is particularly important with taxation – and not just with corporate tax – because the form of that accountability is as yet relatively weak. The strength or weakness of the ex post accountability role, not only of Parliament but also of the judges, is therefore crucial to seeing how prudently corporate tax policy has been conducted.

Within this context, in recent years, politics and the relationship between government and the corporate sector has become associated, not with government as such, but with governance. Uniquely important within the neoliberal ideology is the enrolment of the corporate sector in law-making, in helping to define the public, or national, interest in corporate tax policy. This has its benefits, given the free market premises, to be sure, but it also has its drawbacks. Most importantly, it is difficult sometimes for outsiders to see precisely how politically prudent certain reform initiatives have been, because the respective roles in corporate tax reform of the corporate sector and of government have become blurred. What is certain, following Loughlin's analysis, is that the government's competence in corporation tax policy depends on its capacity, and that depends in turn on the productiveness of the relationship between state and corporate sector.

[6] See above ch 2: M Oakeshott, *On Human Conduct* (Oxford, Clarendon Press, 1975) 200. See also J Le Grand, *Motivation, Agency, and Public Policy: Of Knights and Knaves, Pawns and Queens* (Oxford, Oxford University Press, 2003) 11–16. (My thanks to Dan Priel.)

The body that should be in a position to quiz this rather fuzzy boundary is Parliament, or to be more specific, the House of Commons. I have portrayed the relationship between Commons and Government as one of tension, but there have been early signs that this model, which relies on Government and Parliament to be locked in potential conflict, might have changed under the Coalition Government. Just as it is difficult for an outsider to parse the prudence of particular corporate tax policy decisions, so too it is difficult sometimes for the Commons' Treasury Select Committee. That said, the role of election in the appointment of Select Committees and the absence under the Coalition of a massive single-party majority may facilitate greater accountability in corporate tax matters. Certainly, the initial activities of a highly proactive elected Treasury Committee chairman have indicated that this is the case. It is at the very least possible that the propulsive nature of corporate tax reform under the Labour Government, and its much-criticised outcomes, owed something to the absence of these factors then.

In terms of initiating corporate tax reform, the key institution is the Treasury. Just as Parliament in this respect looks over its shoulder, so the Treasury looks forward. Great prudence is needed from the public servants and ministers involved, because even when equipped with economic modelling techniques, and economics – not politics – is uppermost in their minds, the future is unknown. This is the essence of why corporate tax policy is political economy, and corporate tax legislation the embodiment of the values of political economy. The prudence of Machiavelli and of Smith comes into its own in this context. Although it might be reassuring to find some identity of interest between state and non-state institutions, it would be even more pleasing to think that the apparatus of government could manage significant divergences effectively.

The capacity of Britain's political institutions in this respect centres on the Treasury and HM Revenue and Customs (HMRC), as well as on the effectiveness of Parliament in following their activities. However, effectiveness means different things to different people. For Parliament, the quality resides in its powers of scrutiny, in its ability to hold the government to account for the latter's corporation tax measures. For the Treasury and HMRC, however, it means their policing ability to anticipate and confront unexpected combinations of economic events in such a way as to maintain tax revenues. For judges, it means prudential decisions that reinforce and articulate evolving constitutional understandings. So, if corporation tax reforms fail, and we want to know why, we need to be in a position to find out. Greater ex post accountability would therefore be prudent, and a new House of Commons select committee on taxation, as suggested by a number of observers, seems to be required. The need has become all the more acute because of the Coalition's evident determination to tie the corporate sector and its advisers ever more closely into its counsels, and the possibility of regulatory capture thereby created. It is not necessarily a matter of any sinister motive on the Government's part. It is just possible that a government minister, in a meeting with well-advised corporate tax lobbyists, could actually be persuaded of a policy line that could later be shown to have been demonstrably contrary to the national, or public, interest.

As for the judges, they are closer to the Crown in all of this than might perhaps be imagined. They are in a position to provide an account of the rationale behind corporate tax law in judicial review proceedings, but the same might be said about the prudence involved in everyday cases of statutory interpretation. What is certainly true is that the public law nature of judicial deliberation on corporation tax has been accentuated by the establishment of the Tax Chamber of the Upper and Lower Tribunal. Whether this should causes critics concern depends on the view that one takes of public law. If the taxation judges are there to ensure the accurate implication of the general will on corporate taxation, then the fact that they are experienced professionals should be a cause for reassurance. If, on the other hand, the purpose of judges in tax cases is to submit corporate tax policy to the rigors of legal analysis (perhaps the more contemporary view), then the development will seem less reassuring. What one can conclude, however, from the cases discussed in chapter three is that even before the greater specialisation, there was at least an implicit recognition of the public law nature of judicial decision-making in the corporate tax arena and a commensurate exercise of political prudence on the part of the judges.

The second factor that corporate tax reformers cannot afford to ignore is therefore this: on the footing that corporate tax reform is shaped by prudence as the logic of public law, everything depends on our ability to scan the institutional exercise of that prudence. This argument is subtly different from one based on some vague assertion of the need for transparency. The reason is this: when an institution acts in a policy field, the exercise of its decision-making power is shaped even before the event by the likelihood of meticulous examination afterwards. The less likely the Treasury is to have to mount a rational defence of its actions on corporate tax after the event, the less likely rational factors will be to play an important part in its initial policy decision. More effective accountability would mean that the Treasury would have to deliberate all the more carefully before acting. Its decisions would be all the more likely to be governed, not by short term expediency, but by the effective actualisation of the neoliberal or whatever other economic values the government of the day is charged with promoting. It would be this, rather than a more remote intellectual argument, that would most favour greater public esteem for tax policy in general. This is a really striking area of concern but has probably had less attention than what I want to revisit next, the process by which corporate tax law is made.

III. THE VIRTUOSITY OF PRUDENT CORPORATE TAX REFORM

How, then, do the various stages in which corporation tax reform takes place augment or detract from the state's capacity in the corporate tax policy area? The answer, as constantly re-emphasised, is the degree of political prudence that they reveal. Chapter four sought to show what that quality demanded for several corporate tax reform initiatives. The significance of this point is inextricably bound up in the conviction that in tax as elsewhere, prudence is the indispensable skill of the legislator.

Although the practice of politics in general may be thought of as being mainly about either calculation or deliberation, in relation to the reform of corporate tax, it is probably best thought of as a combination of the two. I have associated this combination with Machiavelli (following Loughlin's lead), but also with Smith and with the arguments of one of his leading modern-day apologists, Amartya Sen.[7] Moreover, managing the ends–means harnessing of deliberation in accordance with a particular policy is historically part of the arcane exercise of the prerogative, the traditional science of police. We should not therefore be surprised by the cloak of secrecy around much, though by no means all corporate tax reform.

Finally, it should be recalled that reform is itself a protean idea: sometimes it is understood as involving the complex reworking of existing material; sometimes it seems to yearn for reviving the spirit of a previous state of affairs. Gordon Brown as Chancellor understood it well, and the early signs have been that George Osborne, his Coalition successor, has the same grasp. There is no denying the strong political instincts of either man. Whether David Gauke, in pursuing the New Approach to tax policy, not to mention the Corporate Tax Road Map, has really deployed the prudential skills of his political master remains to be seen. What is prudential depends on what the political dimension to corporation tax reform is taken to consist of, as well as on the relationship between politics and the adjacent notions of policy and reform.

Whilst under-discussed in the literature, it is plain from both public pronouncements and corporate tax reform measures themselves that the direction of reform has been informed by a particular ideology of the public, or national, interest. This ideology has been conceived of somewhat differently from the common good. First, within a welfare economics framework, it focuses attention on the combination of efficiency and fairness in particular policy decisions; secondly, it strives to put the interests of Britain above those of other countries; and finally, it seeks to put the tax system to work in the service of a vision of combining economic growth with fairness. Interestingly, lawyers have tended either to ignore this ideological dimension or refused to recognise that its furtherance is a legitimate objective of corporate tax legislation.

The fact that legislative proposals tend to be well advanced by the time they are presented for argumentative scrutiny in the House of Commons is entirely compatible with a representative democracy. This is why we need to be aware of the true role, historically speaking, of Parliament in developing corporation tax reform measures. It comes at the end of a multifaceted process, one that requires

[7] A Sen, *The Idea of Justice* (London, Allen Lane, 2009) 44–46; and A Smith, *The Theory of Moral Sentiments* [1759/1790], RP Hanley (ed) (London, Penguin 2009) 255.

the close interaction of public servants with ministers (in clarifying policy objectives), as well as with the public (in terms of public consultation). The arguments mounted by Christopher Wales and by the Institute for Fiscal Studies about 'effective [Parliamentary] scrutiny' fail to recognise the true role of Parliament in a representative democracy. Finance Bill debates do much better than either commentator is willing to recognise in fulfilling the requirement that legislative proposals be subjected to the scrutiny of argumentative debate.[8] That said, a new Commons select committee on tax, supplied with the back-up to familiarise itself better with the technical issues, would greatly strengthen the ex post accountability of the government in tax policy. Such would be a desirable development in itself. There have been many suggestions for something equivalent to the US Congressional Budget Office, and though for the reasons discussed in chapter four, this would not be consistent with the historical characteristics of the British system, it is a better idea than some of the posited alternatives. Extremely imprudent would be any involvement of members of an unelected House of Lords in the enactment of tax legislation. Election, not expertise, is the legitimating quality of the tax legislator. This point has thus far been seriously underestimated in discussions of corporate tax reform. To continue to underestimate it would still further undermine an area of public policy that, in the light of recent public protest, is struggling for legitimacy.

So the third factor that cannot be ignored is as follows: it is absolutely crucial that technical debate about corporate tax reform does not lose sight of the historical significance of the Parliamentary processes that translate ideas into reality. If anything, therefore, even greater emphasis needs to be placed, not as such on the detailed deliberation of individual corporate tax clauses in the House of Commons, but on the quality of Bills presented to Parliament for consideration. Saying 'Parliament', however, underlines the importance of not allowing an unelected House of Lords, however beguiling its expertise may be, to have a greater role in this policy area.

IV. CORPORATION TAX AS POLITICAL JURISPRUDENCE

The discussion of the reform process suggests that at any one time, the boundaries of the corporation tax code are a very good barometer of Britain's sovereignty in taxing corporate income. A key background consideration is the Mirrlees review's (admittedly rather faint) praise of the complex web of public law rights and duties that the legislation contains. '[T]he UK tax system is not, on the whole, a dreadfully bad one'.[9]

[8] B Manin, *The Principles of Representative Government* (Cambridge, Cambridge University Press, 1997) 191.

[9] J Mirrlees, S Adam and T Besley et al, *Tax by Design* (Oxford, Oxford University Press, 2011) 1 (pre-publication draft chapters available at http://www.ifs.org.uk/mirrleesReview/design (accessed 30 November 2010)) chs 1, 8.

Redolent as it is of Britain's tax sovereignty, the corporate tax code should be thought of as political jurisprudence, whose strength is drawn paradoxically from the ideological and institutional constraints under which it is created. It is the embodiment, as argued in chapter five, not of the chaos of Promethean fire unloosed on the world, but rather, so to speak, of the steady course embarked on with Odysseus tied to the mast of the ship of state. Characterising the corporation tax code as political jurisprudence means that it is entirely appropriate for it to be designed to further the ideological objectives of whichever party happens – or whatever parties happen – to have formed the administration. It also means that the code transcends individual morality. Indeed, its role in raising public revenue means that it helps to create the social conditions under which reflecting on such morality is possible. Finally, it is clear both from the code itself and from the approach of the judges to interpreting its provisions that the dominant theory of the corporation tax code is reason of state, and the chief characteristic of the code is political prudence.

Practising such prudence has specific implications for arguments about the complexity and instability of the corporation tax code. Neither of these is relevant to the concept of the rule of law as it inheres to political jurisprudence. Montesquieu's rule of law, the 'freedom from fear', refers to only rule by institutions rather than by men. It does not realistically posit a series of criteria about what 'the rule of law' may require of substantive legislation. The corporation tax code, unstable and complicated though it undoubtedly is, is also undeniably the product of Montesquieu's, not Fuller's, rule of law. So to say does not necessarily endow instability and complexity with the cloak of virtue, however. Levels and degrees of either quality are subject to prudential considerations. Prudence may require a degree of complexity in certain circumstances – to ensure fairness, for example – but not in others. Likewise, prudence may require stability in some cases but not in others. The Corporate Tax Road Map explicitly recognises these points. Prudence in reality means different things at different times, if trust and confidence in government is to be maintained – and possibly even augmented.

So we come to the crux of the matter: corporation tax law, as a form of political jurisprudence, demands prudence; if prudence in turn demands simplicity and stability, this is not in the name of the rule of law but in the name of the prudential management of complexity and of change. These points apply to corporate tax as well as to any other species of public law.

The sketch offered in the latter stages of chapter five should therefore be imagined as a glimpse of the state of affairs on any day when the processes analysed in chapter four are at work. The dominant rationale for tax reform, as famously explained by Adam Smith, is that of effectiveness.[10] In other words, it consists in the successful promotion, if only from day to day, of the sovereign's conception

[10] See the maxims of taxation with which we began: A Smith, *The Wealth of Nations, Books IV–V* [1776], AS Skinner (ed) (London, Penguin, 1999) 418.

of the public, or national, interest. Smith never lived in a democratic state, but he did live in an era of representative institutions. It is not too great a leap, therefore, to associate the eighteenth-century prince's idea of the public good with the national, or public, interest ideology of a governing party or parties in a parliamentary state. Prudence in the advancement of the public, or national, interest is what, I suggest, gives the government sovereignty in corporate tax matters. So long as the prudential conduct of policy continues, and so long as the national interest is demonstrably served by Britain's membership of the European Union, there will subsist the relationship of trust and confidence that we describe as sovereignty. Thus viewed, the relationship is a productive and empowering one. But at the same time, it is our fault and no one else's if, as a society, we seem unable to break free from politically pragmatic neoliberal corporate tax policies.

So, if we have to elaborate on what prudence might mean in the conduct of corporation tax reform, what can we say? Everything, it is suggested, turns on the ability of the government to enlist the reform of corporate taxation in maintaining a state of affairs that bears a plausible relationship with its ideology. The view taken here is that the vision of combining economic growth with social justice is an ideology as strong as any other. It certainly conforms to Oakeshott's characterisation of ideology as a 'formalised abridgement of the supposed substratum of rational truth contained in . . . [a] tradition'.[11] That said, the drawbacks of ideologies are not part of my inquiry. What furthers them, at least in corporate tax terms, *is*, however. In a complex and uncertain world, keeping the vision credible – maintaining trust and confidence – needs 'quick footwork' (we might say prudence) at every turn. The electorate is always ready to enforce a government's duty to make the people richer.

Seen in this light, the value of efficiency, instantiated (though only imperfectly) in the corporation tax code, assumes its proper proportions. For Labour, making the code more efficient meant shaping it to reflect ever more closely the imperatives of post-neoclassical endogenous growth theory. In its closer alignment of taxable profits with commercial profits; in its enhancement of relief for borrowing costs; in its maintenance of generous relief for exchange differences; in the provision of wide relief for intangibles, the corporation tax code might, without exaggeration, be viewed as a vast economic instrument in the service of growth. Instantiating a version of fairness, by contrast, has meant recognising and confronting what is a highly contentious idea: to some extent re-imagining tax law as creating only conventional rights and prudentially managing the relationship of fairness with efficiency. Neither efficiency nor fairness prevails; no conclusive relationship exists between them. Only effectiveness matters, because things are always changing. The effective balancing of efficiency and fairness depends on what is prudential at any given moment, since augmenting trust and confidence is all-important.

[11] M Oakeshott, 'Rationalism in Politics' [1962] in T Fuller (ed), *Rationalism in Politics and Other Essays*, 2nd edn (Indianapolis, Liberty Fund, 1991) 5, 9.

The fourth key factor is therefore this: corporate tax legislation can be adversely criticised from an objective standpoint if it is genuinely unintelligible; but if the criticism of complexity is based simply on its detailed prioritisation of policy issues, then such criticism cannot truly be objective. Everything depends on where the sympathies of readers fall. If you are emphatically not of a neoliberal disposition, there is quite simply no prospect of constructive engagement with corporate tax material as it currently exists. The government will simply see you as one of those who need to be managed because your reaction is one of hostility to the very premises on which the legislation is based. It is not that the system is corrupt. It is just based on ideals or versions of ideals or on priorities among values with which you disagree. If, however, you *are* a neoliberal, this study should have exposed many areas of constructive engagement with the system.

The need to recognise the potential for conflict is always present. So it would be rash to predict where all this goes from here. The process of reform is ongoing. It might be wrecked on the rocks of unforeseen economic contingencies. Rather less likely, it might be destroyed by a reaction to the economic inequalities to which it seems to have contributed. What is clear is that only prudent management in the public, or national, interest can further the corporation tax reform endeavour. That means strengthening accountability, resisting encroachment by any non-elected higher chamber and accepting the rationale for complexity in the corporate tax code itself. It may be, as the Mirrlees review claims, that complexity produces 'an undesirable narrowing of public debate'.[12] However, insofar as it is also coherent and consistent, complexity may actually augment the effectiveness of the system. Little, if any corporation tax reform can command support from everyone affected. Managing conflict is, after all, the essence of politics. And although it may be other things as well, corporate tax law is nothing if not political jurisprudence.

[12] Mirrlees, Adam and Besley et al (above n 9) ch 1, 21.

Bibliography

PRIMARY SOURCES

A. Official Documents

i. Organisation for Economic Co-operation and Development (OECD)

OECD, *The Relationship between Taxation and Financial Reporting: Income Tax Accounting* (Paris, 1987).

——, *Taxing Profits in a Global Economy: Domestic and International Issues* (Paris, 1991).

——, *Harmful Tax Competition: An Emerging Global Issue* (Paris, OECD, 1998).

ii. European Commission

Commission (EC), 'The Application of Anti-abuse Measures in the Area of Direct Taxation within the EU and in Relation to Third Countries' COM (07) 785 FINAL, 10 December 2007.

Commission (EU), 'Proposal for a Council Directive on a Common Consolidated Corporate Tax Base (CCCTB)' COM (11) 121/4, 16 March 2011, available from http://ec.europa.eu/taxation_customs/taxation (accessed 23 March 2011).

iii. International Accounting Standards Committee Foundation (IASCF)

IASCF, *Annual Report 2009* (London, 2010).

iv. British Parliament

Budget 2011 (HC 2010–11, 836).

Lord Fulton (Chairman), *Report of the Committee on the Civil Service, Vol 1, 1966–68* (Cmnd 3638, 1968).

House of Commons Information Office, *Factsheet P10: Programming of Government Bills* (2004), available at http://www.parliament.uk/documents/commons-information-office/p10.pdf (accessed 23 June 2011).

Kelly, R, 'Nominations to Select Committees' (Standard Note SN/PC/3719, House of Commons Library, 2010), available at http://www.parliament.uk/documents/commons/lib/research/briefings/snpc-03719.pdf (accessed 23 June 2011).

National Audit Office, *HM Revenue & Customs: Management of Large Business Corporation Tax* (HC 2006–07, 614).

O'Donnell, G (Chair), *Financing Britain's Future: Review of the Revenue Departments* (Cm 6163, 2004).

Lord Radcliffe (Chair), *Royal Commission on the Taxation of Profits and Income: Final Report* (Cmd 9474, 1955).
Royal Commission on the Constitution, Report: 1969–73, Vol I (Cmnd 5460, 1973).
Select Committee on Corporation Tax, *Report on Corporation Tax, Together with Minutes of Evidence, Appendices and Index* (HC 1970–71, 622).
Select Committee on Economic Affairs, *4th Report: The Finance Bill 2007, Vol II (Evidence)* (HL 2006–07, 121).
HM Treasury, *Corporation Tax* (Green Paper, Cmnd 8456, 1982).
——, *Equipping Britain for Our Long-Term Future: Financial Statement and Budget Report* (HC 1997–98, 85).
Treasury Committee, *10th Report: Inland Revenue Matters* (HC 2002–03, 834).
——, *2nd Report: The 2005 Pre-Budget Report* (HC 2005–06, 739).
——, *4th Report: The 2006 Budget* (HC 2005–06, 994-II).
——, *3rd Special Report: The 2005 Pre-Budget Report: Government Response to the Committee's Second Report of Session 2005–06* (HC 2005–06, 1013).
——, *2nd Report: The 2006 Pre-Budget Report* (HC 2006–07, 115).
——, *5th Report: The 2007 Budget, Volume II (Oral and Written Evidence)* (HC 2006–07, 389-II).
——, *7th Report: Administration and Expenditure of the Chancellor's Departments, 2008–09* (HC 2009–10, 156).
——, *1st Report: June 2010 Budget* (HC 2010–11, 350).
——, 'Letter from the Chairman to the Exchequer Secretary regarding Tax Policy, 4 November 2010', available at http://www.parliament.uk (accessed 20 December 2010).
——, *8th Report: Principles of Tax Policy* (HC 2010–11, 753).

v. HM Government

Cabinet Office, *The 46th Civil Service Year Book* (London, TSO, 2007).
——, *A Draft Civil Service Bill: A Consultation Document* (Cm 6373, 2004).
——, *The Coalition: Our Programme for Government* (2010).
Inland Revenue, *Corporation Tax Reform: The Next Steps* (Inland Revenue Technical Note, December 2003).
——, *Financial Instruments: The Tax Treatment of Financial Instruments for Managing Interest Rate Risk (A Consultative Document)* (1991).
——, *The Path to Tax Simplification: A Background Paper* (1995).
——, *Tax Treatment of Foreign Exchange Gains and Losses: A Consultative Document* (1989).
——, *The Taxation of Gilts and Bonds: A Consultative Document* (1995).
Ministry of Justice, *The Governance of Britain* (Cm 7170, 2007).
Office of Tax Simplification, *Small Business Tax Review: March 2011* (London, HM Treasury, 2011), available at http://www.hm-treasury.gov.uk/ots (accessed 16 March 2011).
Lord Plowden (Chairman), *Control of Public Expenditure* (Cmnd 1432, 1961).
HM Revenue and Customs, *Departmental Report 2009* (Cm 7107, 2009).
——, *Tax Policy Making: Draft Protocol on Announcements Outside Scheduled Fiscal Events* (9 December 2010), available at http://www.hmrc.gov.uk/budget-updates/autumn-tax/tax-policy-other-6655.htm (accessed 22 March 2011).

Sir Colin Southgate (Chair) et al, *Fundamental Review of HM Treasury's Running Costs: A report to the Chancellor of the Exchequer* (1994).

HM Treasury, 'Chancellor Announces Major Review of Inland Revenue and Customs and Excise', Press Release 78/03 (3 July 2003).

——, *The Code for Fiscal Stability* (1998), available at http://archive.treasury.gov.uk/budget/1998/cfs.pdf (accessed 19 July 2011).

——, 'Details of Avoidance Study Group Set Out', Press Release 04/11 (14 January 2011), available at http://www.hm-treasury.gov.uk (accessed 21 January 2011).

——, 'Government Announces Tax Avoidance Clampdown', Press Notice 68/10 (6 December 2010), available at http://www.hm-treasury.gov.uk/press_68_10.htm (accessed 8 January 2011).

——, *Meeting the Aspirations of the British People: 2007 Pre-Budget Report and Comprehensive Spending Review* (Cm 7227, 2007).

——, *Prudent for a Purpose: Working for a Stronger and Fairer Britain (Economic and Fiscal Strategy Report and Financial Statement and Budget Report)* (HC 1999–2000, 346).

——, *Reform of Corporation Tax* (Green Paper, Cmnd 4630, 1971).

——, *Tax Framework for Business: Document for Consultation* (2010), available at http://webarchive.nationalarchives.gov.uk (accessed 10 March 2011).

——, *HM Treasury Annual Report and Accounts, 2008–09* (HC 2008–09, 518).

HM Treasury and Inland Revenue, *Corporation Tax Reform: A Consultation Document* (2003).

——, *Large Business Taxation: HM Government's Strategy and Corporate Tax Reforms (A Consultation Document)* (2001).

——, *Reform of Corporation Tax: A Consultation Document* (2002).

HM Treasury and HM Revenue and Customs (HMRC), *Corporate Tax Reform: Delivering a More Competitive System* (2010), available at http://www.hm-treasury.gov.uk (accessed 30 November 2010).

——, *Review of Links with Large Business: November 2006*, Varney, D (Chair) (2006).

——, *Tax Policymaking: A New Approach* (2010), available at http://hm-treasury.gov.uk (accessed 10 July 2010).

——, *Taxation of the Foreign Profits of Companies: A Discussion Document* (2007).

B. Philosophical and Literary Works

Arendt, H, *The Human Condition*, 2nd edn (Chicago, University of Chicago Press, 1998).

Aristotle, *The Nicomachean Ethics* [c 350 BC], JAK Thomson, H Tredennick and J Barnes (eds and trans) (London, Penguin, 2004).

——, *The Politics* [c 335 BC], S Everson (ed) (Cambridge, Cambridge University Press, 1988).

Bacon, F, 'Of Judicature' in J Pitcher (ed), *The Essays* [1612] (London, Penguin, 1985) 222.

Bentham, J, *An Introduction to the Principles of Morals and Legislation* [1781], JH Burns and HLA Hart (eds) (Oxford, Clarendon Press, 1996).

Bodin, J, *On Sovereignty: Four Chapters from The Six Books of the Commonwealth* [1576], JH Franklin (ed) (Cambridge, Cambridge University Press, 1992).

Burke, E, 'A Letter to a Noble Lord' in I Kramnick (ed), *The Portable Edmund Burke* (New York, Penguin Books, 1999) 213.

——, 'Speech at Mr Burke's Arrival in Bristol' in I Kramnick (ed), *The Portable Edmund Burke* (New York, Penguin Books, 1999) 155.

Cicero, MT, *de Re Publica; de Legibus* [54–51 bc] CW Keyes (ed and trans) (London, William Heinemann, 1928).

Dworkin, R, *Law's Empire* (Cambridge, MA, Belknap Press, 1986).

——, *A Matter of Principle* (Cambridge, MA, Harvard University Press, 1985).

——, *Taking Rights Seriously* (London, Duckworth, 1977).

Finnis, J, *Natural Law and Natural Rights* (Oxford, Clarendon Press, 1980).

Foucault, M, *Security, Territory, Population: Lectures at the Collège de France, 1977–78*, M Senellart (ed) and G Burchell (trans) (London, Palgrave, 2007).

——, 'The Subject and Power' in JD Faubion (ed), *Michel Foucault, Power* (London, Allen Lane Penguin, 2001) 326.

Fuller, LL, *The Morality of Law*, rev edn (London, Yale University Press, 1969).

Gallie, WB, 'Essentially Contested Concepts' (1955–56) 56 *Aristotelian Society (Proceedings)* 167.

Habermas, J, *Between Facts and Norms*, W Rehg (trans) (Cambridge, Polity Press, 1997).

Harrington, J, 'The Prerogative of Popular Government' [1658] in JGA Pocock (ed), *The Political Works of James Harrington* (Cambridge, Cambridge University Press, 1977).

Hart, HLA, *The Concept of Law* (Oxford, Clarendon Press, 1961).

von Hayek, FA, *The Constitution of Liberty* [1960], 2nd edn (London, Routledge, 2006).

Hegel, GWF, *Outlines of the Philosophy of Right* [1821], S Houlgate (ed) and TM Knox (trans) (Oxford, Oxford University Press, 2008).

Hobbes, T, *Leviathan* [1651], M Oakeshott (ed) (Oxford, Basil Blackwell, 1955).

Hume, D, *A Treatise of Human Nature* [1739], LA Selby-Bigge and PH Nidditch (eds) (Oxford, Clarendon Press, 1978).

Justinian, *The Digest of Justinian*, T Mommsen, P Krueger and A Watson (trans and eds) (Philadelphia, Pennsylvania, 1985).

Keynes, JM, *The General Theory of Employment, Interest and Money* [1936] (Basingstoke, Palgrave, 2007).

Lawson, G, *Politica Sacra et Civilis* [1660], C Condren (ed) (Cambridge, Cambridge University Press, 1992).

Locke, J, *Two Treatises of Government* and *A Letter Concerning Toleration* [1690/1689], I Shapiro (ed) (New Haven, Yale University Press, 2003).

Luhmann, N, *Law as a Social System*, F Kastner, R Nobles, D Schiff, and R Ziegert (eds and trans) (Oxford, Oxford University Press, 2004).

——, *A Sociological Theory of Law*, E King and M Albrow (trans) (London, Routledge and Kegan Paul, 1985).

Machiavelli, N, *The Discourses* [1517], B Crick, LJ Walker and B Richardson (eds and trans) (London, Penguin, 2003).

——, *The Prince* [1532], P Bondanella (trans) (Oxford, Oxford University Press, 2005).

Madison, J, 'The Federalist, 57' in A Hamilton, J Madison and J Jay, *The Federalist Papers* [1788], L Goldman (ed) (Oxford, Oxford University Press, 2008).

Mill, JS, 'Considerations on Representative Government' in J Gray (ed), *On Liberty and Other Essays* (Oxford, Oxford University Press, 1991) 203–467.

——, *Principles of Political Economy and Chapters on Socialism* [1848/1873], J Riley (ed) (Oxford, Oxford University Press, 1994).
Millar, J, *An Historical View of the English Government* [1812], MS Phillips and DR Smith (eds) (Indianapolis, Liberty Fund, 2006).
Montesquieu, Baron de, *The Spirit of the Laws* [1748], T Nugent (trans) (New York, Hafner Publishing, 1949).*
Murphy, L and Nagel, T, *The Myth of Ownership* (Oxford, Oxford University Press, 2000).
Nozick, R, *Anarchy, State and Utopia* (Oxford, Blackwell, 1980).
Oakeshott, M, *On Human Conduct* (Oxford, Clarendon Press, 1975).
——, *Rationalism in Politics and Other Essays*, new edn (Indianapolis, Liberty Fund, 1991).
Petty, Sir William, 'A Treatise of Taxes & Contributions' in CH Hull (ed), *The Economic Writings of Sir William Petty: Together with the Observations upon the Bills of Mortality More Probably by Captain John Graunt, 2 vols* (New York, Augustus M Kelley, 1963 and 1964) I 1–97.
Plato, *The Laws* [360 bc], T Saunders (ed) (London, Penguin, 2004).
Pufendorf, S, *On the Duty of Man and Citizen* [1682], J Tully (ed) (Cambridge, Cambridge University Press, 1991).
Rawls, J, *Lectures on the History of Political Philosophy*, S Freeman (ed) (Cambridge, MA, Belknap Press, 2007).
——, *Political Liberalism* (New York, Columbia University Press, 1993).
——, *A Theory of Justice*, rev edn (Oxford, Oxford University Press, 1999).
Rousseau, J-J, *Discourse on Political Economy and The Social Contract* [1755/1762], C Betts (ed and trans) (Oxford, Oxford University Press, 1994).
Savile, G, 'The Character of a Trimmer' [1688] in MN Brown (ed), *The Works of George Savile Marquis of Halifax* (Oxford, Clarendon Press, 1989) I 178.
Schmitt, C, *The Concept of the Political* [1927], G Schwab (trans) (Chicago, University of Chicago Press, 1996).
Sen, A, *Development as Freedom*, 2nd edn (Oxford, Oxford University Press, 2001).
——, *On Economic Inequality*, enlarged edn (Oxford, Clarendon Press, 1997).
——, *The Idea of Justice* (London, Allen Lane, 2009).
Sieyès, EJ, *What is the Third Estate?* [1789], SE Finer (ed) and M Blondel (trans) (London, Pall Mall Press, 1963).
Smith, A, *Lectures on Jurisprudence* [1762–63/1766], RL Meek, DD Raphael and PG Stein (eds) (Indianapolis, Liberty Fund, 1982).
——, *The Theory of Moral Sentiments* [1759/1790], RP Hanley (ed) (London, Penguin, 2009).
——, *The Wealth of Nations* [1776], AS Skinner (ed) (London, Penguin, 1999).
Stewart, D, 'Account of the Life and Writings of Adam Smith, LLD' [1793] in IS Ross, DD Raphael and AS Skinner (eds), *Essays on Philosophical Subjects* (Indianapolis, Liberty Fund, 1982) 263–351.
Stiglitz, JE, *Making Globalization Work* (London, Penguin, 2007).
——, *Globalization and its Discontents* (London, Penguin, 2002).

* Thomas Nugent's original translation of 1750 was entitled *The Spirit of Laws*, which is a rendition generally preferred among Montesquieu specialists; this 1949 reprint has *The Spirit of the Laws* on the title page, with *The Spirit of Laws* in the text itself.

Todorov, T, *In Defence of the Enlightenment*, G Walker (trans) (London, Atlantic, 2009).
Waldron, J, 'The Core of the Case against Judicial Review' (2006) 115 *Yale Law Journal* 1346–1406.
——, *The Dignity of Legislation* (Cambridge, Cambridge University Press, 1999).

SECONDARY SOURCES

A. Books

Adamson, J, *The Noble Revolt: The Overthrow of Charles I* (London, Weidenfeld & Nicolson, 2007).
Allen, CK, *Law in the Making*, 7th edn (Oxford, Clarendon Press, 1964).
Arnold, BJ and McIntyre, MJ, *International Tax Primer*, 2nd edn (The Hague, Kluwer, 2002).
Arnold, NS, *Imposing Values: An Essay on Liberalism and Regulation* (Oxford, Oxford University Press, 2009).
Association of Chartered Certified Accountants (ACCA), *Tax Principles: From Adam Smith to Barack Obama* (London, ACCA, 2009), available at http://www.accaglobal.com/pubs (accessed 22 March 2011).
Atkinson, AB and Stiglitz, JE, *Lectures on Public Economics* (London, McGraw-Hill, 1980).
Augar, P, *The Greed Merchants: How the Investment Banks Played the Free Market Game* (London, Allen Lane, 2005).
Avery Jones, JF, 'Taxing Foreign Income from Pitt to the Tax Law Rewrite: The Decline of the Remittance Basis' in J Tiley (ed), *Studies in the History of Tax Law* (Oxford, Hart Publishing, 2004).
Avi-Yonah, RS, *International Tax as International Law: An Analysis of the International Tax Regime* (Cambridge, Cambridge University Press, 2007).
Aylmer, GE, *Rebellion or Revolution? England 1640–1660* (Oxford, Oxford University Press, 1986).
Bagehot, W, *The English Constitution* [1867] (London, Kegan Paul, 1919).
Baker, JH, *An Introduction to English Legal History*, 4th edn (London, Butterworths, 2002).
Baldwin, R and Cave, M, *Understanding Regulation: Theory, Strategy and Practice* (Oxford, Oxford University Press, 1999).
Baldwin, R, Scott, C and Hood, C (eds), *A Reader on Regulation* (Oxford, Oxford University Press, 1998).
Barker, R, *Political Ideas in Modern Britain* (London, Methuen, 1978).
Barnard, T, *The English Republic, 1649–1660* (Harlow, Longman, 1982).
Barry, B, *Political Argument: A Reissue with a New Introduction* (Berkeley, University of California Press, 1990).
Beetham, D, *The Legitimation of Power* (Basingstoke, Palgrave, 1991).
Berle, AA and Means, GC, *The Modern Corporation and Private Property*, rev edn (New York, Harcourt, Brace and World, 1967).
Bernstein, RJ, *The Restructuring of Social and Political Theory* (Oxford, Basil Blackwell, 1976).

Besley, T, *Principled Agents? The Political Economy of Good Government* (Oxford, Oxford University Press, 2006).

Bingham, T, *The Rule of Law* (London, Allen Lane, 2010).

Bohman, J, *Public Deliberation: Pluralism, Complexity, and Democracy* (Cambridge, MA, MIT Press, 1996).

Bower, T, *Gordon Brown* (London, HarperCollins, 2004).

Bradshaw, K and Pring, D, *Parliament and Congress* (London, Constable, 1972).

Bramwell, R, James, A, Hardwick, M and Lindsay, J, *Taxation of Companies and Company Reconstructions*, 8th edn (London, Sweet and Maxwell, 2002).

Brewer, M, Goodman, A, Myck, M, Shaw, J and Shephard, A (eds), *Poverty and Inequality in Britain: 2004* (London, Institute for Fiscal Studies, 2004).

Brewer, M, Sibieta, L and Wren-Lewis, L, *Racing Away? Income Inequality and the Evolution of High Incomes* (London, Institute for Fiscal Studies, 2008).

Brown, G, *Beyond the Crash: Overcoming the First Crisis of Globalisation* (London, Simon and Schuster, 2010).

Buckle, M and Thompson, J, *The UK Financial System: Theory and Practice*, 4th edn (Manchester, Manchester University Press, 2004).

Buckley, PJ and Casson, M, *The Future of the Multinational Enterprise*, 3rd edn (Basingstoke, Palgrave Macmillan, 2002).

van Caenegem, RC, *An Historical Introduction to Western Constitutional Law* (Cambridge, Cambridge University Press, 1995).

Canavan, FP, *The Political Reason of Edmund Burke* (Durham, NC, Duke University Press, 1960).

Chapman, RA, *The Treasury in Public Policymaking* (London, Routledge, 1997).

Chartered Institute of Taxation (CIOT), *Taxed by Law, Untaxed by Concession* (London, CIOT, 2005).

Coates, D, *Models of Capitalism: Growth and Stagnation in the Modern Era* (Cambridge, Polity Press, 2000).

Cohen, MR and Nagel, E, *An Introduction to Logic and Scientific Method* (London, Routledge and Kegan Paul, 1963).

Collini, S, Winch, D and Burrow, J, *That Noble Science of Politics: A Study in Nineteenth-Century Intellectual History* (Cambridge, Cambridge University Press, 1983).

Connolly, WE, *The Terms of Political Discourse*, 3rd edn (Oxford, Blackwell, 1993).

Coyle, D, *The Soulful Science: What Economists Really Do and Why It Matters* (Princeton, Princeton University Press, 2007).

Daintith, T and Page, A, *The Executive in the Constitution: Structure, Autonomy and Internal Control* (Oxford, Oxford University Press, 1999).

Devereux, MP and Loretz, S, *Corporation Tax in the United Kingdom* (Oxford, Oxford University Centre for Business Taxation, 2011), available at http://www.sbs.ox.ac.uk/centres/tax (accessed 19 April 2011).

Dicey, AV, *Introduction to the Study of the Law of the Constitution* [1885], 10th edn, ECS Wade (ed) (London, Macmillan, 1965).

Dorey, P, *Policy-Making in Britain: An Introduction* (London, Sage, 2005).

Dowding, K, *The Civil Service* (London, Routledge, 1995).

Dowell, S, *A History of Taxation and Taxes in England from the Earliest Times to the Present Day*, 3rd edn, 6 vols, AR Ilersic (rev) (London, Frank Cass, 1965).

Drucker, PF, *The Concept of the Corporation* (New York, Mentor, 1964).

——, *The Frontiers of Management* (London, Heinemann, 1987).

Dunn, J (ed), *The Economic Limits to Modern Politics* (Cambridge, Cambridge University Press, 1990).
Elliott, M (ed), *Beatson, Matthews and Elliott's Administrative Law Text and Materials*, 3rd edn (Oxford University Press, Oxford, 2005).
Elster, J (ed), *Deliberative Democracy* (Cambridge, Cambridge University Press, 1998).
Eriksen, EO and Weigård, J, *Understanding Habermas: Communicative Action and Deliberative Democracy* (London, Continuum, 2003).
Farmer, P and Lyal, R, *EC Tax Law* (Oxford, Clarendon Press, 1994).
Finer, H, *The Theory and Practice of Modern Government*, 4th edn (London, Methuen, 1961).
Fischer, F, *Technocracy and the Politics of Expertise* (London, Sage, 1990).
Foster, CD and Plowden, FJ, *The State under Stress* (Buckingham, Open University Press, 1996).
Fox, CJ and Miller, HT, *Postmodern Public Administration: Toward Discourse* (Thousand Oaks, Sage, 1995).
Frampton, D, *Practical Tax Administration* (Bath, Fiscal Publications, 1993).
Franco, P, *The Political Philosophy of Michael Oakeshott* (London, Yale University Press, 1990).
Freeman, MDA (ed), *Lloyd's Introduction to Jurisprudence*, 7th edn (London, Sweet and Maxwell, 2001).
French, PA, *Collective and Corporate Responsibility* (New York, Columbia University Press, 1984).
Gamble, A, *Politics and Fate* (Cambridge, Polity, 2000).
Gammie, M, *The Enactment of Tax Legislation: An Analysis of the Consultative Process and the Finance Acts 1979 to 1987* (London, Law Society of England and Wales, 1988).
Gardiner, SR, *Constitutional Documents of the Puritan Revolution 1625–1660*, 3rd edn (Oxford, Clarendon Press, 1906).
Ghosh, J, Johnson, I and Miller, P, *Ghosh, Johnson and Miller on the Taxation of Corporate Debt and Derivatives* (London, LexisNexis, 2010).
Giddens, A, *The Third Way and its Critics* (Cambridge, Polity Press, 2000).
——, *The Third Way: The Renewal of Social Democracy* (Oxford, Polity Press, 1998).
Glenn, HP, *Legal Traditions of the World*, 2nd edn (Oxford, Oxford University Press, 2004).
Goldsworthy, J, *The Sovereignty of Parliament: History and Philosophy* (Oxford, Clarendon Press, 1999).
Grant, W, *Economic Policy in Britain* (Basingstoke, Palgrave, 2002).
Graves, MAR, *The Tudor Parliaments: Crown, Lords and Commons, 1485–1603* (London, Longman, 1985).
Gray, J, *False Dawn: The Delusions of Global Capitalism*, 2nd edn (London, Granta, 2002).
Greenleaf, WH, *The British Political Tradition, Volume Three: A Much Governed Nation (Part I)* (London, Methuen, 1987).
Greenspan, A, *The Age of Turbulence: Adventures in a New World* (London, Allen Lane, 2007).
Griffith, JAG, *The Politics of the Judiciary*, 5th edn (London, Fontana, 1997).
Haakonssen, K, *The Science of a Legislator: The Natural Jurisprudence of David Hume and Adam Smith* (Cambridge, Cambridge University Press, 1981).

Harden, I and Lewis, N, *The Noble Lie: The British Constitution and the Rule of Law* (London, Hutchinson, 1986).
Hardin, R, *David Hume: Moral and Political Theorist* (Oxford, Oxford University Press, 2007).
Hardt, M and Negri, A, *Empire* (London, Harvard University Press, 2000).
Hausman, DM and McPherson, MS, *Economic Analysis and Moral Philosophy* (Cambridge, Cambridge University Press, 1996).
Henderson Global Investors, *Responsible Tax* (London, Henderson, 2005).
Hennessy, P, *Whitehall* (London, Fontana, 1990).
Lord Hewart of Bury, *The New Despotism* (London, Ernest Benn, 1929).
Hillman, AL, *Public Finance and Public Policy: Responsibilities and Limitations of Government* (Cambridge, Cambridge University Press, 2003).
Hilson, C, *Regulating Pollution: A UK and EC Perspective* (Oxford, Hart Publishing, 2000).
Himmelfarb, G, *The Roads to Modernity: The British, French and American Enlightenments* (London, Vintage, 2008).
Holmes, S, *Passions and Constraint: On the Theory of Liberal Democracy* (Chicago, University of Chicago Press, 1995).
Holt, JC, *Magna Carta*, 2nd edn (Cambridge, Cambridge University Press, 1992).
Holt, R, *Second amongst Equals: Chancellors of the Exchequer since the Second World War* (London, Profile Books, 2002).
Hood, C, *Explaining Economic Policy Reversals* (Buckingham, Open University Press, 1994).
Lord Howe (chair), *Making Taxes Simpler: The Final Report of a Working Party Chaired by Lord Howe of Aberavon* (London, Conservative Party, 2008).
Hughes, OE, *Public Management and Administration: An Introduction*, 2nd edn (London, Macmillan, 1998).
Hutton, W, *The State We're In*, rev edn (London, Vintage, 1996).
——, *Them and Us: Changing Britain – Why We Need a Fair Society* (London, Little, Brown, 2010).
Institute of Chartered Accountants in England and Wales (ICAEW), *Towards a Better Tax System: Practical Consideration of the Ten Tenets* (London, ICAEW, 2000).
Institute for Fiscal Studies (IFS), *Equity for Companies: A Corporation Tax for the 1990s – A Report of the IFS Capital Taxes Group chaired by Malcolm Gammie*, Commentary No 26 (London, IFS, 1991).
Ipsos Mori, *UK Corporate Taxation and International Competitiveness* (London, Confederation of British Industry, 2006).
Israel, J, *A Revolution of the Mind: Radical Enlightenment and the Intellectual Origins of Modern Democracy* (Princeton, Princeton University Press, 2010).
Jackson, P and Leopold, P, *O Hood Phillips & Jackson: Constitutional and Administrative Law*, 8th edn (London, Sweet and Maxwell, 2001).
Jacob, JM, *The Republican Crown: Lawyers and the Making of the State in Twentieth-Century Britain* (Aldershot, Dartmouth, 1996).
James, S and Nobes, C, *The Economics of Taxation: Principles, Policy and Practice*, 7th edn (Harlow, Financial Times and Prentice Hall, 2000).
Jensen, NM, *Nation-States and the Multinational Corporation: A Political Economy of Foreign Direct Investment* (Woodstock, Princeton University Press, 2006).
Jones, WJ, *Politics and the Bench: The Judges and the Origins of the English Civil War* (London, George Allen and Unwin, 1971).

Jordan, B, *The Common Good: Citizenship, Morality and Self-Interest* (Oxford, Basil Blackwell, 1989).
Judge, D, *Political Institutions in the United Kingdom* (Oxford, Oxford University Press, 2005).
Julius, D, *Global Companies and Public Policy: The Growing Challenge of Foreign Direct Investment* (London, Pinter, 1990).
Kaletsky, A, *Capitalism 4.0: The Birth of a New Economy* (London, Bloomsbury, 2010).
Kay, JA and King, MA, *The British Tax System*, 5th edn (Oxford, Oxford University Press, 1990).
Keegan, W, *The Prudence of Mr Gordon Brown* (Chichester, John Wiley, 2003).
Kiesling, H, *Taxation and Public Goods: A Welfare-Economic Critique of Tax Policy Analysis* (Ann Arbor, University of Michigan Press, 1992).
King, A, *The British Constitution* (Oxford, Oxford University Press, 2007).
King, M and Thornhill, C, *Niklas Luhmann's Theory of Politics and Law* (Basingstoke, Palgrave Macmillan, 2003).
Knowles, D, *Hegel and the Philosophy of Right* (London, Routledge, 2002).
Kynaston, D, *The City of London, Volume IV: A Club No More, 1945–2000* (London, Chatto and Windus, 2001).
Laws, D and Marshall, P (eds), *The Orange Book: Reclaiming Liberalism* (London, Profile, 2004).
Lawson, N, *The View from No. 11: Memoirs of a Tory Radical* (London, Bantam Press, 1992).
Lee, N (ed), *Revenue Law: Principles and Practice*, 27th edn (Haywards Heath, Bloomsbury Professional, 2009).
Lee, S, *Best for Britain? The Politics and Legacy of Gordon Brown* (Oxford, Oneworld, 2007).
Le Grand, J, *Motivation, Agency, and Public Policy: Of Knights and Knaves, Pawns and Queens* (Oxford, Oxford University Press, 2003).
Lewis, ND, *Choice and the Legal Order: Rising above Politics* (London, Butterworths, 1996).
——, *Law and Governance: The Old Meets the New* (London, Cavendish Publishing, 2001).
Leys, C, *Market-Driven Politics: Neoliberal Democracy and the Public Interest* (London, Verso, 2001).
Lipsey, D, *The Secret Treasury* (London, Viking, 2000).
Loughlin, M, *Foundations of Public Law* (Oxford, Oxford University Press, 2010).
——, *The Idea of Public Law* (Oxford, Oxford University Press, 2003).
——, *Public Law and Political Theory* (Oxford, Clarendon Press, 1992).
——, *Sword and Scales: An Examination of the Relationship between Law and Politics* (Oxford, Hart Publishing, 2000).
Lukes, S, *Power: A Radical View*, 2nd edn (Basingstoke, Palgrave Macmillan, 2005).
McAllister TV, *Revolt against Modernity: Leo Strauss, Eric Voegelin, and the Search for a Postliberal Order* (Lawrence, University Press of Kansas, 1997).
McEldowney JF, *Public Law*, 3rd edn (London, Sweet and Maxwell, 2002).
McEldowney, JF and McEldowney, S, *Environmental Law and Regulation* (London, Blackstone Press, 2001).
McKay W, et al, *Erskine May's Treatise on The Law, Privileges, Proceedings and Usage of Parliament*, 23rd edn (London, LexisNexis UK, 2004).

McLean, I, *Adam Smith, Radical and Egalitarian: An Interpretation for the Twenty-First Century* (Edinburgh, Edinburgh University Press, 2006).
McMillan, E, *Complexity, Organisations and Change* (London, Routledge, 2004).
Majone, G, *Regulating Europe* (London, Routledge, 1996).
Malcolm, N, *Reason of State, Propaganda, and the Thirty Years' War: An Unknown Translation by Thomas Hobbes* (Oxford, Clarendon Press, 2007).
Manin, B, *The Principles of Representative Government* (Cambridge, Cambridge University Press, 1997).
March, JG and Olsen, JP, *Rediscovering Institutions: The Organizational Basis of Politics* (New York, Free Press, 1989).
Marquand, D, *The Unprincipled Society: New Demands and Old Politics* (London, Fontana, 1988).
Matthew, HCG, *Gladstone: 1809–1874* (Oxford, Clarendon Press, 1986).
——, *Gladstone: 1875–1898* (Oxford, Clarendon Press, 1995).
Maturana, HR and Varela, FJ, *Autopoiesis and Cognition: The Realization of the Living* (Dordrecht, Reidel Publishing, 1980).
Meade, JE (ed), *The Structure and Reform of Direct Taxation: Report of a Committee Chaired by Professor JE Meade* (London, George Allen and Unwin, 1978).
Messere, K, de Kam, F and Heady, C, *Tax Policy: Theory and Practice in OECD Countries* (Oxford, Oxford University Press, 2003).
Metcalfe, L and Richards, S, *Improving Public Management*, 2nd edn (London, Sage, 1990).
Micklethwait, J and Wooldridge, A, *The Company: A Short History of a Revolutionary Idea* (London, Phoenix, 2005).
Mills, CW, *The Power Elite* (New York, Oxford University Press, 1959).
Milward, AS, *The European Rescue of the Nation-State*, 2nd edn (London, Routledge, 2000).
Mirrlees, J, Adam, S and Besley, T et al, *Tax by Design* (Oxford, Oxford University Press, 2011) (draft chapters available at http://www.ifs.org.uk/mirrleesReview/design (accessed 30 November 2010)).
Moffat, G, *Trusts Law: Text and Materials*, 5th edn (Cambridge, Cambridge University Press, 2009).
Monbiot, G, *Captive State: The Corporate Takeover of Britain* (London, Macmillan, 2000).
Monroe, H, *Intolerable Inquisition? Reflections on the Law of Tax* (London, Stevens, 1981).
Morse, G and Williams, D, *Davies: Principles of Tax Law*, 5th edn (London, Sweet and Maxwell, 2004).
Mosley, L, *Global Capital and National Governments* (Cambridge, Cambridge University Press, 2003).
Mouffe, C, *On the Political* (London, Routledge, 2005).
Mumford, A, *Taxing Culture: Towards a Theory of Tax Collection Law* (Aldershot, Ashgate Dartmouth, 2002).
Musgrave, RA, *The Theory of Public Finance: A Study in Public Economy* (London, McGraw-Hill, 1959).
Musgrave, RA and Musgrave, PB, *Public Finance in Theory and Practice*, 5th edn (New York, McGraw-Hill, 1989).
Myrdal, G, *The Political Element in the Development of Economic Theory*, P Streeten (trans) (London, Routledge and Kegan Paul, 1953).

Naughtie, J, *The Rivals: The Intimate Story of a Political Marriage* (London, Fourth Estate, 2001).
O'Brien, DP, *The Classical Economists* (Oxford, Clarendon Press, 1975).
Ogus, A, *Regulation: Legal Form and Economic Theory* (Oxford, Oxford University Press, 1994).
Ohmae, K, *The End of the Nation State: The Rise of Regional Economies* (London, HarperCollins, 1995).
Pannick, D, *Judges* (Oxford, Oxford University Press, 1987).
Parsons, W, *Public Policy: An Introduction to the Theory and Practice of Policy Analysis* (Cheltenham, Edward Elgar, 1995).
Perkin, H, *The Rise of Professional Society: England since 1880* (London, Routledge, 1989).
——, *The Third Revolution: Professional Elites in the Modern World* (London, Routledge, 1996).
Peston, R, *Brown's Britain* (London, Short Books, 2005).
——, *Who Runs Britain?* (London, Hodder and Stoughton, 2008).
Peters, BG, *Institutional Theory in Political Science: The 'New Institutionalism'*, 2nd edn (London, Continuum, 2005).
——, *The Politics of Taxation: A Comparative Perspective* (Oxford, Blackwell, 1991).
Petsoulas, C, *Hayek's Liberalism and its Origins: His Idea of Spontaneous Order and the Scottish Enlightenment* (London, Routledge, 2001).
Picciotto, S, *International Business Taxation* (London, Weidenfeld and Nicolson, 1992).
Pierre, J and Peters, BG, *Governance, Politics and the State* (Basingstoke, Macmillan, 2000).
Pigou, AC, *A Study in Public Finance*, 3rd edn (London, Macmillan, 1962).
Plant, R, *The Neo-liberal State* (Oxford, Oxford University Press, 2010).
Pocock, JGA, *The Machiavellian Moment: Florentine Political Thought and the Atlantic Republican Tradition* (Princeton, Princeton University Press, 1975).
Pollard, AF, *The Evolution of Parliament*, 2nd edn (London, Longmans, 1926).
Porter, R, *Enlightenment: Britain and the Creation of the Modern World* (London, Penguin, 2000).
Powell, J, *The New Machiavelli: How to Wield Power in the Modern World* (London, Bodley Head, 2010).
PricewaterhouseCoopers LLP and World Bank Group, *Paying Taxes: The Global Picture* (London, PricewaterhouseCoopers, 2006).
Prosser, T, *Law and the Regulators* (Oxford, Clarendon Press, 1997).
Pym, H and Kochan, N, *Gordon Brown: The First Year in Power* (London, Bloomsbury, 1998).
Radaelli, CM, *The Politics of Corporate Taxation in the European Union: Knowledge and International Policy Agendas* (London, Routledge, 1997).
——, *Technocracy in the European Union* (London, Longman, 1999).
Redston, A (conslt ed), *Tolley's Yellow Tax Handbook, 2010–11*, 51st edn, (London, LexisNexis, 2010).
Rhodes, RAW, *Understanding Governance: Policy Networks, Governance, Reflexivity and Accountability* (Maidenhead, Open University Press, 1997).
Richards, D and Smith, MJ, *Governance and Public Policy in the UK* (Oxford, Oxford University Press, 2002).
Richards, S, *Whatever it Takes: The Real Story of Gordon Brown and New Labour* (London, Fourth Estate, 2010).

Richardson, JJ and Jordan, AG, *Governing under Pressure: The Policy Process in a Post-Parliamentary Democracy* (Oxford, Basil Blackwell, 1985).

Ringen, S, *The Economic Consequences of Mr. Brown: How a Strong Government Was Defeated by a Weak System of Governance* (Oxford, Bardwell, 2009).

Robertson, D, *Judicial Discretion in the House of Lords* (Oxford, Clarendon Press, 1998).

Robinson, A and Sandford, C, *Tax Policy-Making in the United Kingdom: A Study of Rationality, Ideology and Politics* (London, Heinemann, 1983).

Rush, M, *Parliament Today* (Manchester, Manchester University Press, 2005).

Sampson, A, *Anatomy of Britain Today* (London, Hodder and Stoughton, 1965).

——, *Who Runs This Place? The Anatomy of Britain in the 21st Century* (London, John Murray, 2004).

Sandford, C, *The Economics of Public Finance: An Economic Analysis of Government Expenditure and Revenue in the United Kingdom*, 4th edn (Oxford, Pergamon Press, 1992).

Sandford, C, Godwin, M and Hardwick, P, *Administrative and Compliance Costs of Taxation* (Bath, Fiscal Publications, 1989).

Sands, P and Klein, P (eds), *Bowett's Law of International Institutions*, 5th edn (London, Sweet and Maxwell, 2001).

Sassen, S, *Losing Control? Sovereignty in an Age of Globalization* (New York, Columbia University Press, 1996).

Schmidt, J, *Disciplined Minds* (Oxford, Rowman and Littlefield, 2000).

Schwarzmantel, J, *Ideology and Politics* (London, Sage, 2008).

Sennett, R, *The Corrosion of Character: The Personal Consequences of Work in the New Capitalism* (New York, WW Norton, 1998).

Servan-Schreiber, J-J, *The American Challenge*, R Steel (trans) (London, Hamish Hamilton, 1968).

Scheuerman, WE, *Liberal Democracy and the Social Acceleration of Time* (London, Johns Hopkins University Press, 2004).

Scholte, JA, *Globalization: A Critical Introduction*, 2nd edn (Basingstoke, Palgrave Macmillan, 2005).

Schumpeter, JA, *History of Economic Analysis*, EB Schumpeter (ed) (London, George Allen and Unwin, 1954).

Seligman, ERA, *Essays in Taxation*, 9th edn (London, Macmillan, 1923).

——, *Progressive Taxation in Theory and Practice*, 2nd edn (Princeton, American Economic Association, 1908).

Shavell, S, *Foundations of Economic Analysis of Law* (Cambridge, MA, Belknap Press, 2004).

Shaxson, N, *Treasure Islands: Tax Havens and the Men Who Stole the World* (London, Bodley Head, 2011).

Skinner, Q, *Machiavelli* (Oxford, Oxford University Press, 1981).

Slater, D and Tonkiss, F, *Market Society: Markets and Modern Social Theory* (Cambridge, Polity Press, 2001).

Slemrod, J and Bakija, J, *Taxing Ourselves: A Citizen's Guide to the Debate over Taxes*, 3rd edn (Cambridge, MA, MIT Press, 2004).

Smith, C, *Adam Smith's Political Philosophy: The Invisible Hand and Spontaneous Order* (London, Routledge, 2006).

Southern, D, *Taxation of Corporate Debt, Foreign Exchange and Derivative Contracts*, 7th edn (London, Lexis Nexis, 2004).

——, *Tolley's Taxation of Corporate Debt and Financial Instruments*, 2nd edn (Croydon, Tolley Publishing, 1998).
Stamp, Sir J, *The Fundamental Principles of Taxation in the Light of Modern Developments: The Newmarch Lectures for 1919* (London, Macmillan and Co, 1921).
Steger, MB and Roy, RK, *Neoliberalism: A Very Short Introduction* (Oxford, Oxford University Press, 2010).
Stevens, R, *The English Judges: Their Role in the Changing Constitution* (Oxford, Hart Publishing, 2005).
Stewart, A, *Theories of Power and Domination: The Politics of Empowerment in Late Modernity* (London, Sage, 2001).
Strange, S, *The Retreat of the State: The Diffusion of Power in the World Economy* (Cambridge, Cambridge University Press, 1996).
Tamanaha, BZ, *On the Rule of Law: History, Politics, Theory* (Cambridge, Cambridge University Press, 2004).
Tawney, RH, *Equality*, 4th edn (London, George Allen and Unwin, 1952).
Terra, BJM and Wattel, PJ, *European Tax Law*, 4th edn (The Hague, Kluwer Law, 2005).
Thatcher, M, *The Downing Street Years* (London, HarperCollins, 1993).
——, *The Path to Power* (London, HarperCollins, 1995).
Theakston, K, *The Civil Service since 1945* (Oxford, Blackwell, 1995).
Thomas, R, *The British Philosophy of Administration: A Comparison of British and American Ideas, 1900–1939* (Cambridge, Centre for Business and Public Sector Ethics, 1989).
Thompson, EP, *Whigs and Hunters: The Origin of the Black Act* (London, Penguin, 1990).
Thompson, N, *Political Economy and the Labour Party: The Economics of Democratic Socialism, 1884–1995* (London, University College London Press, 1996).
Thuronyi, V, *Comparative Tax Law* (The Hague, Kluwer Law, 2003).
—— (ed), *Tax Law Design and Drafting* (Washington, DC, International Monetary Fund, 1996).
Tiley, J, *Revenue Law*, 5th edn (Oxford, Hart Publishing, 2005).
—— (ed), *Studies in the History of Tax Law* (Oxford, Hart Publishing, 2004).
Tomkins, A, *Public Law* (Oxford, Oxford University Press, 2003).
——, *Our Republican Constitution* (Oxford, Hart Publishing, 2005).
Tsebelis, G and Money, J, *Bicameralism* (Cambridge, Cambridge University Press, 1997).
Tugendhat, C, *The Multinationals* (Harmondsworth, Penguin, 1973).
Turner, A, *Just Capital: The Liberal Economy*, rev edn (London, Pan Books, 2002).
Turpin, C and Tomkins, A, *British Government and the Constitution: Text and Materials*, 6th edn (Cambridge, Cambridge University Press, 2007).
Ussher, K, *The Spectre of Tax Harmonisation* (London, Centre for European Reform, 2000).
Ussher, K and Walford, I, *National Treasure* (London, Demos, 2011).
Vernon, R, *In the Hurricane's Eye: The Troubled Prospects of Multinational Enterprises* (London, Harvard University Press, 1998).
——, *Sovereignty at Bay: The Multinational Spread of US Enterprises* (London, Longman, 1971).
Watterston, J, *Core Tax Annuals: Corporation Tax 2010/11* (Haywards Heath, Bloomsbury Professional, 2010).
Weaver, RK and Rockman, BA, *Do Institutions Matter? Government Capabilities in the United States and Abroad* (Washington, DC, Brookings Institution, 1993).

Weinrib, EJ, *The Idea of Private Law* (Cambridge, MA, Harvard University Press, 1995).
Wheeler, S, *Corporations and the Third Way* (Oxford, Hart Publishing, 2002).
Whitehouse, C, Narain, L, Watson, L and Lee, N, *Revenue Law: Principles and Practice*, 19th edn (Croydon, Tolley Lexis Nexis, 2001).
Whitehouse, C, Watson, L, Narain, L and Lee, N, *Revenue Law: Principles and Practice*, 18th edn (Croydon, Butterworths Tolley, 2000).
Whiting, S, *Corporation Tax 2005/2006* (Kingston upon Thames, Commerce Clearing House, 2005).
Williams, DF, *EC Tax Law* (London, Longman, 1998).
Williams, H, *Britain's Power Elites: The Rebirth of a Ruling Class* (London, Constable, 2006).
Wilson, G, *Cases and Materials on Constitutional and Administrative Law*, 2nd edn (Cambridge, Cambridge University Press, 1976).
Winch, D, *Adam Smith's Politics: An Essay in Historiographic Revision* (Cambridge, Cambridge University Press, 1978).
Wolf, M, *Why Globalization Works* (London, Yale University Press, 2005).
Zander, M, *The Law-Making Process*, 6th edn (Cambridge, Cambridge University Press, 2004).
Zolo, D, *Democracy and Complexity: A Realist Approach*, D McKie (trans) (Cambridge, Polity Press, 1992).

B. Papers, Book Chapters, Pamphlets, Journal Notes, etc

Alt, J, Preston, I and Sibieta, L, 'The Political Economy of Tax Policy' in S Adam, T Besley et al (eds), *Dimensions of Tax Design: The Mirrlees Review* (Oxford, Oxford University Press, 2010).
Altshuler, R, Grubert, H and Newlon, TS, 'Has US Investment Abroad Become More Sensitive to Tax Rates?' in JR Hines Jr (ed), *International Taxation and Multinational Activity* (London, University of Chicago Press, 2001) 9.
Alworth, JS, 'Taxation and Integrated Financial Markets: The Challenges of Derivatives and Other Financial Innovations' (1998) 5 *International Tax and Public Finance* 507.
Auerbach, AJ, Devereux, MP and Simpson, H, 'Taxing Corporate Income' in S Adam, T Besley et al (eds), *Dimensions of Tax Design: The Mirrlees Review* (Oxford, Oxford University Press, 2010) 837.
Avery Jones, JF, 'Tax Law: Rules or Principles?' (1996) *British Tax Review* 580.
Baker, P, 'United Kingdom' in GTK Meussen (ed), *The Principle of Equality in European Taxation* (The Hague, Kluwer Law International, 1999) 165.
Barendt, E, 'Constitutional Fundamentals' in D Feldman (ed), *English Public Law* (Oxford, Oxford University Press, 2004) 3.
Barro, RJ, 'Economic Growth in a Cross Section of Countries' (1991) 106 *Quarterly Journal of Economics* 407.
Beighton, L, 'Tax Policy and Management: The Role of the Inland Revenue' (1987) 8 *Fiscal Studies* 1.
Berlin, I, 'Does Political Theory Still Exist?' in H Hardy and R Hausheer (eds), *The Proper Study of Mankind: An Anthology of Essays* (London, Pimlico, 1998) 59.
Lord Bingham, 'The Rule of Law' (2007) *Cambridge Law Journal* 67.

Black, JM, 'An Economic Analysis of Regulation: One View of the Cathedral' (1996) 16 *Oxford Journal of Legal Studies* 699.
Bond, SR, 'Levelling Up or Levelling Down? Some Reflections on the ACE and CBIT Proposals and the Future of the Corporate Tax Base' in S Cnossen (ed), *Taxing Capital Income in the European Union: Issues and Options for Reform* (Oxford, Oxford University Press, 2000) 161.
Bowler, T, 'Tax Policymaking in the UK' Tax Law Review Committee (TLRC) Discussion Paper No 8 (Institute for Fiscal Studies, 2010).
Bracewell-Milnes, B, 'A Liberal Tax Policy: Tax Neutrality and Freedom of Choice' (1976) *British Tax Review* 110.
Brauner, Y, 'National Report: The United States' in M Lang, J Herdin and I Hofbauer (eds), *WTO and Direct Taxation* (The Hague, Kluwer Law, 2005) 727.
Bräutigam, D, 'Building Leviathan: Revenue, State Capacity and Governance' (2002) 33(3) *IDS Bulletin* 10.
Brown, G, 'Advancing the Public Interest' in W Stevenson (ed), *Gordon Brown: Moving Britain Forward – Selected Speeches, 1997–2006* (London, Bloomsbury, 2006) 136.
Chartered Institute of Taxation (CIOT), *The Making of Tax Law: Proposals for Reform from the Chartered Institute of Taxation, June 2010* (London, CIOT, 2010).
——, *Fair Is Efficient: A Socialist Agenda for Fairness (Fabian Pamphlet 563)* (London, Fabian Society, 1994).
Cini, M, 'Intergovernmentalism' in M Cini (ed), *European Union Politics* (Oxford, Oxford University Press, 2003) 93.
Cane, P, 'Theory and Values in Public Law' in P Craig and R Rawlings (eds), *Law and Administration in Europe: Essays in Honour of Carol Harlow* (Oxford, Oxford University Press, 2003) 3.
Cook, S, 'The Taxation of Financial Instruments: New Rules' (1993) *British Tax Review* 429.
Craig, P, 'Theory and Values in Public Law: A Response' in P Craig and R Rawlings (eds), *Law and Administration in Europe: Essays in Honour of Carol Harlow* (Oxford, Oxford University Press, 2003) 23.
Daintith, T, 'Public Law and Economic Policy' (1974) *Journal of Business Law* 9.
Devereux, M and Freeman, H, 'A General Neutral Profits Tax' (1991) 12(3) *Fiscal Studies* 1.
Devereux, MP, Griffith, R and Klemm, A, 'Why Has the UK Corporation Tax Raised So Much Revenue?' (2004) 25 *Fiscal Studies* 367.
Devereux, MP, Lockwood, B and Redoano, M, 'Do Countries Compete over Corporate Tax Rates?' (2008) *Journal of Public Economics* 1210.
Diamond, P, 'The Political Power of Economic Ideas: Understanding Relations between "New" Labour and the City in the Post-war Era' in S Barber (ed), *The City in Europe and the World* (London, European Research Forum, 2005) 65.
Dickson, B, 'The Processing of Appeals in the House of Lords' (2007) 123 *Law Quarterly Review* 571.
Diplock, K, 'The Courts as Legislators' in BW Harvey (ed), *The Lawyer and Justice* (London, Sweet and Maxwell, 1978) 263.
Drewry, G, 'The New Public Management' in J Jowell and D Oliver (eds), *The Changing Constitution*, 4th edn (Oxford, Oxford University Press, 2000) 167.
Dunn, J, 'Trust and Political Agency' in J Dunn, *Interpreting Political Responsibility: Essays, 1981–1989* (Cambridge, Polity Press, 1990) 26.

Eichengreen, B, 'Conclusion: The Tobin Tax – What Have We Learned?' in M ul Haq, I Kaul and I Grunberg (eds), *The Tobin Tax: Coping With Financial Volatility* (New York, Oxford University Press, 1996) 273.

Feldstein, M, 'On the Theory of Tax Reform' (1976) 6 *Journal of Public Economics* 77.

Fisher, E, 'Book Review' (2001) 13 *Journal of Environmental Law* 115.

Fleisher, M, 'A Passion for Politics: The Vital Core of the World of Machiavelli' in M Fleisher (ed), *Machiavelli and the Nature of Political Thought* (London, Croom Helm, 1973) 114.

Frecknall Hughes, J, 'The Concept of Taxation and the Age of Enlightenment' in J Tiley (ed), *Studies in the History of Tax Law: Volume 2* (Oxford, Hart Publishing, 2007) 253.

Freedman, J, 'Aligning Taxable Profits and Accounting Profits: Accounting Standards, Legislators and Judges' (2004) 2 *eJournal of Tax Research* 71.

——, 'Defining Taxable Profit in a Changing Accounting Environment' (1995) *British Tax Review* 434.

——, 'Defining Taxpayer Responsibility: In Support of a General Anti-Avoidance Principle' (2004) *British Tax Review* 332.

——, 'The Role of Realisation: Accounting, Company Law and Taxation' in P Thorell (ed), *The Influence of Corporate Law and Accounting Principles in Determining Taxable Income* (London, Kluwer Law, 1997) 29.

——, 'Taxation Research as Legal Research' in M Lamb et al (eds), *Taxation: An Interdisciplinary Approach to Research* (Oxford, Oxford University Press, 2005) 13.

Freshfields, 'Taxation of Financial Instruments' (1991) 5 *Corporate Briefing* 284.

Gamble, A, 'Economic Governance' in J Pierre (ed), *Debating Governance* (Oxford, Oxford University Press, 2000) 110.

——, 'Theories of British Politics' (1990) 38 *Political Studies* 404.

Gammie, M, 'Has Nigel Lawson Really Reformed Business Taxation?' (1984) *Fiscal Studies* 82.

——, 'The Process of Fiscal Reform in the United Kingdom' (1989) *British Tax Review* 252.

——, 'Reforming Corporate Taxation: An Evaluation of the United States Treasury Integration Proposals and other Corporate Tax Systems in an International Context: Part 1' (1992) *British Tax Review* 148.

——, 'Tax Avoidance and the Rule of Law: a Perspective from the United Kingdom' in GS Cooper (ed), *Tax Avoidance and the Rule of Law* (Amsterdam, IBFD Publications, 1997) 181.

——, 'Tax Simplification' in R Chote, C Emmerson, D Miles and J Shaw (eds), *The IFS Green Budget: January 2008* (London, Institute for Fiscal Studies, 2007) 260.

Gauke, D, 'Check against Delivery', Philip Hardman Memorial Lecture (16 November 2010), available at http://www.hm-treasury.gov.uk/speech_xst_161110.htm (accessed 18 April 2011).

——, 'Check against Delivery', speech by the Exchequer Secretary to the Treasury to the Centre for Business Taxation, Oxford University (2 July 2010), available at http://www.hm-treasury.gov.uk/speech_xst_020710.htm (accessed 2 March 2011).

Goldberg, D, 'Between the Taxpayer and the Executive; Law's Inadequacy; Democracy's Failure?' (1996) *British Tax Review* 9.

Lord Healey of Riddlesden, 'Why the Treasury is so Difficult' in H Davies (ed), *The Chancellors' Tales: Managing the British Economy* (Cambridge, Polity, 2006) 52.

Heclo, HH, 'Review Article: Policy Analysis' (1972) 2 *British Journal of Political Science* 83.
Hole, D, 'Finance Act Notes: Corporate and Government Debt – Sections 80–105 and Schedules 7–15' (1996) *British Tax Review* 347.
——, 'The Taxation of Gilts and Bonds' (1995) *British Tax Review* 511.
Hope, D (Lord), 'Voices from the Past: The Law Lords' Contribution to the Legislative Process' (2007) 123 *Law Quarterly Review* 547.
Howe, Sir G, 'Reform of Taxation Machinery' (1977) *British Tax Review* 97.
Lord Howe of Aberavon, 'Can 364 Economists all be Wrong?' in H Davies (ed), *The Chancellors' Tales: Managing the British Economy* (Cambridge, Polity, 2006) 76.
——, 'Simplicity and Stability: the Politics of Tax Policy' (2001) *British Tax Review* 113.
Isaac, J, 'Development of Tax Policy Formulation and Presentation: A Retrospect' (2006) *British Tax Review* 222.
Jackson, D, 'Thomas Hobbes' Theory of Taxation' (1973) 21 *Political Studies* 175.
Johnson, P, 'Defining a Tax Strategy' in M Brewer, C Emmerson and H Miller (eds), *The Institute for Fiscal Studies Green Budget: February 2011* (London, IFS, 2011) 207.
Judge, D, Stoker, G and Wolman, H, 'Urban Politics and Theory: An Introduction' in D Judge, G Stoker and H Wolman (eds), *Theories of Urban Politics* (London, Sage, 1995) 1.
Kaul, I, Grunberg, I and ul Haq, M, 'Overview' in M ul Haq, I Kaul, I Grunberg (eds), *The Tobin Tax: Coping with Financial Volatility* (New York, Oxford University Press, 1996) 1.
Kay, J and Sen, J, 'The Comparative Burden of Business Taxation' (1983) 4(3) *Fiscal Studies* 23.
Keeling, E, 'Taxing Foreign Exchange Gains and Losses: Past Doubts and Future "Solutions"' (1995) *British Tax Review* 122.
Keen, M, Klemm, A and Perry, V, 'Tax and the Crisis' (2010) 31(1) *Fiscal Studies* 43.
Kelly, R, 'Taxing the Speculator: The Route to Forex Stability', Fabian Society Discussion Paper No 15 (London, Fabian Society, 1993).
Kerridge, R, 'The Income Tax (Earnings and Pensions) Act 2003' (2003) *British Tax Review* 257.
King, JR, 'Debt and Equity Financing' in P Shome (ed), *Tax Policy Handbook* (Washington, DC, International Monetary Fund, 1995) 158.
Kingston, S, 'A Light in the Darkness; Recent Developments in the ECJ's Direct Tax Jurisprudence' (2007) 44 *Common Market Law Review* 1321.
Kooiman, J, 'Social-Political Governance: Introduction' in J Kooiman (ed), *Modern Governance: New Government–Society Interactions* (London, Sage, 1993) 1.
——, 'Societal Governance: Levels, Modes, and Orders of Social-Political Interaction' in J Pierre (ed), *Debating Governance* (Oxford, Oxford University Press, 2000) 138.
Kooiman, J and van Vliet, M, 'Governance and Public Management' in KA Eliassen and J Kooiman (eds), *Managing Public Organizations: Lessons from Contemporary European Experience*, 2nd edn (London, Sage, 1993) 58.
Law Society, 'Tax: Good Governance and Better Law-Making: A Manifesto for Improving Tax Law' (3 March 2010), available at http://www.lawsociety.org.uk (accessed 22 March 2011).
Lawson, N, 'Changing the Consensus' in H Davies (ed), *The Chancellors' Tales: Managing the British Economy* (Cambridge, Polity, 2006) 113.
Lever, A, 'Is Judicial Review Undemocratic?' (2007) *Public Law* 280.

Likhovski, A, 'A Map of Society: Defining Income in British, British Colonial and American Tax Legislation' (2005) *British Tax Review* 158.

——,'Tax Law and Public Opinion: Explaining *IRC v Duke of Westminster*' in J Tiley (ed), *Studies in the History of Tax Law: Volume 2* (Oxford, Hart Publishing, 2007) 183.

Loughlin, M, 'Constituent Power Subverted: From English Constitutional Argument to British Constitutional Practice' in M Loughlin and N Walker (eds), *The Paradox of Constitutionalism: Constituent Power and Constitutional Form* (Oxford, Oxford University Press, 2007) 27.

——,'Constitutional Law: The Third Order of the Political' in N Bamforth and P Leyland (eds), *Public Law in a Multi-layered Constitution* (Oxford, Hart Publishing, 2003) 27.

——,'The Functionalist Style in Public Law' (2005) 55 *University of Toronto Law Journal* 361.

——,'Review Article' (1988) 51 *Modern Law Review* 531.

——,'The State, the Crown and the Law' in M Sunkin and S Payne (eds), *The Nature of the Crown: A Legal and Political Analysis* (Oxford, Oxford University Press, 1999).

——,'Theory and Values in Public Law: An Interpretation' (2005) *Public Law* 48.

Lowi, TJ, 'Four Systems of Policy, Politics, and Choice' (1972) 32 *Public Administration Review* 298.

Lucas, RE, 'On the Mechanics of Economic Development' (1988) 22 *Journal of Monetary Economics* 3.

Luhmann, N, 'The Unity of the Legal System' in *Autopoietic Law: A New Approach to Law and Society* (Berlin, Walter de Gruyter, 1988) 12.

Luja, RHC, 'WTO Agreements versus the EC Fiscal Aid Regime: Impact on Direct Taxation' (1999) 27 *Intertax* 207.

Macdonald, G, '*Revenue and Customs Commissioners v William Grant and Sons Distillers Ltd* and *Small (Inspector of Taxes) v Mars (UK) Ltd*: Accountancy Practice and the Computation of Profit' (2007) *British Tax Review* 366.

Macpherson, N, 'Evolution of the Modern Treasury' ESRC Seminar, All Souls College, Oxford (9 December 2009), available at http://www.treasuryproject.org/NickMac.pdf (accessed 17 July 2011).

Maier, CS, 'Introduction: Political Economy and History' in CS Maier (ed), In Search of Stability: Explorations in Historical Political Economy (Cambridge, Cambridge University Press, 1987).

Marsh, D and Rhodes, RAW, 'Policy Communities and Issue Networks: Beyond Typology' in D Marsh and RAW Rhodes (eds), *Policy Networks in British Government* (Oxford, Clarendon Press, 1992) 249.

McCubbins, MD and Schwartz, T, 'Congressional Oversight Overlooked: Police Patrols versus Fire Alarms' (1984) 28 *American Journal of Political Science* 165.

Mintz, J, 'The Corporation Tax' in MP Devereux (ed), *The Economics of Tax Policy* (Oxford, Oxford University Press, 1996) 137.

Moran, BI, 'Taxation' in P Cane and M Tushnet (eds), *The Oxford Handbook of Legal Studies* (Oxford, Oxford University Press, 2003) 377.

Mulgan, R, '"Accountability": An Ever-Expanding Concept?' (2000) 78 *Public Administration* 555.

Musgrave, RA, 'The Public Interest: Efficiency in the Creation and Maintenance of Material Welfare' in CJ Friedrich (ed), *Nomos V: The Public Interest* (New York, Atherton Press, 1962) 107.

Niemeyer, G, 'Public Interest and Private Utility' in CJ Friedrich (ed), *Nomos V: The Public Interest* (New York, Atherton Press, 1962) 1.
Norton, P, 'Barons in a Shrinking Kingdom: Senior Ministers in British Government' in RAW Rhodes (ed), *Transforming British Government, Volume 2: Changing Roles and Relationships* (Basingstoke, Macmillan, 2000) 101.
Ogus, A, 'Corrective Taxes and Financial Impositions as Regulatory Instruments' (1998) 61 *Modern Law Review* 767.
Pagan, J, 'Foreign Exchange Gains and Losses' (1993) *British Tax Review* 276.
Parker, C and Braithwaite, J, 'Regulation' in P Cane and M Tushnet (eds), *The Oxford Handbook of Legal Studies* (Oxford, Oxford University Press, 2003) 119.
Parry-Wingfield, M, 'The Chicken or the Egg?' (2000) *British Tax Review* 597.
Parsons, T, 'On the Concept of Political Power' in R Bell, DV Edwards and RH Wagner (eds), *Political Power: A Reader in Theory and Research* (London, Free Press, 1969) 251.
Paul, DL, 'The Sources of Tax Complexity: How Much Simplicity Can Fundamental Tax Reform Achieve?' (1997) 76 *North Carolina Law Review* 151.
Pemberton, H, 'Policy Networks and Policy Learning: UK Economic Policy in the 1960s and 1970s' (2000) 78 *Public Administration* 771.
Peters, BG, 'Managing the Hollow State' in KA Eliassen and J Kooiman (eds), *Managing Public Organisations: Lessons from Contemporary European Experience*, 2nd edn (London, Sage, 1993) 46.
——, 'Politics is about Governing' in A Leftwich (ed), *What is Politics?* (Cambridge, Polity, 2004) 23.
Pierre, J, 'Introduction: Understanding Governance' in J Pierre (ed), *Debating Governance* (Oxford, Oxford University Press, 2000) 1.
Pollock, AM, Price, D and Player, S, 'An Examination of the UK Treasury's Evidence Base for Cost and Time Overrun Data in UK Value-for-Money Policy and Appraisal' (April 2007) *Public Money and Management* 1.
Potter, C, 'Reflections on *Sharkey v Wernher*' (1964) *British Tax Review* 438.
Prebble, J, 'Should Tax Legislation be Written from a Principles and Purpose Point of View or a Precise and Detailed Point of View?' (1998) *British Tax Review* 112.
——, 'Why is Tax Law Incomprehensible?' (1994) *British Tax Review* 380.
Radaelli, CM, 'The Political Economy of EU Direct Tax Policy' in A Lymer and D Salter (eds), *Contemporary Issues in Taxation Research* (Aldershot, Ashgate Publishing, 2003) 145.
Rhodes, RAW, 'The Civil Service' in A Seldon (ed), *The Blair Effect* (London, Little Brown, 2001) 97.
——, 'The New Governance: Governing without Government' (1996) 44 *Political Studies* 652.
Rhodes, RAW and Marsh, D, 'Policy Networks in British Politics: A Critique of Existing Approaches' in D Marsh and RAW Rhodes (eds), *Policy Networks in British Government* (Oxford, Clarendon Press, 1992) 1.
Riddell, P, 'Commentary [on Alt, Preston and Sibieta]' in S Adam, T Besley et al (eds), *Dimensions of Tax Design: The Mirrlees Review* (Oxford, Oxford University Press, 2010) 1280.
Romer, PM, 'Increasing Returns and Long-Run Growth' (1986) 94 *Journal of Political Economy* 1002.
Rush, M, 'Influencing the 1986 Budget' in M Rush (ed), *Parliament and Pressure Politics* (Oxford, Clarendon Press, 1990).

Salter, D, 'Pre-Parliamentary Procedure, Consultation and the Tax Law Rewrite' (1997) 16 *Civil Justice Quarterly* 294.

——, 'Towards a Parliamentary Procedure for the Tax Law Rewrite' (1998) 19 *Statute Law Review* 65.

Sanger, C, 'Corporate Tax Road Map' (2011) *British Tax Review* 2.

Schneider, DM, 'Interpreting the Interpreters: Assessing Forty-Five Years of Tax Literature' (1999) 4 *Florida Tax Review* 483.

Sentance, A, 'UK Macroeconomic Policy and Economic Performance' in T Buxton, P Chapman and P Temple (eds), *Britain's Economic Performance*, 2nd edn (London, Routledge, 1998) 35.

Shklar, J, 'Political Theory and the Rule of Law' in AC Hutchinson and P Monahan (eds), *The Rule of Law: Ideal or Ideology?* (Toronto, Carswell, 1987) 1.

Simester, AP and Chan, W, 'Review Article' (2003) 23 *Oxford Journal of Legal Studies* 711.

Simpson, E, 'Making Sense of the *Ramsay* Principle: a Novel Role for Public Law?' in M Freedland and J-B Auby (eds), *The Public Law/Private Law Divide: Une entente assez cordiale?* (Oxford, Hart Publishing, 2006) 165.

Smithies, A, 'Memorial: Joseph Alois Schumpeter (1883–1950)' (1950) 40(4) *American Economic Review* 628.

Snape, J, 'Corporation Tax Reform: Politics and Public Law' (2007) *British Tax Review* 374.

——, 'Tax and the City: The UK's Proposals for a Bank Levy' in JR LaBrosse, R Olivares-Caminal and D Singh (eds), *Managing Risk in the Financial System* (Cheltenham, Edward Elgar, 2011).

Solow, RM, 'A Contribution to the Theory of Economic Growth' (1956) 70 *Quarterly Journal of Economics* 65.

Southern, D, 'The Taxation of Derivatives' (1998) *British Tax Review* 348.

Stary, E, 'The March of the Tax Profession' (2006) *British Tax Review* 249.

Stephens, P, 'The Treasury under Labour' in A Seldon (ed), *The Blair Effect* (London, Little Brown, 2001) 185.

Stoker, G, 'Governance as Theory: Five Propositions' (1998) 50 *International Social Science Journal* 17.

Taylor, C, 'Interpretation and the Sciences of Man' in *Philosophy and the Human Sciences: Philosophical Papers 2* (Cambridge, Cambridge University Press, 1985) 15.

Thain, C, 'Economic Policy' in P Dunleavy, A Gamble, I Holliday and G Peele (eds), *Developments in British Politics, Vol 6* (Basingstoke, Macmillan, 2002) 219.

——, 'Economic Policy' in P Dorey (ed), *Developments in British Public Policy* (Cambridge, Sage, 2005) 24.

——, 'Treasury Rules OK? The Further Evolution of a British Institution' (2004) 6 *British Journal of Politics and International Relations* 123.

Thain, C and Christie, R, 'Treasury Power: Past, Present and Future', presented at JUC PAC Conference (Belfast, 3–5 September 2007), available at http://colinthain.com/images/pub_uploads/pacpaper.pdf (accessed 5 July 2011).

Thompson, H, 'The Modern State and its Adversaries' (2006) 41 *Government and Opposition* 23.

Tiley, J, 'Barclays and Scottish Provident: Avoidance and Highest Courts; Less Chaos but more Uncertainty' (2005) *British Tax Review* 273.

——, 'One Way of Improving the Judges: Law Clerks?' (2000) *British Tax Review* 133.

'TL' [Timothy Lyons], 'What Will the ECJ Decide Tomorrow?' (2006) *British Tax Review* 399.

Tomkins, A, 'In Defence of the Political Constitution' (2002) 22 *Oxford Journal of Legal Studies* 157.

Tomkins, A, 'The Struggle to Delimit Executive Power in Britain' in P Craig and A Tomkins (eds), *The Executive and Public Law: Power and Accountability in Comparative Perspective* (Oxford, Oxford University Press, 2006) 16.

——, 'What is Parliament for?' in N Bamforth and P Leyland (eds), *Public Law in a Multi-layered Constitution* (Oxford, Hart Publishing, 2003) 53.

HM Treasury, *Microeconomic Reform in Britain: Delivering Opportunities for All*, E Balls, J Grice and G O'Donnell (eds) (Basingstoke, Palgrave Macmillan, 2004).

——, *Reforming Britain's Economic and Financial Policy: Towards Greater Economic Stability*, E Balls and G O'Donnell (eds) (Basingstoke, Palgrave, 2002).

Troup, E, 'Finance Act Notes: Fiscal Stability – Sections 155 and 156' (1998) *British Tax Review* 490.

Turpin, C, 'Ministerial Responsibility' in J Jowell and D Oliver (eds), *The Changing Constitution*, 3rd edn (Oxford, Clarendon Press, 1994) 109.

Väljemark, C, 'National Report United Kingdom' in M Lang, J Herdin and I Hofbauer (eds), *WTO and Direct Taxation* (The Hague, Kluwer Law, 2005) 685.

Vanistendael, F, 'The Role of the European Court of Justice as the Supreme Judge in Tax Cases' (1996) *EC Tax Review* 114.

Wales, C, 'Commentary [on Alt, Preston and Sibieta]' in S Adam, T Besley et al (eds), *Dimensions of Tax Design: The Mirrlees Review* (Oxford, Oxford University Press, 2010) 1300.

——, 'The Implications of the O'Donnell Review for the Making of Tax Policy in the UK' (2004) *British Tax Review* 543.

——, 'The Making of Tax Policy in the Post-O'Donnell World: Can the HMT–HMRC "Policy Partnership" Meet the Challenge?' (2009) *British Tax Review* 245.

Walker, N, 'Post-Constituent Constitutionalism? The Case of the European Union' in M Loughlin and N Walker (eds), *The Paradox of Constitutionalism: Constituent Power and Constitutional Form* (Oxford, Oxford University Press, 2007) 247.

Warren Jr, AC, 'Commentary: Financial Contract Innovation and Income Tax Policy' (1993) 107 *Harvard Law Review* 460.

Weiler, JHH, 'A Quiet Revolution: The European Court of Justice and its Interlocutors' (1994) 26(4) *Comparative Political Studies* 510.

Wenman, MA, 'Power' in I MacKenzie (ed), *Political Concepts: A Reader and Guide* (Edinburgh, Edinburgh University Press, 2005) 370.

Williams, DF, 'Avoidance through the Creation and Use of Capital Losses by Companies' (2006) *British Tax Review* 23.

——, 'Developing the Concept of Tax Governance', KPMG's Tax Business School discussion paper (London, KPMG, 2007).

Winch, D, 'Adam Smith's "Enduring Particular Result": A Political and Cosmopolitan Perspective' in I Hont and M Ignatieff (eds), *Wealth and Virtue: The Shaping of Political Economy in the Scottish Enlightenment* (Cambridge, Cambridge University Press, 1983) 253.

Wolf, M, 'Does Globalisation Render States Impotent?' (2000) *Wealth and Virtue: The Shaping of Political* 537.

Woodhouse, D, 'The Constitutional and Political Implications of a United Kingdom Supreme Court' (2004) 24(1) & (2) *Legal Studies* 134.
Lord Woolf, 'Tax and Judicial Review' (1993) *British Tax Review* 219.
Young, GM, 'The Liberal Mind in Victorian England' in *Last Essays* (London, Rupert Hart-Davis, 1950) 206.

C. Newspaper and Professional Articles

Adams, C, 'Energy Industry Angry at Rise in Corporation Tax' *Financial Times* (6 December 2005) 5.
——, 'MM02 Chief to Head Merged Revenue' *Financial Times* (14 May 2004) 3.
——, 'Ussher Aims to Give City a Whitehall Voice' *Financial Times* (30 July 2007) 3.
Anonymous (*Financial Times* Editors), 'Britain's Growing Inequality Problem: The UK has a Problem with its Widening Rich–Poor Gap' *Financial Times* (28 January 2010) 14.
——, 'Departmental Drift at the Treasury' (editorial) *Financial Times* (20 December 2007) 12.
——, 'Editorial' *Financial Times* (31 March 2004) 17.
——, 'Low-Tax Lessons from Cadbury's Court Cases: ECJ Judgment should Prompt Deep Corporate Tax Review' (editorial) *Financial Times* (14 September 2006) 16.
——, 'Mandelson Rises from Political Dead: Return of New Labour's Spin-Doctor is an Audacious Bet (Editorial)' *Financial Times* (4–5 October 2008) 14.
——, 'New Transatlantic War – on Accounting: Battle over International Standards Threatens Convergence' (editorial) *Financial Times* (10 March 2005) 18.
——, 'Non-dom Dismay: Minister's Warning on Tax Crackdown Carries Some Weight' (editorial) *Financial Times* (8 February 2008) 12.
——, 'Tax Threat to UK plc: Revenue Crackdown will have Consequences for Investment' (editorial) *Financial Times* (9 November 2005) 18.
Anonymous (*Private Eye* editors), 'In the Back: Tax Avoidance – Haven Sent' *Private Eye*, No 1277 (10–23 December 2010) 28.
——, 'In the Back: Tax – Dodge City' *Private Eye*, No 1204 (22 February–6 March 2008) 28.
——, 'Called to Ordure' *Private Eye*, No 1281 (4–17 February 2011) 8.
——, 'Street of Shame' *Private Eye*, No 1279 (7–20 January 2011) 7.
Ashley, J, 'Glimpses of the Real Gordon' *Guardian G2* (30 May 2007) 4.
Ballard, R and Staveley, B, 'New Relationships: Part 1' *Tax Journal* (7 December 1995) 4.
Barber, B, 'Europe Must Rein in the Power of Private Equity' *Financial Times* (16 March 2007) 15.
Barber, L, Blitz, J and Giles, C, 'Stability is Darling's Watchword' *Financial Times* (4 July 2007) 3.
Beattie, A and Minder, R, 'EU Threatens Sanctions over US Tax Breaks' *Financial Times* (14 February 2006) 6.
Blitz, J, 'This is More about Politics than Policy' *Financial Times* (12 July 2007) 2.
Boxell, J and Jones, A, 'Domecq Chief Attacks Brown over Tax' *Financial Times* (5 December 2003) 1.

Brittan, S, '"Competitiveness" Rears its Ugly Head' *Financial Times* (31 August 2007) 11.
——, 'A Credo for a Revived Capitalism' *Financial Times* (7 May 2010) 13.
——, 'The Many Faces of Liberalism' *Financial Times* 'Life and Arts' (23–24 January 2010) 13.
——, 'The Pitfalls of Confidential Advice' *Financial Times* (5 March 2010) 15.
——, 'Please Spare Us This Vision Thing' *Financial Times* (23 November 2007) 15.
——, 'The Tragedy of the Pre-Budget Report' *Financial Times* (12 October 2007) 17.
Brittan, S, 'Why There Are Two Kinds of Conservatism' *Financial Times* (4 March 2011) 13.
——, 'Why This Should Be the last "Budget"' *Financial Times* (23 March 2007) 15.
Broadley, P and Collier-Keywood, R, 'The Hundred Group and Its Total Tax Contribution' *Tax Journal* (12 February 2007) 7.
Buck, T and Jopson, B, 'Brussels Seeks Greater Role in IASB Decisions' *Financial Times* (3 February 2005) 27.
Buck, T, Parker, G and Mai, C, 'EU Internal Market Chief Fuels Debate over Accounts Rules' *Financial Times* (17 January 2005) 6.
Burns, J and Eaglesham, J, 'Police to End Hunt for Lost Data CDs' *Financial Times* (14 December 2007) 2.
Cable, V, 'Britain's Fiscal Policy Network Needs to be Less Opaque' *Financial Times* (6 December 2006) 19.
Cameron, S, 'Mandarin Dynasty' *Financial Times Magazine* (8–9 April 2006) 16.
——, 'Supertaxman Can't Avoid the Leakers' *Financial Times* (22 December 2010) 11.
Chapman, J, 'House of Lords to be Abolished and Replaced by Elected Senate' *Daily Mail* (4 December 2010) 20.
Christie, R, 'Continuity and Change' (January 2008) 3 *The Treasury under New Labour Project Bulletin* 10.
Collins, J and Dixon, D, 'Open and Shut Case?' *Tax Journal* (9 April 2007) 6.
Croft, J, Jolliffe, A and Davies, PJ, 'Action on Loopholes will Target Financial Products' *Financial Times* (17 March 2005) 9.
Cullinane, J, 'Chaos Theory in Corporate Decisions and Tax' *Financial Times* (20 April 2006) 11.
——, 'Rule of Law' *Taxation* (11 May 2006) 147.
Dodwell, B, 'Budget Analysis: Corporate Tax Reform' *Tax Journal* (5 July 2010) 22.
——, 'The UK: New Holding Company for the World?' *Tax Journal* (2 July 2007) 15.
Doran, N and Greenbank, A, 'Be Vigilant on Tax Reforms' *The Times* (11 April 1996).
Dromey, J, 'Protect Workers from the Private Equiteers' *Financial Times* (3 July 2007) 13.
Eaglesham, J, 'CBI Launches Savage Attack on Treasury' *Financial Times* (27 February 2008) 2.
——, 'CBI Warns of Multinational Exodus' *Financial Times* (10 October 2006) 4.
——, 'Chancellor Rebuffs Pleas for Delay' *Financial Times* (14 February 2008) 2.
——, 'Employers' Chief Warns over Drive against Tax Dodging' *Financial Times* (6 December 2005) 4.
——, 'Lords Reform Slips off Labour Priorities' *Financial Times* (20 July 2007) 2.
Eaglesham, J and Guthrie, J, 'Business on Attack after Concessions' *Financial Times* (25 January 2008) 4.
Eaglesham, J and Houlder, V, 'Four in Ten Companies Make Errors in Corporation Tax Returns' *Financial Times* (31 January 2006) 4.

Edge, S, 'Paragraph 13: Unlucky Only for Some?' *Tax Journal* (14 December 1995) 4.
Fearnley, S and Hines, T, 'Accountability at the Heart of a Complex Debate' *Financial Times* (25 May 2006) 12.
Felsted, A, 'Framework Change will Affect Insurance Industry' *Financial Times* (5 January 2005) 21.
——, 'IASB Taken to Task over IAS 39' *Financial Times* (18 January 2005) 31.
Ferrier, I, 'Tax Editor's Notes (July/August)' (2003) *Conveyancer and Property Lawyer* 346.
'Gavel Basher', 'Called to Ordure' *Private Eye*, No 1194 (28 September–11 October 2007) 6.
Giles, C, 'Brown Yet to Grasp Thorny Problem of Corporation Tax' *Financial Times* (21 October 2004) 3.
——, 'Chancellor Pledges to Simplify Tax System' *Financial Times* (26 July 2007) 2.
——, 'Inequality Rose under Labour, Says IFS' *Financial Times* (8 April 2010) 3.
——, 'Master of Illusion's Debt Vanishing Act' *Financial Times* (21 October 2005) 3.
——, 'Treasury Culture Needs Shake-Up, Says Demos Study' *Financial Times* (8 March 2011) 2.
——, 'Treasury to Retain Key Role, Darling Insists' *Financial Times* (16 January 2008) 2.
——, 'Very Rich Get Richer under Labour' *Financial Times* (18 January 2008) 3.
Goodall, A, 'Knowledge Gap Hinders Debate' *Tax Journal* (2 March 2009) 10.
——, 'Tax Avoidance under Scrutiny' *Tax Journal* (23 February 2009) 5.
Gray, J, 'Maggie's Gift to Gordon' *New Statesman* (24 September 2007) 46.
Greenwood, J, 'Defuse Your Pensions "Time Bomb"' *Daily Telegraph* (2 April 2010), available from http://www.telegraph.co.uk (accessed 14 February 2011).
Guthrie, J, 'A Boisterous Brummie in Brown's Big Tent' *Financial Times* (12 July 2007) 13.
——, 'Tax Treatment of Private Equity? Don't Ask' *Financial Times* (26 April 2007) 15.
Hargreaves, D and Tricks, H, 'New Accounting Rules Raise Questions of Accountability' *Financial Times* (9 December 2004) 20.
Hargreaves, D, Tricks, H and Arnold, M, 'Bolkestein Says New Accounts Rules could Mean Two Years of Confusion' *Financial Times* (18 October 2004) 1.
Houlder, V, 'Britain Remains Competitive on Tax Even as Law Book Expands' *Financial Times* (8 November 2006) 4.
——, 'Brown Urged to Consider Foreign Dividend Tax Reform' *Financial Times* (4 December 2006) 3.
——, 'Businesses Say Volume of Tax Changes Deters Growth' *Financial Times* (21 March 2011) 10.
——, 'Cadbury Tax Case could Hit EU Coffers' *Financial Times* (15 December 2005) 1.
——, 'CBI Team to Assess Corporate Tax Risks' *Financial Times* (14 May 2007) 3.
——, 'A Charm Offensive from the Taxman' *Financial Times* (17 November 2006) 3.
——, 'Companies Anchored to Tax Regime in Spite of Discontent' *Financial Times* (20 June 2006) 3.
——, '"Confusion Layered on Complexity" with Growth of Legislation' *Financial Times* (24 March 2006) 2.
——, 'Crackdown in Structured Finance Arena' *Financial Times* (15 March 2006) 21.
——, 'Experts Attack Rewrite of Arcane Legislation' *Financial Times* (25 February 2008) 4.
——, 'Fewer Tax Laws as Treasury Reacts to Criticism' *Financial Times* (15 August 2007) 3.

——, 'Foreign Profits Tax Reform Fear' *Financial Times* (5 October 2007) 2.
——, 'Fright could Turn to Flight as Tax Regime Gets Tighter' *Financial Times* (23 December 2005) 4.
——, 'Global Corporate Tax Rates Fall' *Financial Times* (23 July 2007) 7.
——, 'Gold Star Tax Award Proposed' *Financial Times* (31 March 2006) 5.
——, 'HSBC Says Tax Regime May Force It to Move' *Financial Times* (6 October 2006) 3.
Houlder, V, 'Inquiries into "Closed" Returns Prompt Alarm' *Financial Times* (21 August 2006) 3.
——, 'Large Companies Pay Lower Rate of Corporation Tax' *Financial Times* (2 March 2011) 3.
——, 'One-Third of Biggest Businesses Pays No Tax' *Financial Times* (28 August 2007) 1.
——, 'Penalty-Based Revenue under Attack' *Financial Times* (20 November 2007) 2.
——, 'Revenue Study Explores Roots of Aggressive Tax Planning' *Financial Times* (30 July 2007) 3.
——, 'Revenue's Uneven Reach Has Its Risks' *Financial Times* (28 August 2007) 3.
——, 'Rules Getting "More and More Complicated"' *Financial Times* (21 October 2004) 3.
——, 'Security Breach a Sign of Deep-Rooted Problems' *Financial Times* (21 November 2007) 2.
——, 'Simpler, Lower, Fairer: Brown's Tax Demand from Business' *Financial Times* (3 October 2005) 17.
——, 'Sweeping Reforms in Corporate Taxation Proposed' *Financial Times* (22 June 2007) 2.
——, 'The Tax Avoidance Story as a Morality Tale' *Financial Times* (22 November 2004) 9.
——, 'Tax Base Changes Seek to Tempt Back Multinationals' *Financial Times* (24 March 2011) 7.
——, 'Tax Claims Hit at Reputation as well as the Coffers' *Financial Times* (9 November 2010) 16.
——, 'Tax System Complexities Threaten to Dull Competitive Edge, Say Directors' *Financial Times* (21 April 2006) 3.
——, 'Tax System Grows More Complicated' *Financial Times* (11 December 2009) 4.
——, 'Treasury Hands Compound Political Errors' *Financial Times* (11 February 2008) 3.
——, 'Treasury Weighs Up Loss of Tax Revenue' *Financial Times* (19 September 2008) 7.
——, 'Trouble to Avoid' *Financial Times* (7 February 2011) 9.
——, 'Victory is Sweet but Result could be Bitter' *Financial Times* (13 September 2006) 3.
——, 'Warning to Groups over Tax Reform Debate' *Financial Times* (20 July 2007) 3.
——, 'Watchdog Criticises Excessive Business Tax Probes' *Financial Times* (25 July 2007) 4.
——, 'Why the Broad of Shoulder have a Wider Range of Options' *Financial Times* (12–13 December 2009) 3.
Houlder, V, Parker, G and Murphy, M, 'Big Banks Meet Tax Code of Conduct Deadline' *Financial Times* (1 December 2010) 2.
Houlder, V and Tait, N, 'European Corporate Tax Plans under Fire' *Financial Times* (7 February 2011) 5.

Lord Howe, 'Bipartisan Support is Needed to Clear the Tax Jungle' *Financial Times* (22 March 2006) 17.

Hubbard, A, 'Interpreting Interventions' *Taxation* (2 November 2006) 111.

Hume, N, 'Why It Is in the National Interest to be Neighbourly' *Financial Times* (21 November 2010) 25.

Johnson, B, 'AV Was a Last Gasp from Brown's Bunker – and It's a Gigantic Fraud' *Daily Telegraph* (28 February 2011) 22.

Jopson, B, 'Banks and IASB in Stalemate on Derivatives' *Financial Times* (17 September 2005) 30.

——, 'EU Calls for Caution over IFRS Move' *Financial Times* (21 October 2005) 30.

——, 'IASB Committee Expands Europe Representation' *Financial Times* (22 February 2005) 30.

——, 'McCreevy Turns on the IASB' *Financial Times* (27 January 2005) 26.

——, 'New Draft of IAS 39 "Workable"' *Financial Times* (17 March 2005) 50.

——, 'New IASB Trustee Calms Nerves' *Financial Times* (30 January 2006) 26.

Jopson, B and Felsted, A, 'IASB Hopes New Rule will End Stand-Off' *Financial Times* (15 March 2005) 30.

Kaletsky, A, 'Goodbye, Homo Economicus' (April 2009) *Prospect* 46.

Kay, J, 'The Failure of Market Failure' (August 2007) *Prospect* 36.

——, 'It may be a Rembrandt to You, but Markets can Beg to Differ' *Financial Times* (21 July 2010) 11.

——, 'Talk of Raising the Corporate Burden Taxes Logic' *Financial Times* (25 October 2005) 19.

Lawson, N, 'Five Myths and a Menace' *Standpoint* (January/February 2011) 36.

Levy, J, 'Dextra, Tax Avoidance and the Courts' *Tax Journal* (25 July 2005) 9.

Maas, R, 'The Great Tax Avoidance "Debate"' *Tax Journal* (16 March 2009) 9.

Marquand, D, 'The Creator' *New Statesman* (24 September 2007) 36.

Minder, R and Alden, E, 'WTO Rules US has Failed to Dismantle Tax Subsidy' *Financial Times* (1–2 October 2005) 7.

Monbiot, G, 'They Still Rage about the Class War, but Keep Funding Their Class Enemies' *Guardian* (10 July 2007) 29.

Moore, S, 'Group Hug' *New Statesman* (24 September 2007) 43.

Muggeridge, S, 'Trust Fosters Relationship between Parliament and City (Letter)' *Financial Times* (31 July 2007) 10.

Mulholland, H and Watt, N, 'Spending Review 2010: George Osborne Announces Extra £7bn of Welfare Cuts' *Guardian* (20 October 2010), available at http://www.guardian.co.uk/politics/2010/oct/20/spending-review-2010-osborne-cuts (accessed 13 July 2011).

Murphy, R and Christensen, J, 'This Change on Tax Avoidance Rules Could Create a Real Economic Advantage for the UK (Letter)' *Financial Times* (12 March 2004) 18.

Murphy, R and Picciotto, S, 'Tax Co-operation is Essential for Global Business (Letter)' *Financial Times* (27 September 2007) 14.

Parker, A, 'Revenue and Business to Thrash Out Tax Problems' *Financial Times* (24 February 2004) 1.

——, 'Tax Collectors Clash with "Aggressive Avoidance Promoter"' *Financial Times* (4 May 2004) 4.

——, 'Tax Probe to Centre on 30 Top Companies' *Financial Times* (4 May 2004) 1.

Parker, A and Budden, R, 'Business Warning over Tax Crackdown Tactic' *Financial Times* (2 April 2004) 2.
Parker, G, 'Brown Weakened by 10p Tax Climbdown' *Financial Times* (24 April 2008) 1.
——, 'A Firefighter under Fire' *Financial Times* (22–23 September 2007) 11.
——, 'Labour Unease over Darling Reforms' *Financial Times* (12 February 2008) 2.
——, 'Mandelson Recall is "in National Interest"' *Financial Times* (4–5 October 2008) 2.
——, 'Osborne's Long Game' *FT Weekend Magazine* (19–20 March 2011) 15.
Parker, G and Eaglesham, J, '"Committee of Chairmen" Set for Select Role' *Financial Times* (11 June 2010) 2.
Parker, G and Houlder, V, 'Osborne Adopts "Robin Hood" Tactics' *Financial Times* (22 March 2011) 10.
Parker, G, Jacobs, E and Pickard, J, 'A Quiet Rebellion' *Financial Times* (12–13 February 2011) 11.
Parker, G, Thal Larsen, P, Giles, C and Saigol, L, 'Darling Caught Off-Guard by first Big Test' *Financial Times* (19 September 2007) 3.
Parry-Wingfield, M, 'Depreciation in Stock: Where Next?' *Tax Journal* (28 May 2007) 13.
Pickard, J, 'More than 100 Labour MPs Defy Miliband on Alternative Vote' *Financial Times* (17 March 2011) 6.
——, 'Notably Global Set of Owners' *Financial Times* (3 April 2007) 19.
——, 'Query on £14m Stirs Spectre of Expenses Scandal' *Financial Times* (16 December 2010) 2.
Pickard, J and Barker, A, 'Legg Orders 390 MPs to Repay £1.1m' *Financial Times* (5 February 2010) 2.
Pierce, J and Knight, R, 'International Accounting Board's Standards and Their Implications must be Assessed by the EU (Letter)' *Financial Times* (7 April 2004) 16.
Pimlott, D, 'Tax Receipts Ease Public Borrowing' *Financial Times* (20 August 2010) 3.
Plender, J, 'Beware the Side-Effects of a Tax Clampdown' *Financial Times* (18 March 2004) 18.
——, 'Counting the Cost of Globalisation: How Companies Keep Tax Low and Stay within the Law' *Financial Times* (21 July 2004) 15.
——, 'Double Non-taxation is a Global Issue' *Financial Times* (17 March 2005) 19.
——, 'Top Banks Eliminate UK Tax Liabilities' *Financial Times* (21 July 2004) 1.
Plender, J and Simons, M, 'A Big Squeeze for Governments: How Transfer Pricing Threatens Global Tax Revenues' *Financial Times* (22 July 2004) 15.
Porter, A and Reece, D, 'Chancellor Who Wants a Return to Prudence' *Daily Telegraph* (13 September 2007) 14.
Rifkind, M, 'In Some Areas, Sovereignty Should Be Shared in Europe' *Financial Times* (13 December 2006) 15.
Rigby, E, 'Lords Reform could See Elected Senators by 2015' *Financial Times* (10 March 2011) 3.
Rumbelow, H, Webster, P and Harding, J, 'Man Who Stepped into Limelight on the Darkest of All Mondays' *The Times* (22 September 2007) 6.
Sakoui, A, 'Ineos Looks to Cut Tax Bill with Swiss Relocation' *Financial Times* (4 March 2010) 1.
Sanger, C, 'Business Tax Policy: A Vision for the Future?' *Tax Adviser* (April 2002) 12.

Sedley, S, 'Judicial Discretion in the House of Lords (Book Review)' (1999) *Cambridge Law Journal* 627.

Southern, D, 'Big Bang for Bonds' *Tax Journal* (23 November 1995) 6.

Stafford, P, 'Swiss Tax Rules Lure McDonald's from UK' *Financial Times* (13 July 2009) 15.

Stephens, P, 'A Dispiriting Return to Europe's Trenches' *Financial Times* (15 January 2008) 17.

——, 'Europe is Unravelling in a Tangle of National Interests' *Financial Times* (30 April 2010) 13.

Strauss, D, 'Short, Measured and No Word of Prudence' *Financial Times* (10 October 2007) 2.

Tait, N, 'Influential Rulings and Modern Attitudes in Court Win Plaudits' *Financial Times Innovative Lawyers Report 2007* (6 July 2007) 12.

Taylor, M, Lewis, P and Gabbatt, A, 'Tax Activists to Target Topshop Boss' *Guardian* (30 November 2010) 17.

Thain, C, 'The Real Question on Treasury's Role (Letter)' *Financial Times* (18 February 2008) 10.

Thain, C and Christie, R, 'A New-Look Treasury under its New Boss: Mr Brown' *Parliamentary Brief* (February 2008) 21, available at http://www.treasuryproject.org (accessed 21 February 2008).

Thal Larsen, P, 'Accounting Bodies under Fire' *Financial Times* (13 June 2005) 21.

——, 'Sprinter's Dash for Tax Advantages Has Admirers Watching in the Stands' *Financial Times* (15 March 2006) 21.

Timmins, N, 'Draft Bill on Civil Service Finally Published' *Financial Times* (16 November 2004) 4.

——, 'Need to Rebuild Trust after Data Loss' *Financial Times* (18 December 2007) 3.

——, ' "Stalinist" Brown, by Ex-Cabinet Secretary' *Financial Times* (20 March 2007) 1.

Tyrrall, DE, 'Can Accountants Figure a Way to Global Standards? (Letter)' *Financial Times* (17 March 2005) 42.

Wales, C, 'Building or Bombing Bridges?' *Tax Journal* (20 November 2006) 9.

Watts, R, 'Chancellor "Ruthlessly Rejected" Warnings on Pensions' *Sunday Telegraph* (8 April 2007) 2.

Willman, J, 'Business Relieved Its Voice is Heard at Last' *Financial Times* (23 March 2007) 3.

——, 'Criticism of Non-dom Tax Move Grows' *Financial Times* (9–10 February 2008) 2.

——, 'Ears and Eyes in Business for No 10' *Financial Times* (8 February 2008) 3.

——, 'Rock and Tax Wobble City's Financial Crown' *Financial Times* (29 February 2008) 2.

Willman, J and Eaglesham, J, 'A Wilting Relationship: Fiscal Fumbles Leave Business Feeling Less Enamoured of Labour' *Financial Times* (28 January 2008) 9.

Wintour, P, 'No 10 Strategy Unit, Headed by Birt, Wanted Brown to Go to Foreign Office' *Guardian* (9 May 2007) 1.

Wolf, M, 'Diligent, Dull and Politically Defensive' *Financial Times* (10 October 2007) 10.

——, 'Two Brave Gambles in a Huge Fiscal Tightening' *Financial Times* (23 June 2010) 20.

——, 'Why We Should Choose the Alternative Vote' *Financial Times* (25 February 2011) 15.

D. Miscellaneous

BBC 2, 'No Tax Please, We're Rich!' *The Money Programme* (2 March 2006), available at http://news.bbc.co.uk/2/hi/business/4763984.stm (accessed 13 July 2011).

BBC Radio 4, 'Companies "Looting" a Continent' *File on Four* (29 July 2007), available at http://news.bbc.co.uk/2/hi/programmes/file_on_4/6908997.stm (accessed 13 July 2011).

BBC Radio 4, *Evan Loves Tax* (three episodes) (13–15 September 2010), details available at http://www.bbc.co.uk/news/business-11275040 (accessed 30 March 2011).

——,'The Orange Book: Clegg's Political Lemon?' *Analysis* (27 February 2011), available at http://www.bbc.co.uk/programmes/b00yqjtj (accessed 13 July 2011.)

——, *The Report* (30 December 2010), summary available at http://www.bbc.co.uk/programmes/b00wr9vx (accessed 13 July 2011).

Catholic Church, *Catechism*, rev edn (London, Geoffrey Chapman, 1999).

Channel 4, 'Oil Company Speaks Out on "Easy Hit" Tax' *Channel 4 News* (Siobhan Kennedy) (4 April 2011), available at http://www.channel4.com/news/catch-up/display/playlistref/040411/clipid/040411_OIL_04 (accessed 6 April 2011).

Financial Times Reporters, *Responsible Business: Financial Times Special Report* (London, 3 July 2007).

Institute for Fiscal Studies (IFS) Tax Law Review Committee, *Making Tax Law: Report of a Working Party on the Institutional Processes for the Parliamentary Scrutiny of Tax Proposals and for the Enactment of Tax Legislation*, Sir Alan Budd (chair) (London, Institute for Fiscal Studies, 2003).

Law Society, *A Guide to the Treaty of Lisbon: European Union Insight* (January 2008), available at http://www.lawsociety.org.uk/documents/downloads/guide_to_treaty_of_lisbon.pdf (accessed 9 July 2011).

Index

www.ingramcontent.com/pod-product-compliance
Ingram Content Group UK Ltd.
Pitfield, Milton Keynes, MK11 3LW, UK
UKHW020905190926
475560UK00010B/269